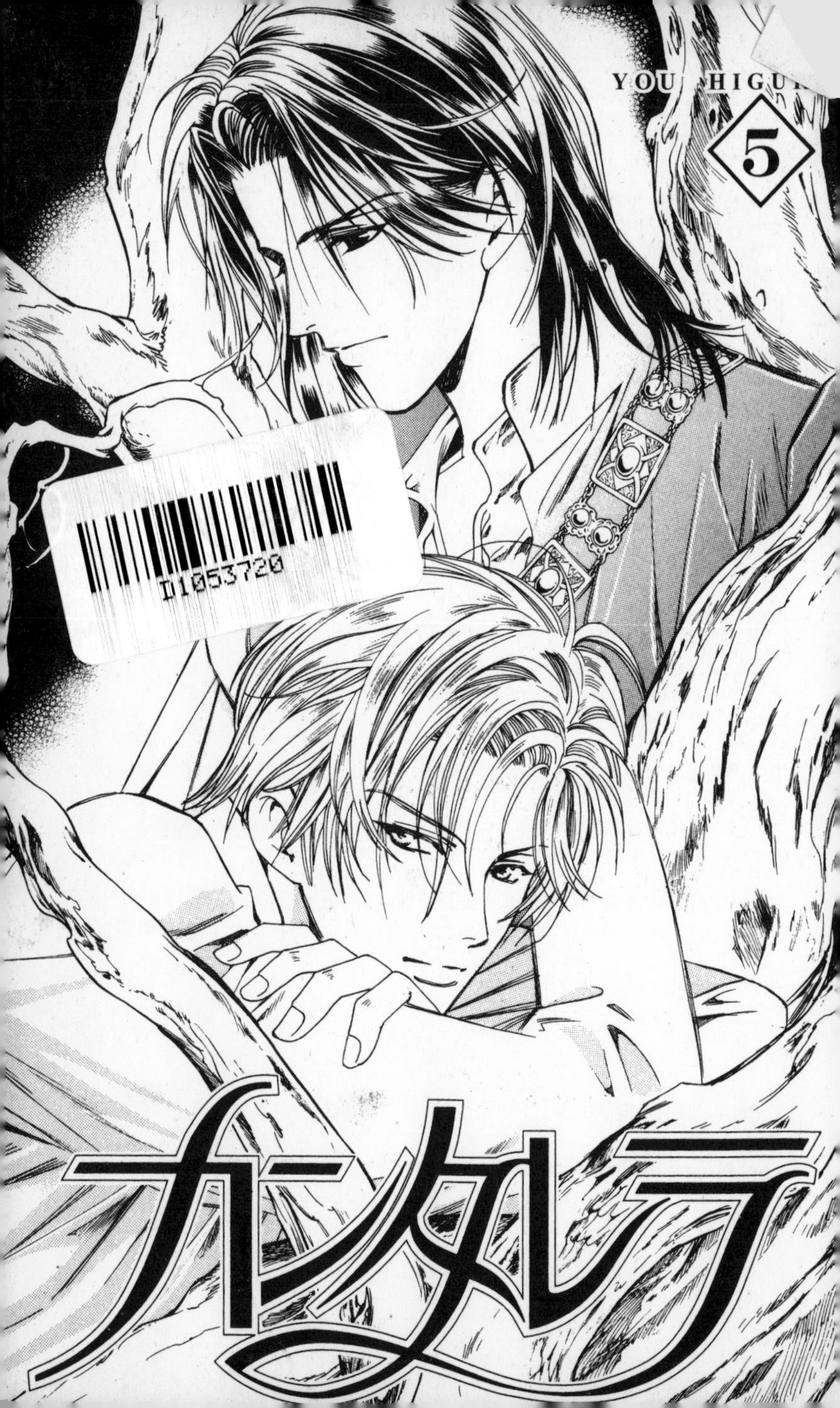
YOU HIGU
5
D1053720

Translation – Christine Schilling
Adaptation – Audry Taylor
Production Assistant – Mallory Reaves
Lettering & Design– Fawn Lau
Production Manager – James Dashiell
Editor – Audry Taylor

A Go! Comi manga

Published by Go! Media Entertainment, LLC

Cantarella Volume 5
© YOU HIGURI 2003
Originally published in Japan in 2003 by Akita Publishing Co., Ltd., Tokyo.
English translation rights arranged with Akita Publishing Co., Ltd.
through TOHAN CORPORATION, Tokyo.

Visit us online at www.gocomi.com
e-mail: info@gocomi.com

ISBN 1-933617-08-X

First printed in December 2006

1 2 3 4 5 6 7 8 9

Manufactured in the United States of America

Cantarella

STORY AND ART BY

YOU HIGURI

VOLUME 5

go!comi

TABLE OF
CONTENTS

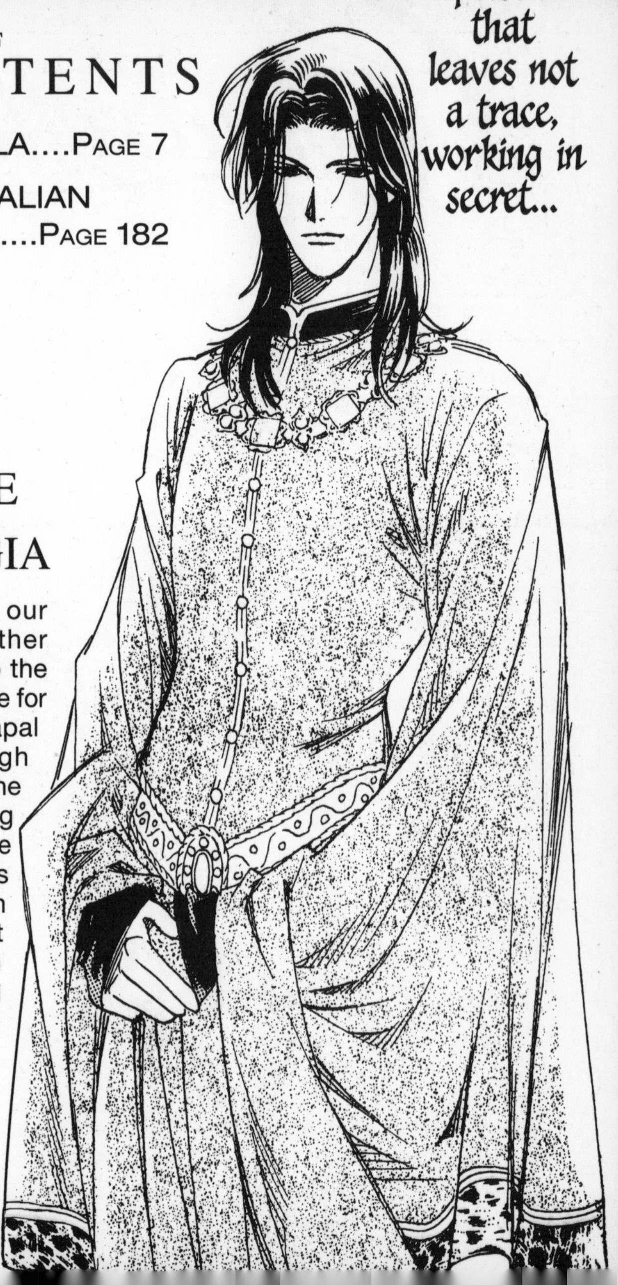

that leaves not a trace, working in secret...

CESARE BORGIA

The hero of our story. His father sold his soul to the devil in exchange for gaining the Papal throne. Though constantly on the brink of being consumed by the demonic powers that dwell within him, he will let nothing stop him from fulfilling his ambition of unifying Italy.

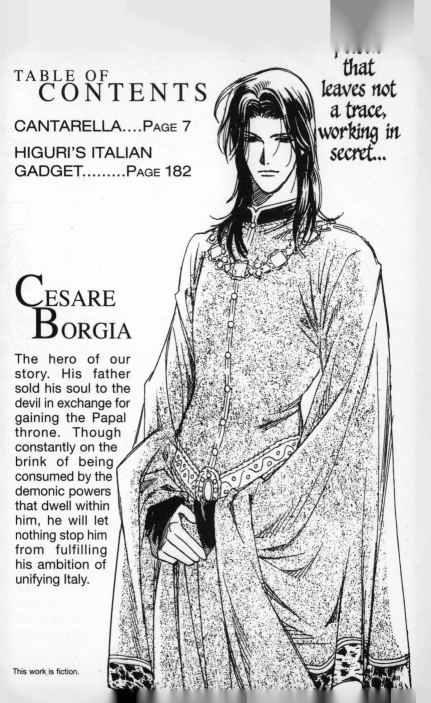

This work is fiction.

◆ Pope Alexander VI ◆

An ambitious man who sold his own son's soul to the devil in exchange for the Papal throne. He has solidified the foundation of his authority through nepotism.

◆ Michelotto (Chiaro) ◆

A legendary assassin who wears the mask of "Michelotto." Chiaro is Cesare's closest confidant -- and the only thing standing between him and madness.

◆ Juan Borgia ◆

Cesare's little brother is favored by their father and thus leads a blessed life. He is the Duke of Gandia and has nothing but scorn for his older brother Cesare.

◆ Lucrezia Borgia ◆

A sweet girl who adores her older brother Cesare. She was forced into an arranged marriage with Lord Pesaro, but now calls a quiet monastery home.

◆ Volpe ◆

Cesare's loyal retainer who's been by his side since childhood. He idolizes Cesare's tyrannical nature.

◆ Sancia d'Aragon ◆

The wife of Jofre, third son in the Borgia family. She has an uninhibited personality and a unique "relationship" with Cesare.

Story So Far

Reunited with her brother Cesare, Lucrezia struggles to keep secret the forbidden feelings she has for him. After being provoked by Sancia's jealous words, she confesses her sinful love to Cesare, who gently rejects it. The distraught Lucrezia is abducted by her ex-husband, whose attempt to rape her is thwarted by the noble Chiaro. Feeling truly alone, Cesare turns to the adulterous Sancia for comfort...

Various cities and territories of Italy during *Cantarella* period

(end of the 15th century)

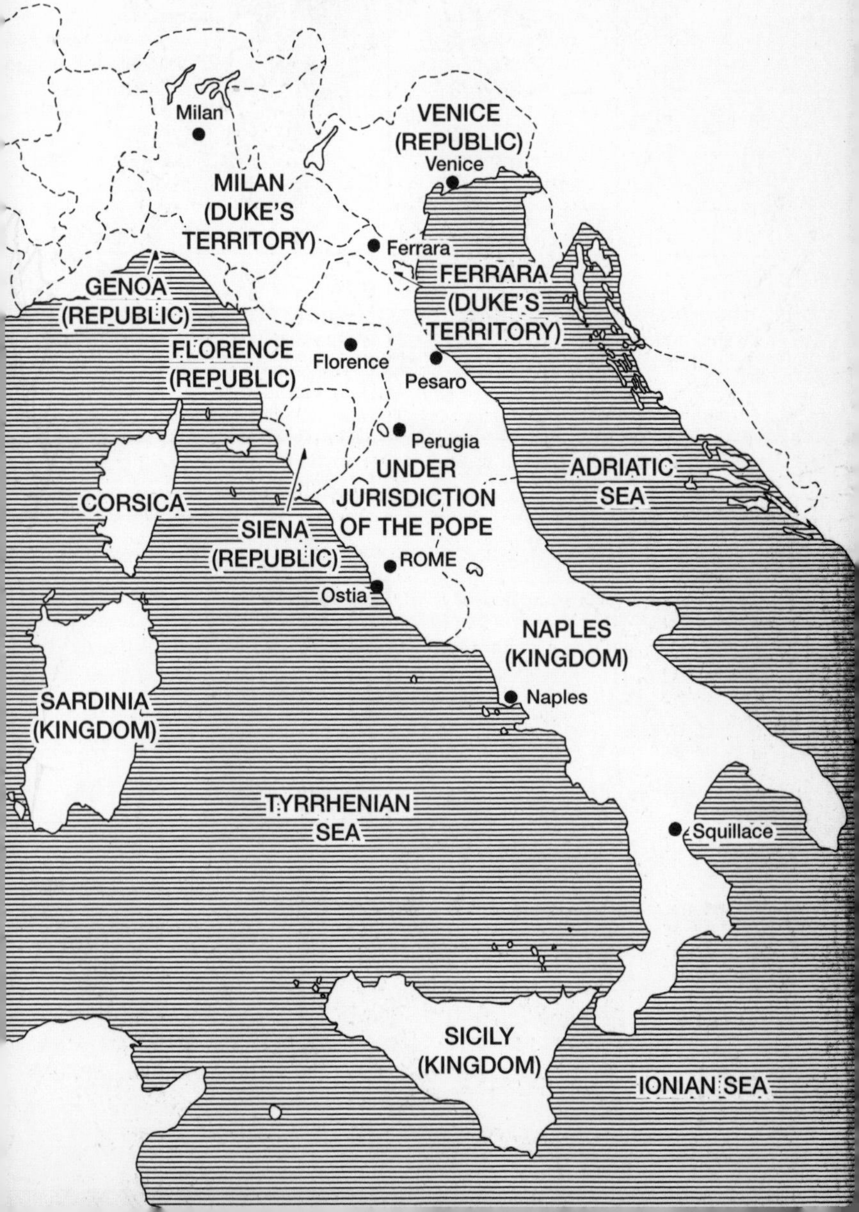

Milan
VENICE (REPUBLIC)
Venice
MILAN (DUKE'S TERRITORY)
Ferrara
FERRARA (DUKE'S TERRITORY)
GENOA (REPUBLIC)
FLORENCE (REPUBLIC)
Florence
Pesaro
Perugia
UNDER JURISDICTION OF THE POPE
ADRIATIC SEA
CORSICA
SIENA (REPUBLIC)
ROME
Ostia
NAPLES (KINGDOM)
Naples
SARDINIA (KINGDOM)
TYRRHENIAN SEA
Squillace
SICILY (KINGDOM)
IONIAN SEA

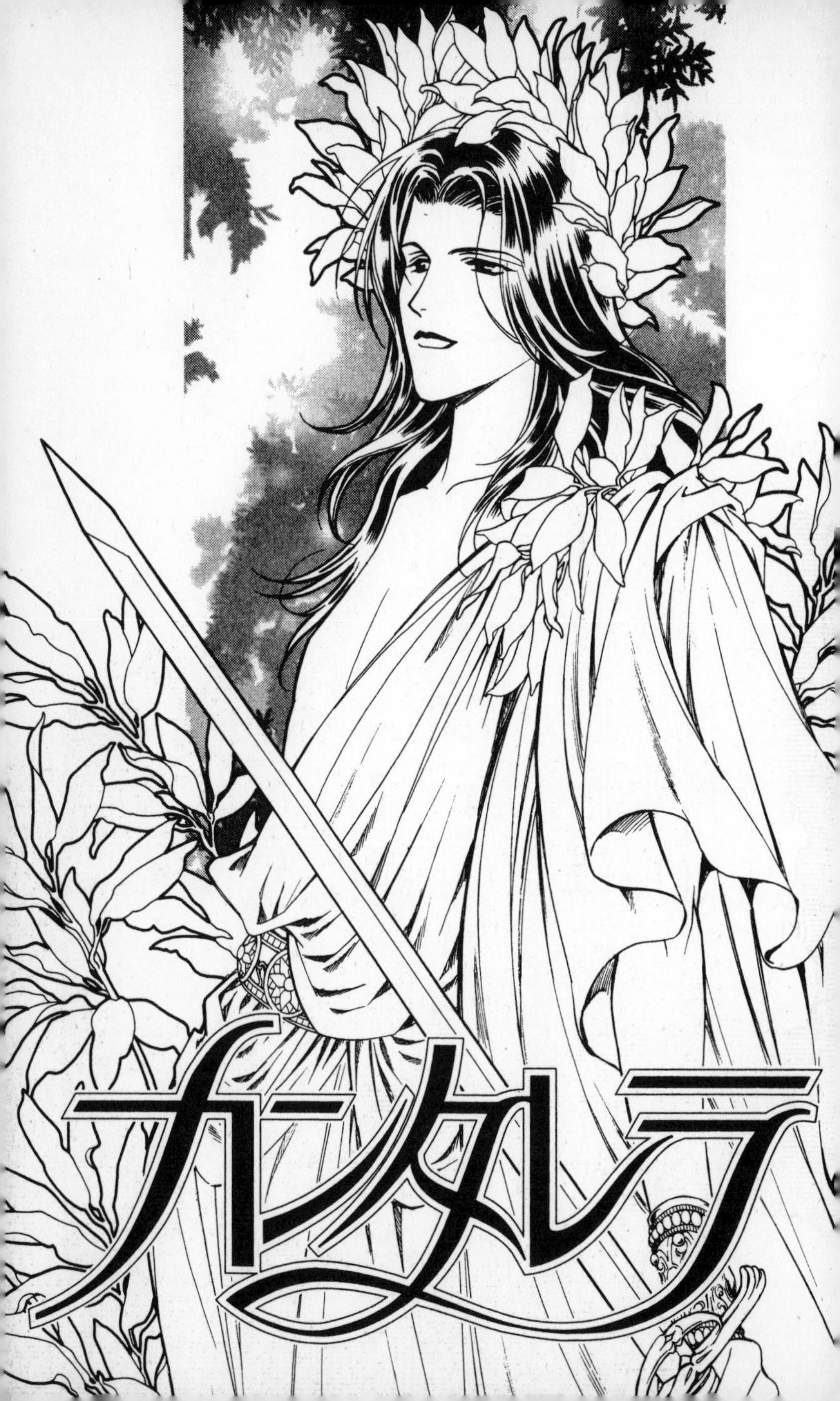

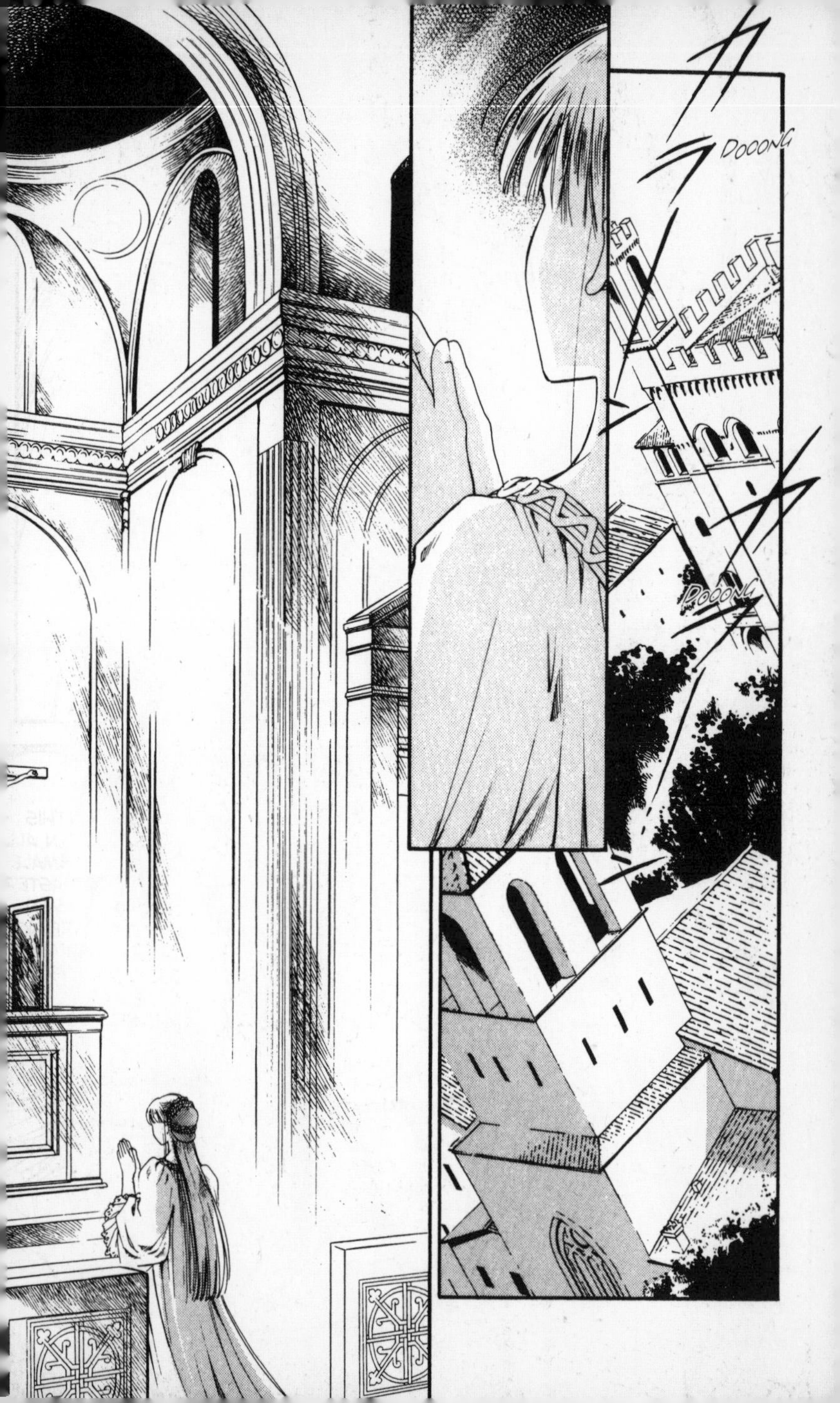
DOOONG
DOOONG

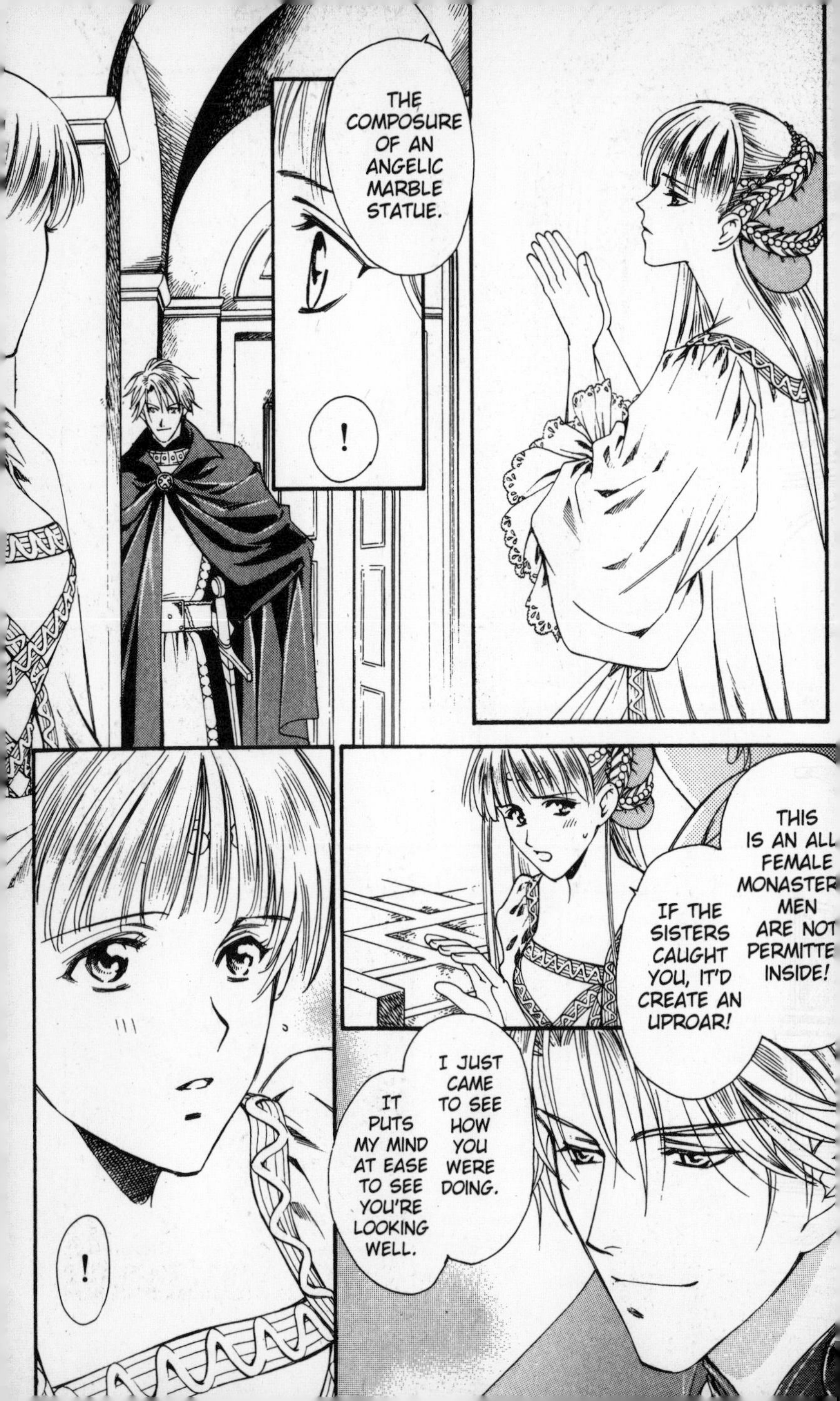
THE COMPOSURE OF AN ANGELIC MARBLE STATUE.
!
THIS IS AN ALL FEMALE MONASTER MEN ARE NOT PERMITTE INSIDE!
IF THE SISTERS CAUGHT YOU, IT'D CREATE AN UPROAR!
I JUST CAME TO SEE HOW YOU WERE DOING.
IT PUTS MY MIND AT EASE TO SEE YOU'RE LOOKING WELL.
!

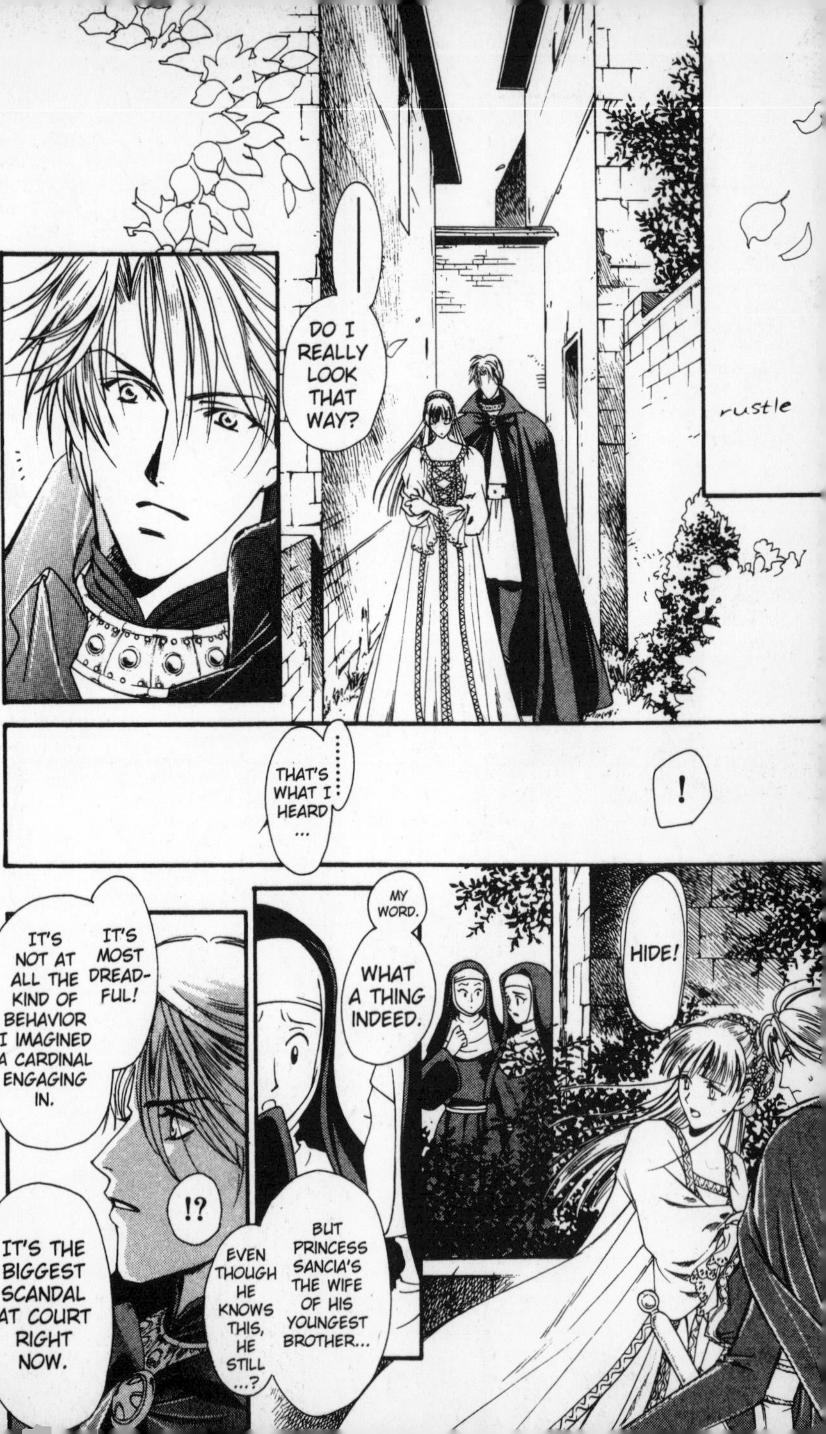
!
DO I REALLY LOOK THAT WAY?
rustle
!
......
THAT'S WHAT I HEARD...
HIDE!
MY WORD.
WHAT A THING INDEED.
IT'S MOST DREAD-FUL!
IT'S NOT AT ALL THE KIND OF BEHAVIOR I IMAGINED A CARDINAL ENGAGING IN.
!?
BUT PRINCESS SANCIA'S THE WIFE OF HIS YOUNGEST BROTHER...
EVEN THOUGH HE KNOWS THIS, HE STILL ...?
IT'S THE BIGGEST SCANDAL AT COURT RIGHT NOW.

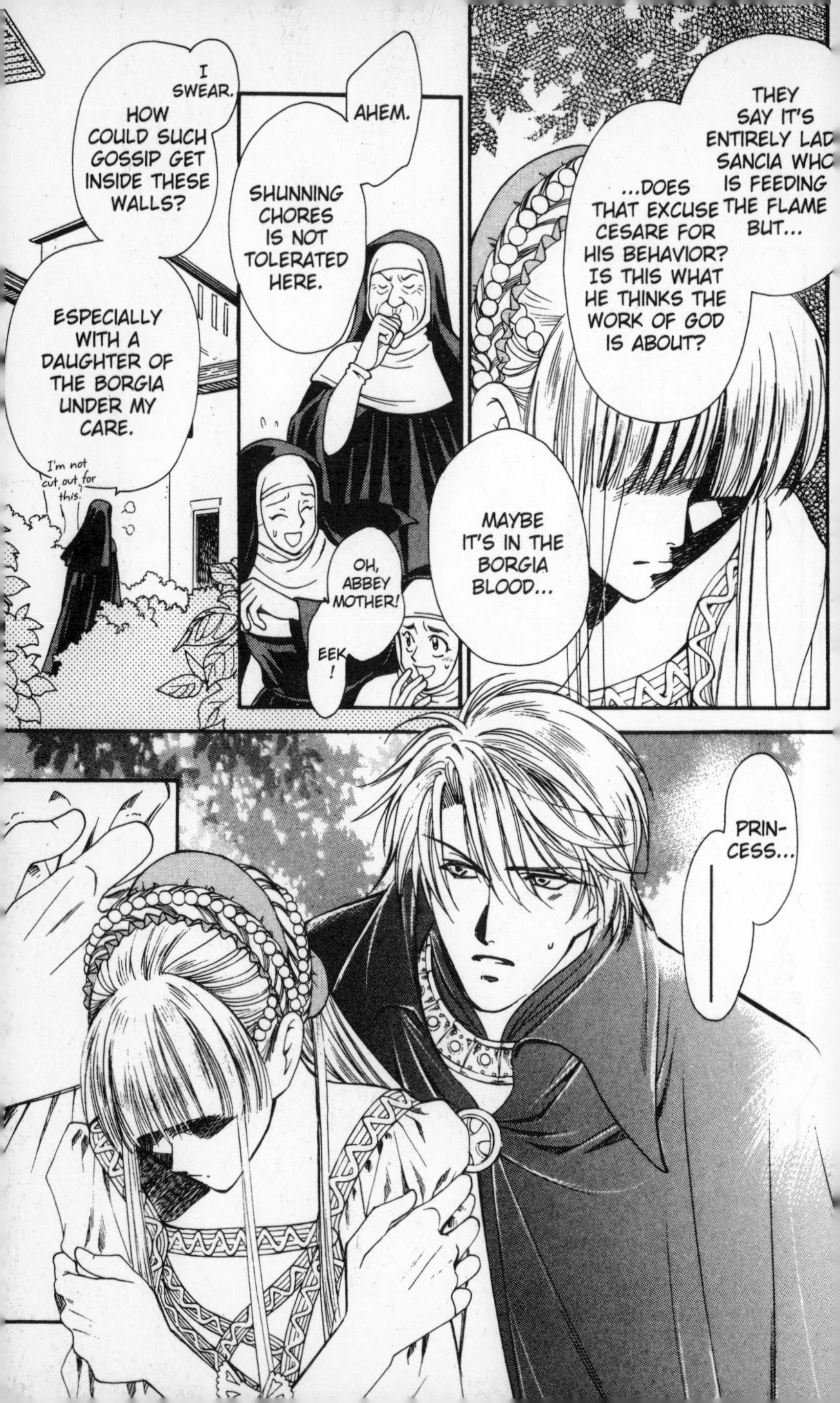
THEY SAY IT'S ENTIRELY LAD SANCIA WHO IS FEEDING THE FLAME BUT...
...DOES THAT EXCUSE CESARE FOR HIS BEHAVIOR? IS THIS WHAT HE THINKS THE WORK OF GOD IS ABOUT?
MAYBE IT'S IN THE BORGIA BLOOD...
AHEM.
SHUNNING CHORES IS NOT TOLERATED HERE.
OH, ABBEY MOTHER!
EEK!
I SWEAR. HOW COULD SUCH GOSSIP GET INSIDE THESE WALLS?
ESPECIALLY WITH A DAUGHTER OF THE BORGIA UNDER MY CARE.
I'm not cut out for this.
PRIN-CESS...

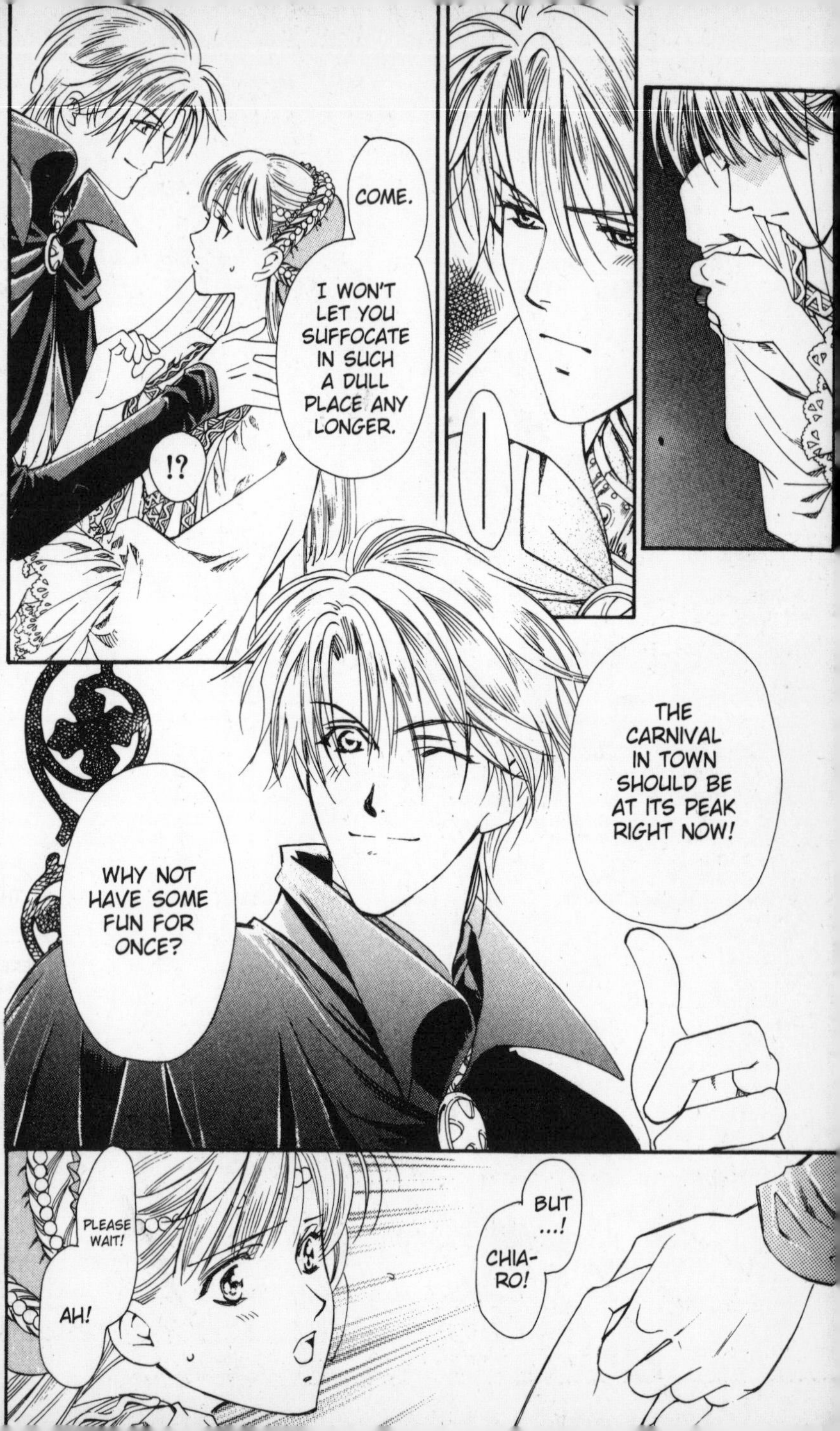
COME.
I WON'T LET YOU SUFFOCATE IN SUCH A DULL PLACE ANY LONGER.
!?
THE CARNIVAL IN TOWN SHOULD BE AT ITS PEAK RIGHT NOW!
WHY NOT HAVE SOME FUN FOR ONCE?
BUT ...!
CHIA-RO!
PLEASE WAIT!
AH!

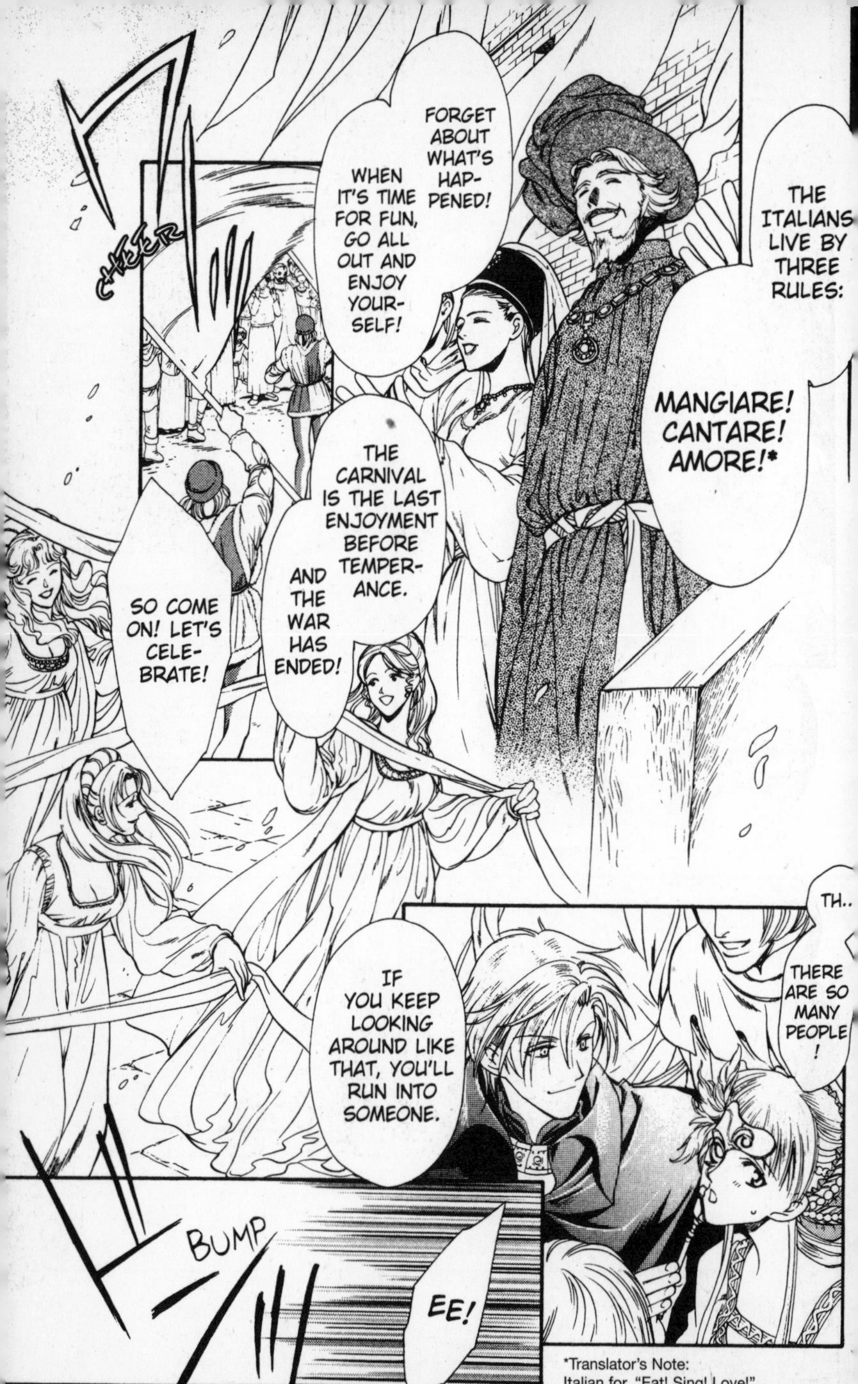
THE ITALIANS LIVE BY THREE RULES:
MANGIARE! CANTARE! AMORE!*
FORGET ABOUT WHAT'S HAP-PENED!
WHEN IT'S TIME FOR FUN, GO ALL OUT AND ENJOY YOUR-SELF!
THE CARNIVAL IS THE LAST ENJOYMENT BEFORE TEMPER-ANCE.
AND THE WAR HAS ENDED!
SO COME ON! LET'S CELE-BRATE!
CHEER
TH..
THERE ARE SO MANY PEOPLE!
IF YOU KEEP LOOKING AROUND LIKE THAT, YOU'LL RUN INTO SOMEONE.
EE!
BUMP

*Translator's Note:
Italian for, "Eat! Sing! Love!"

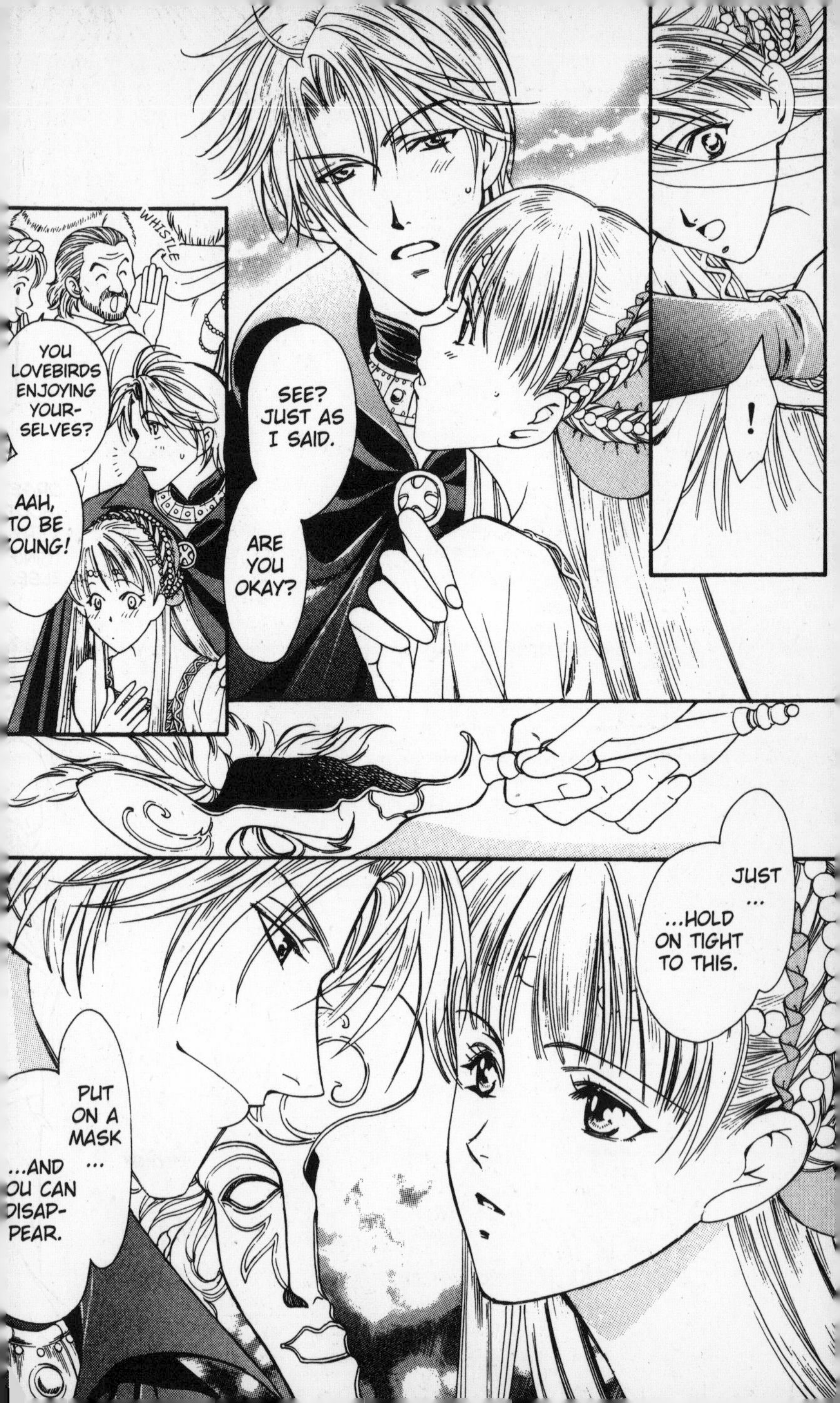
!
SEE? JUST AS I SAID.
ARE YOU OKAY?
WHISTLE
YOU LOVEBIRDS ENJOYING YOUR-SELVES?
AAH, TO BE OUNG!
JUST ...
...HOLD ON TIGHT TO THIS.
PUT ON A MASK ...
...AND OU CAN DISAP-PEAR.

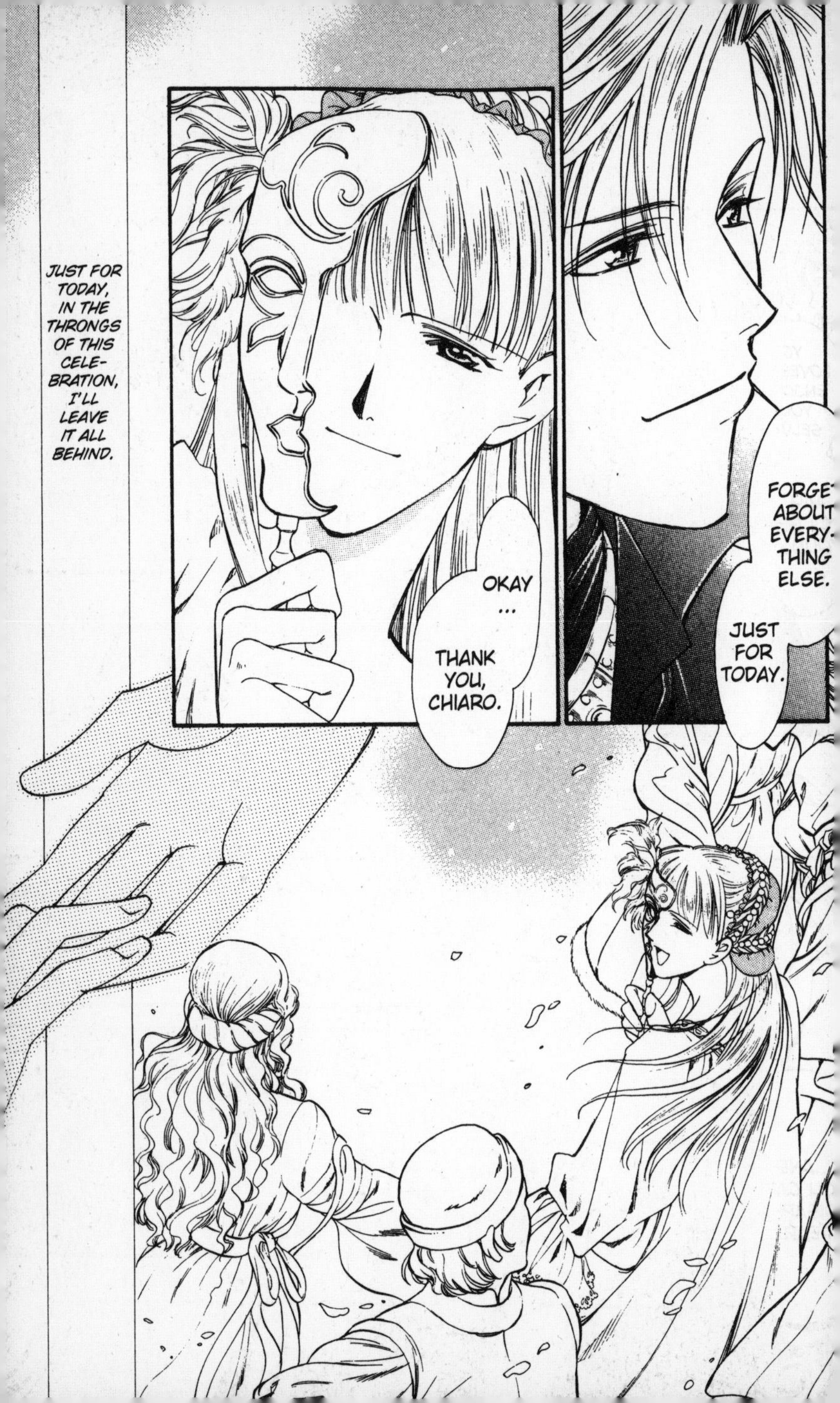
FORGET ABOUT EVERYTHING ELSE.
JUST FOR TODAY.
OKAY ...
THANK YOU, CHIARO.
JUST FOR TODAY, IN THE THRONGS OF THIS CELEBRATION, I'LL LEAVE IT ALL BEHIND.

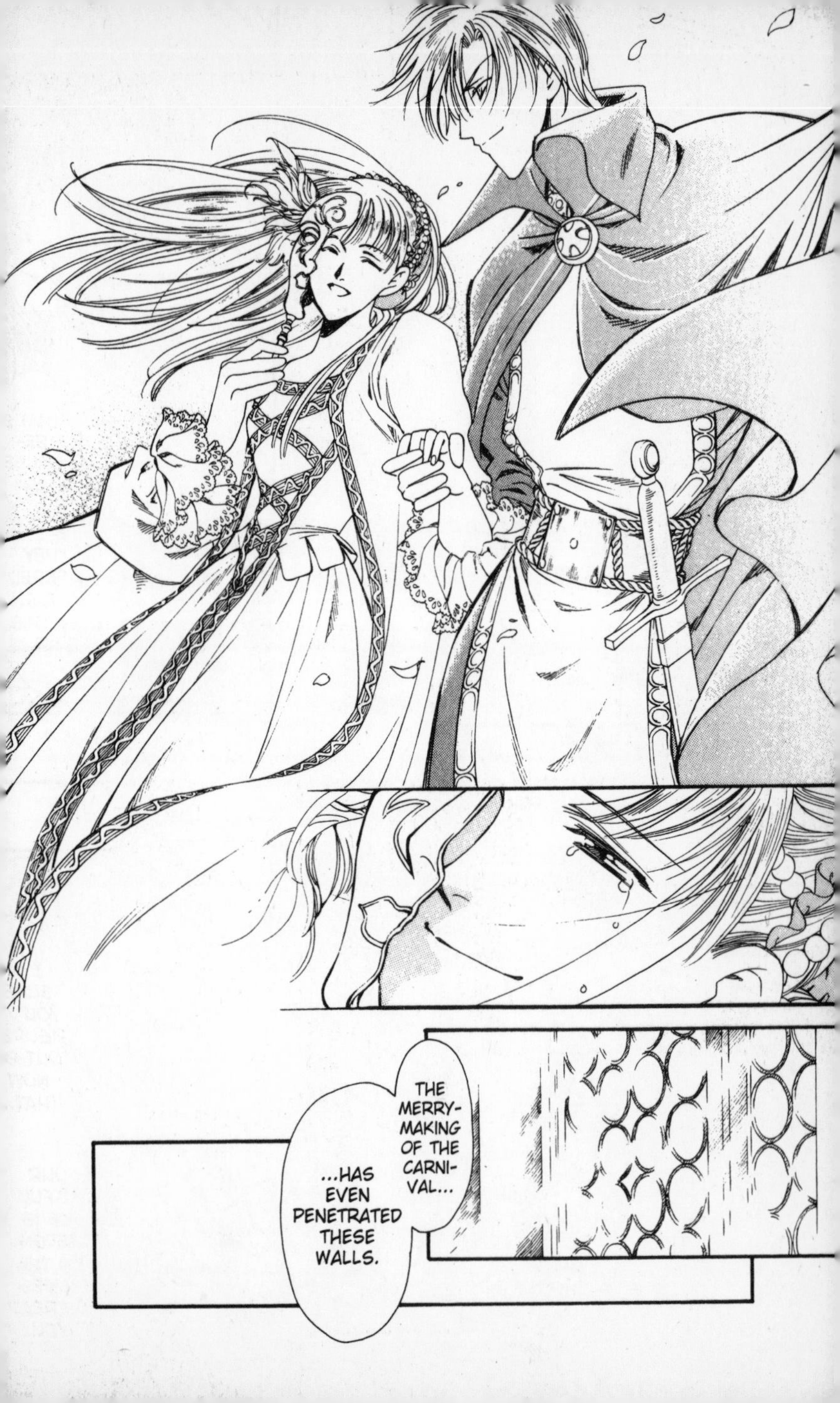
THE MERRY-MAKING OF THE CARNI-VAL...
...HAS EVEN PENETRATED THESE WALLS.

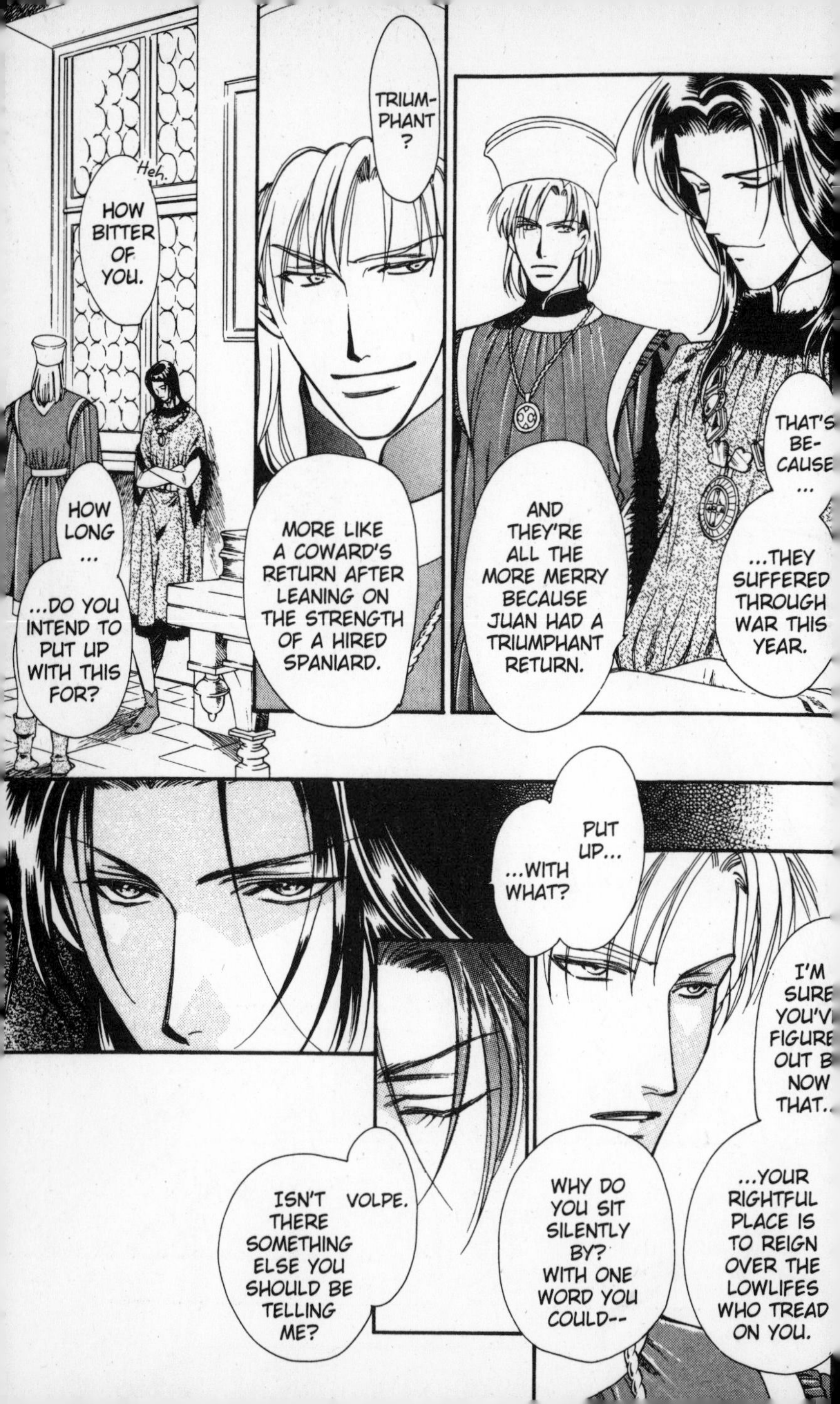
THAT'S BE-CAUSE ...
...THEY SUFFERED THROUGH WAR THIS YEAR.
AND THEY'RE ALL THE MORE MERRY BECAUSE JUAN HAD A TRIUMPHANT RETURN.
TRIUM-PHANT ?
MORE LIKE A COWARD'S RETURN AFTER LEANING ON THE STRENGTH OF A HIRED SPANIARD.
Heh.
HOW BITTER OF YOU.
HOW LONG ...
...DO YOU INTEND TO PUT UP WITH THIS FOR?
PUT UP...
...WITH WHAT?
I'M SURE YOU'V FIGURE OUT B NOW THAT..
...YOUR RIGHTFUL PLACE IS TO REIGN OVER THE LOWLIFES WHO TREAD ON YOU.
WHY DO YOU SIT SILENTLY BY? WITH ONE WORD YOU COULD--
VOLPE.
ISN'T THERE SOMETHING ELSE YOU SHOULD BE TELLING ME?

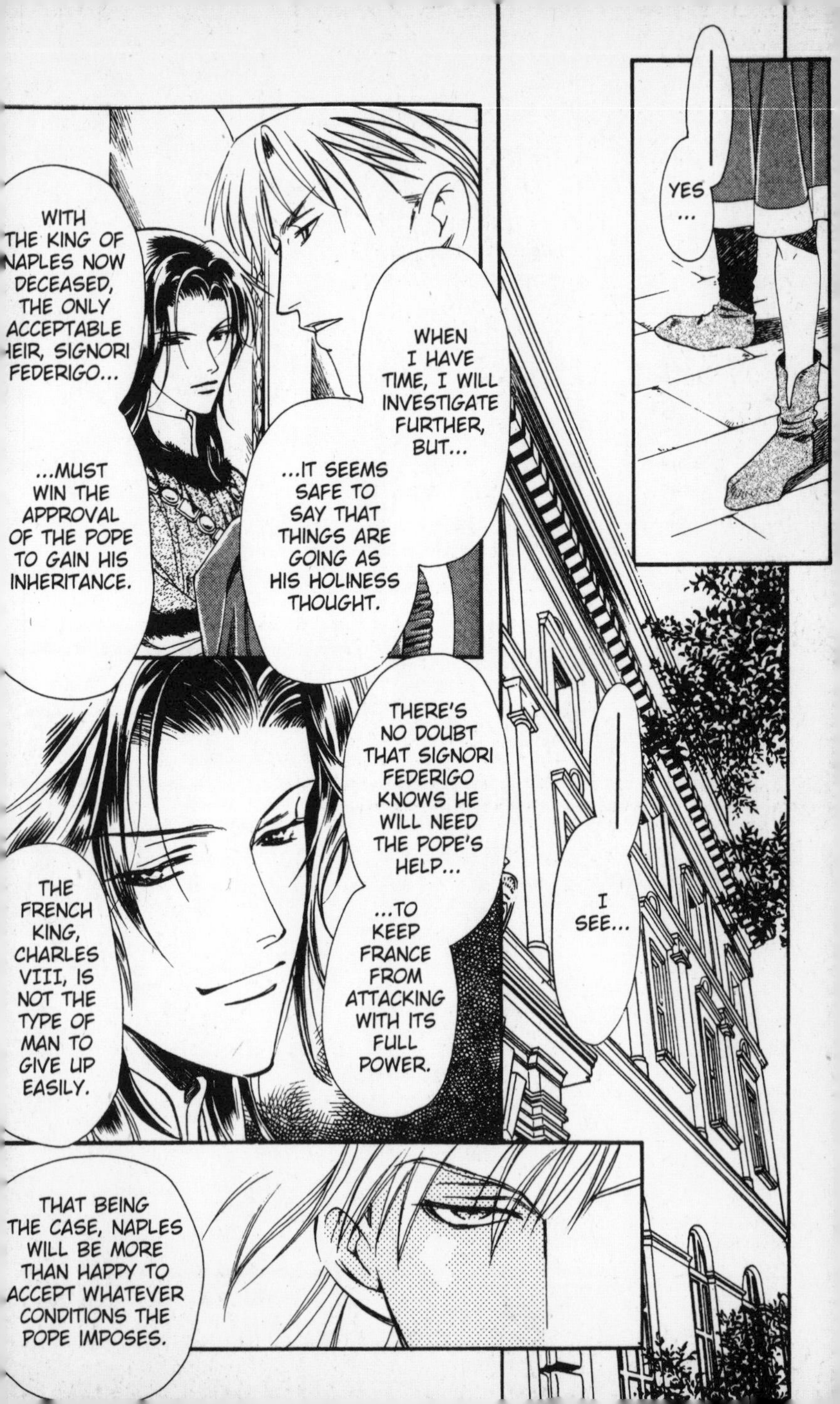
YES...
WHEN I HAVE TIME, I WILL INVESTIGATE FURTHER, BUT...
...IT SEEMS SAFE TO SAY THAT THINGS ARE GOING AS HIS HOLINESS THOUGHT.
WITH THE KING OF NAPLES NOW DECEASED, THE ONLY ACCEPTABLE HEIR, SIGNORI FEDERIGO...
...MUST WIN THE APPROVAL OF THE POPE TO GAIN HIS INHERITANCE.
I SEE...
THERE'S NO DOUBT THAT SIGNORI FEDERIGO KNOWS HE WILL NEED THE POPE'S HELP...
...TO KEEP FRANCE FROM ATTACKING WITH ITS FULL POWER.
THE FRENCH KING, CHARLES VIII, IS NOT THE TYPE OF MAN TO GIVE UP EASILY.
THAT BEING THE CASE, NAPLES WILL BE MORE THAN HAPPY TO ACCEPT WHATEVER CONDITIONS THE POPE IMPOSES.

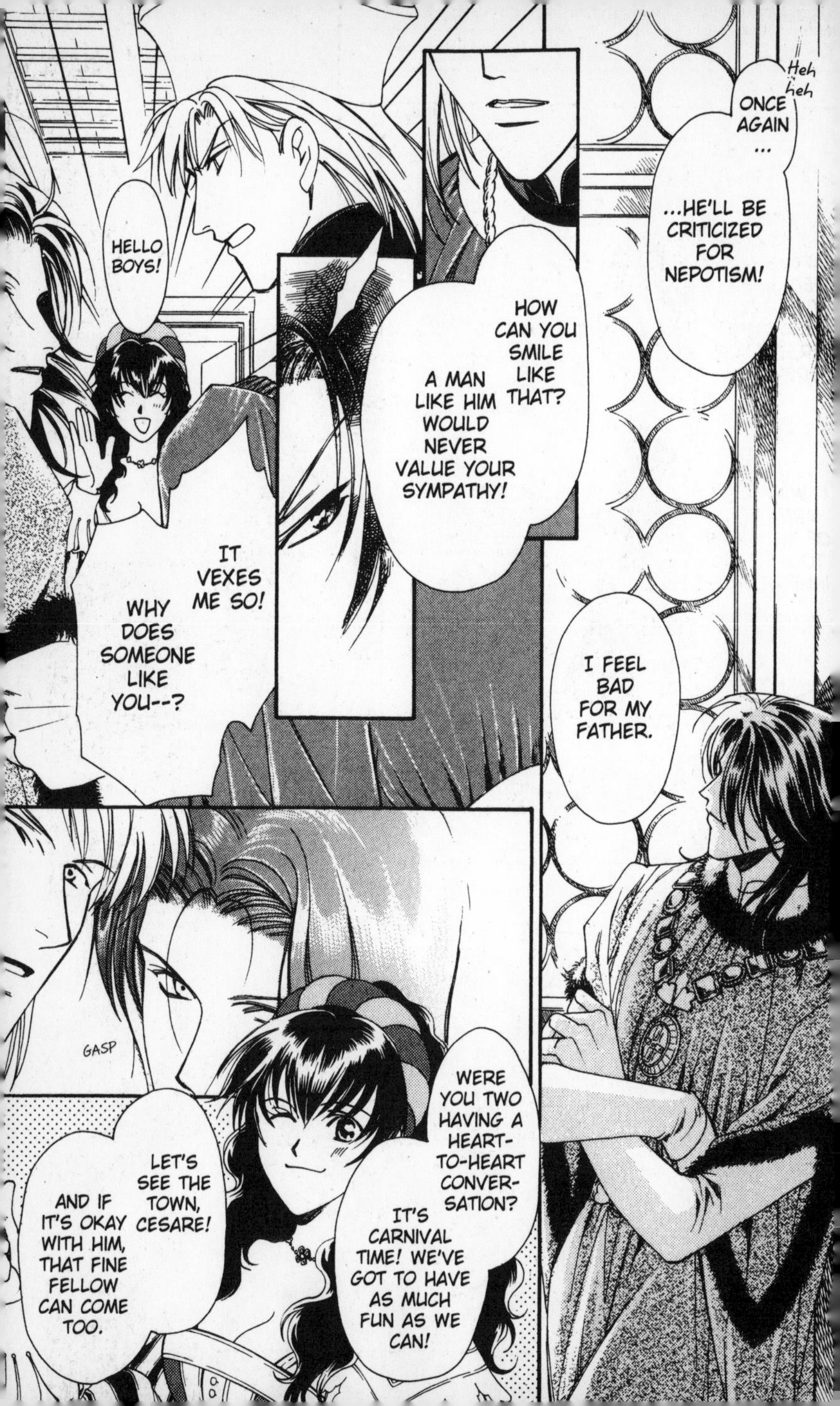
Heh heh
ONCE AGAIN ...
...HE'LL BE CRITICIZED FOR NEPOTISM!
I FEEL BAD FOR MY FATHER.
HOW CAN YOU SMILE LIKE THAT?
A MAN LIKE HIM WOULD NEVER VALUE YOUR SYMPATHY!
IT VEXES ME SO!
WHY DOES SOMEONE LIKE YOU--?
HELLO BOYS!
GASP
WERE YOU TWO HAVING A HEART-TO-HEART CONVER-SATION?
IT'S CARNIVAL TIME! WE'VE GOT TO HAVE AS MUCH FUN AS WE CAN!
LET'S SEE THE TOWN, CESARE!
AND IF IT'S OKAY WITH HIM, THAT FINE FELLOW CAN COME TOO.

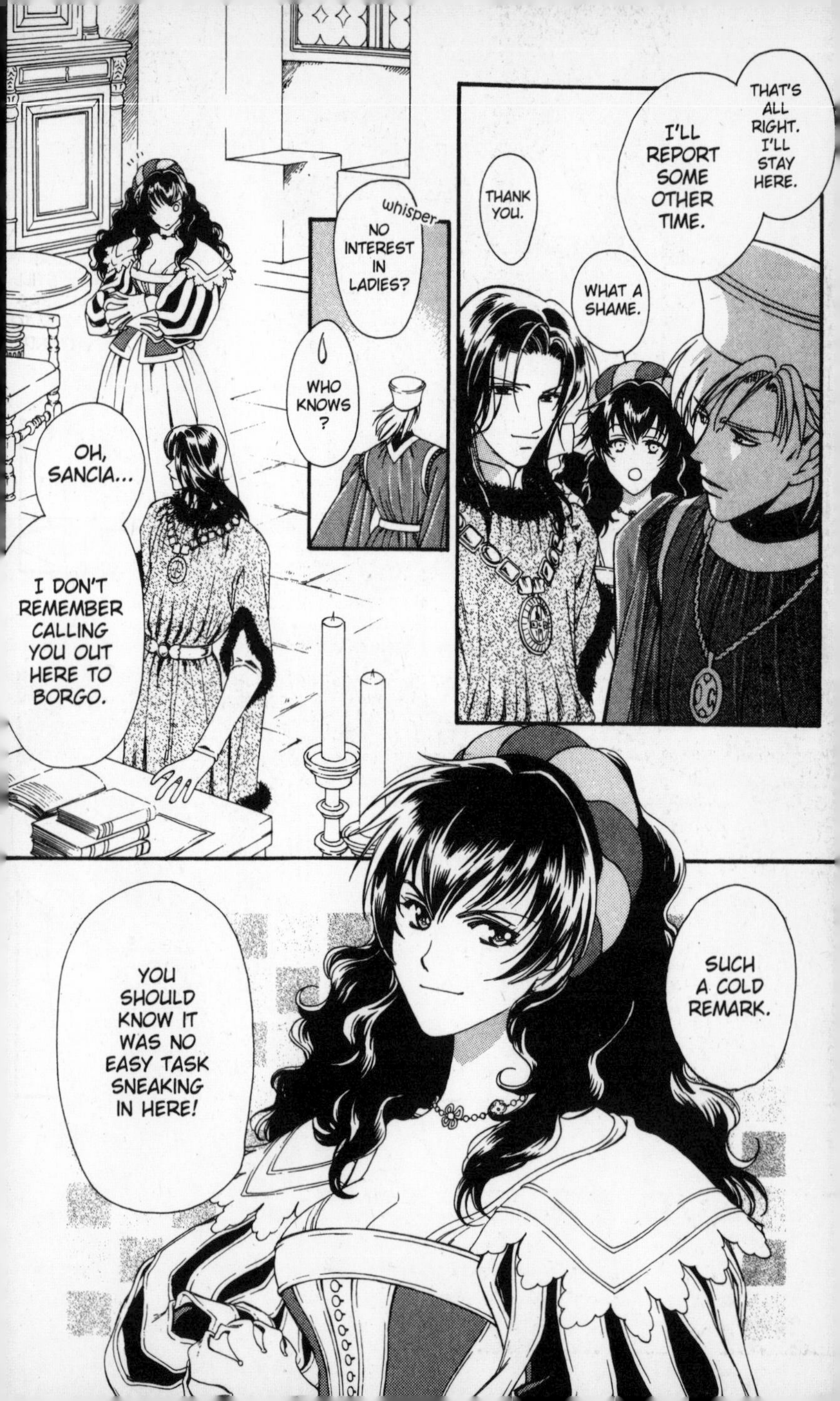
THAT'S ALL RIGHT. I'LL STAY HERE.
I'LL REPORT SOME OTHER TIME.
THANK YOU.
WHAT A SHAME.
whisper
NO INTEREST IN LADIES?
WHO KNOWS?
OH, SANCIA...
I DON'T REMEMBER CALLING YOU OUT HERE TO BORGO.
SUCH A COLD REMARK.
YOU SHOULD KNOW IT WAS NO EASY TASK SNEAKING IN HERE!

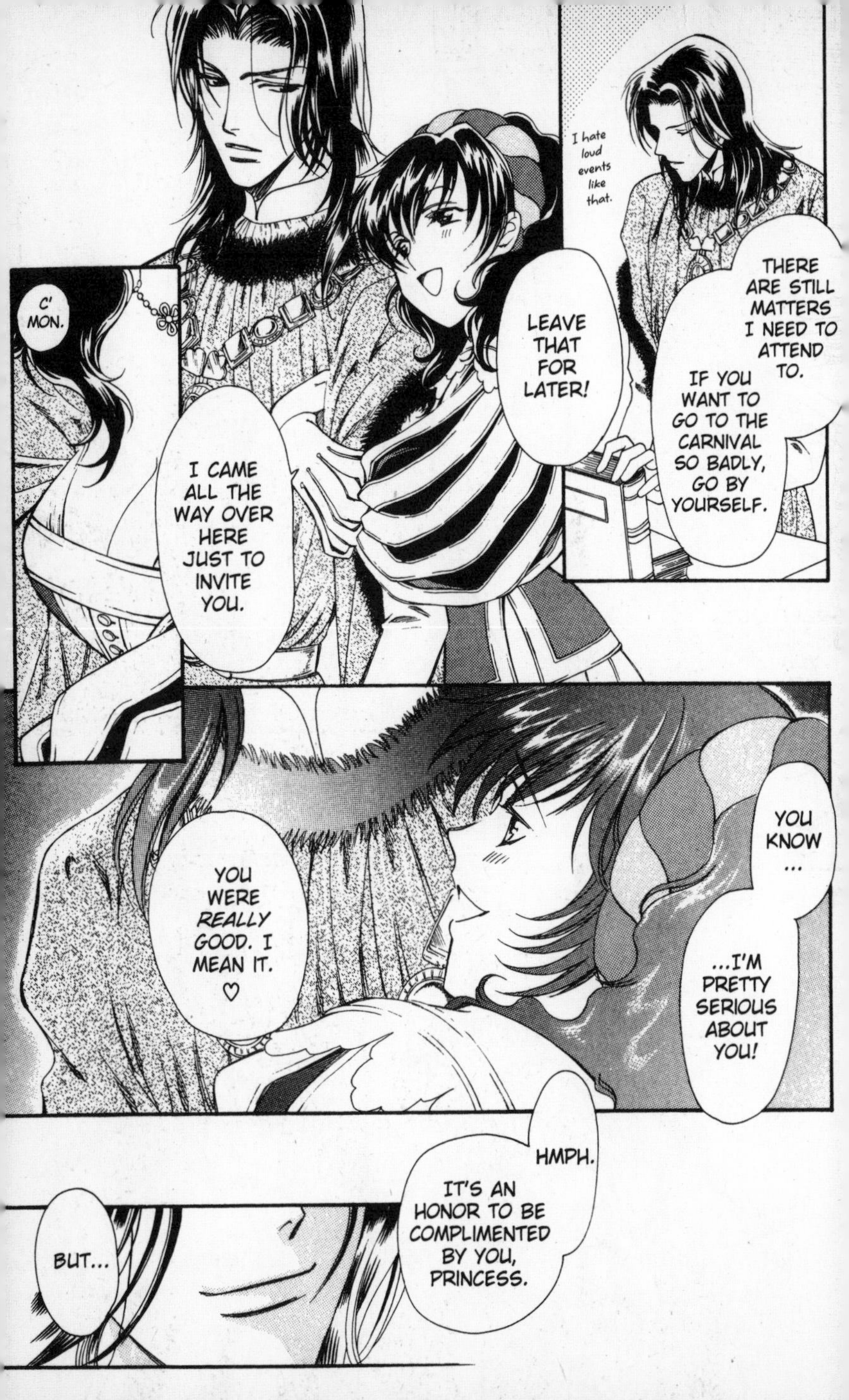
I hate loud events like that.
THERE ARE STILL MATTERS I NEED TO ATTEND TO.
IF YOU WANT TO GO TO THE CARNIVAL SO BADLY, GO BY YOURSELF.
LEAVE THAT FOR LATER!
I CAME ALL THE WAY OVER HERE JUST TO INVITE YOU.
C'MON.
YOU KNOW...
...I'M PRETTY SERIOUS ABOUT YOU!
YOU WERE REALLY GOOD. I MEAN IT. ♡
HMPH.
IT'S AN HONOR TO BE COMPLIMENTED BY YOU, PRINCESS.
BUT...

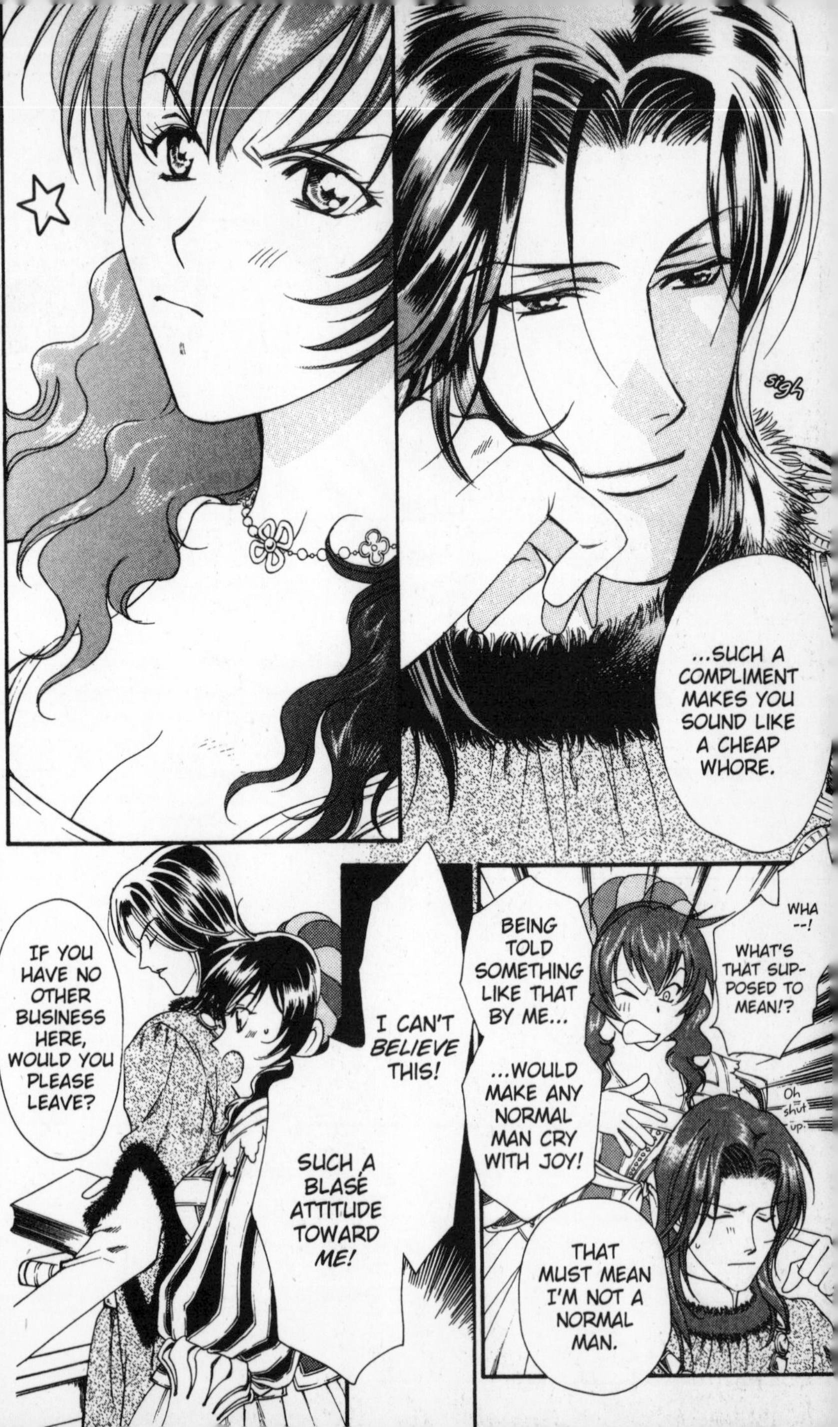
sigh
...SUCH A COMPLIMENT MAKES YOU SOUND LIKE A CHEAP WHORE.
WHA --!
WHAT'S THAT SUP- POSED TO MEAN!?
BEING TOLD SOMETHING LIKE THAT BY ME...
...WOULD MAKE ANY NORMAL MAN CRY WITH JOY!
Oh shut up.
THAT MUST MEAN I'M NOT A NORMAL MAN.
I CAN'T *BELIEVE* THIS!
SUCH A BLASÉ ATTITUDE TOWARD *ME*!
IF YOU HAVE NO OTHER BUSINESS HERE, WOULD YOU PLEASE LEAVE?

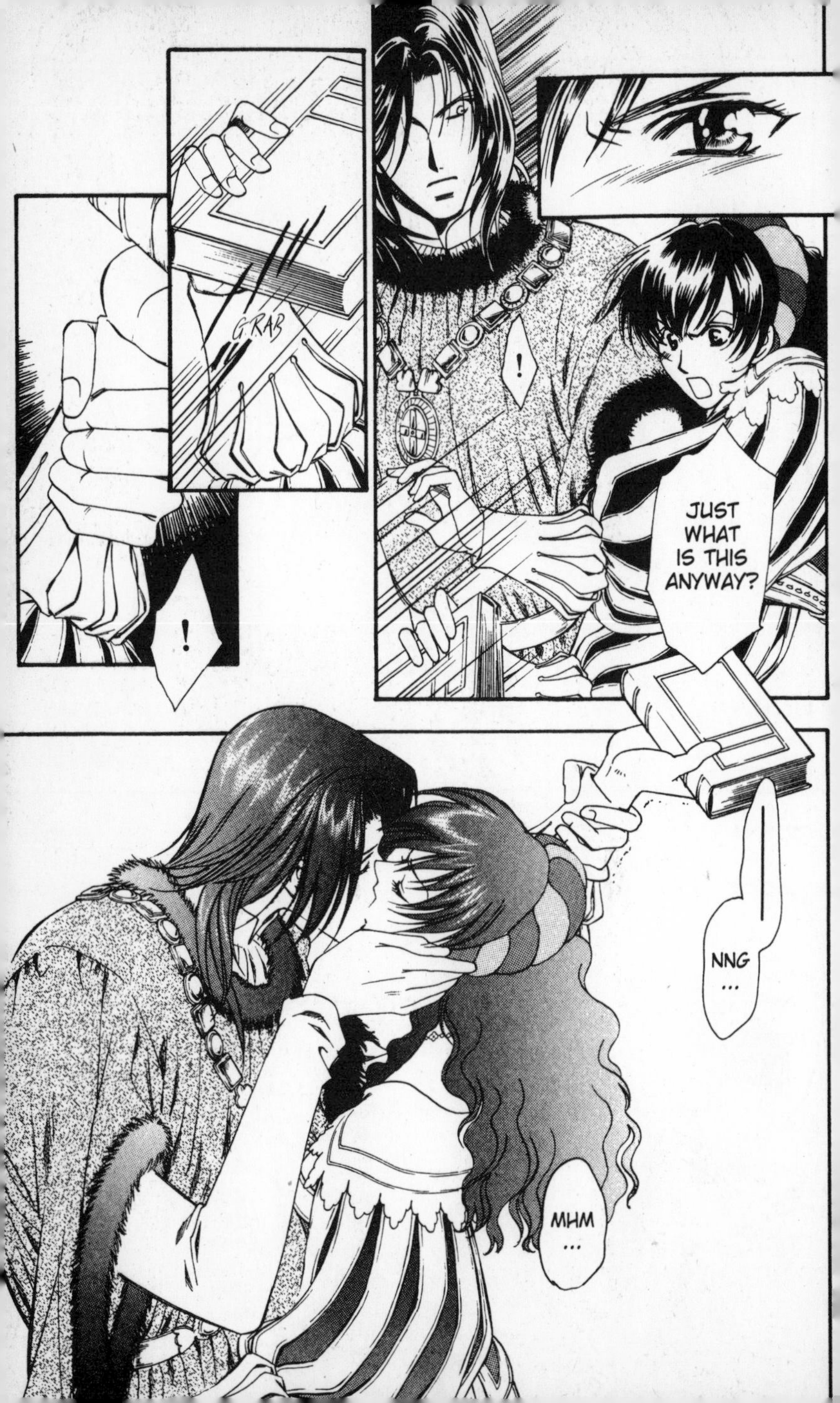
!
JUST WHAT IS THIS ANYWAY?
GRAB
!
NNG ...
MHM ...

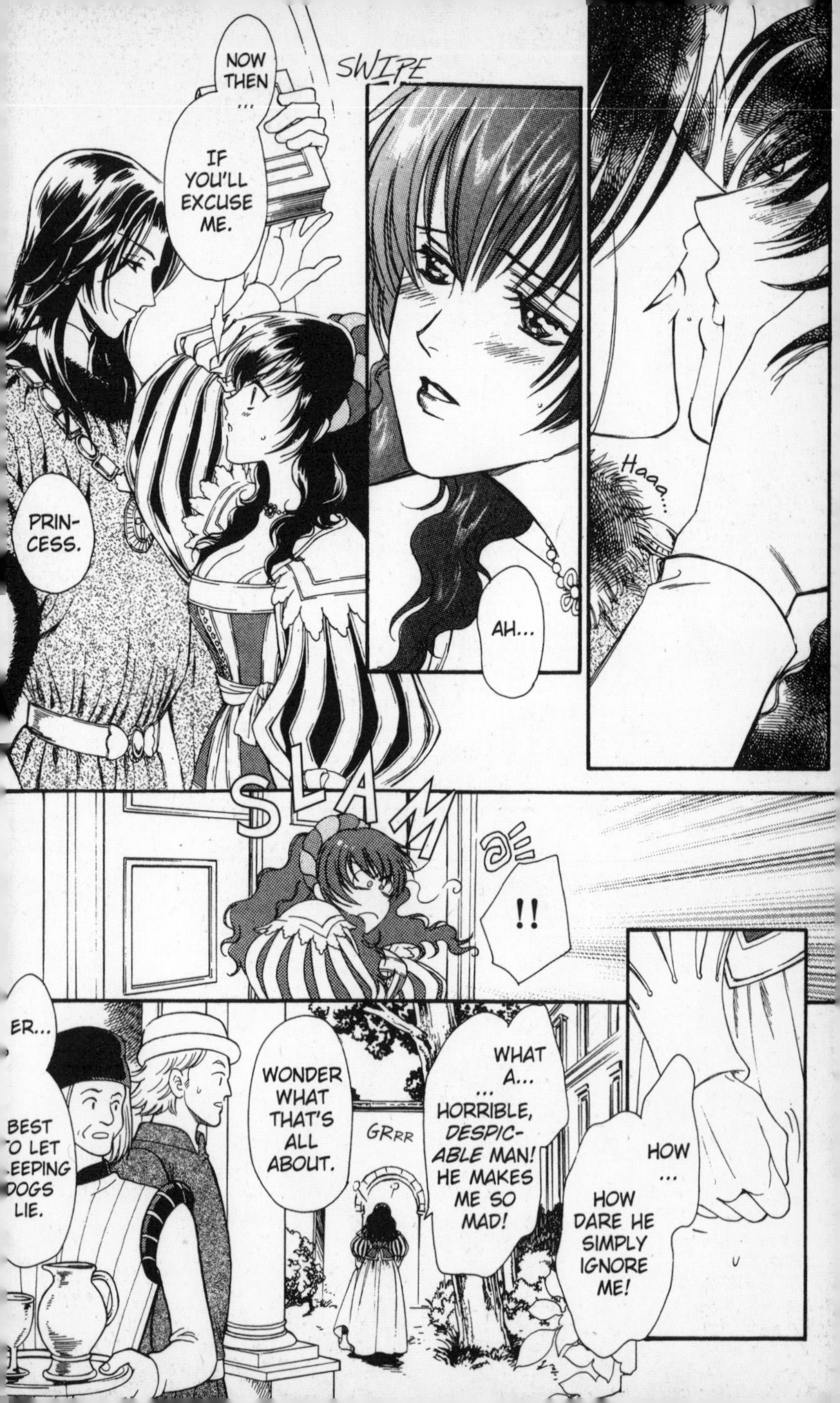
Haaa...
AH...
SWIPE
NOW THEN ...
IF YOU'LL EXCUSE ME.
PRINCESS.
SLAM
!!
HOW ...
HOW DARE HE SIMPLY IGNORE ME!
WHAT A... ... HORRIBLE, DESPICABLE MAN! HE MAKES ME SO MAD!
GRrr
WONDER WHAT THAT'S ALL ABOUT.
ER...
BEST O LET LEEPING DOGS LIE.

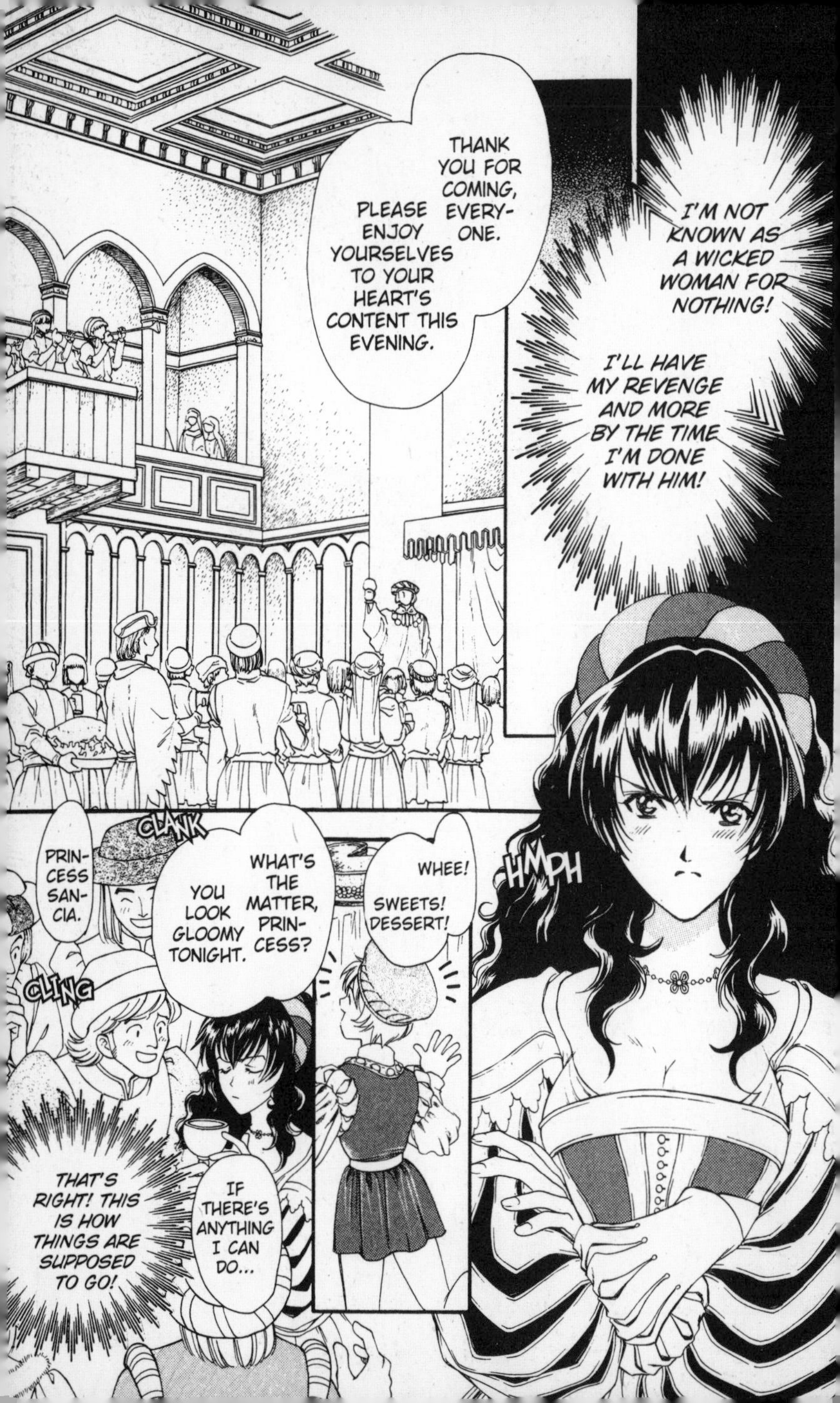
I'M NOT KNOWN AS A WICKED WOMAN FOR NOTHING!
I'LL HAVE MY REVENGE AND MORE BY THE TIME I'M DONE WITH HIM!
HMPH
THANK YOU FOR COMING, EVERY-ONE.
PLEASE ENJOY YOURSELVES TO YOUR HEART'S CONTENT THIS EVENING.
WHEE!
SWEETS! DESSERT!
CLANK
WHAT'S THE MATTER, PRIN-CESS?
YOU LOOK GLOOMY TONIGHT.
PRIN-CESS SAN-CIA.
CLING
IF THERE'S ANYTHING I CAN DO...
THAT'S RIGHT! THIS IS HOW THINGS ARE SUPPOSED TO GO!

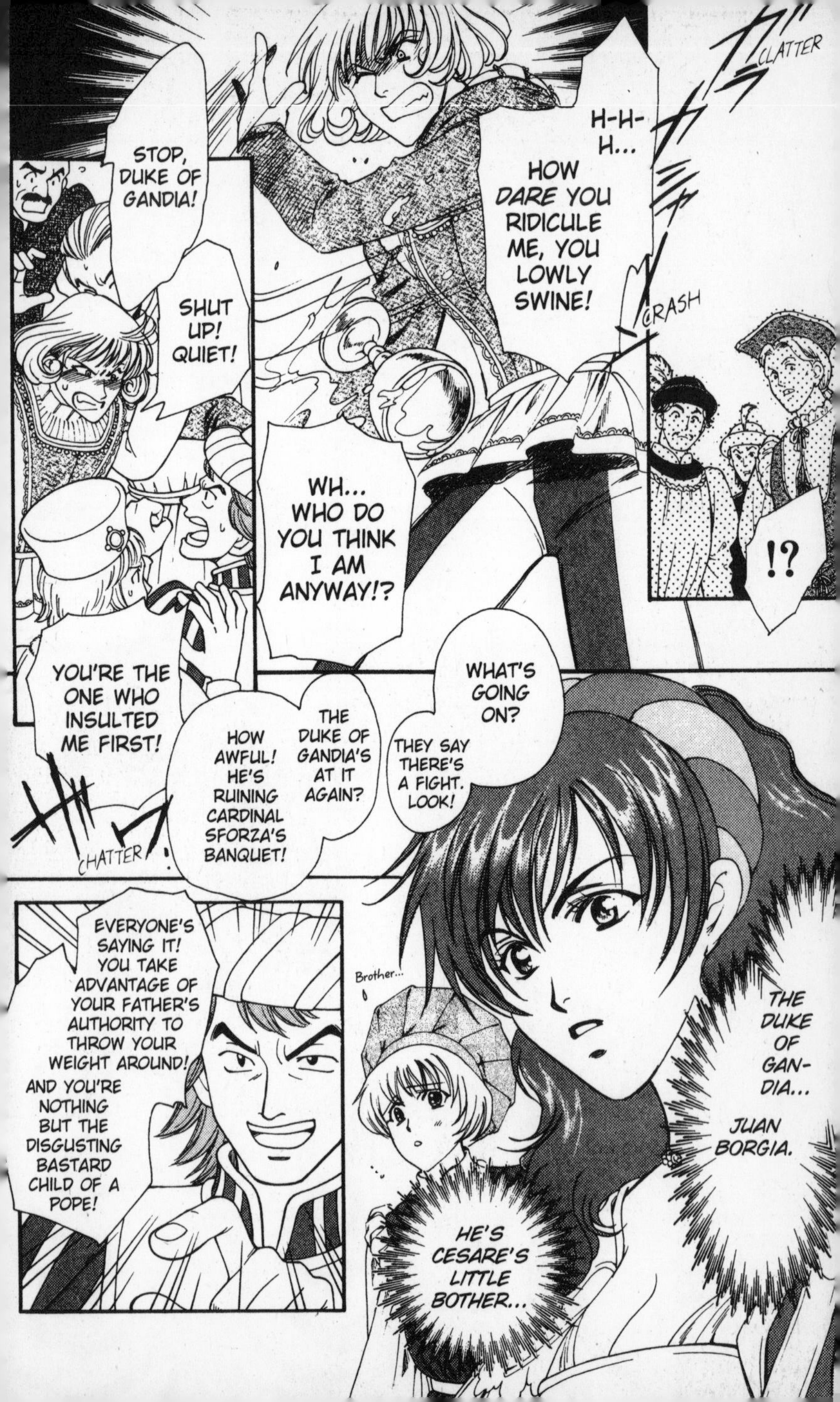
CLATTER
H-H-H... HOW DARE YOU RIDICULE ME, YOU LOWLY SWINE!
CRASH
!?
STOP, DUKE OF GANDIA!
SHUT UP! QUIET!
WH... WHO DO YOU THINK I AM ANYWAY!?
YOU'RE THE ONE WHO INSULTED ME FIRST!
WHAT'S GOING ON?
THEY SAY THERE'S A FIGHT. LOOK!
THE DUKE OF GANDIA'S AT IT AGAIN?
HOW AWFUL! HE'S RUINING CARDINAL SFORZA'S BANQUET!
CHATTER
THE DUKE OF GAN-DIA... JUAN BORGIA.
Brother...
HE'S CESARE'S LITTLE BOTHER...
EVERYONE'S SAYING IT! YOU TAKE ADVANTAGE OF YOUR FATHER'S AUTHORITY TO THROW YOUR WEIGHT AROUND!
AND YOU'RE NOTHING BUT THE DISGUSTING BASTARD CHILD OF A POPE!

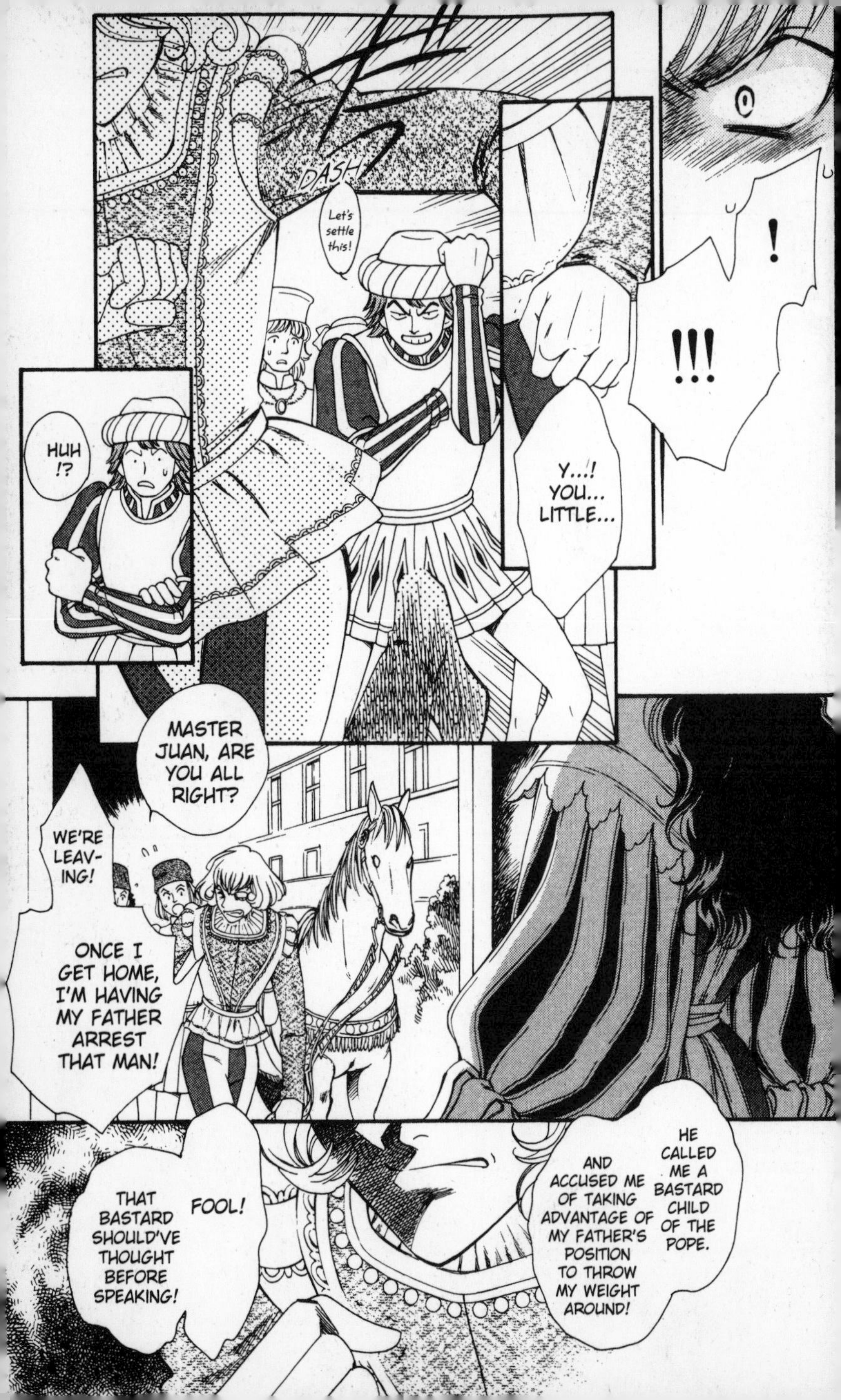
!
!!!
Y...! YOU... LITTLE...
DASH
Let's settle this!
HUH !?
MASTER JUAN, ARE YOU ALL RIGHT?
WE'RE LEAV-ING!
ONCE I GET HOME, I'M HAVING MY FATHER ARREST THAT MAN!
HE CALLED ME A BASTARD CHILD OF THE POPE.
AND ACCUSED ME OF TAKING ADVANTAGE OF MY FATHER'S POSITION TO THROW MY WEIGHT AROUND!
FOOL!
THAT BASTARD SHOULD'VE THOUGHT BEFORE SPEAKING!

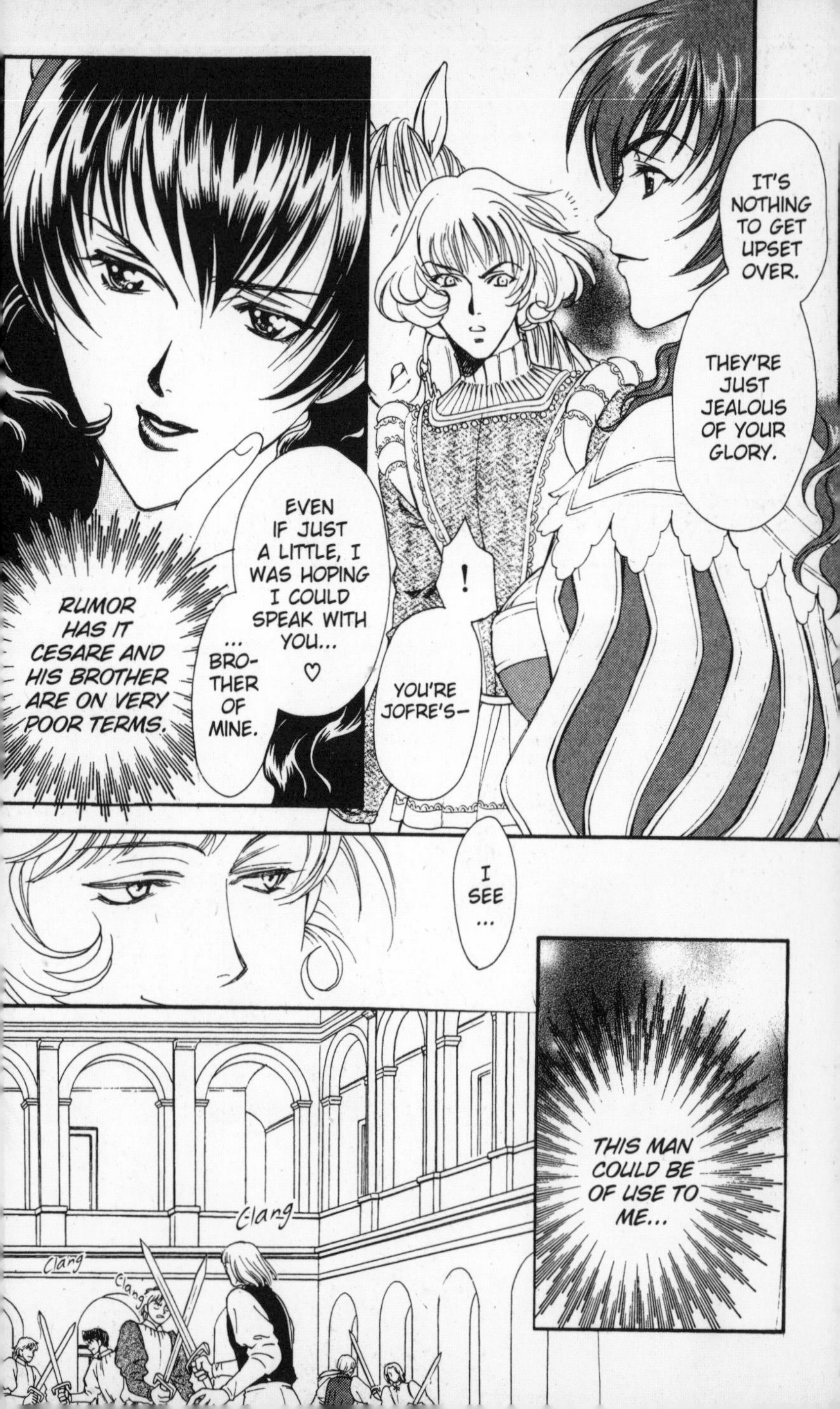
IT'S NOTHING TO GET UPSET OVER.
THEY'RE JUST JEALOUS OF YOUR GLORY.
!
YOU'RE JOFRE'S—
EVEN IF JUST A LITTLE, I WAS HOPING I COULD SPEAK WITH YOU... ♡
...BROTHER OF MINE.
RUMOR HAS IT CESARE AND HIS BROTHER ARE ON VERY POOR TERMS.
I SEE...
THIS MAN COULD BE OF USE TO ME...
Clang
Clang
Clang

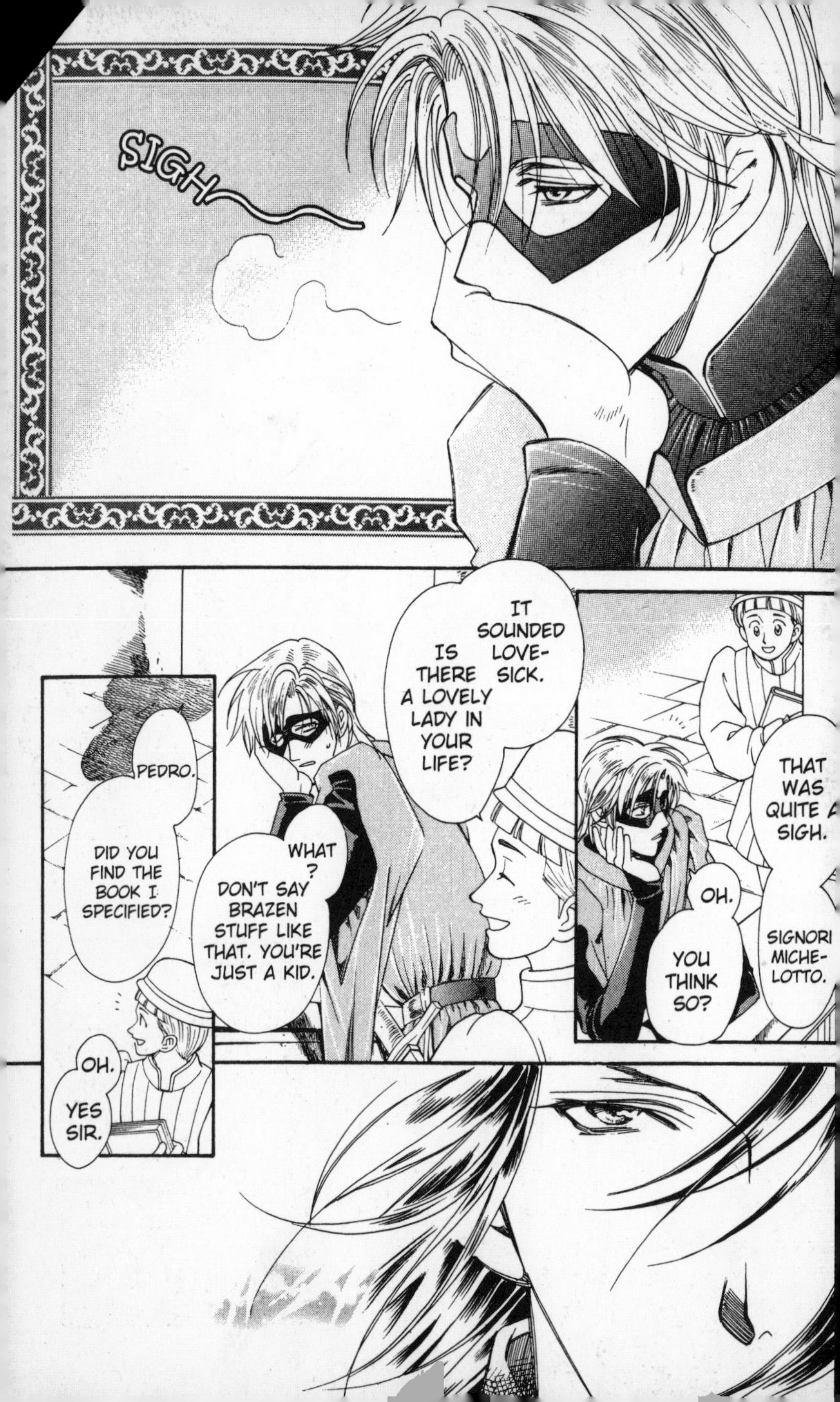

SIGH
THAT WAS QUITE A SIGH.
SIGNORI MICHE-LOTTO.
OH.
YOU THINK SO?
IT SOUNDED LOVE-SICK.
IS THERE A LOVELY LADY IN YOUR LIFE?
WHAT? DON'T SAY BRAZEN STUFF LIKE THAT. YOU'RE JUST A KID.
PEDRO.
DID YOU FIND THE BOOK I SPECIFIED?
OH.
YES SIR.

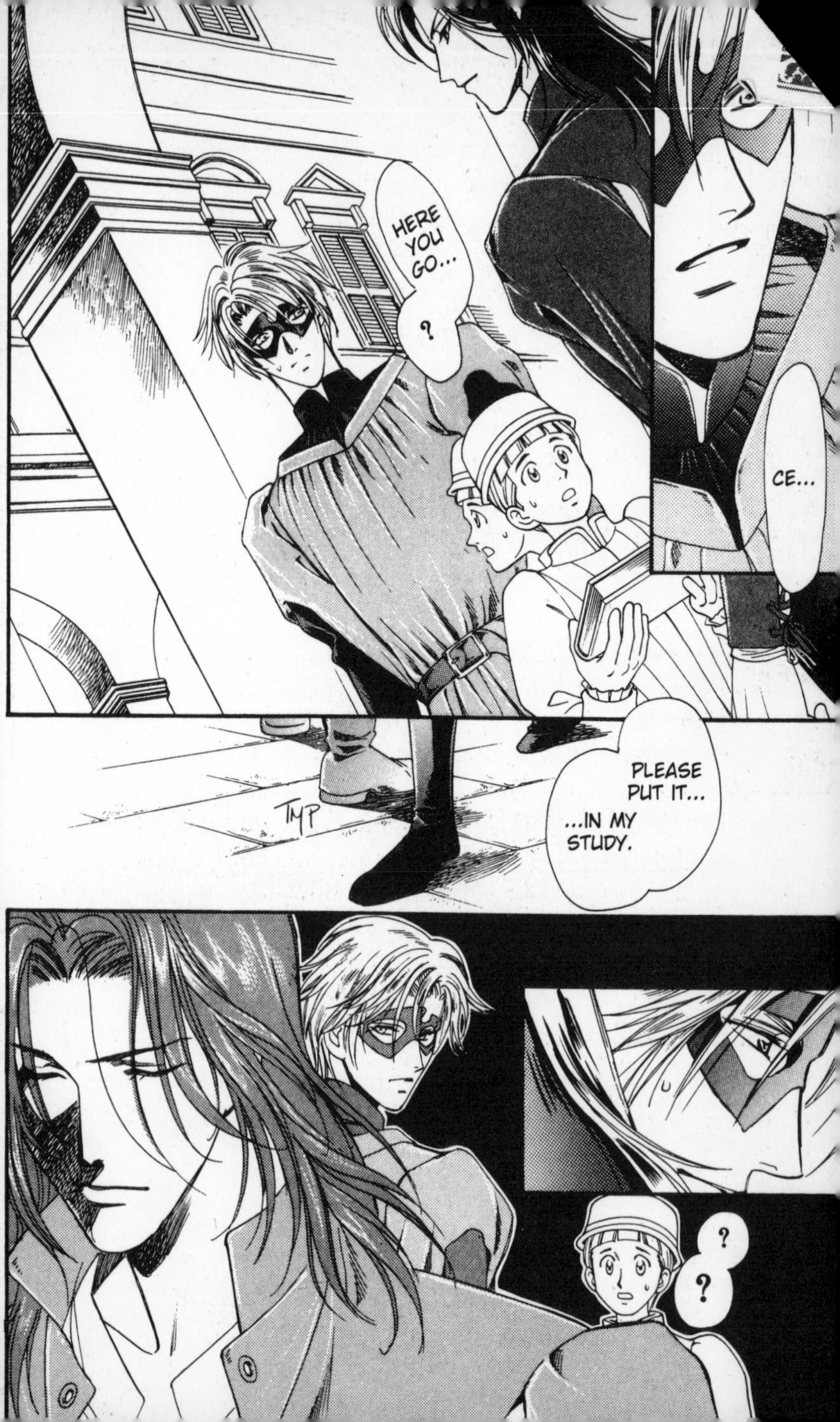
CE...
HERE YOU GO...
?
PLEASE PUT IT...
...IN MY STUDY.
TMP
?
?

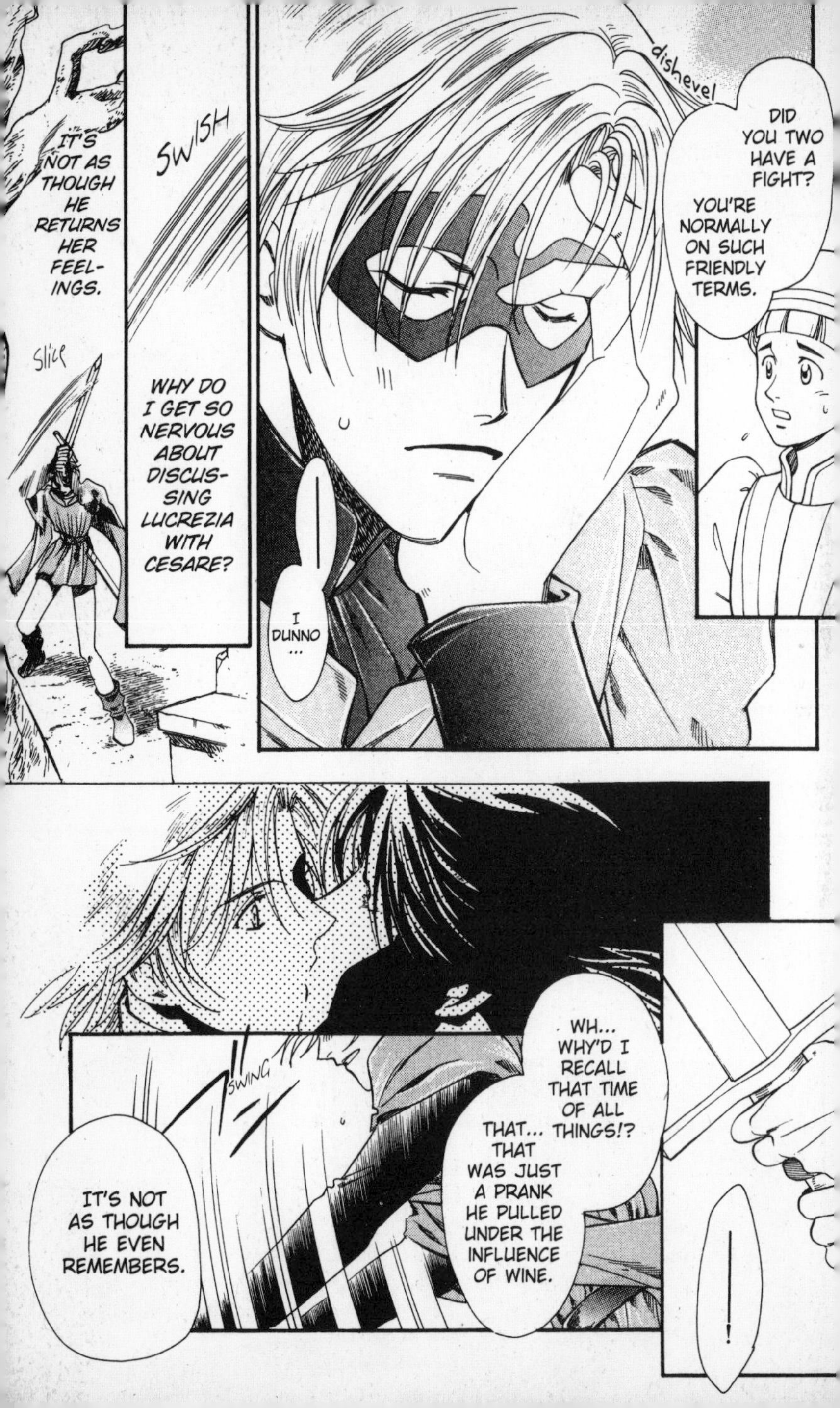
dishevel
DID YOU TWO HAVE A FIGHT?
YOU'RE NORMALLY ON SUCH FRIENDLY TERMS.
SWISH
I DUNNO...
WHY DO I GET SO NERVOUS ABOUT DISCUSSING LUCREZIA WITH CESARE?
IT'S NOT AS THOUGH HE RETURNS HER FEELINGS.
Slice
!
WH... WHY'D I RECALL THAT TIME OF ALL THINGS!?
THAT... THAT WAS JUST A PRANK HE PULLED UNDER THE INFLUENCE OF WINE.
SWING
IT'S NOT AS THOUGH HE EVEN REMEMBERS.

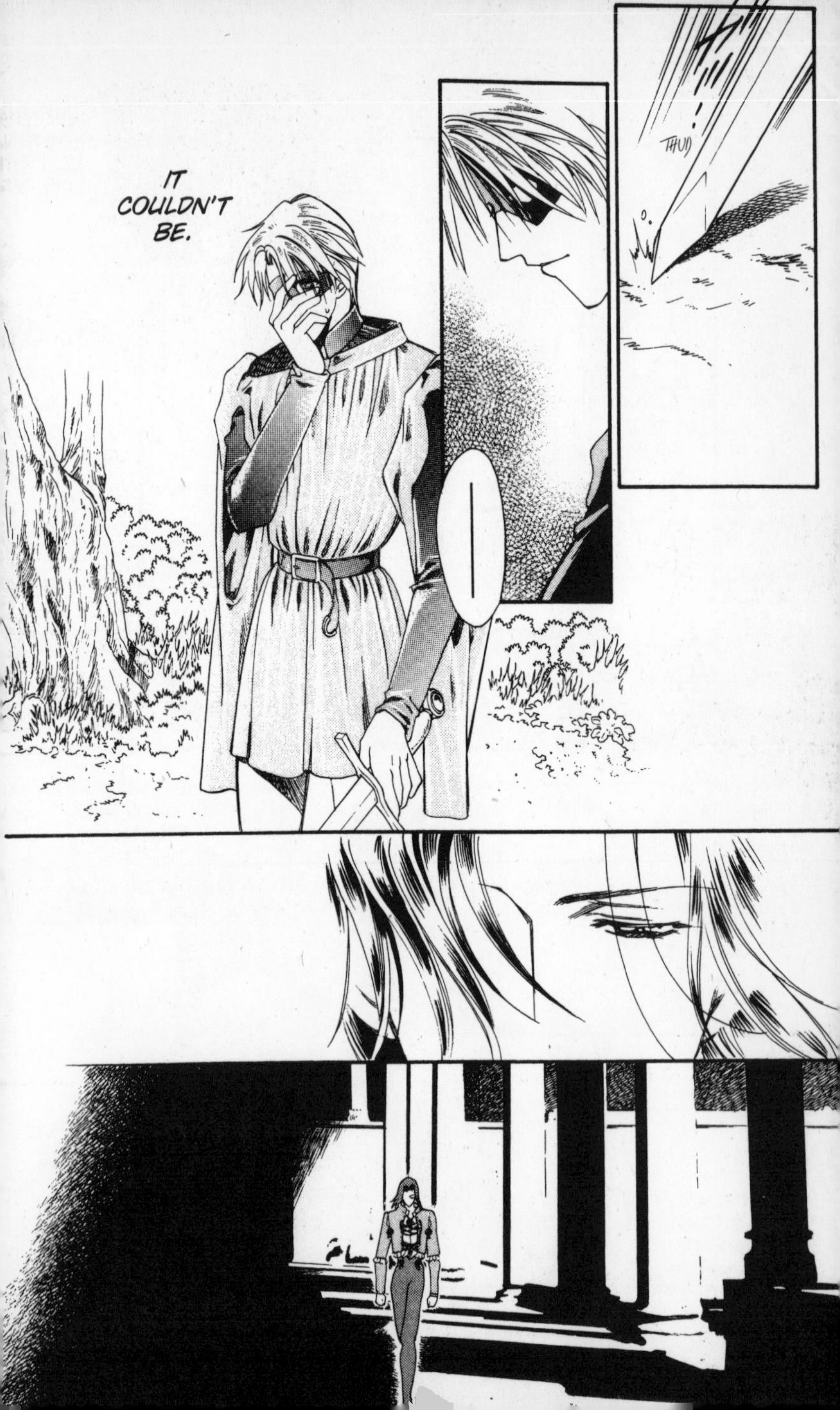
THUD
IT COULDN'T BE.

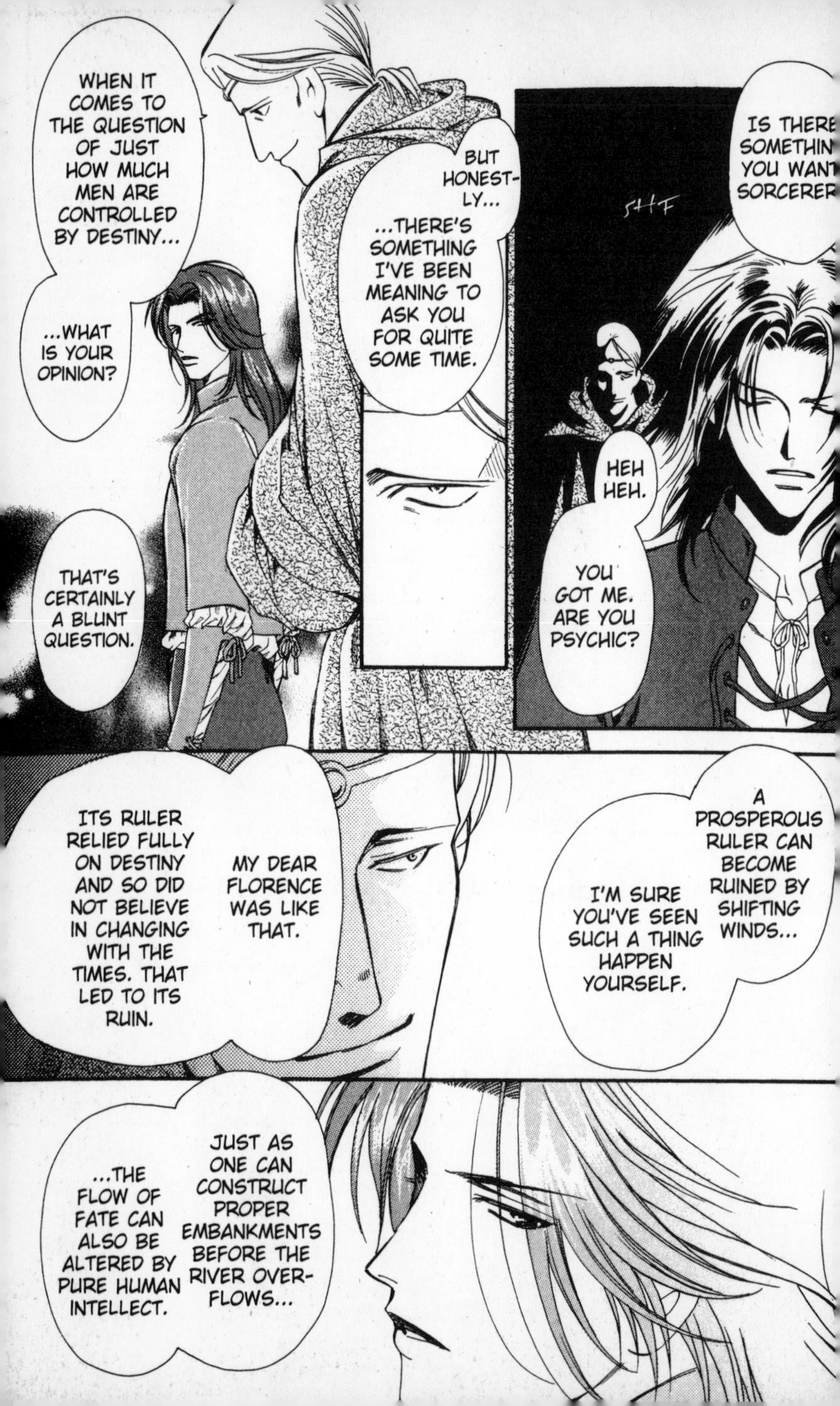
IS THERE SOMETHIN YOU WANT SORCERER
SHF
HEH HEH.
YOU GOT ME. ARE YOU PSYCHIC?
BUT HONESTLY...
...THERE'S SOMETHING I'VE BEEN MEANING TO ASK YOU FOR QUITE SOME TIME.
WHEN IT COMES TO THE QUESTION OF JUST HOW MUCH MEN ARE CONTROLLED BY DESTINY...
...WHAT IS YOUR OPINION?
THAT'S CERTAINLY A BLUNT QUESTION.
A PROSPEROUS RULER CAN BECOME RUINED BY SHIFTING WINDS...
I'M SURE YOU'VE SEEN SUCH A THING HAPPEN YOURSELF.
MY DEAR FLORENCE WAS LIKE THAT.
ITS RULER RELIED FULLY ON DESTINY AND SO DID NOT BELIEVE IN CHANGING WITH THE TIMES. THAT LED TO ITS RUIN.
JUST AS ONE CAN CONSTRUCT PROPER EMBANKMENTS BEFORE THE RIVER OVERFLOWS...
...THE FLOW OF FATE CAN ALSO BE ALTERED BY PURE HUMAN INTELLECT.

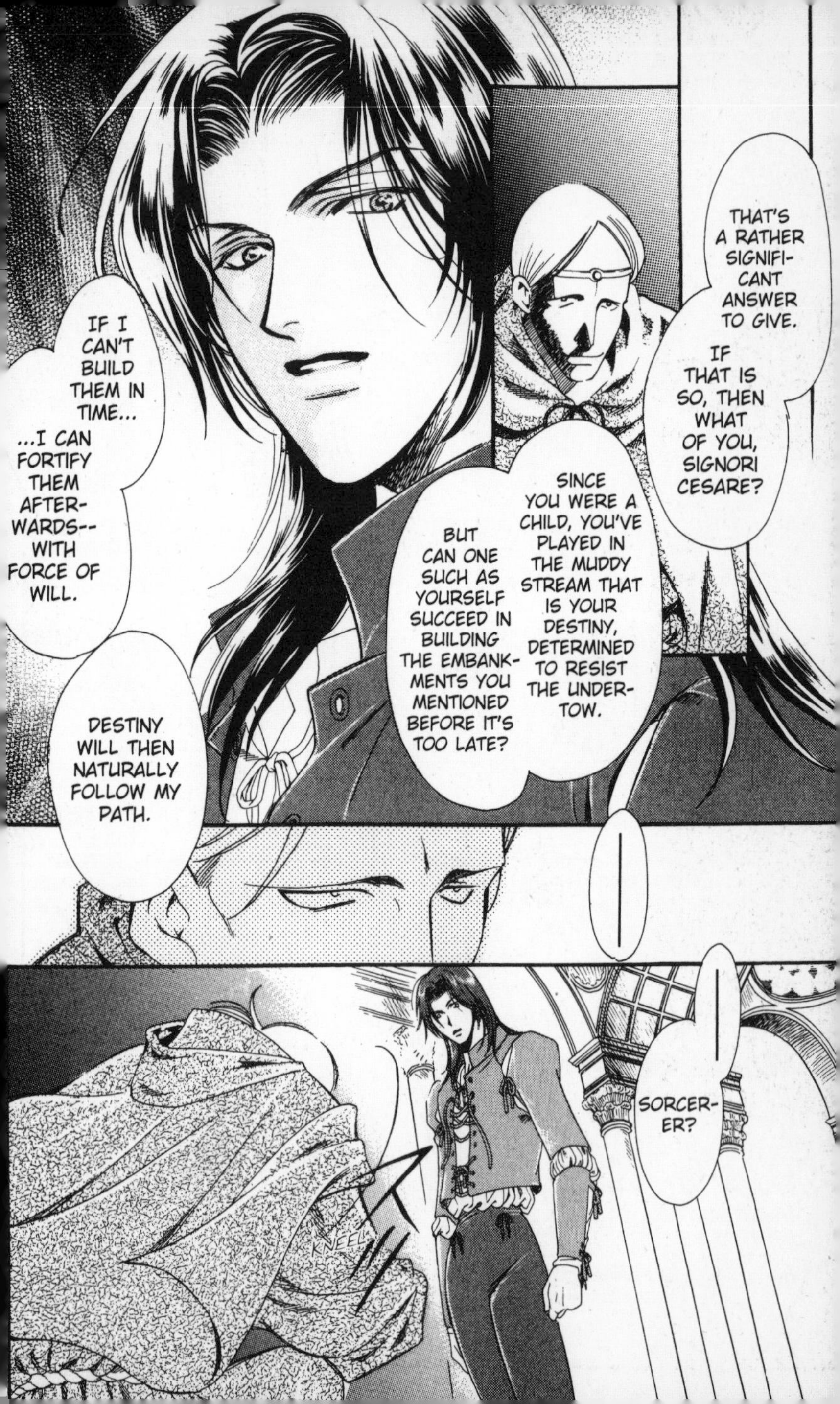

THAT'S A RATHER SIGNIFICANT ANSWER TO GIVE.
IF THAT IS SO, THEN WHAT OF YOU, SIGNORI CESARE?
SINCE YOU WERE A CHILD, YOU'VE PLAYED IN THE MUDDY STREAM THAT IS YOUR DESTINY, DETERMINED TO RESIST THE UNDERTOW.
BUT CAN ONE SUCH AS YOURSELF SUCCEED IN BUILDING THE EMBANKMENTS YOU MENTIONED BEFORE IT'S TOO LATE?
IF I CAN'T BUILD THEM IN TIME...
...I CAN FORTIFY THEM AFTERWARDS--WITH FORCE OF WILL.
DESTINY WILL THEN NATURALLY FOLLOW MY PATH.
—
—
SORCERER?
KNEEL

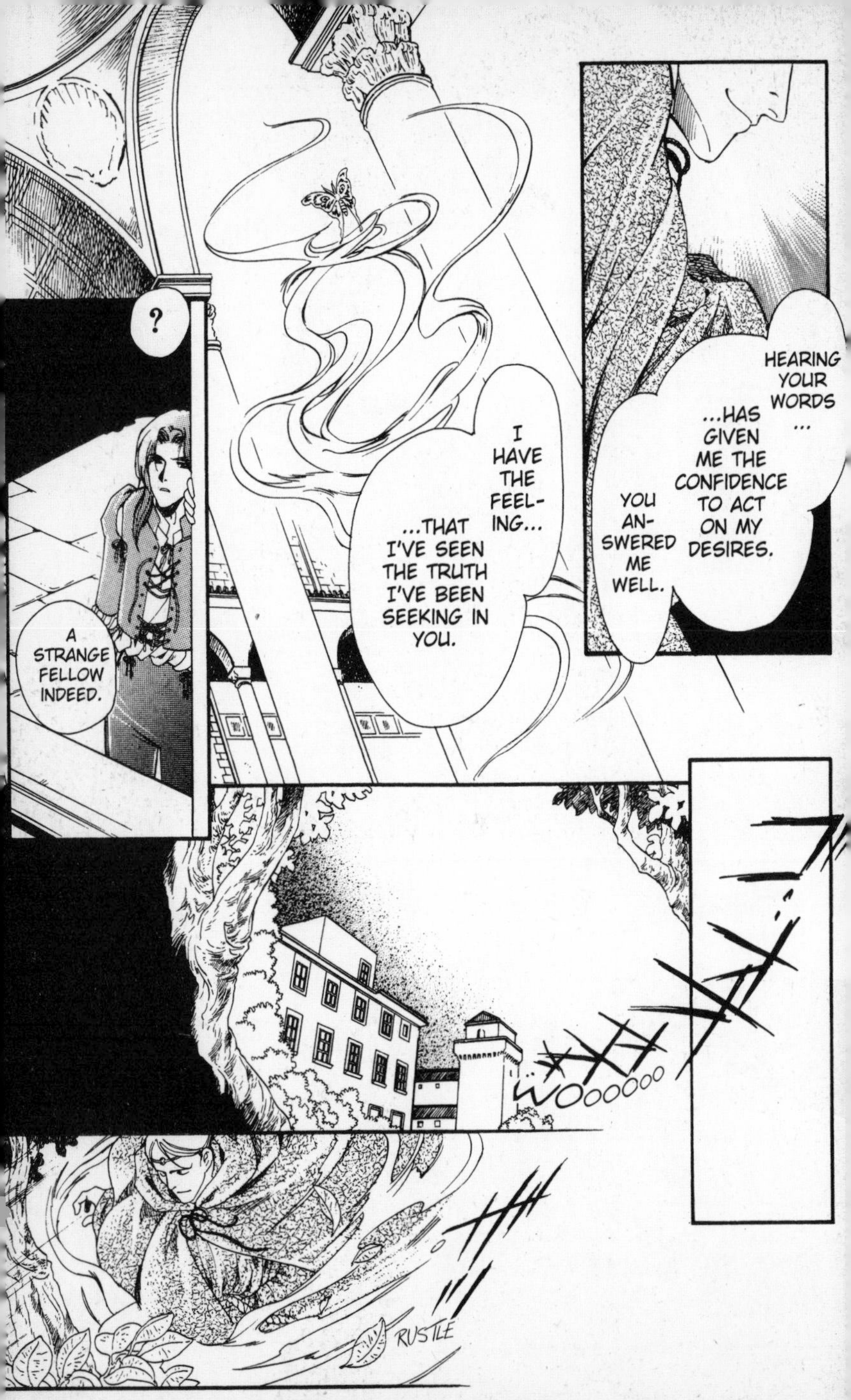
HEARING YOUR WORDS...
...HAS GIVEN ME THE CONFIDENCE TO ACT ON MY DESIRES.
YOU AN-SWERED ME WELL.
I HAVE THE FEEL-ING...
...THAT I'VE SEEN THE TRUTH I'VE BEEN SEEKING IN YOU.
?
A STRANGE FELLOW INDEED.
WOOOOOO
RUSTLE

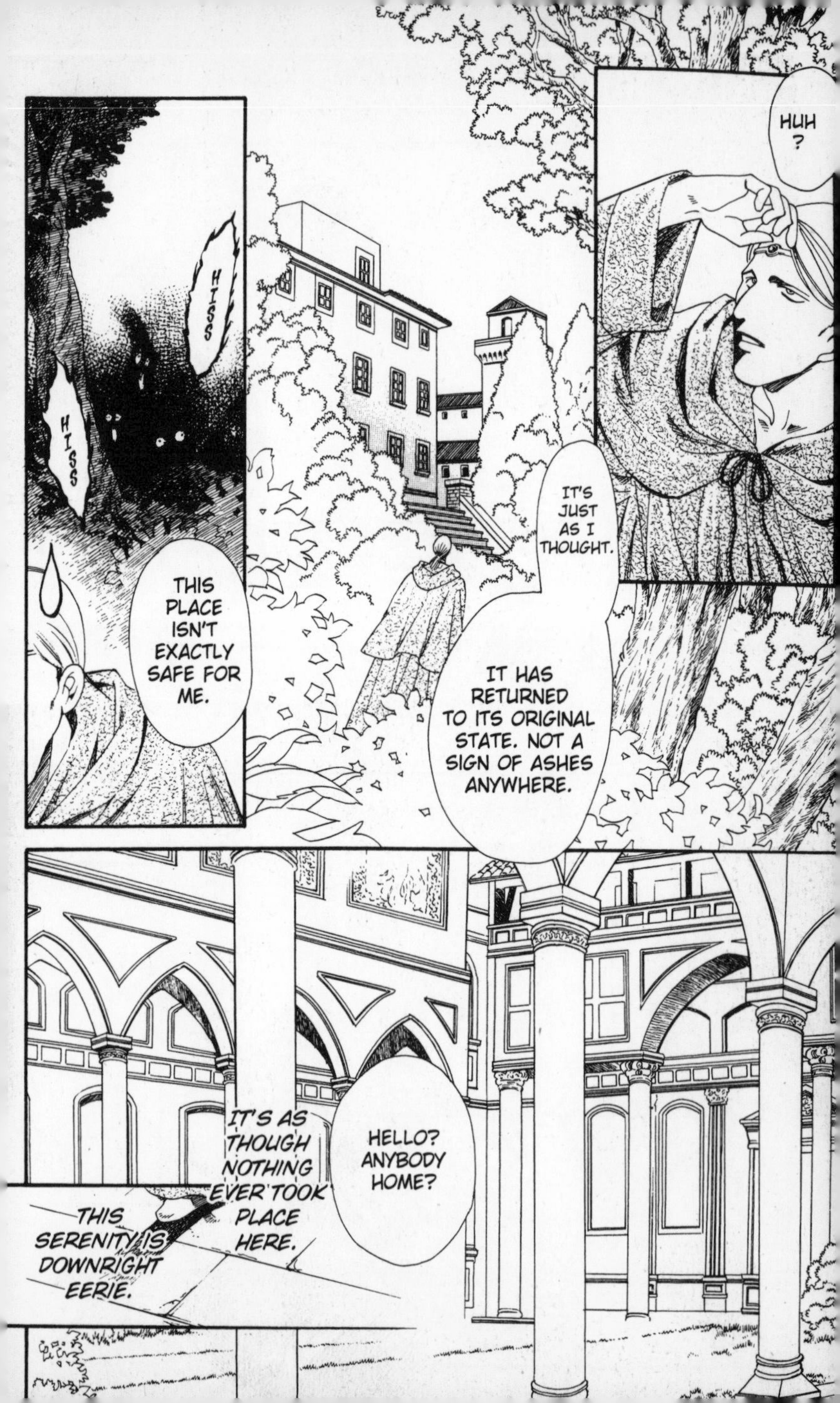
HUH?
IT'S JUST AS I THOUGHT.
IT HAS RETURNED TO ITS ORIGINAL STATE. NOT A SIGN OF ASHES ANYWHERE.
HISS
HISS
THIS PLACE ISN'T EXACTLY SAFE FOR ME.
HELLO? ANYBODY HOME?
IT'S AS THOUGH NOTHING EVER TOOK PLACE HERE.
THIS SERENITY IS DOWNRIGHT EERIE.

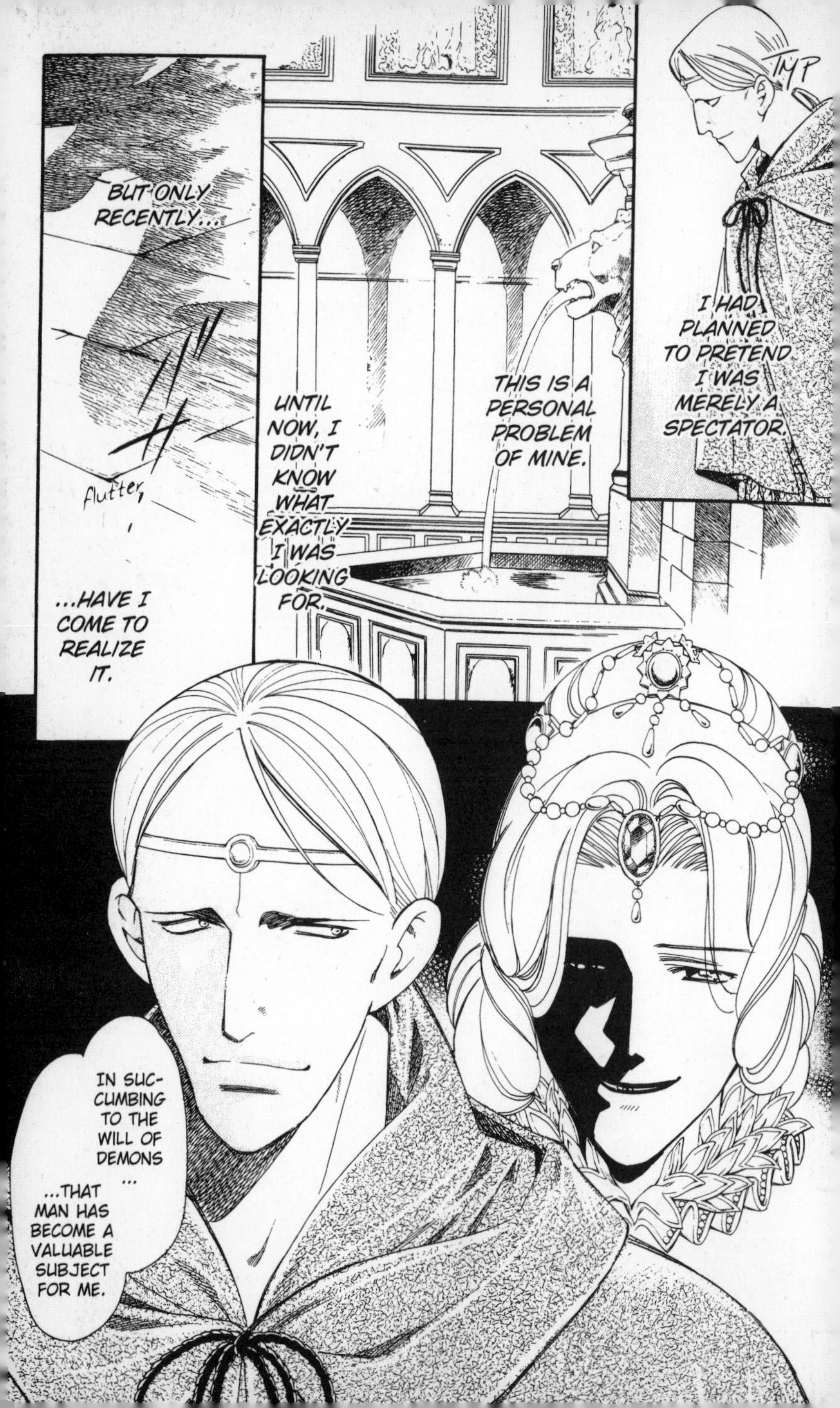
TMP
I HAD PLANNED TO PRETEND I WAS MERELY A SPECTATOR.
THIS IS A PERSONAL PROBLEM OF MINE.
UNTIL NOW, I DIDN'T KNOW WHAT EXACTLY I WAS LOOKING FOR.
BUT ONLY RECENTLY...
flutter
...HAVE I COME TO REALIZE IT.
IN SUCCUMBING TO THE WILL OF DEMONS...
...THAT MAN HAS BECOME A VALUABLE SUBJECT FOR ME.

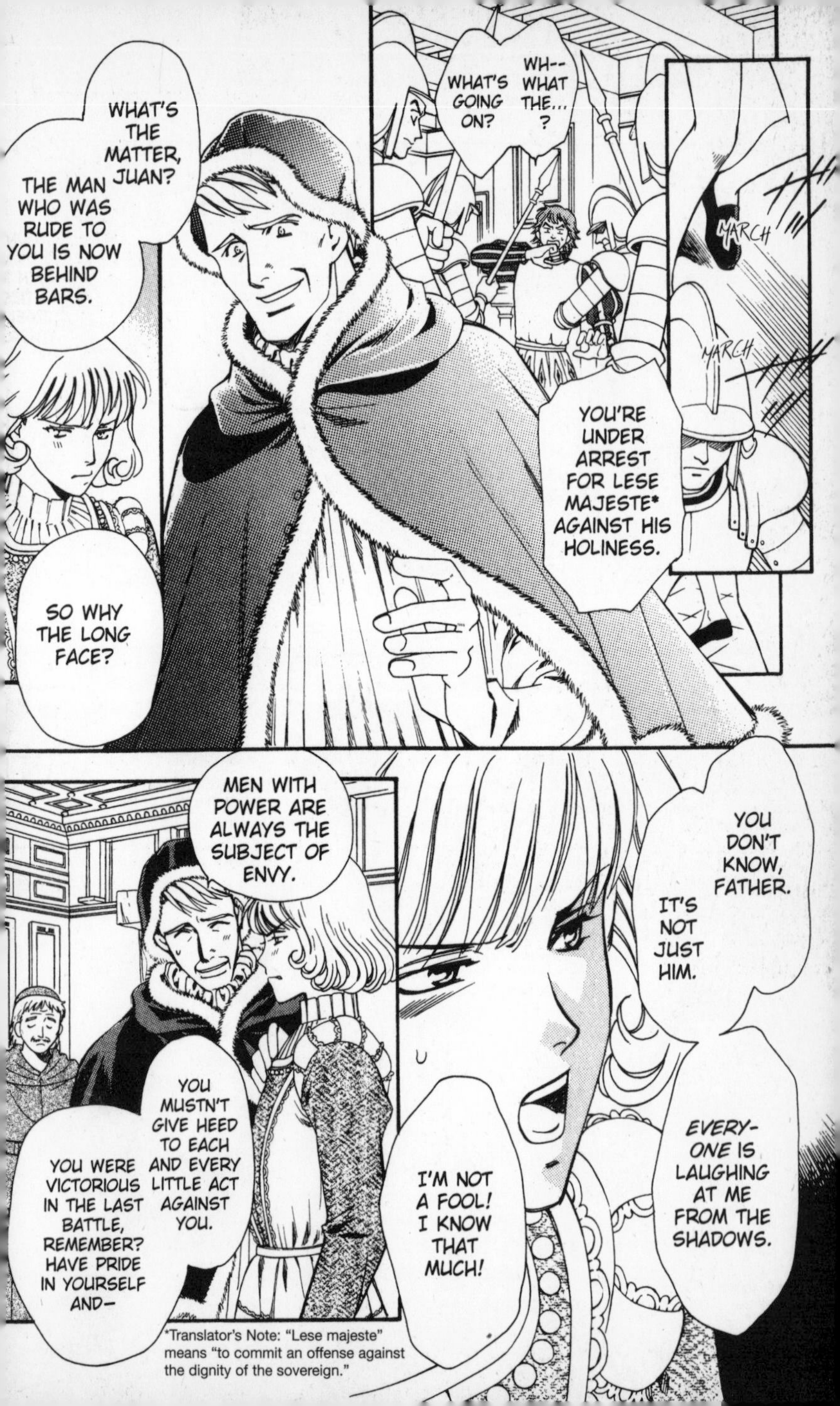
MARCH
MARCH
WH-- WHAT THE... ?
WHAT'S GOING ON?
YOU'RE UNDER ARREST FOR LESE MAJESTE* AGAINST HIS HOLINESS.
WHAT'S THE MATTER, JUAN?
THE MAN WHO WAS RUDE TO YOU IS NOW BEHIND BARS.
SO WHY THE LONG FACE?
YOU DON'T KNOW, FATHER.
IT'S NOT JUST HIM.
EVERYONE IS LAUGHING AT ME FROM THE SHADOWS.
I'M NOT A FOOL! I KNOW THAT MUCH!
MEN WITH POWER ARE ALWAYS THE SUBJECT OF ENVY.
YOU MUSTN'T GIVE HEED TO EACH AND EVERY LITTLE ACT AGAINST YOU.
YOU WERE VICTORIOUS IN THE LAST BATTLE, REMEMBER? HAVE PRIDE IN YOURSELF AND–

*Translator's Note: "Lese majeste" means "to commit an offense against the dignity of the sovereign."

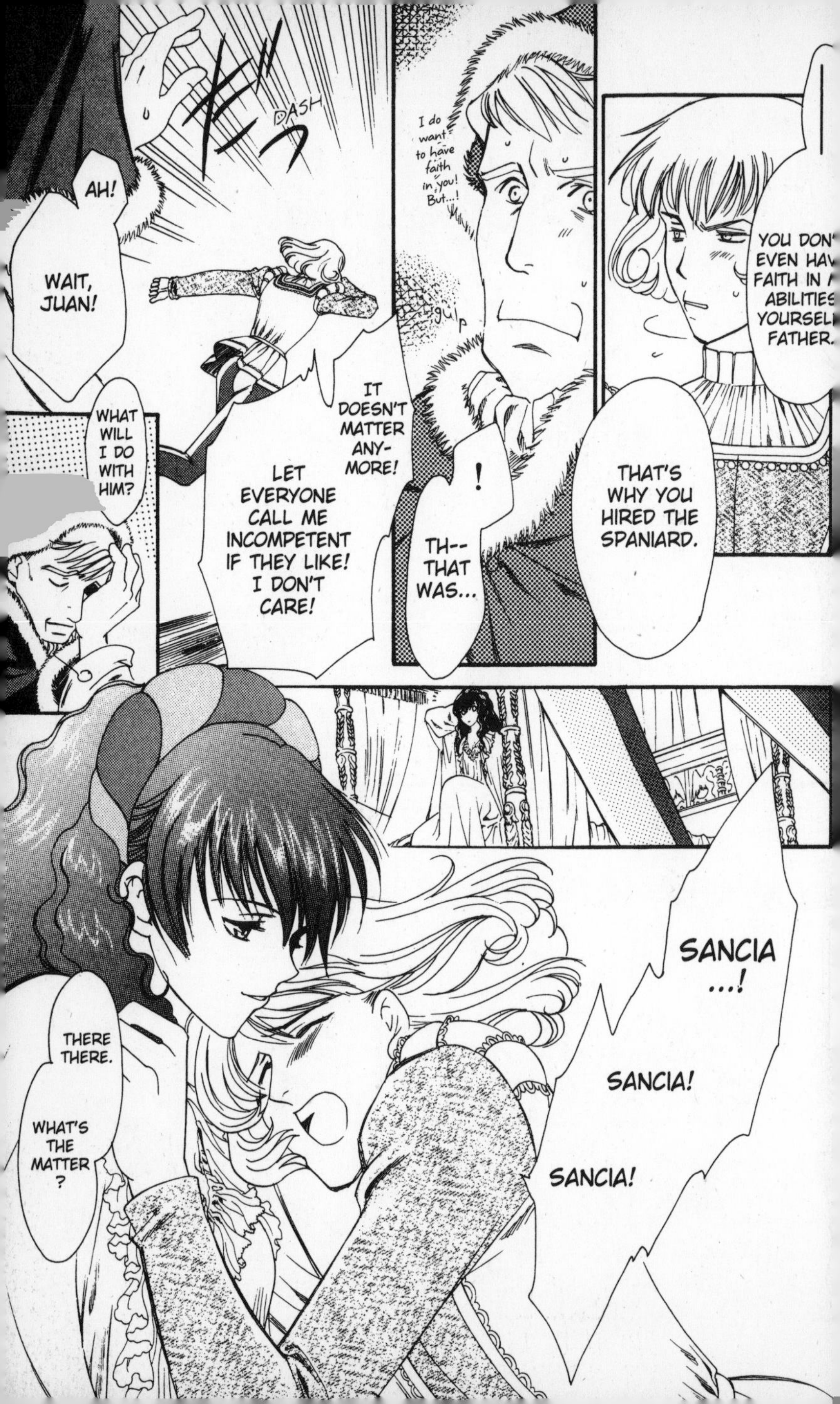
YOU DON' EVEN HAV FAITH IN A ABILITIES YOURSEL FATHER.
THAT'S WHY YOU HIRED THE SPANIARD.
I do want to have faith in you! But...!
GULP
!
TH-- THAT WAS...
DASH
AH!
WAIT, JUAN!
IT DOESN'T MATTER ANY-MORE!
LET EVERYONE CALL ME INCOMPETENT IF THEY LIKE! I DON'T CARE!
WHAT WILL I DO WITH HIM?
SANCIA ...!
SANCIA!
SANCIA!
THERE THERE.
WHAT'S THE MATTER?

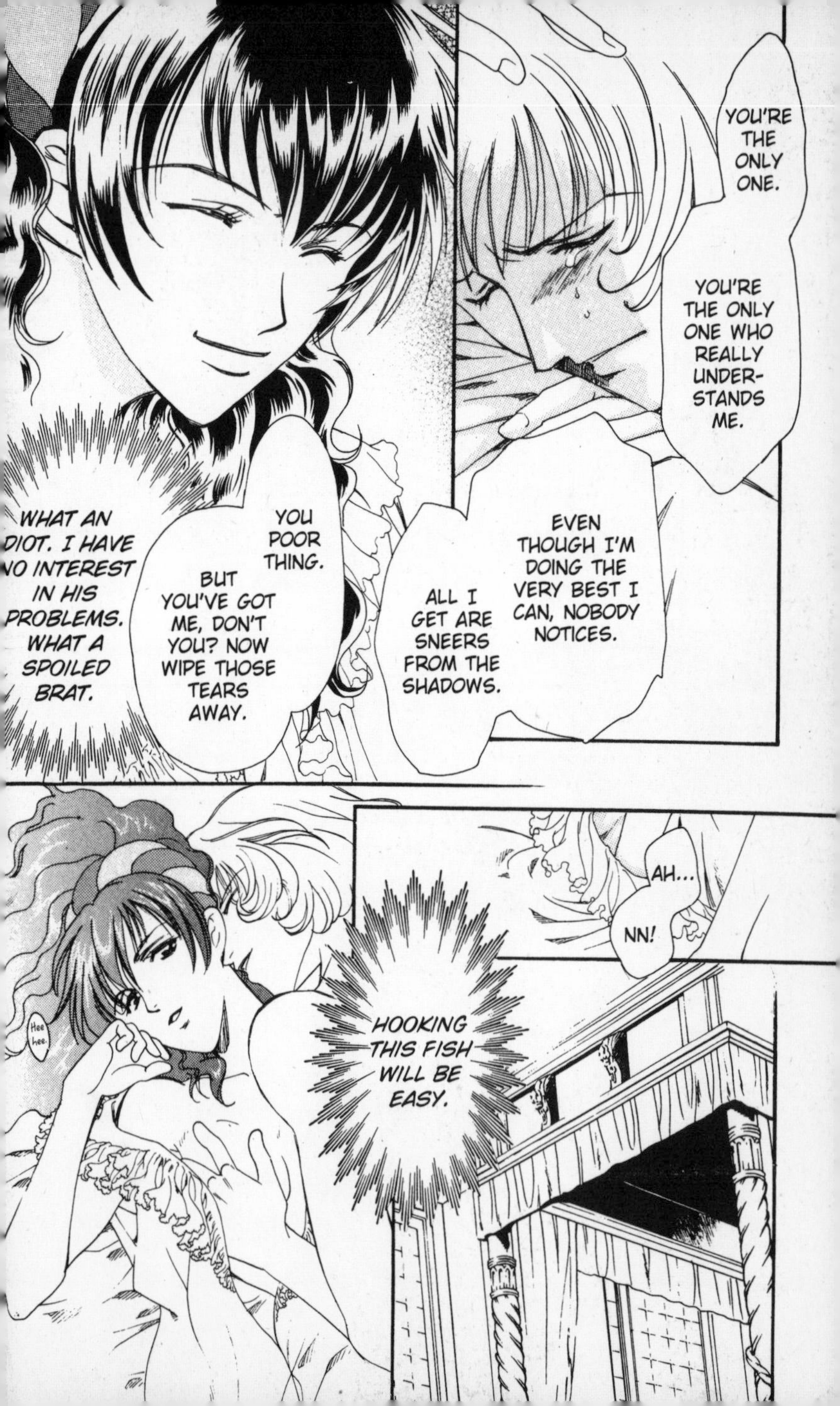

YOU'RE THE ONLY ONE.
YOU'RE THE ONLY ONE WHO REALLY UNDER-STANDS ME.
EVEN THOUGH I'M DOING THE VERY BEST I CAN, NOBODY NOTICES.
ALL I GET ARE SNEERS FROM THE SHADOWS.
YOU POOR THING.
BUT YOU'VE GOT ME, DON'T YOU? NOW WIPE THOSE TEARS AWAY.
WHAT AN DIOT. I HAVE NO INTEREST IN HIS PROBLEMS. WHAT A SPOILED BRAT.
AH...
NN!
HOOKING THIS FISH WILL BE EASY.
Hee hee.

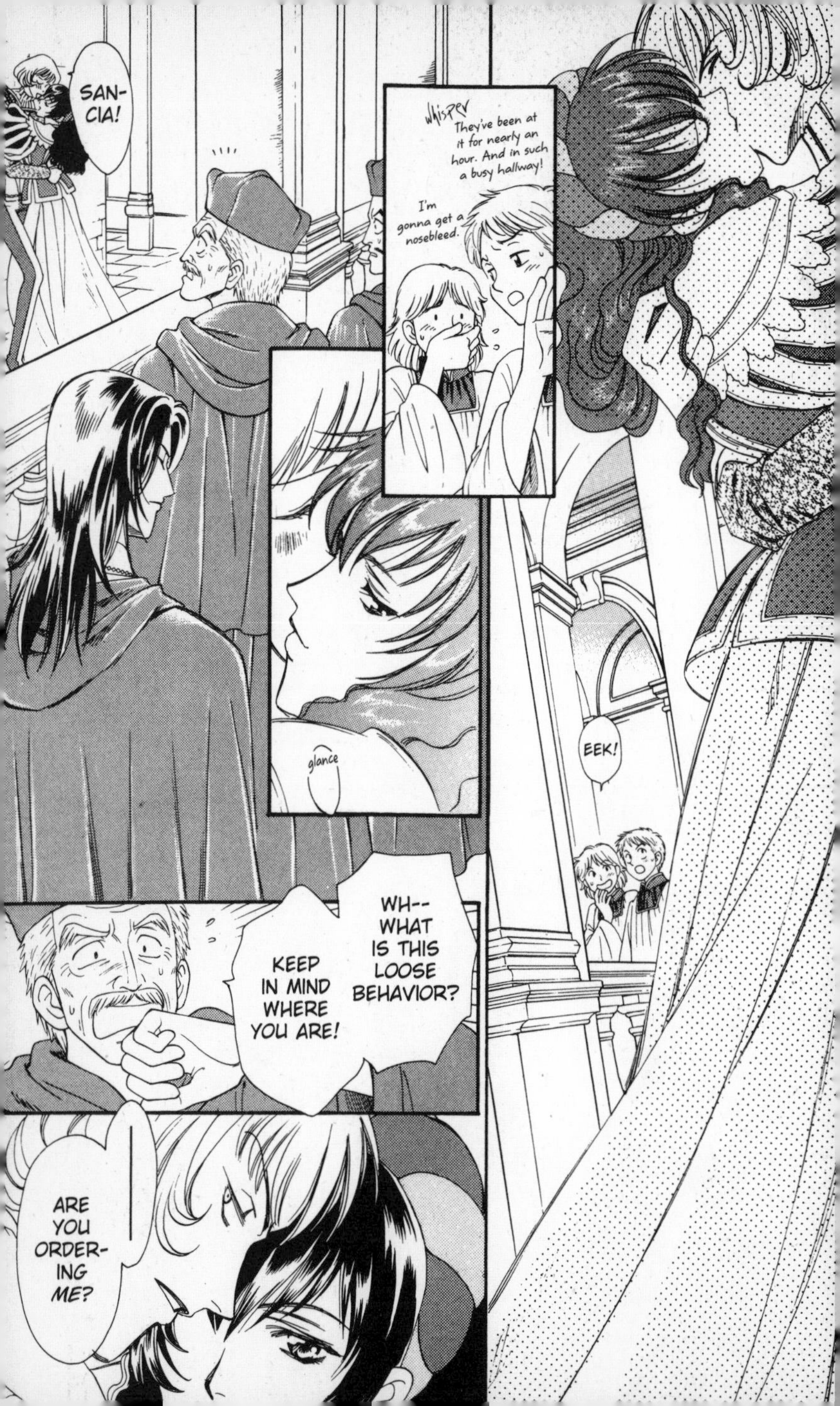
EEK!
SAN-CIA!
whisper
They've been at it for nearly an hour. And in such a busy hallway!
I'm gonna get a nosebleed.
glance
WH-- WHAT IS THIS LOOSE BEHAVIOR?
KEEP IN MIND WHERE YOU ARE!
ARE YOU ORDERING ME?

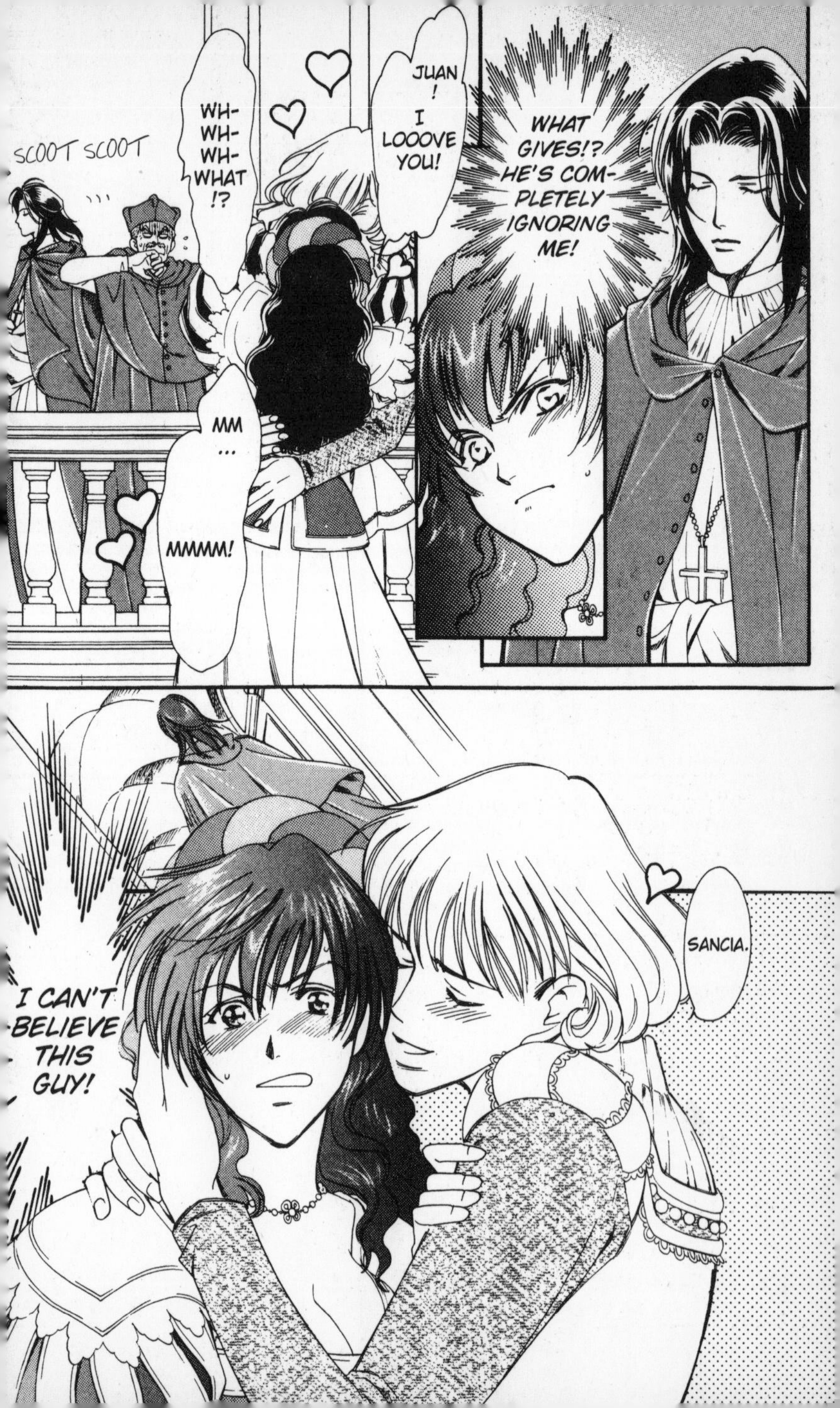
WHAT GIVES!? HE'S COMPLETELY IGNORING ME!
JUAN! I LOOOVE YOU!
WH-WH-WH-WHAT!?
SCOOT SCOOT
MM... MMMM!
SANCIA.
I CAN'T BELIEVE THIS GUY!

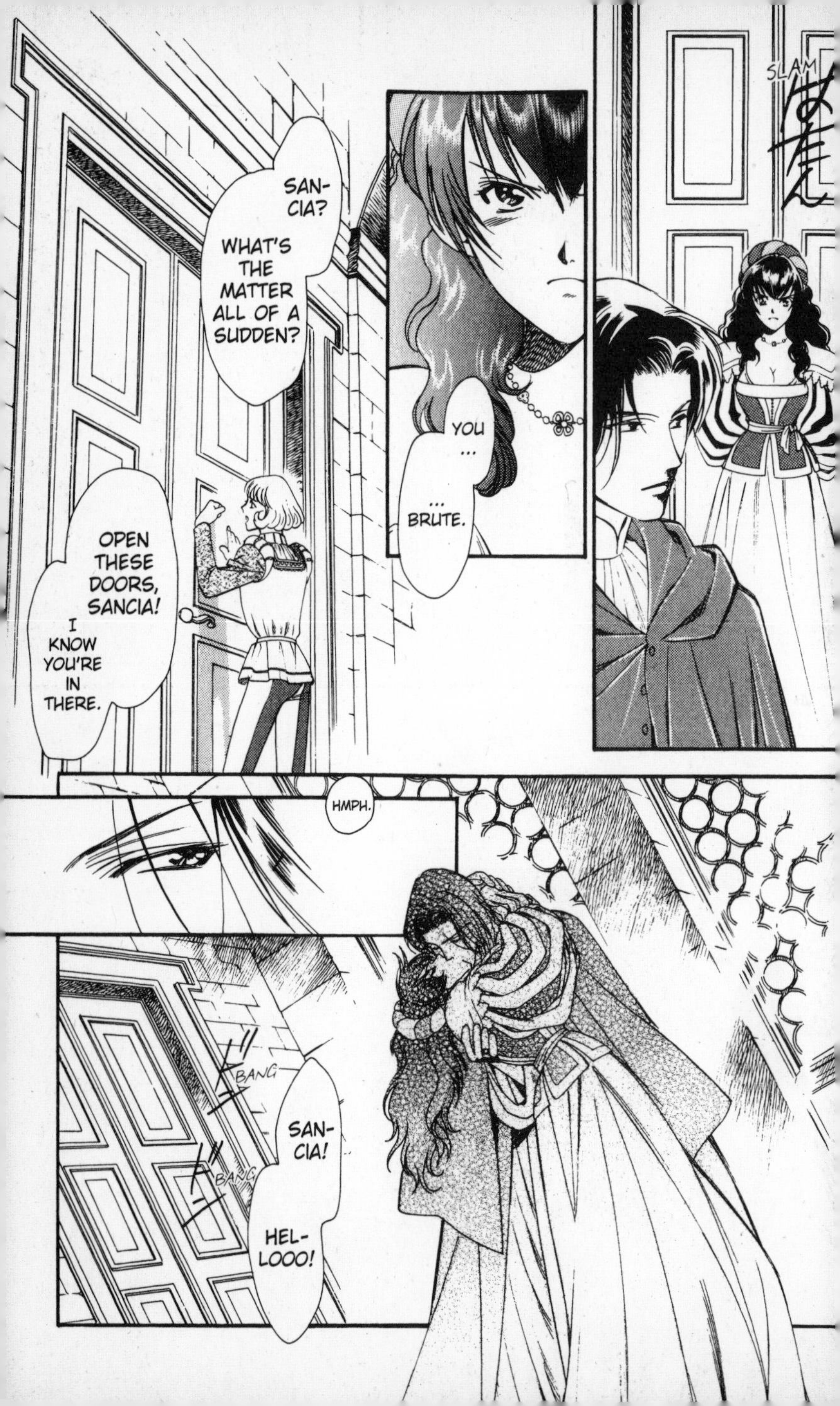

SLAM
YOU ...
... BRUTE.
SAN-CIA?
WHAT'S THE MATTER ALL OF A SUDDEN?
OPEN THESE DOORS, SANCIA!
I KNOW YOU'RE IN THERE.
HMPH.
BANG
BANG
SAN-CIA!
HEL-LOOO!

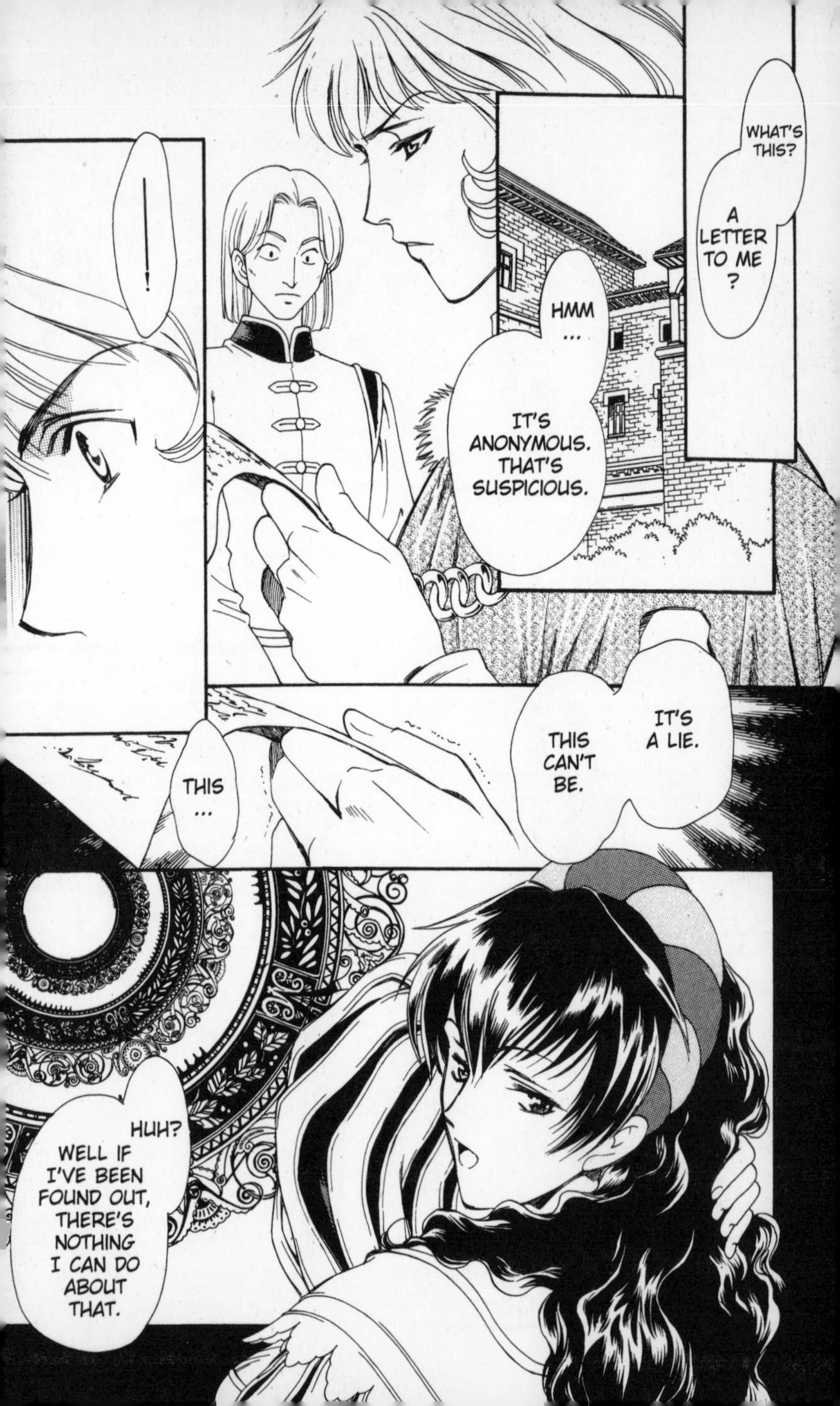
WHAT'S THIS?
A LETTER TO ME ?
HMM ...
IT'S ANONYMOUS. THAT'S SUSPICIOUS.
!
IT'S A LIE. THIS CAN'T BE.
THIS ...
HUH? WELL IF I'VE BEEN FOUND OUT, THERE'S NOTHING I CAN DO ABOUT THAT.

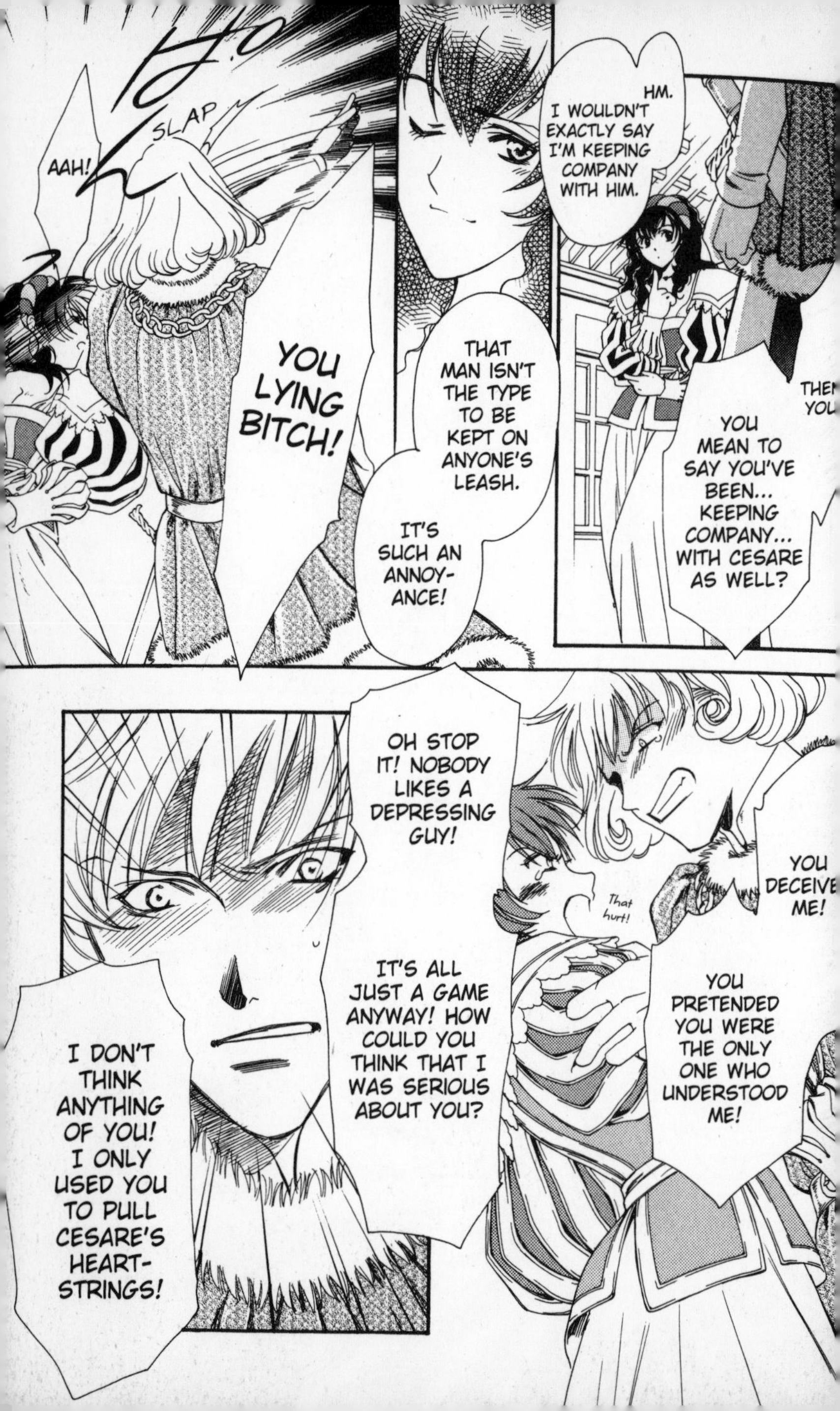
YOU MEAN TO SAY YOU'VE BEEN... KEEPING COMPANY... WITH CESARE AS WELL?
HM. I WOULDN'T EXACTLY SAY I'M KEEPING COMPANY WITH HIM.
THAT MAN ISN'T THE TYPE TO BE KEPT ON ANYONE'S LEASH.
IT'S SUCH AN ANNOY-ANCE!
YOU LYING BITCH!
SLAP
AAH!
YOU DECEIVE ME!
YOU PRETENDED YOU WERE THE ONLY ONE WHO UNDERSTOOD ME!
That hurt!
OH STOP IT! NOBODY LIKES A DEPRESSING GUY!
IT'S ALL JUST A GAME ANYWAY! HOW COULD YOU THINK THAT I WAS SERIOUS ABOUT YOU?
I DON'T THINK ANYTHING OF YOU! I ONLY USED YOU TO PULL CESARE'S HEART-STRINGS!

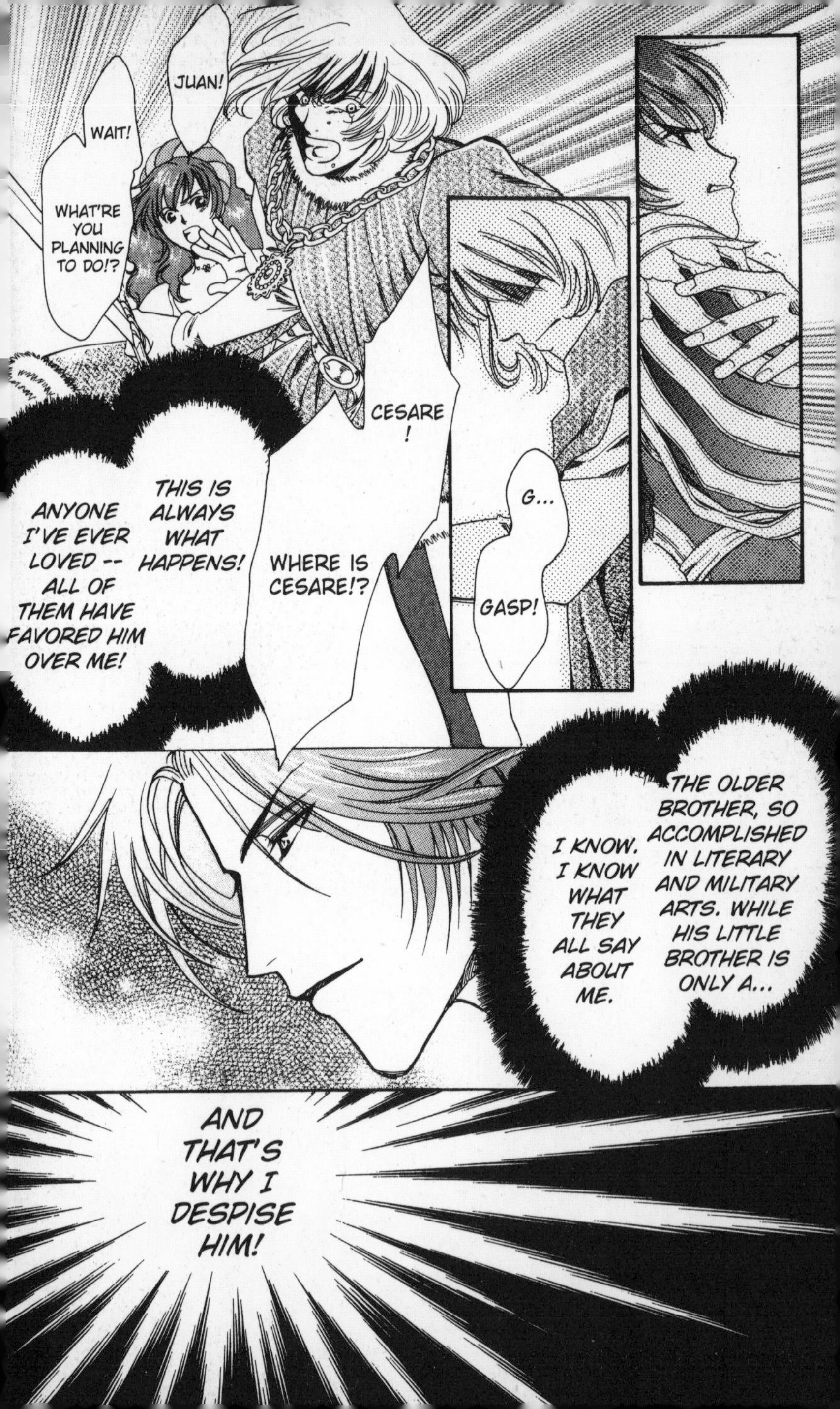
G...
GASP!
JUAN!
WAIT!
WHAT'RE YOU PLANNING TO DO!?
CESARE!
WHERE IS CESARE!?
THIS IS ALWAYS WHAT HAPPENS!
ANYONE I'VE EVER LOVED -- ALL OF THEM HAVE FAVORED HIM OVER ME!
THE OLDER BROTHER, SO ACCOMPLISHED IN LITERARY AND MILITARY ARTS. WHILE HIS LITTLE BROTHER IS ONLY A...
I KNOW. I KNOW WHAT THEY ALL SAY ABOUT ME.
AND THAT'S WHY I DESPISE HIM!

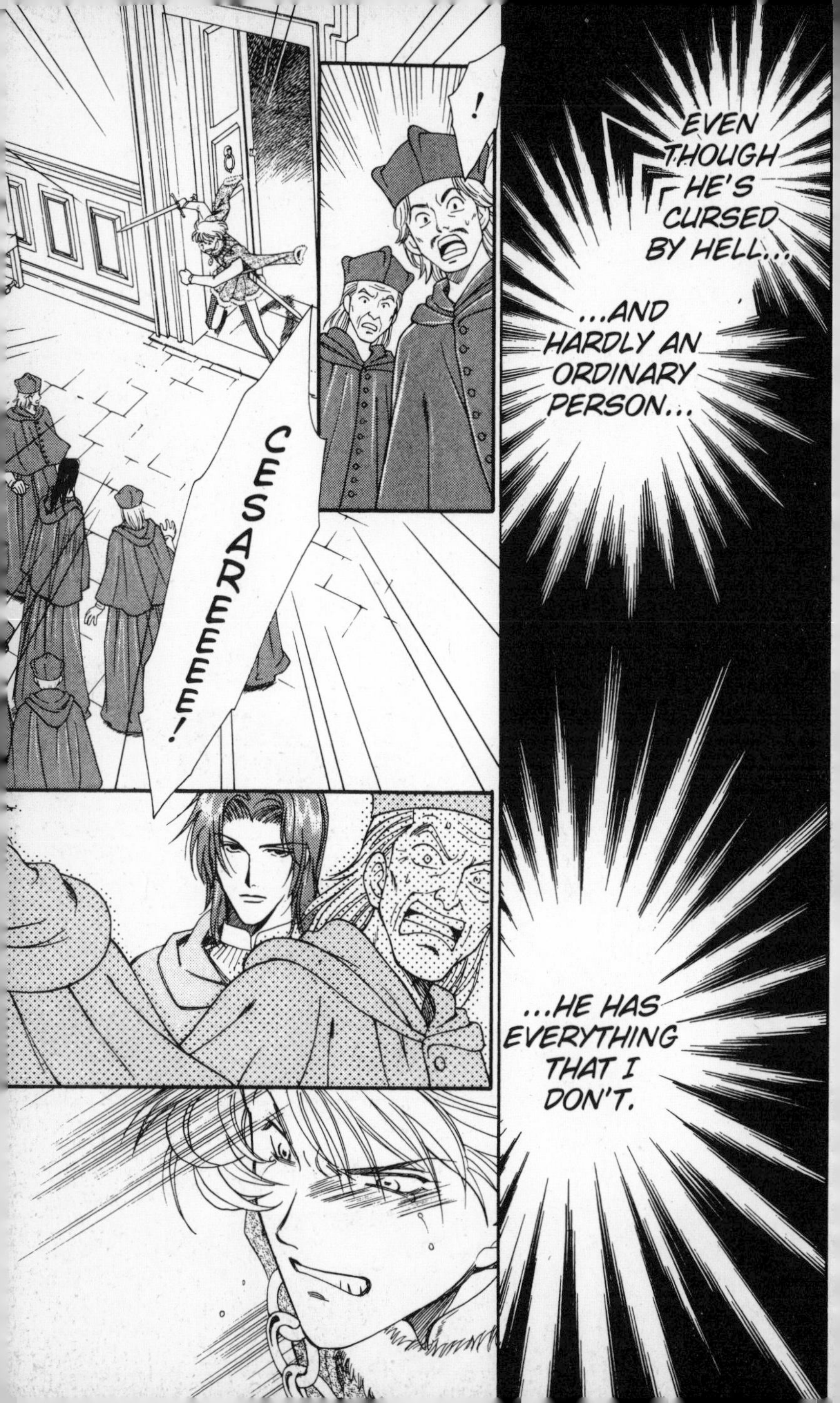
EVEN THOUGH HE'S CURSED BY HELL...
...AND HARDLY AN ORDINARY PERSON...
...HE HAS EVERYTHING THAT I DON'T.
!
CESAREEEEE!

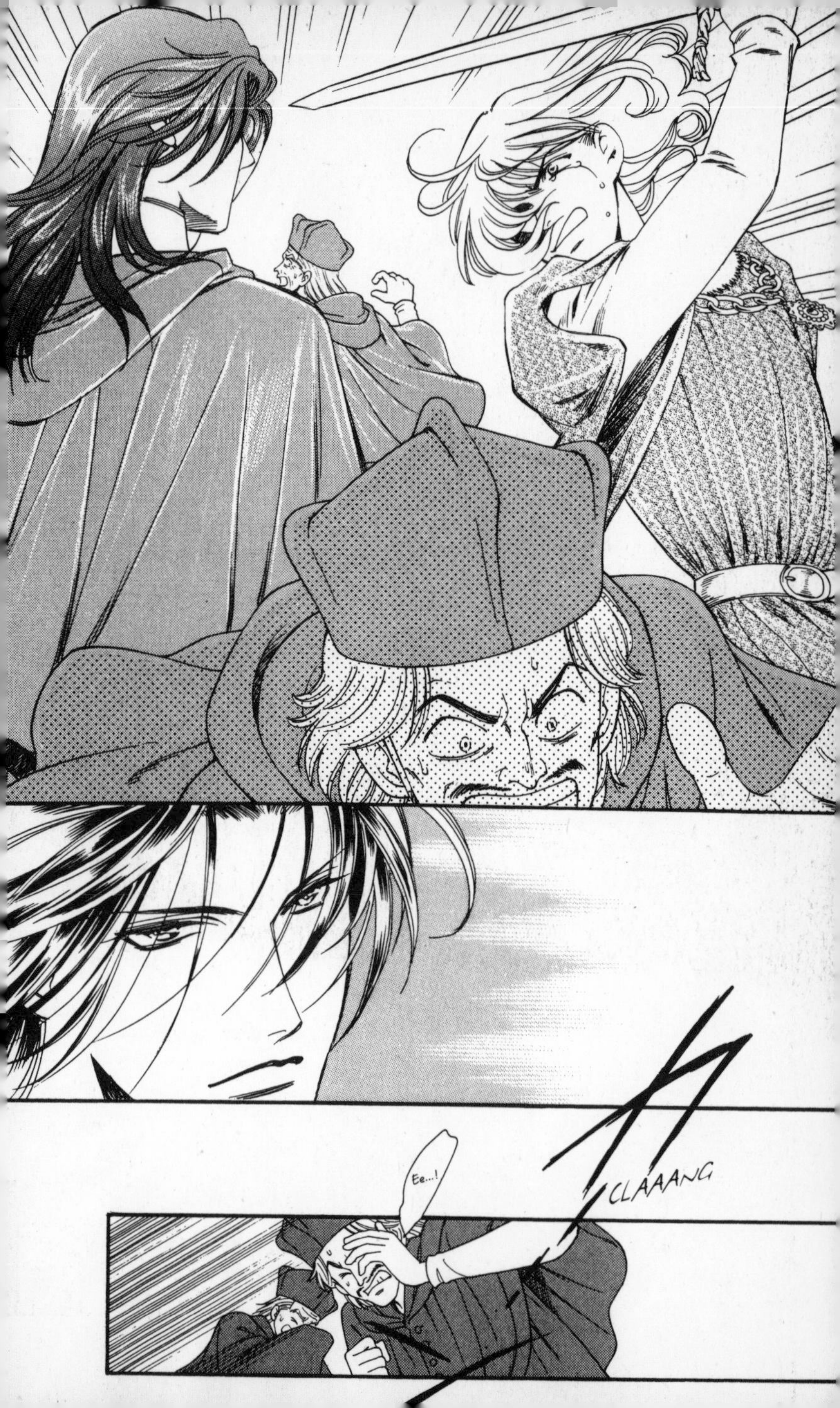

CLAAANG
Ee...!

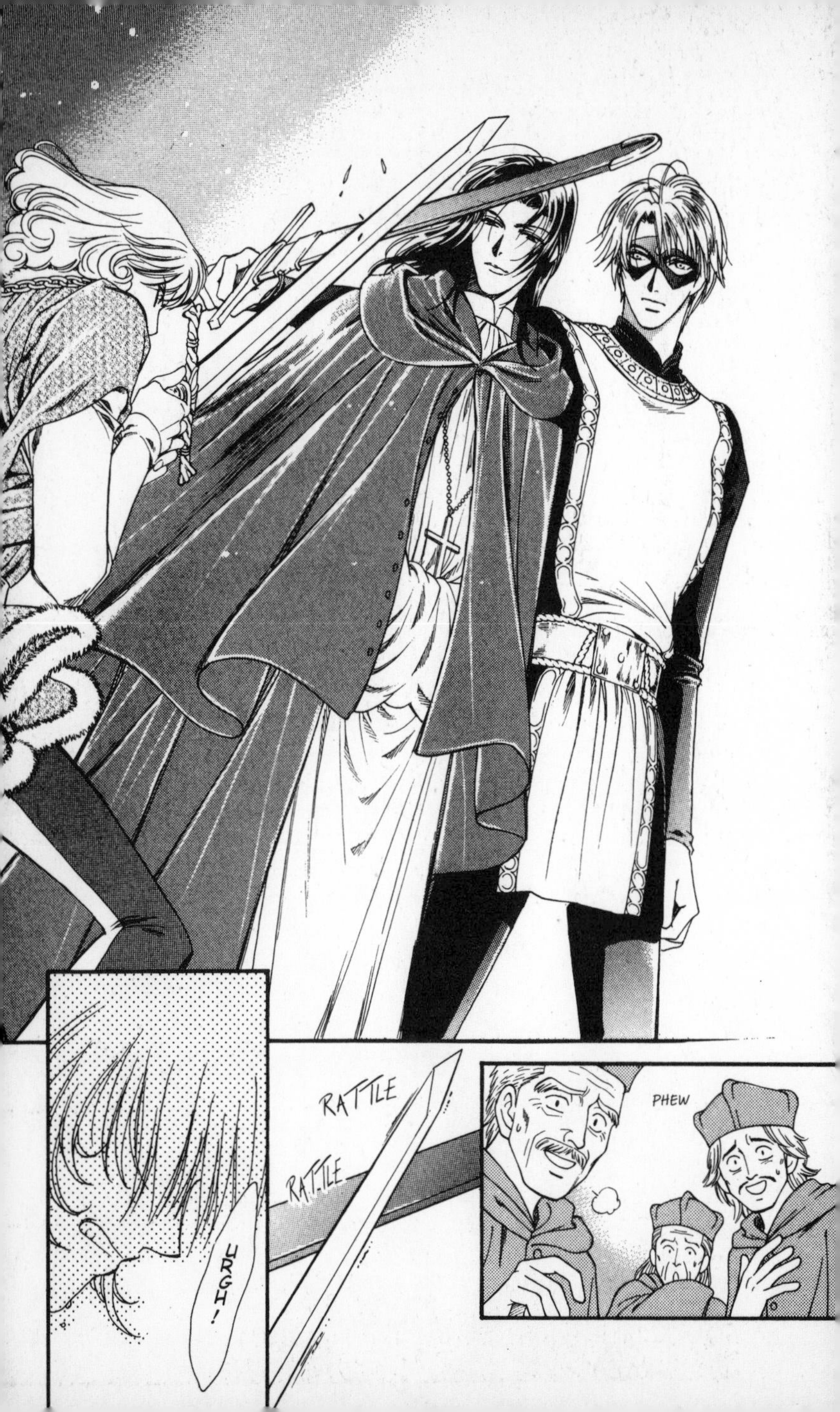
PHEW
RATTLE
RATTLE
URGH!

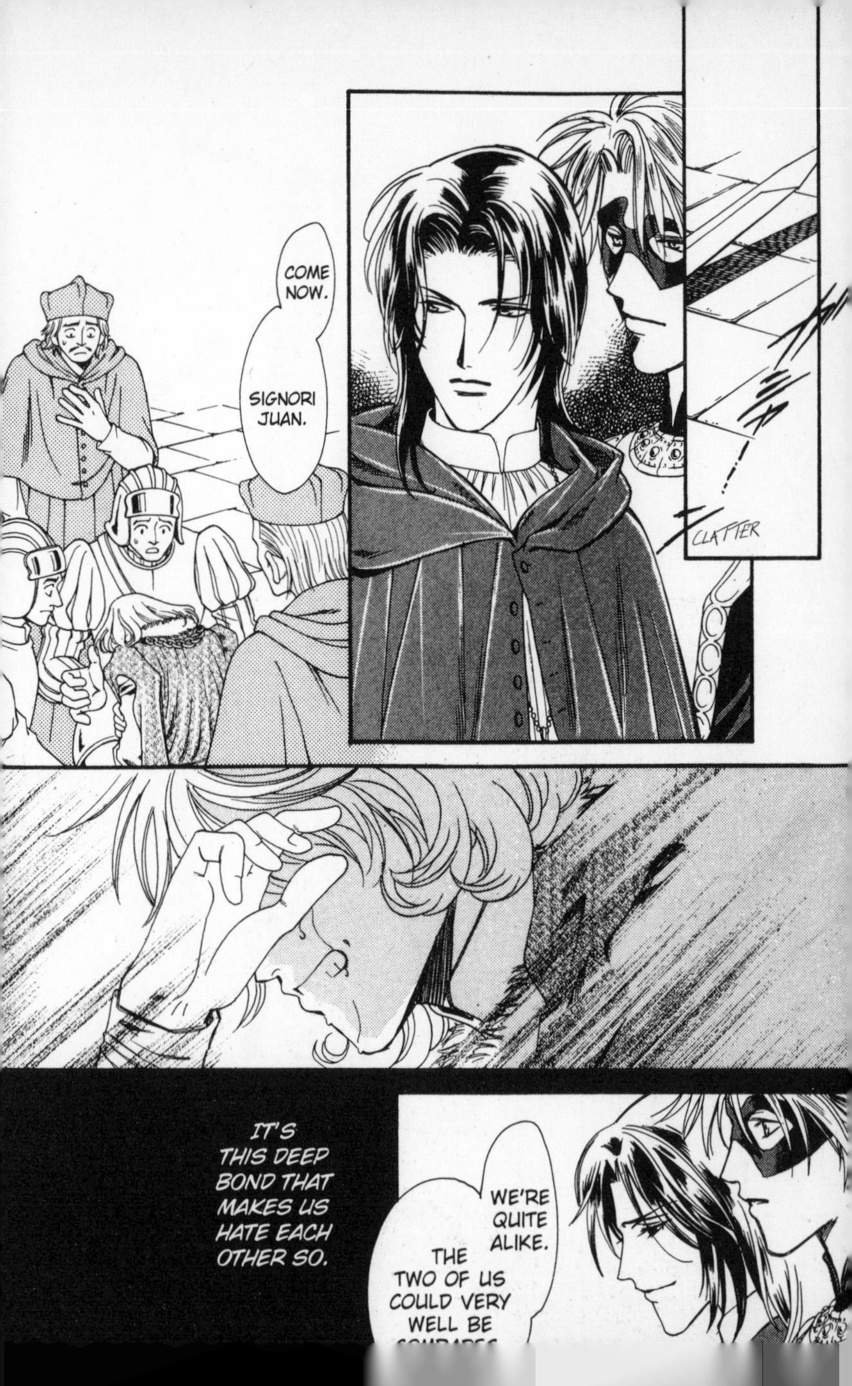
CLATTER
COME NOW.
SIGNORI JUAN.
WE'RE QUITE ALIKE.
THE TWO OF US COULD VERY WELL BE
IT'S THIS DEEP BOND THAT MAKES US HATE EACH OTHER SO.

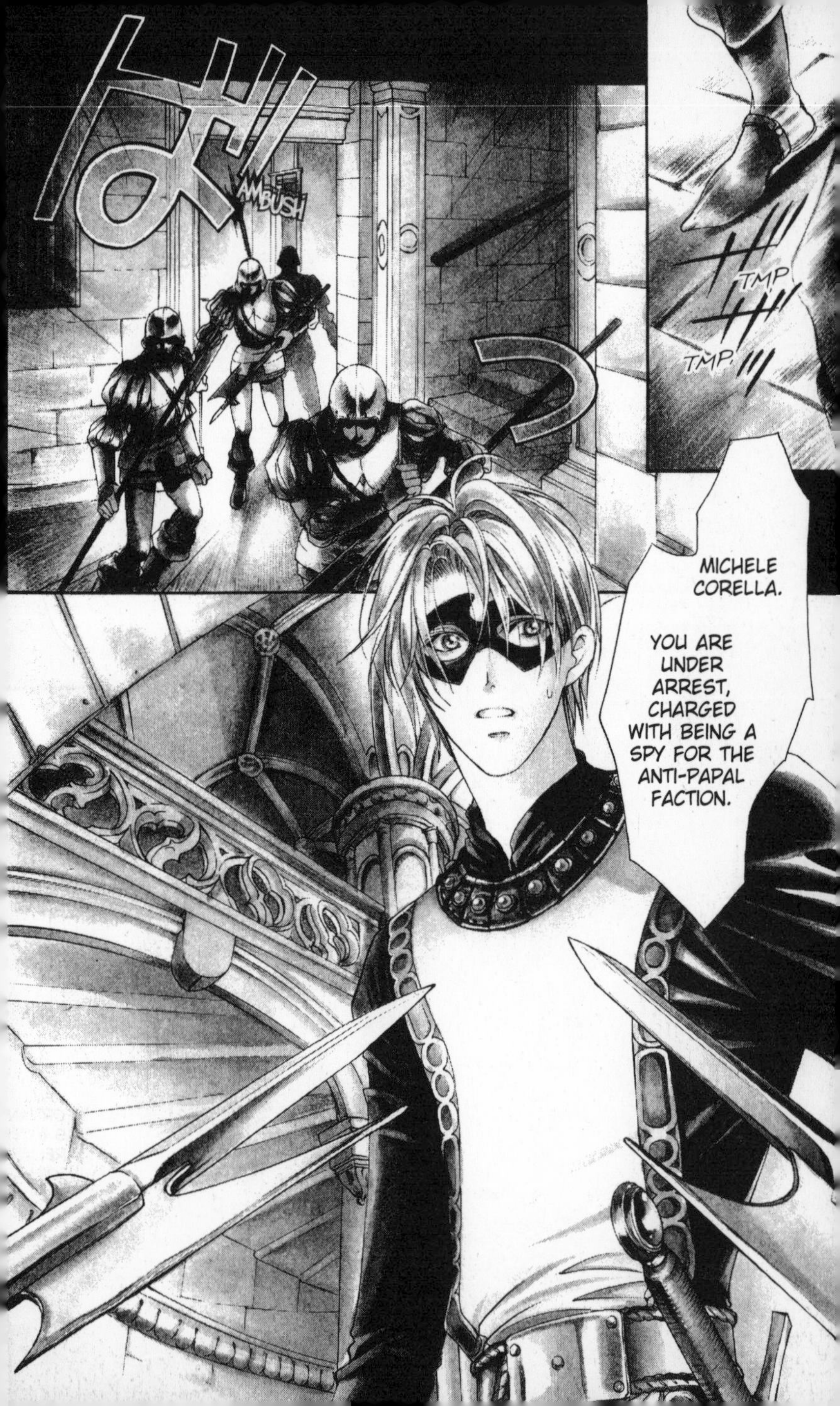
TMP
TMP
AMBUSH
MICHELE CORELLA.
YOU ARE UNDER ARREST, CHARGED WITH BEING A SPY FOR THE ANTI-PAPAL FACTION.

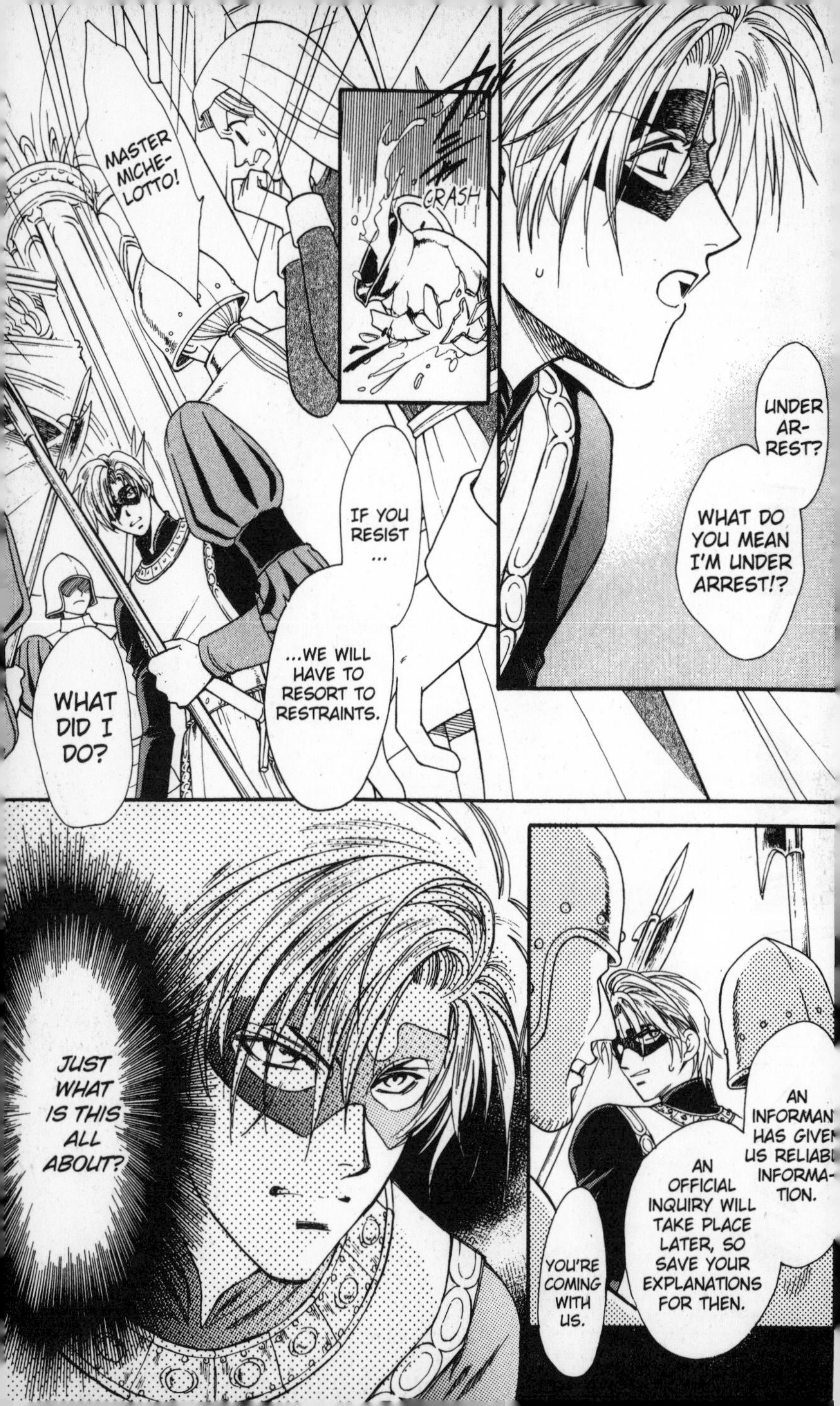
UNDER ARREST?
WHAT DO YOU MEAN I'M UNDER ARREST!?
CRASH
MASTER MICHELOTTO!
IF YOU RESIST...
...WE WILL HAVE TO RESORT TO RESTRAINTS.
WHAT DID I DO?
AN INFORMAN HAS GIVEN US RELIABL INFORMATION.
AN OFFICIAL INQUIRY WILL TAKE PLACE LATER, SO SAVE YOUR EXPLANATIONS FOR THEN.
YOU'RE COMING WITH US.
JUST WHAT IS THIS ALL ABOUT?

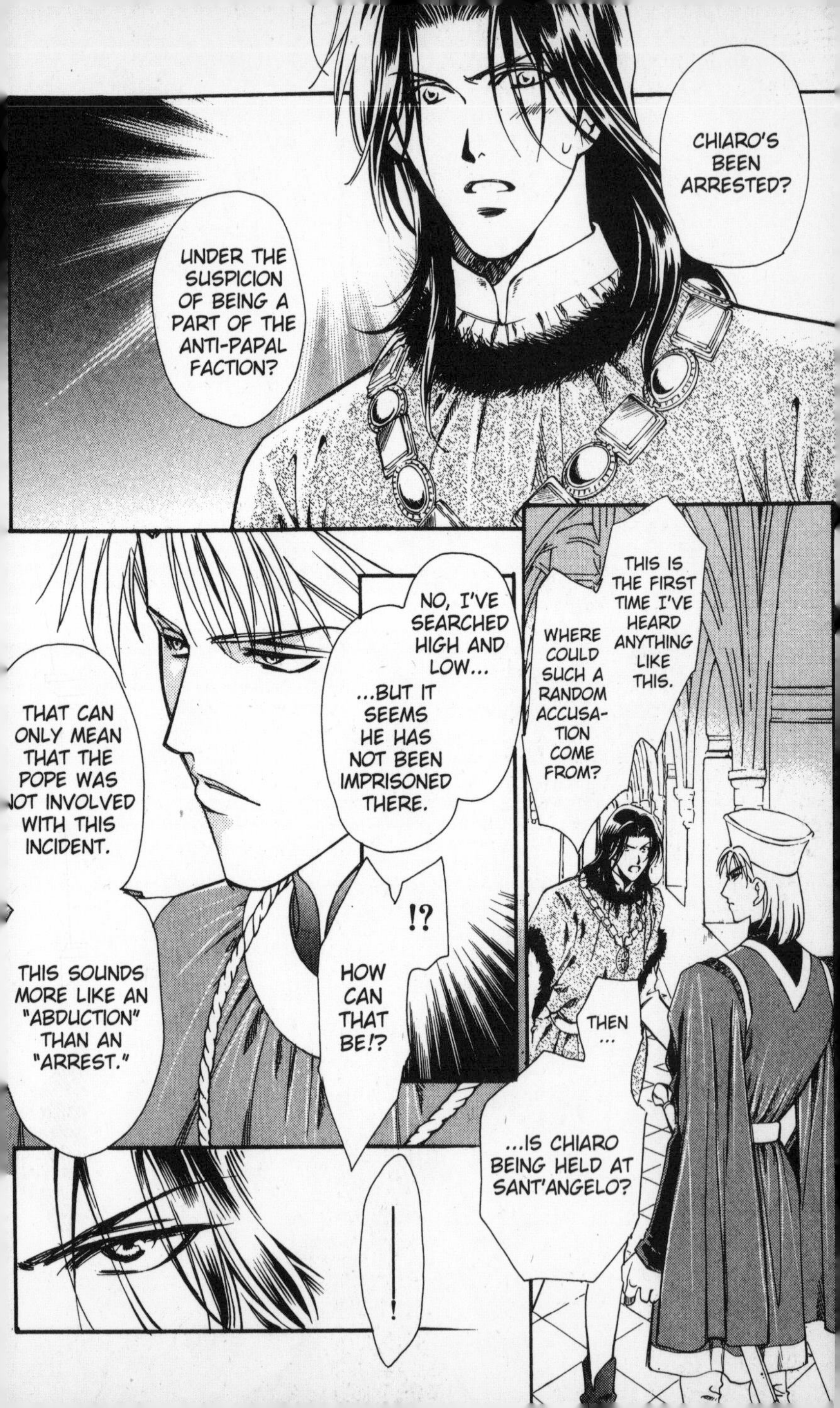

CHIARO'S BEEN ARRESTED?
UNDER THE SUSPICION OF BEING A PART OF THE ANTI-PAPAL FACTION?
THIS IS THE FIRST TIME I'VE HEARD ANYTHING LIKE THIS.
WHERE COULD SUCH A RANDOM ACCUSA-TION COME FROM?
THEN ...
...IS CHIARO BEING HELD AT SANT'ANGELO?
NO, I'VE SEARCHED HIGH AND LOW...
...BUT IT SEEMS HE HAS NOT BEEN IMPRISONED THERE.
!?
HOW CAN THAT BE!?
THAT CAN ONLY MEAN THAT THE POPE WAS NOT INVOLVED WITH THIS INCIDENT.
THIS SOUNDS MORE LIKE AN "ABDUCTION" THAN AN "ARREST."
!

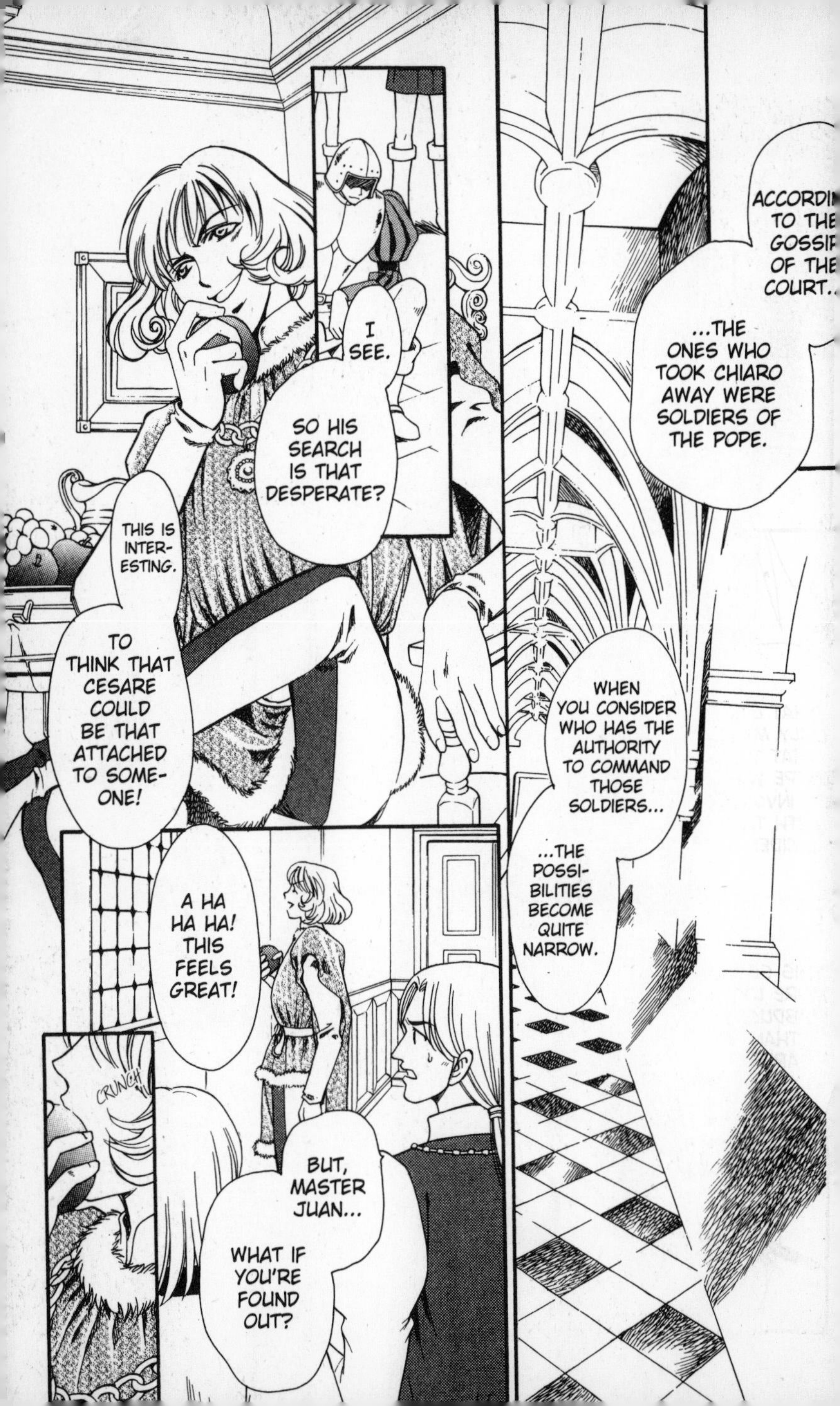
ACCORDI TO THE GOSSI OF THE COURT...
...THE ONES WHO TOOK CHIARO AWAY WERE SOLDIERS OF THE POPE.
WHEN YOU CONSIDER WHO HAS THE AUTHORITY TO COMMAND THOSE SOLDIERS...
...THE POSSIBILITIES BECOME QUITE NARROW.
I SEE.
SO HIS SEARCH IS THAT DESPERATE?
THIS IS INTERESTING.
TO THINK THAT CESARE COULD BE THAT ATTACHED TO SOMEONE!
A HA HA HA! THIS FEELS GREAT!
BUT, MASTER JUAN...
WHAT IF YOU'RE FOUND OUT?
CRUNCH

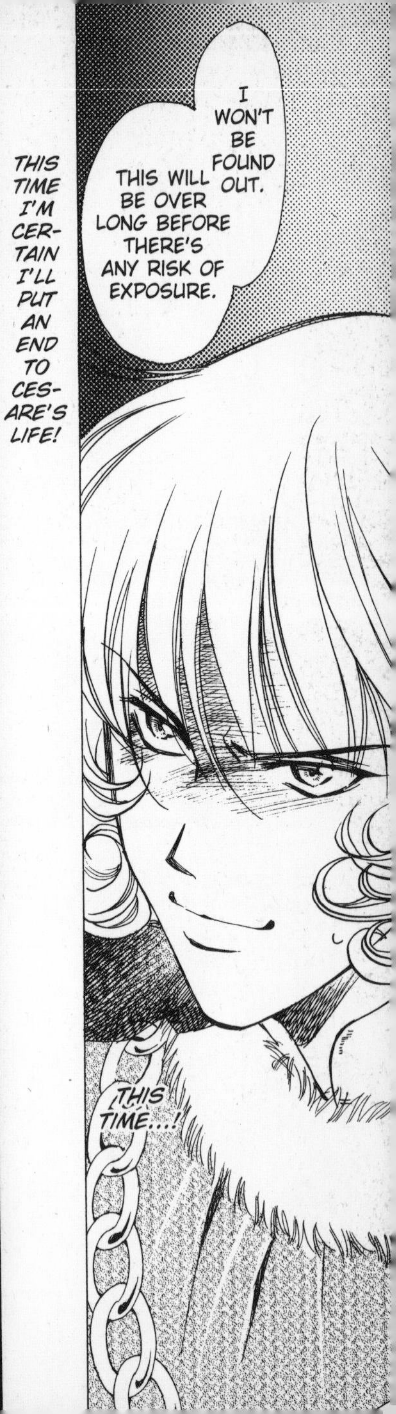
I WON'T BE FOUND OUT. THIS WILL BE OVER LONG BEFORE THERE'S ANY RISK OF EXPOSURE.
THIS TIME I'M CER-TAIN I'LL PUT AN END TO CES-ARE'S LIFE!
THIS TIME...!

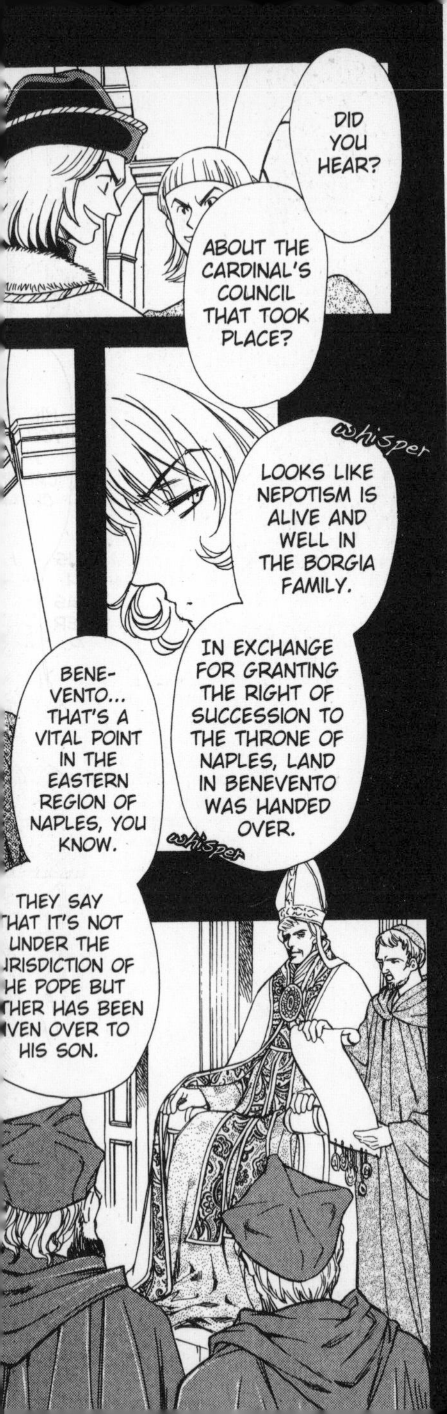
DID YOU HEAR?
ABOUT THE CARDINAL'S COUNCIL THAT TOOK PLACE?
whisper
LOOKS LIKE NEPOTISM IS ALIVE AND WELL IN THE BORGIA FAMILY.
IN EXCHANGE FOR GRANTING THE RIGHT OF SUCCESSION TO THE THRONE OF NAPLES, LAND IN BENEVENTO WAS HANDED OVER.
BENE-VENTO... THAT'S A VITAL POINT IN THE EASTERN REGION OF NAPLES, YOU KNOW.
whisper
THEY SAY HAT IT'S NOT UNDER THE IRISDICTION OF HE POPE BUT THER HAS BEEN IVEN OVER TO HIS SON.

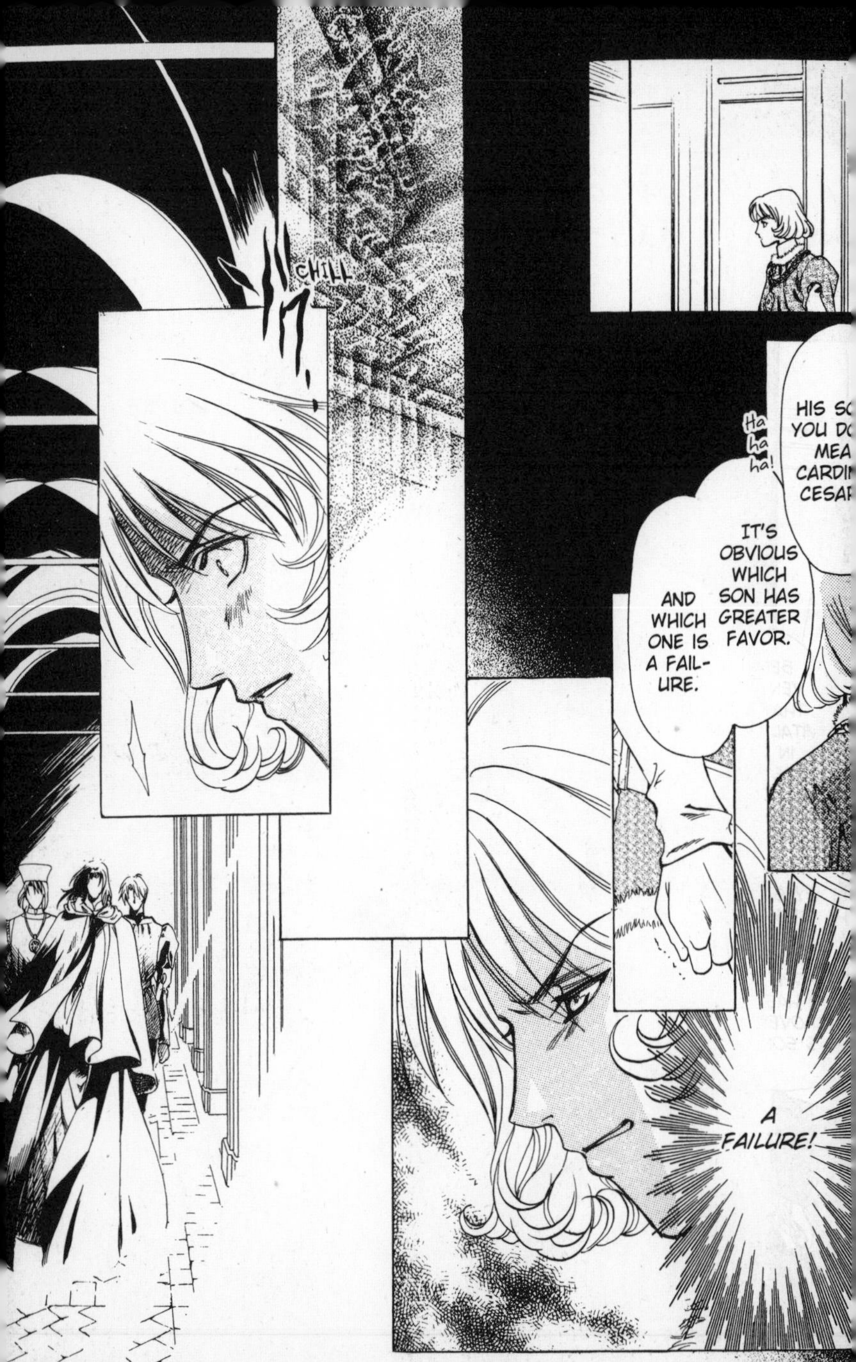
HIS SO
YOU DO
MEA
CARDIN
CESAR
Ha ha ha!
IT'S OBVIOUS WHICH SON HAS GREATER FAVOR.
AND WHICH ONE IS A FAIL-URE.
A FAILURE!
CHILL

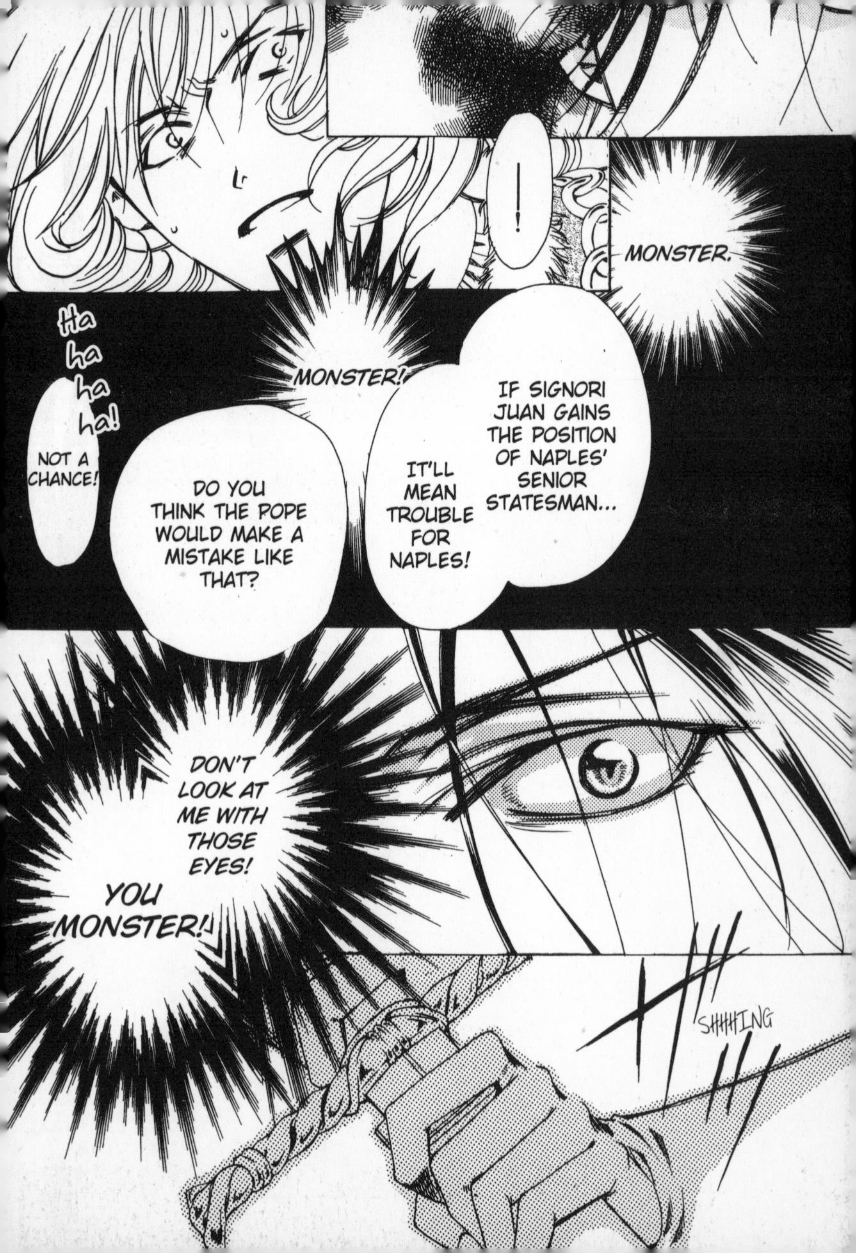
!
MONSTER.
IF SIGNORI JUAN GAINS THE POSITION OF NAPLES' SENIOR STATESMAN...
IT'LL MEAN TROUBLE FOR NAPLES!
MONSTER!
DO YOU THINK THE POPE WOULD MAKE A MISTAKE LIKE THAT?
Ha ha ha ha!
NOT A CHANCE!
DON'T LOOK AT ME WITH THOSE EYES!
YOU MONSTER!
SHHHING

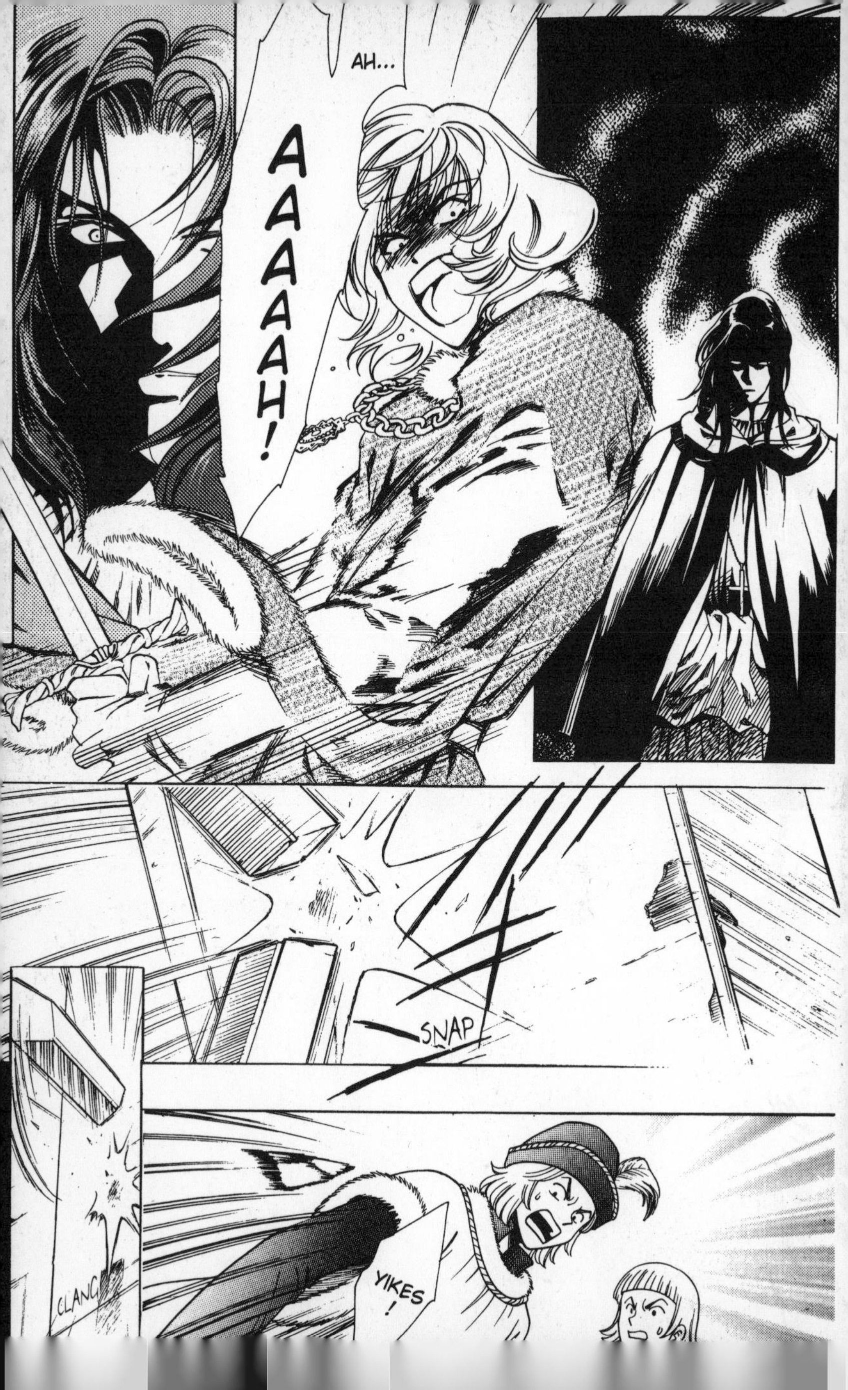
AH...
AAAAAAH!
SNAP
YIKES!
CLANG

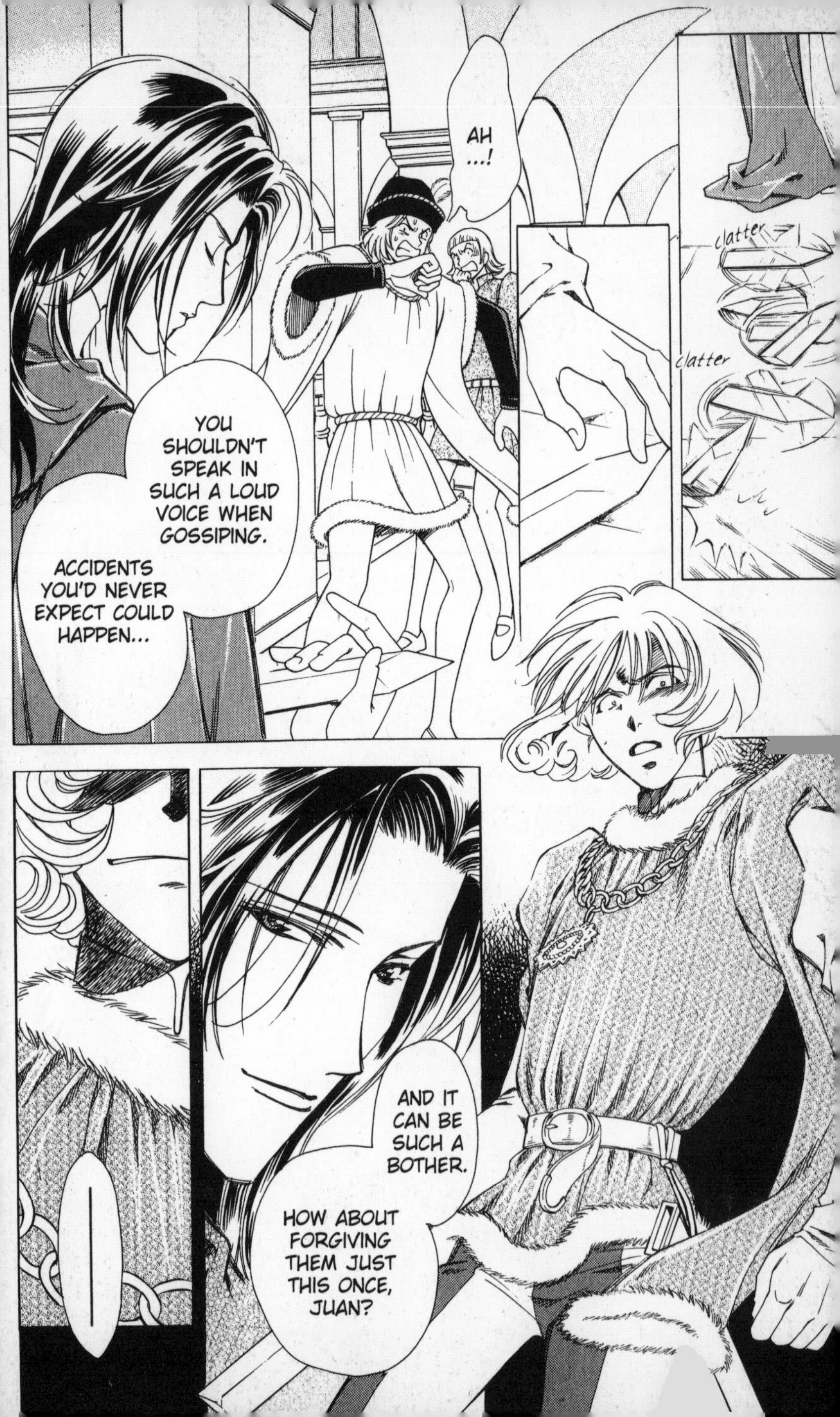
clatter
clatter
AH ...!
YOU SHOULDN'T SPEAK IN SUCH A LOUD VOICE WHEN GOSSIPING.
ACCIDENTS YOU'D NEVER EXPECT COULD HAPPEN...
AND IT CAN BE SUCH A BOTHER.
HOW ABOUT FORGIVING THEM JUST THIS ONCE, JUAN?

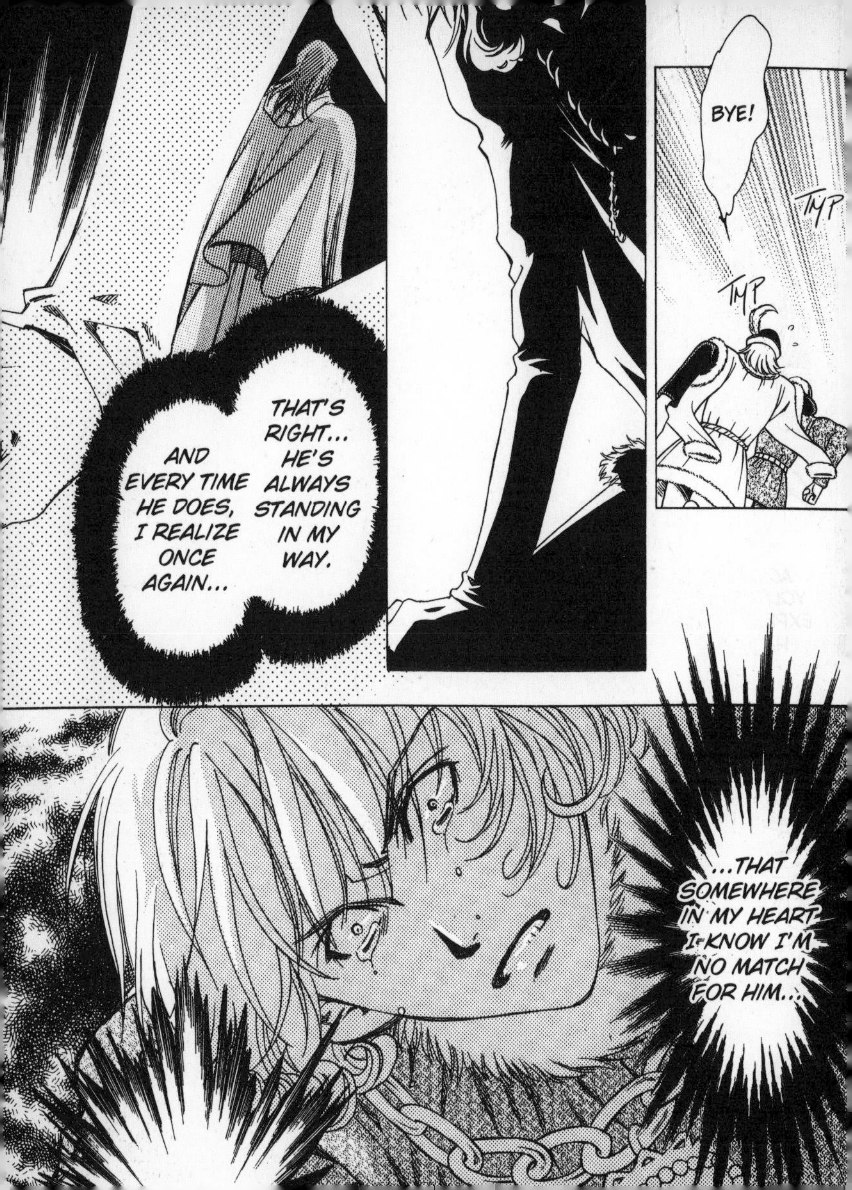
BYE!
TMP
TMP
THAT'S RIGHT... HE'S ALWAYS STANDING IN MY WAY.
AND EVERY TIME HE DOES, I REALIZE ONCE AGAIN...
...THAT SOMEWHERE IN MY HEART I KNOW I'M NO MATCH FOR HIM...

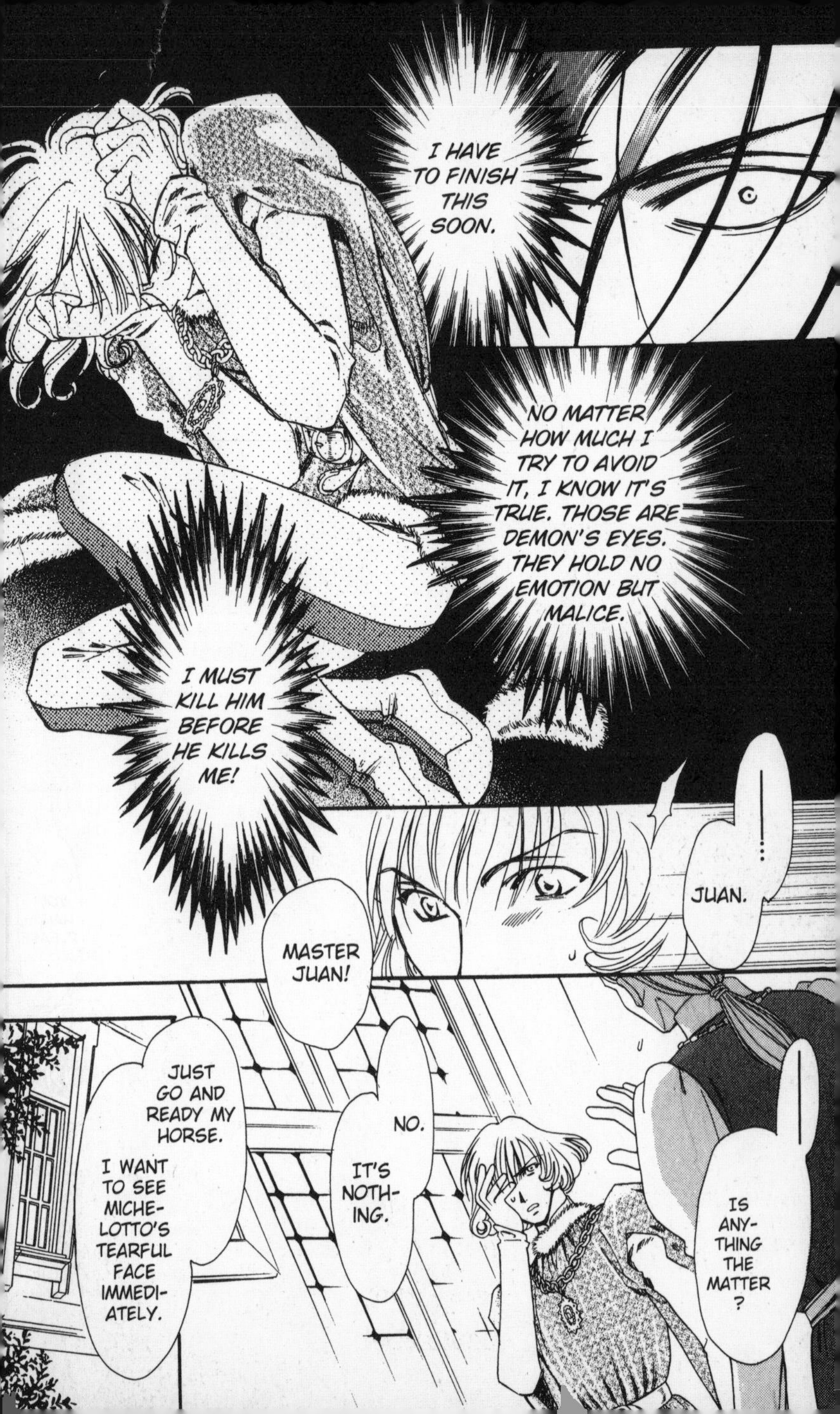
I HAVE TO FINISH THIS SOON.
NO MATTER HOW MUCH I TRY TO AVOID IT, I KNOW IT'S TRUE. THOSE ARE DEMON'S EYES. THEY HOLD NO EMOTION BUT MALICE.
I MUST KILL HIM BEFORE HE KILLS ME!
...!
JUAN.
MASTER JUAN!
IS ANYTHING THE MATTER?
NO.
IT'S NOTHING.
JUST GO AND READY MY HORSE.
I WANT TO SEE MICHELOTTO'S TEARFUL FACE IMMEDIATELY.

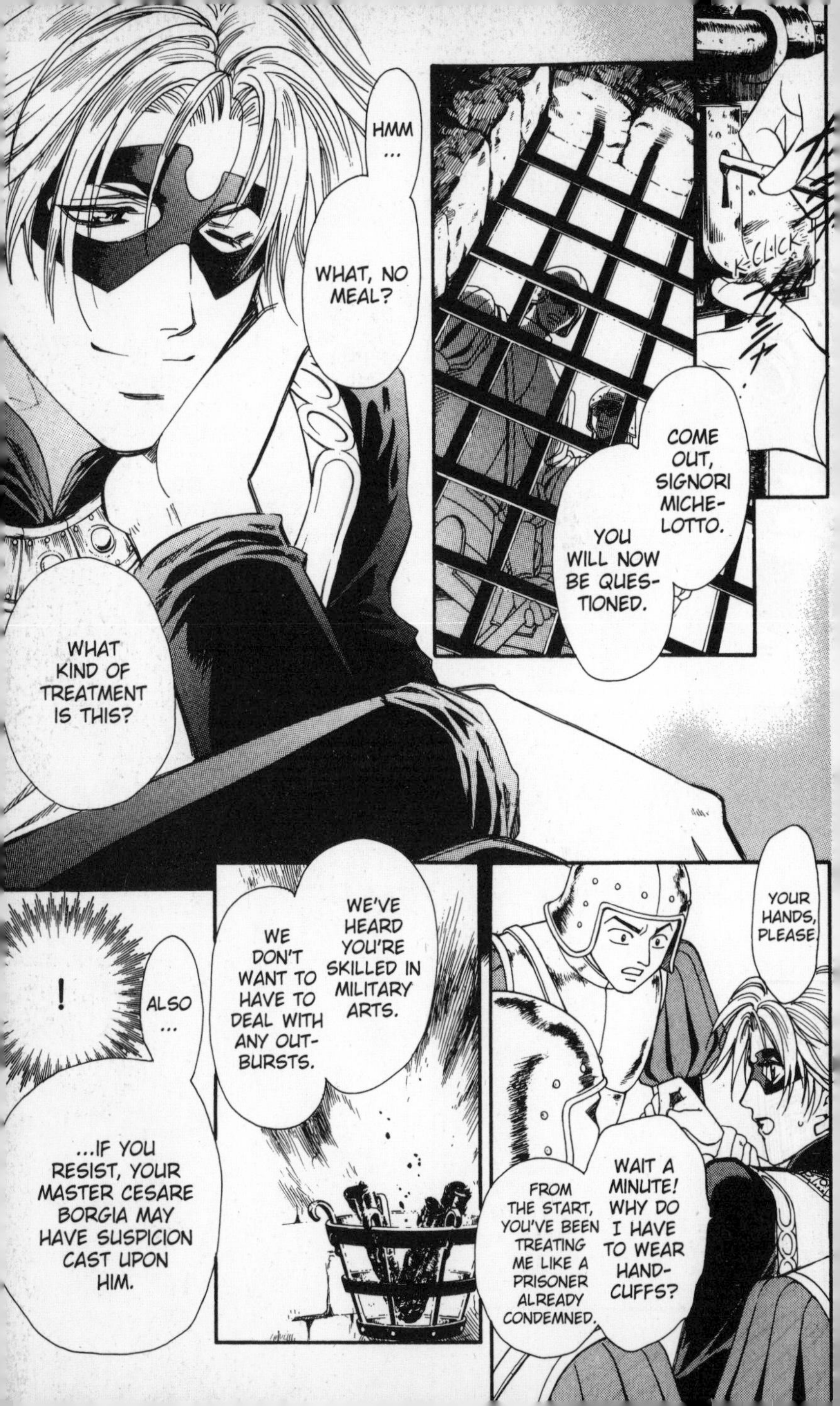
K-CLICK
COME OUT, SIGNORI MICHELOTTO.
YOU WILL NOW BE QUESTIONED.
HMM ...
WHAT, NO MEAL?
WHAT KIND OF TREATMENT IS THIS?
YOUR HANDS, PLEASE.
WAIT A MINUTE! WHY DO I HAVE TO WEAR HANDCUFFS?
FROM THE START, YOU'VE BEEN TREATING ME LIKE A PRISONER ALREADY CONDEMNED.
WE'VE HEARD YOU'RE SKILLED IN MILITARY ARTS.
WE DON'T WANT TO HAVE TO DEAL WITH ANY OUTBURSTS.
!
ALSO ...
...IF YOU RESIST, YOUR MASTER CESARE BORGIA MAY HAVE SUSPICION CAST UPON HIM.

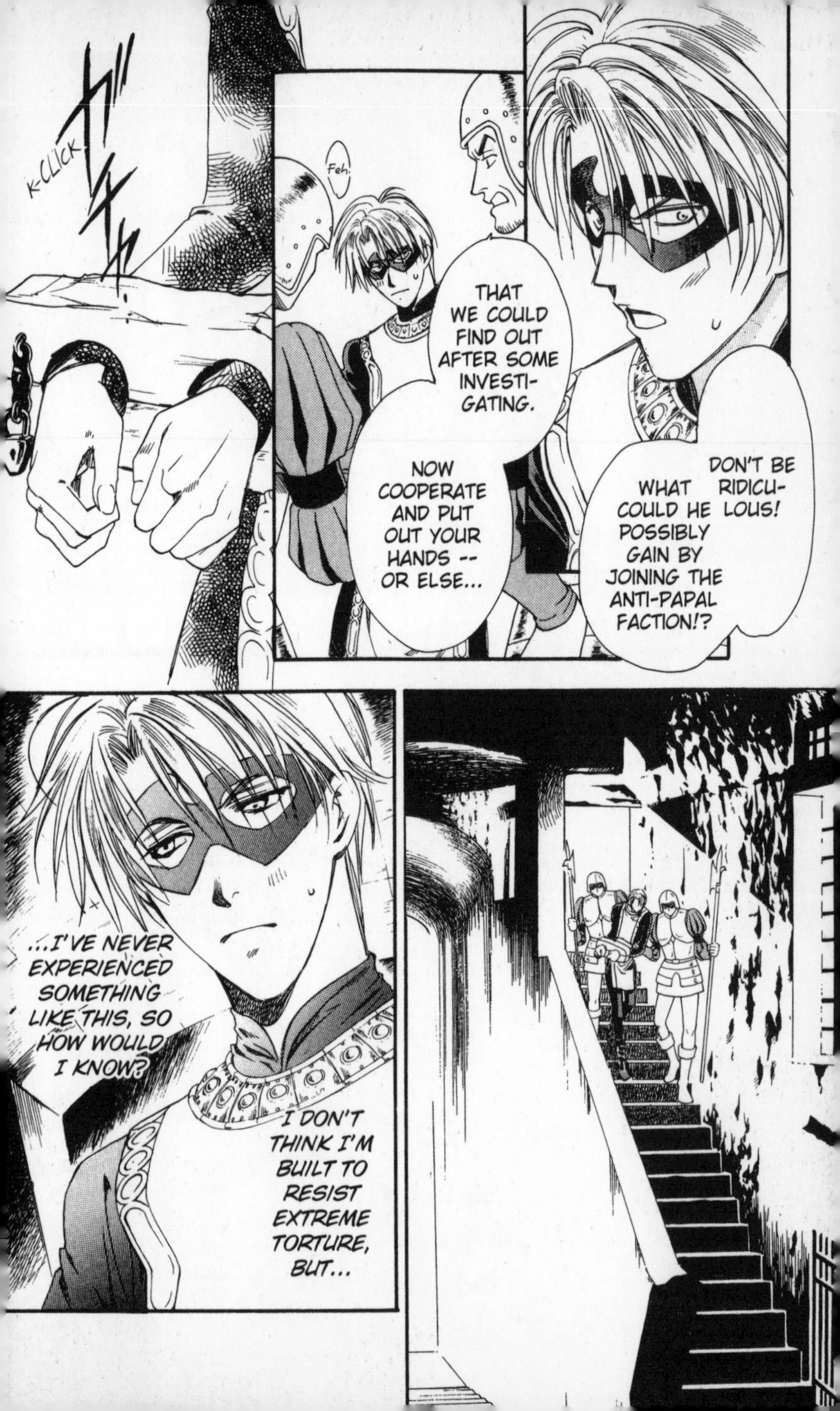
DON'T BE RIDICULOUS!
WHAT COULD HE POSSIBLY GAIN BY JOINING THE ANTI-PAPAL FACTION!?
THAT WE COULD FIND OUT AFTER SOME INVESTIGATING.
Feh.
NOW COOPERATE AND PUT OUT YOUR HANDS -- OR ELSE...
K-CLICK
I DON'T THINK I'M BUILT TO RESIST EXTREME TORTURE, BUT...
...I'VE NEVER EXPERIENCED SOMETHING LIKE THIS, SO HOW WOULD I KNOW?

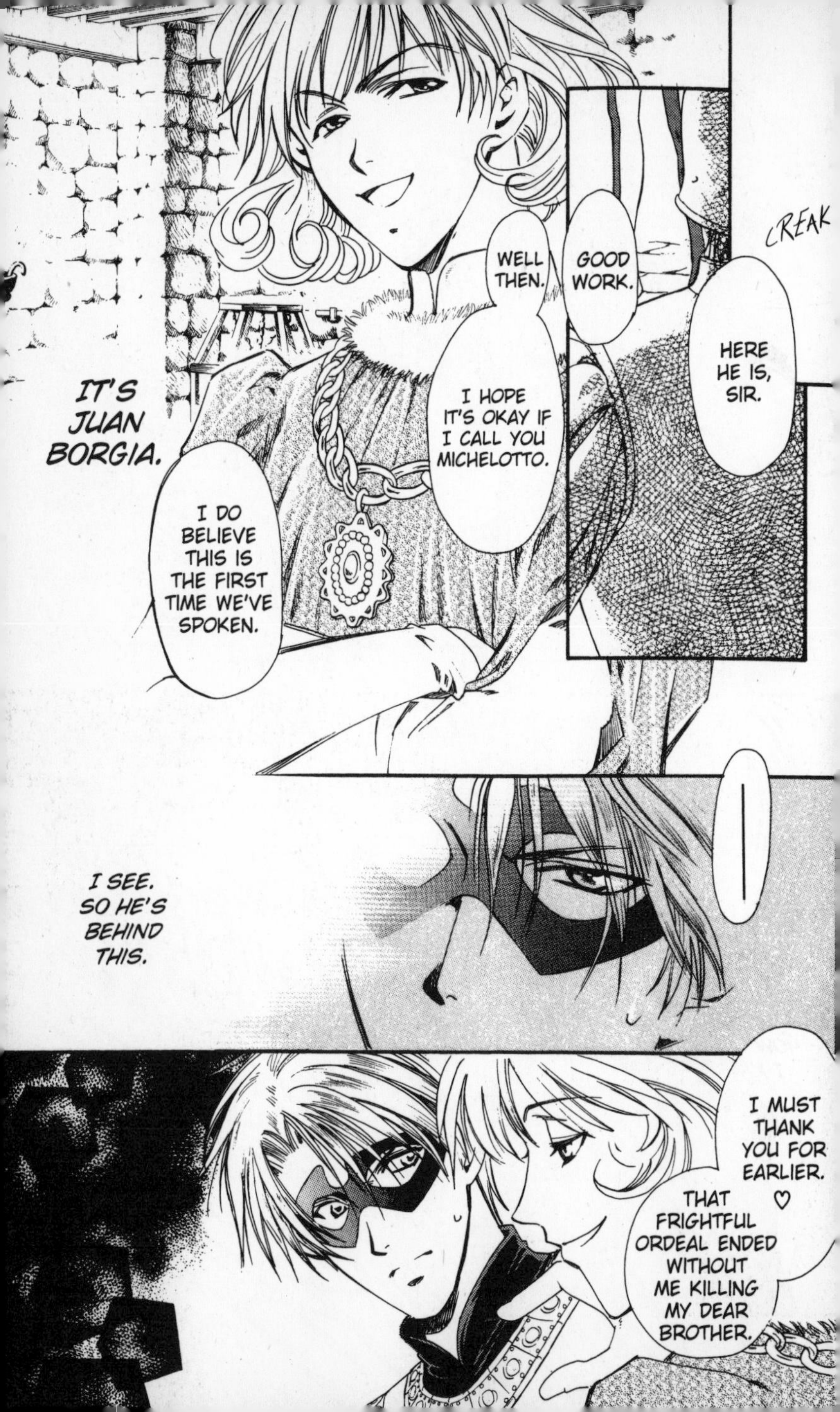
CREAK
HERE HE IS, SIR.
GOOD WORK.
WELL THEN.
I HOPE IT'S OKAY IF I CALL YOU MICHELOTTO.
I DO BELIEVE THIS IS THE FIRST TIME WE'VE SPOKEN.
IT'S JUAN BORGIA.
—
I SEE. SO HE'S BEHIND THIS.
I MUST THANK YOU FOR EARLIER. ♡
THAT FRIGHTFUL ORDEAL ENDED WITHOUT ME KILLING MY DEAR BROTHER.

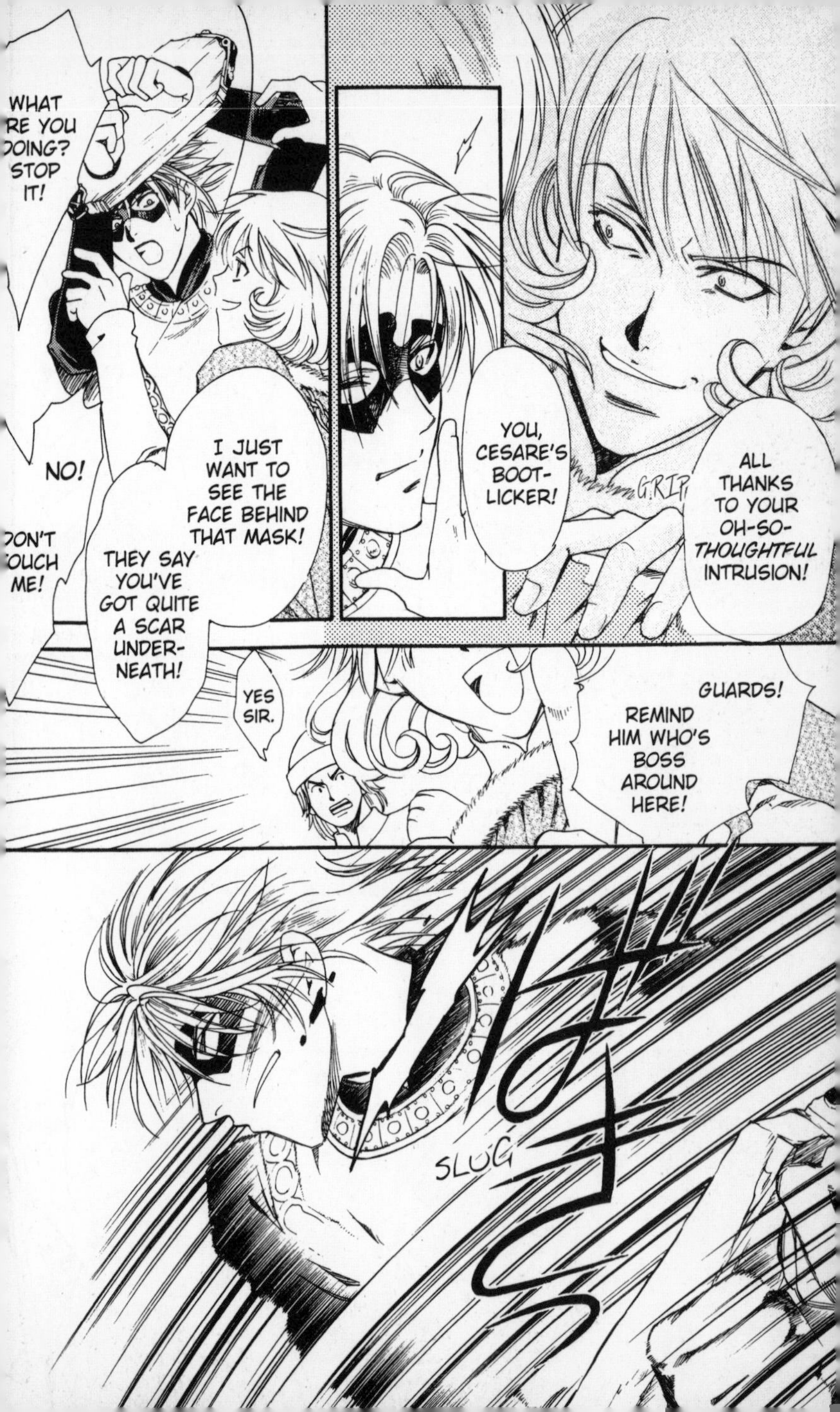
GRIP
ALL THANKS TO YOUR OH-SO-*THOUGHTFUL* INTRUSION!
YOU, CESARE'S BOOT-LICKER!
I JUST WANT TO SEE THE FACE BEHIND THAT MASK!
THEY SAY YOU'VE GOT QUITE A SCAR UNDER-NEATH!
WHAT RE YOU OING? STOP IT!
NO!
ON'T OUCH ME!
GUARDS!
REMIND HIM WHO'S BOSS AROUND HERE!
YES SIR.
SLUG

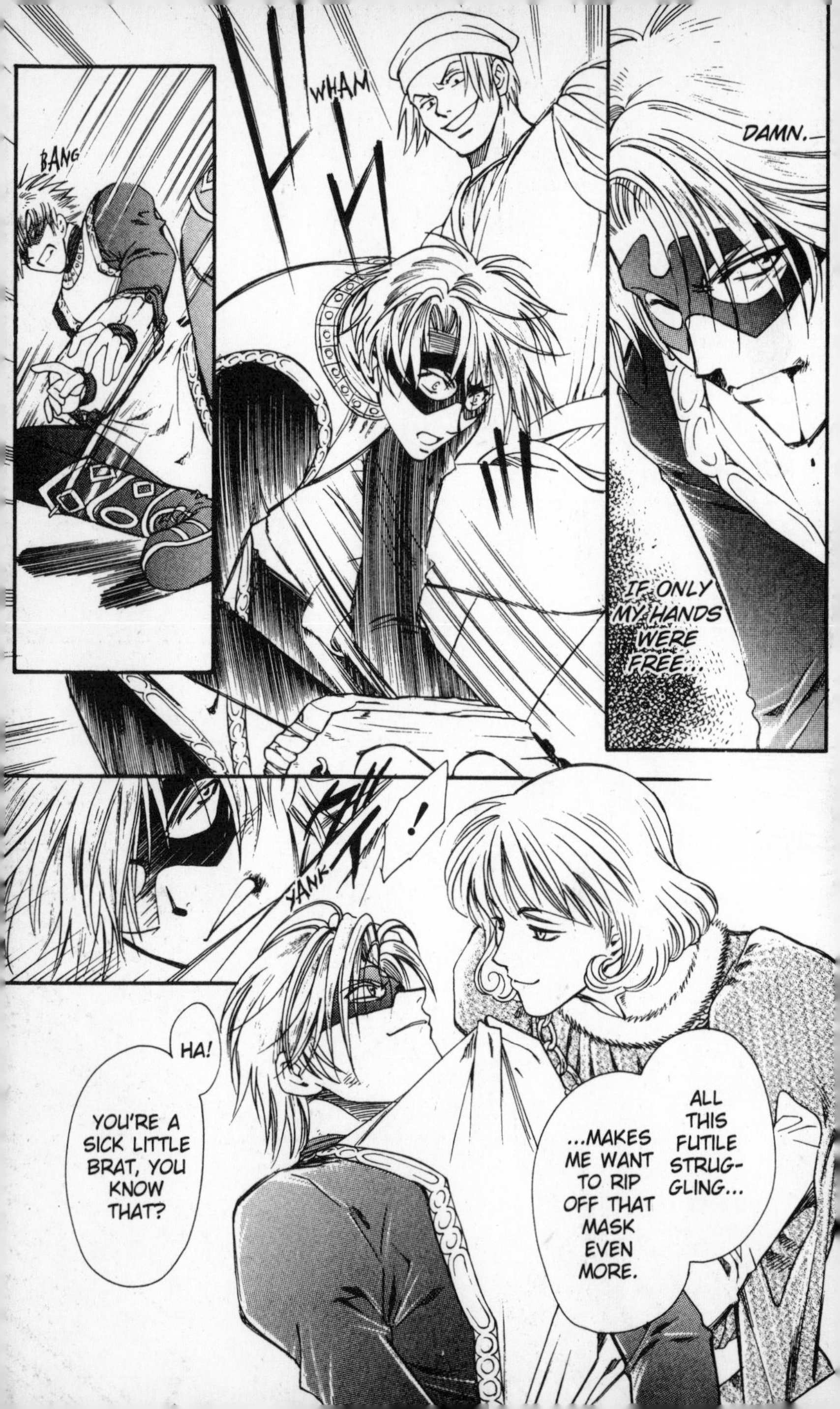
DAMN.
IF ONLY MY HANDS WERE FREE...
WHAM
BANG
YANK
!
ALL THIS FUTILE STRUGGLING...
...MAKES ME WANT TO RIP OFF THAT MASK EVEN MORE.
HA!
YOU'RE A SICK LITTLE BRAT, YOU KNOW THAT?

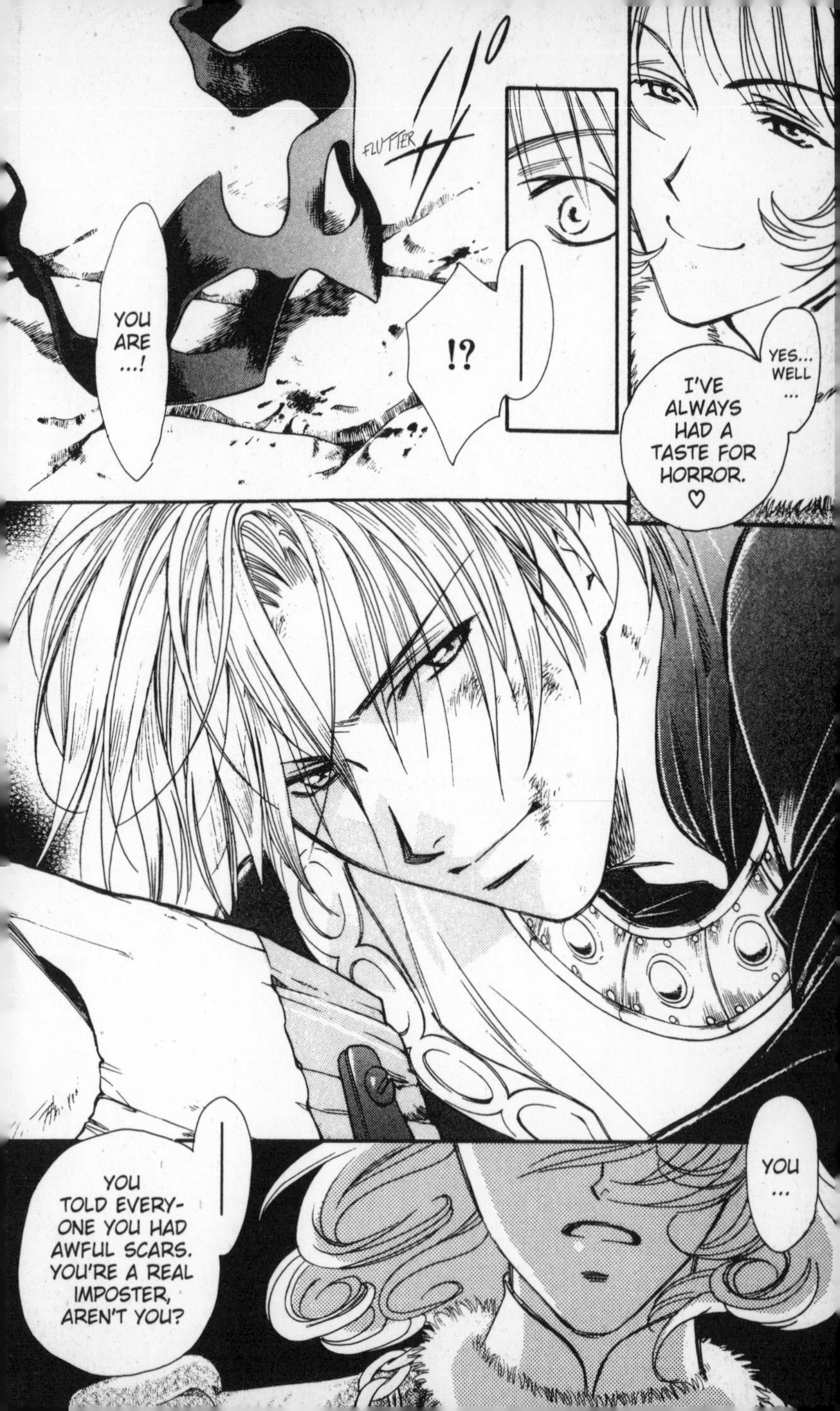
YES... WELL ...
I'VE ALWAYS HAD A TASTE FOR HORROR. ♡
!?
FLUTTER
YOU ARE ...!
YOU ...
YOU TOLD EVERY-ONE YOU HAD AWFUL SCARS. YOU'RE A REAL IMPOSTER, AREN'T YOU?

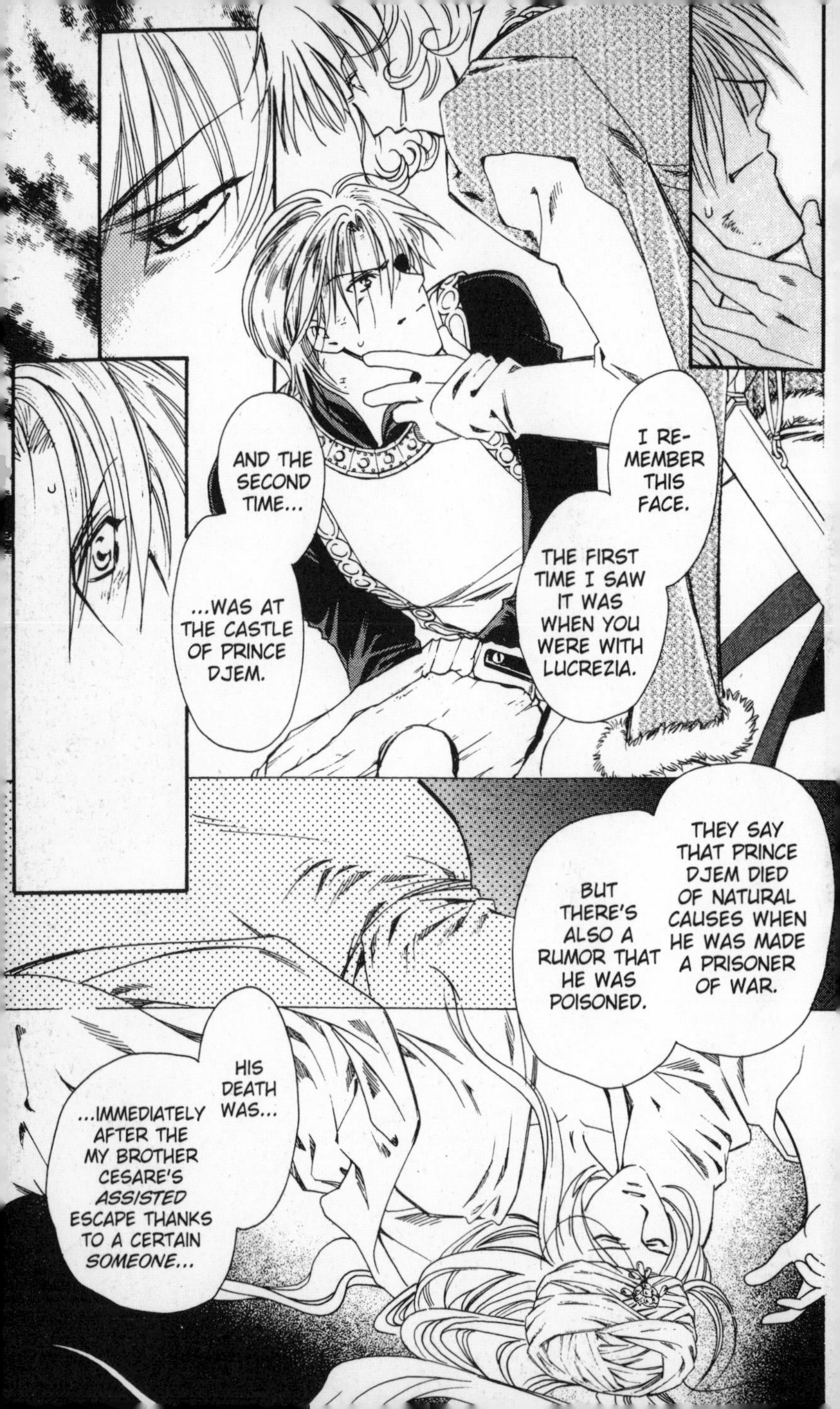

I RE-MEMBER THIS FACE.
THE FIRST TIME I SAW IT WAS WHEN YOU WERE WITH LUCREZIA.
AND THE SECOND TIME...
...WAS AT THE CASTLE OF PRINCE DJEM.
THEY SAY THAT PRINCE DJEM DIED OF NATURAL CAUSES WHEN HE WAS MADE A PRISONER OF WAR.
BUT THERE'S ALSO A RUMOR THAT HE WAS POISONED.
HIS DEATH WAS...
...IMMEDIATELY AFTER THE MY BROTHER CESARE'S *ASSISTED* ESCAPE THANKS TO A CERTAIN *SOMEONE*...

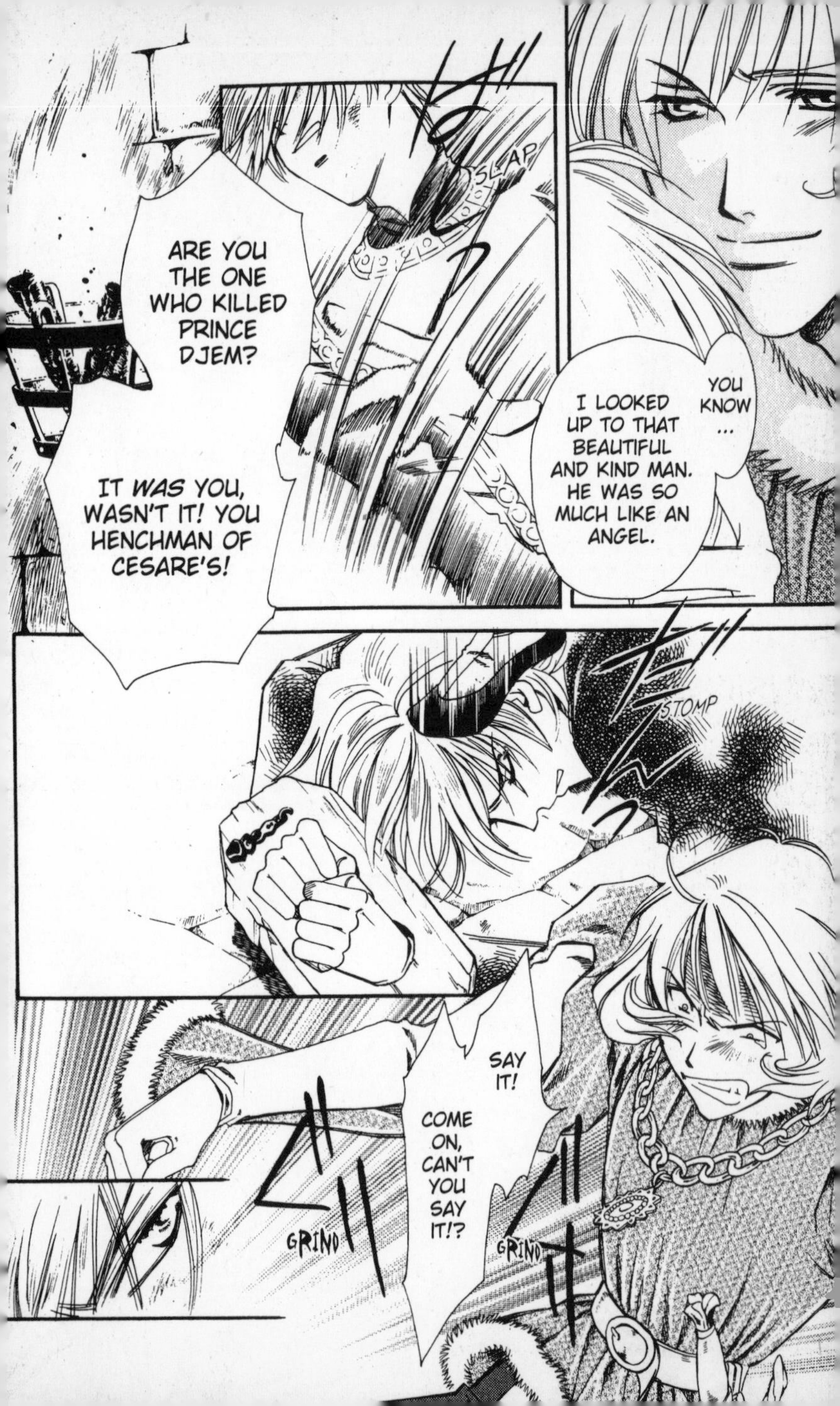
YOU KNOW ...
I LOOKED UP TO THAT BEAUTIFUL AND KIND MAN. HE WAS SO MUCH LIKE AN ANGEL.
SLAP
ARE YOU THE ONE WHO KILLED PRINCE DJEM?
IT *WAS* YOU, WASN'T IT! YOU HENCHMAN OF CESARE'S!
STOMP
SAY IT!
COME ON, CAN'T YOU SAY IT!?
GRIND
GRIND

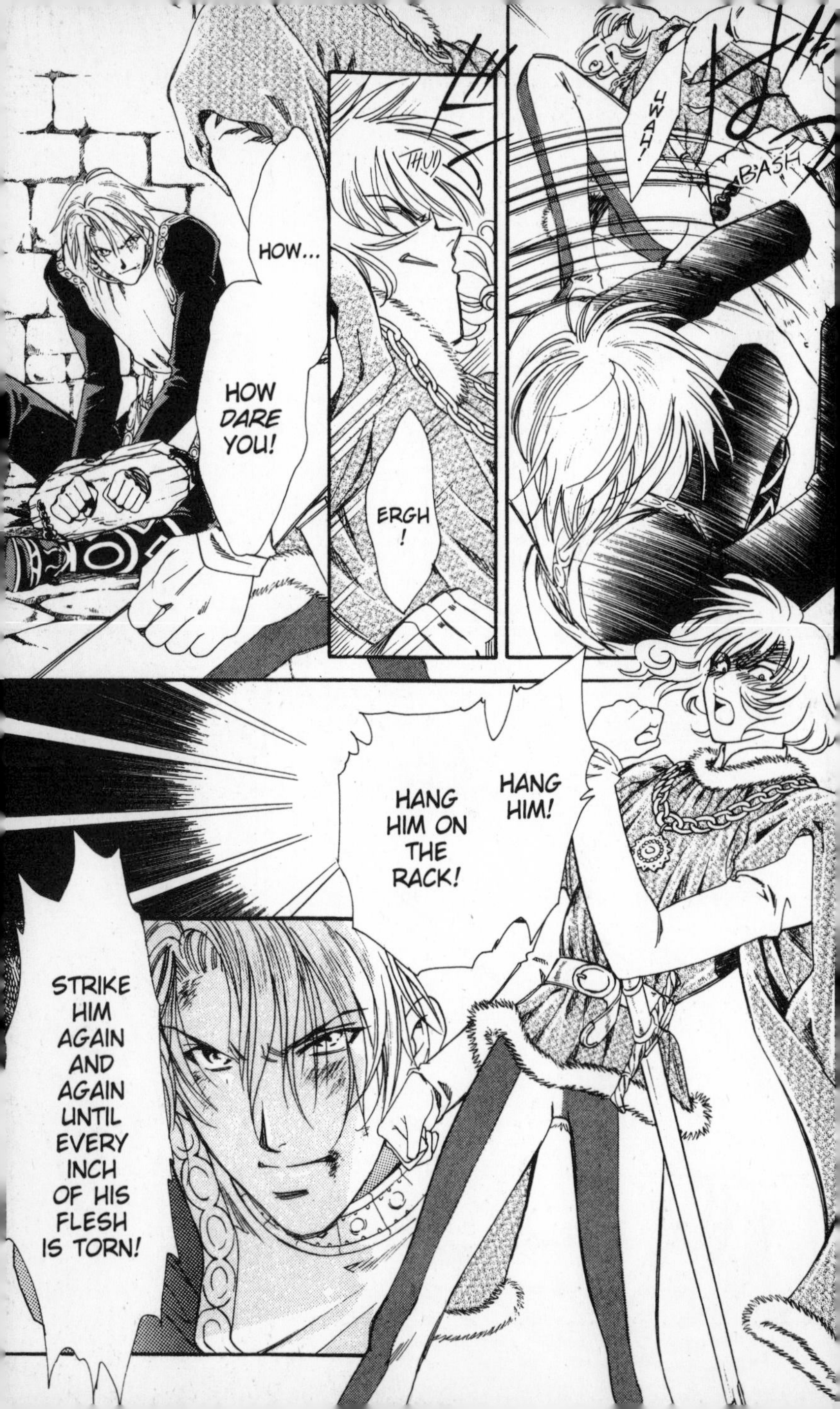
UWAH!
BASH
THUD
ERGH!
HOW...
HOW DARE YOU!
HANG HIM!
HANG HIM ON THE RACK!
STRIKE HIM AGAIN AND AGAIN UNTIL EVERY INCH OF HIS FLESH IS TORN!

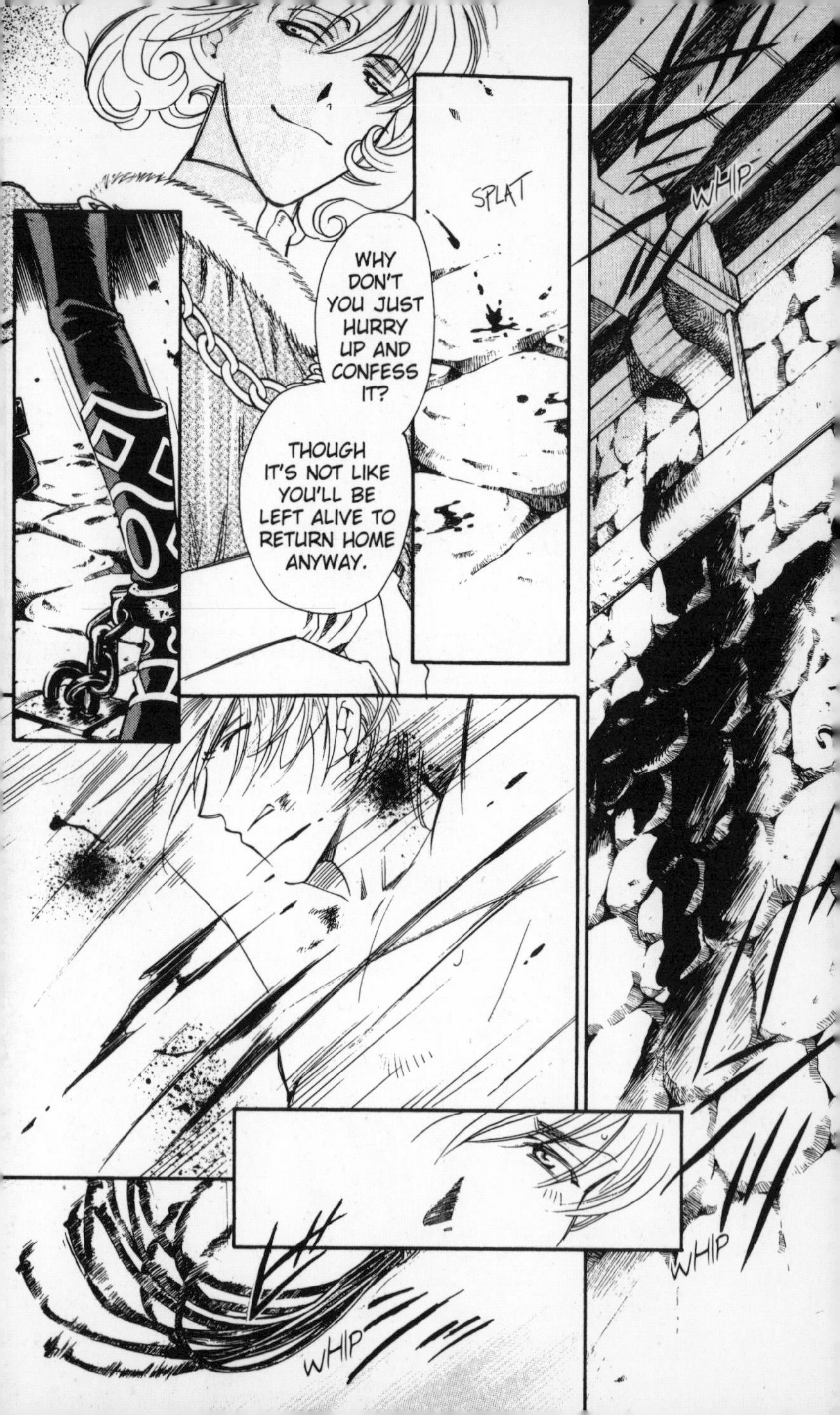
WHIP
SPLAT
WHY DON'T YOU JUST HURRY UP AND CONFESS IT?
THOUGH IT'S NOT LIKE YOU'LL BE LEFT ALIVE TO RETURN HOME ANYWAY.
WHIP
WHIP

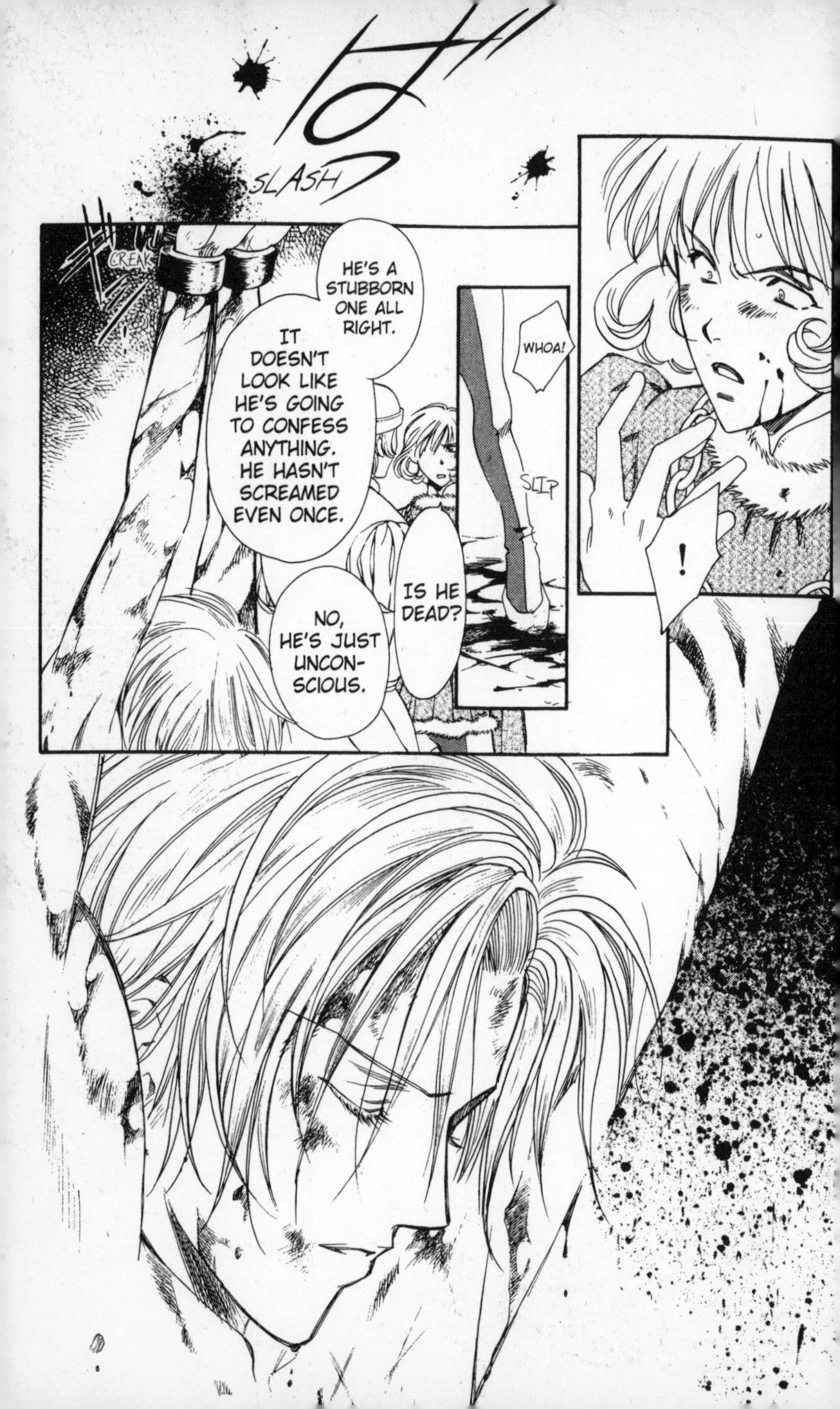
SLASH
CREAK
HE'S A STUBBORN ONE ALL RIGHT.
IT DOESN'T LOOK LIKE HE'S GOING TO CONFESS ANYTHING. HE HASN'T SCREAMED EVEN ONCE.
IS HE DEAD?
NO, HE'S JUST UNCON-SCIOUS.
WHOA!
SLIP
!

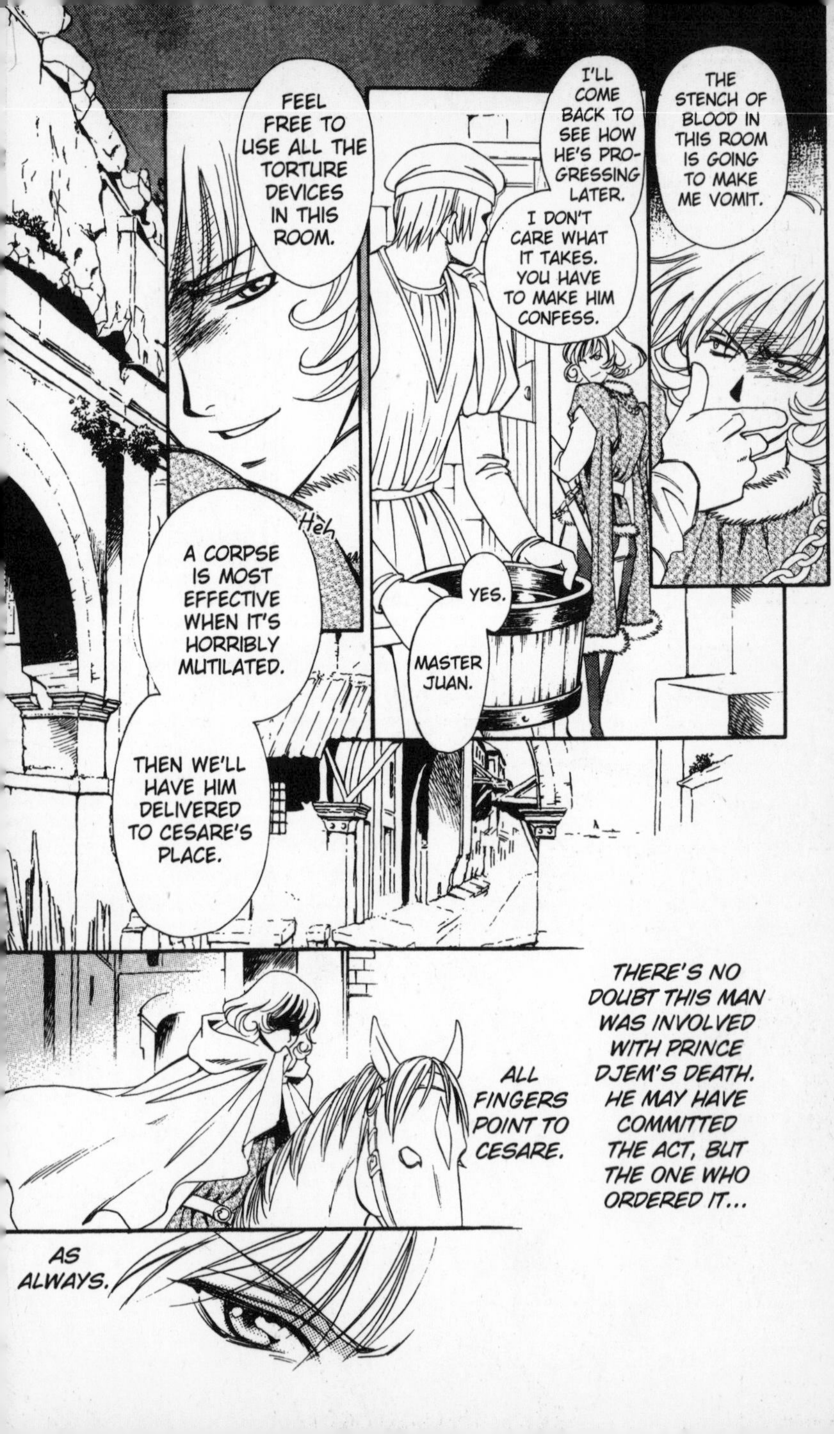
THE STENCH OF BLOOD IN THIS ROOM IS GOING TO MAKE ME VOMIT.
I'LL COME BACK TO SEE HOW HE'S PRO-GRESSING LATER.
I DON'T CARE WHAT IT TAKES. YOU HAVE TO MAKE HIM CONFESS.
YES.
MASTER JUAN.
FEEL FREE TO USE ALL THE TORTURE DEVICES IN THIS ROOM.
Heh
A CORPSE IS MOST EFFECTIVE WHEN IT'S HORRIBLY MUTILATED.
THEN WE'LL HAVE HIM DELIVERED TO CESARE'S PLACE.
THERE'S NO DOUBT THIS MAN WAS INVOLVED WITH PRINCE DJEM'S DEATH. HE MAY HAVE COMMITTED THE ACT, BUT THE ONE WHO ORDERED IT...
ALL FINGERS POINT TO CESARE.
AS ALWAYS.

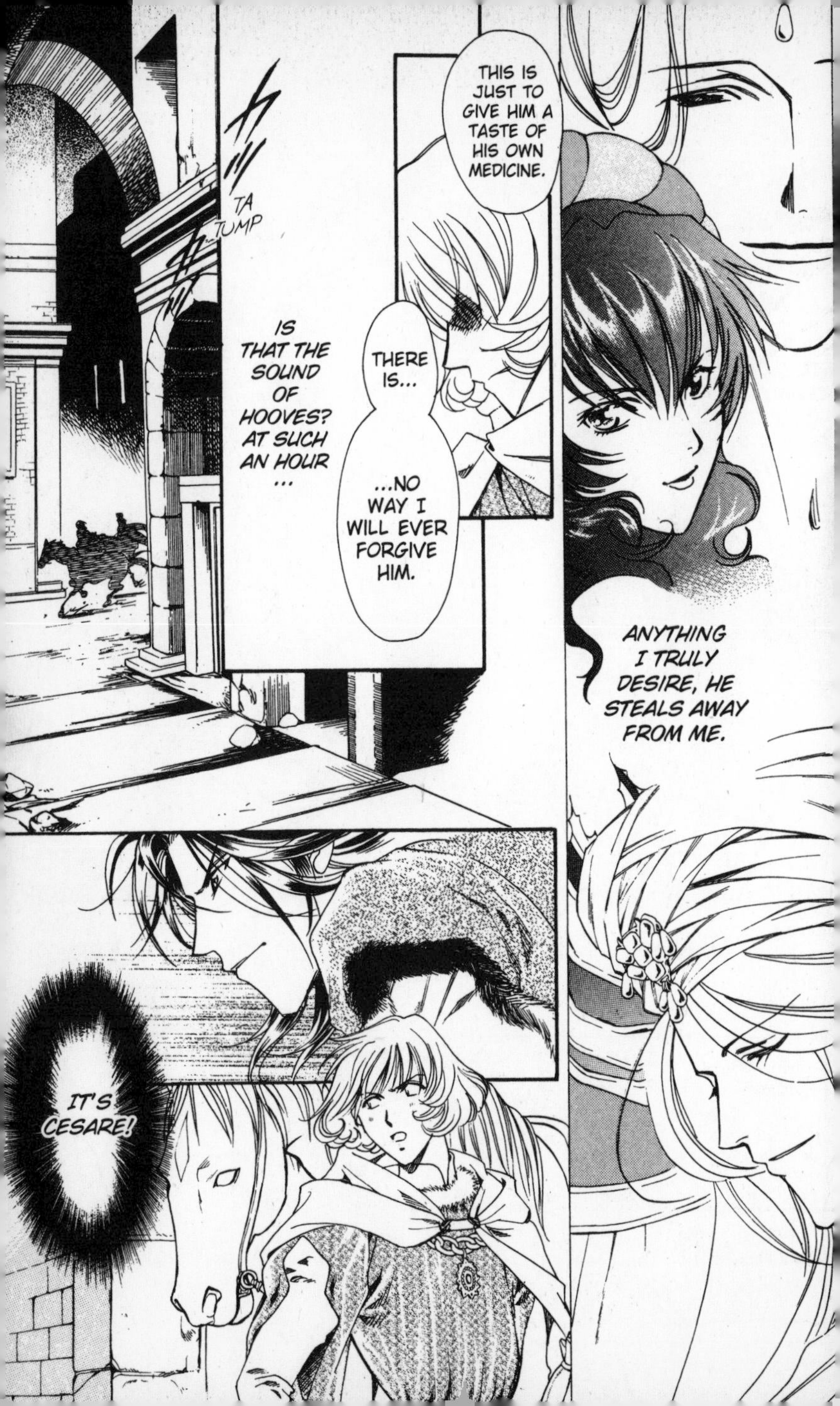
ANYTHING I TRULY DESIRE, HE STEALS AWAY FROM ME.
THIS IS JUST TO GIVE HIM A TASTE OF HIS OWN MEDICINE.
THERE IS...
...NO WAY I WILL EVER FORGIVE HIM.
TA TUMP
IS THAT THE SOUND OF HOOVES? AT SUCH AN HOUR ...
IT'S CESARE!

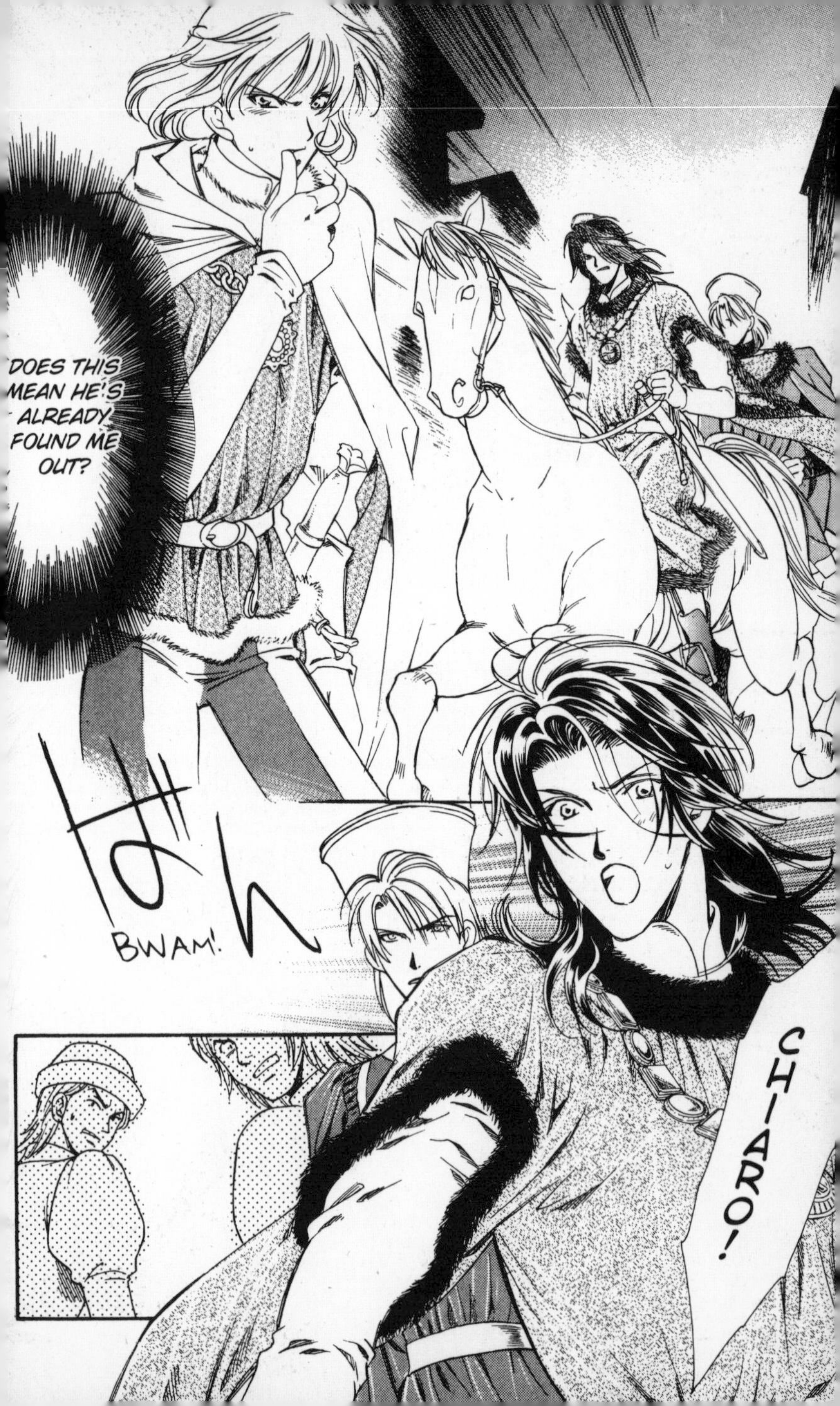
DOES THIS MEAN HE'S ALREADY FOUND ME OUT?
BWAM!
CHIARO!

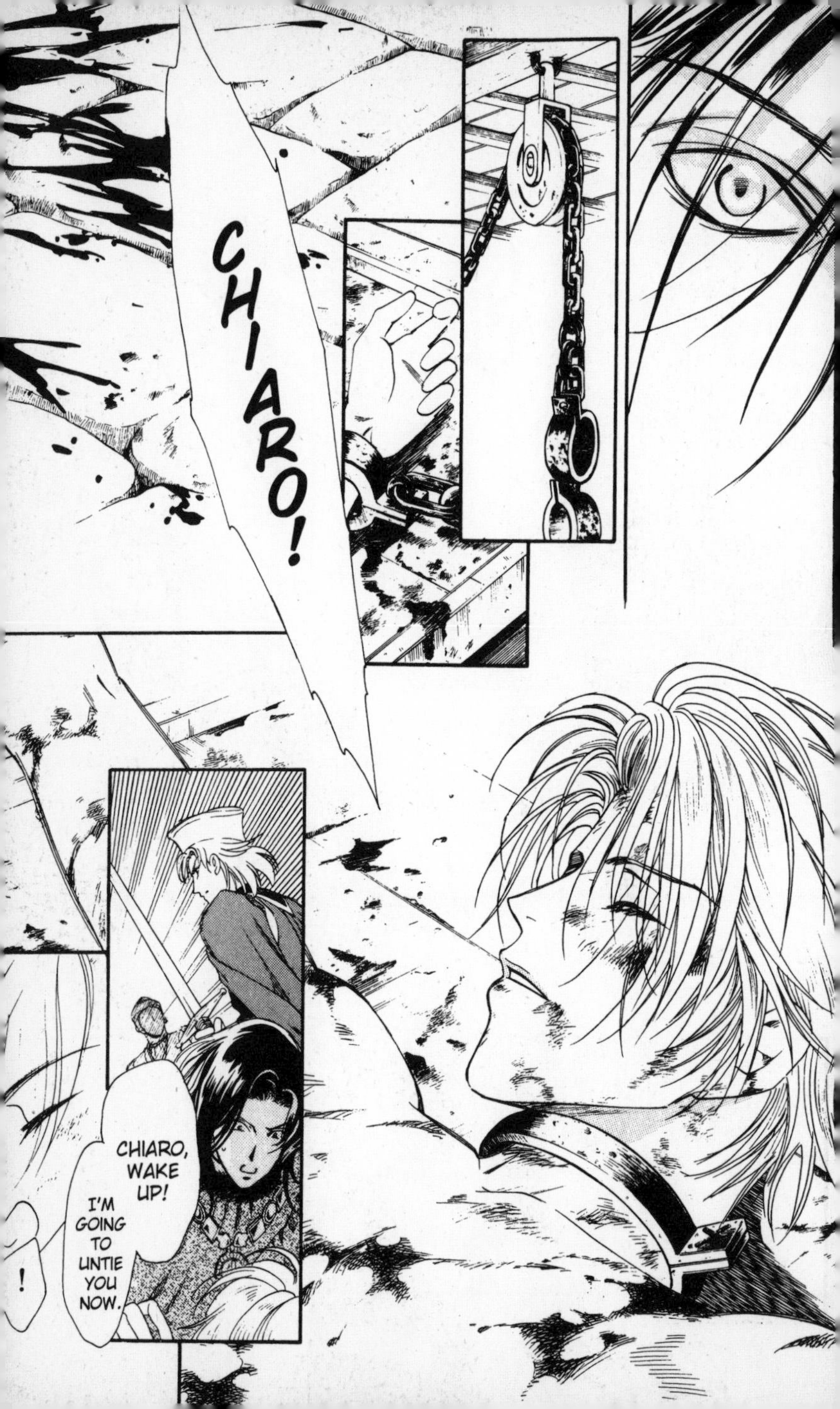
CHIARO!
CHIARO, WAKE UP!
I'M GOING TO UNTIE YOU NOW.
!

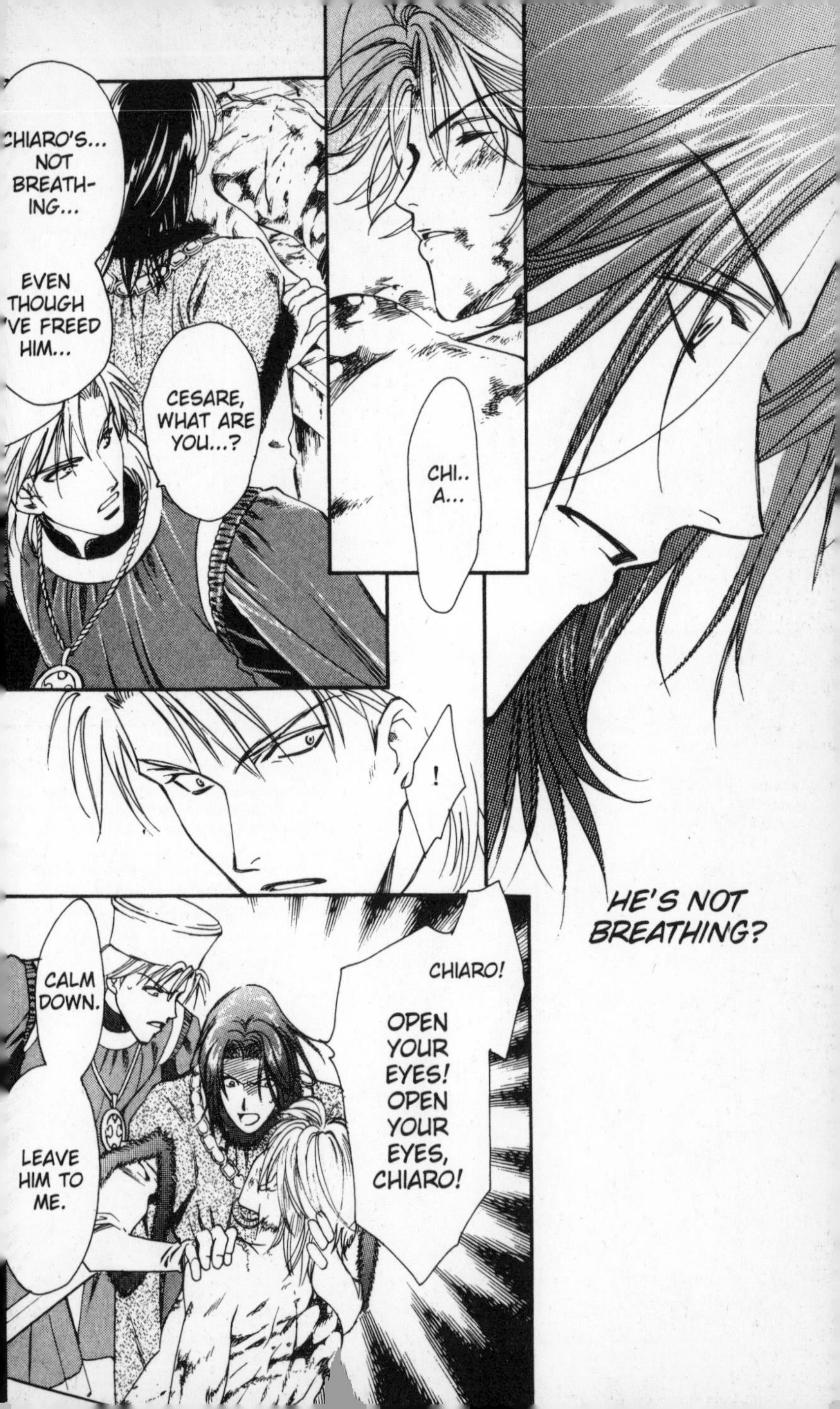

CHI.. A...
CHIARO'S... NOT BREATHING...
EVEN THOUGH 'VE FREED HIM...
CESARE, WHAT ARE YOU...?
!
HE'S NOT BREATHING?
CHIARO!
OPEN YOUR EYES! OPEN YOUR EYES, CHIARO!
CALM DOWN.
LEAVE HIM TO ME.

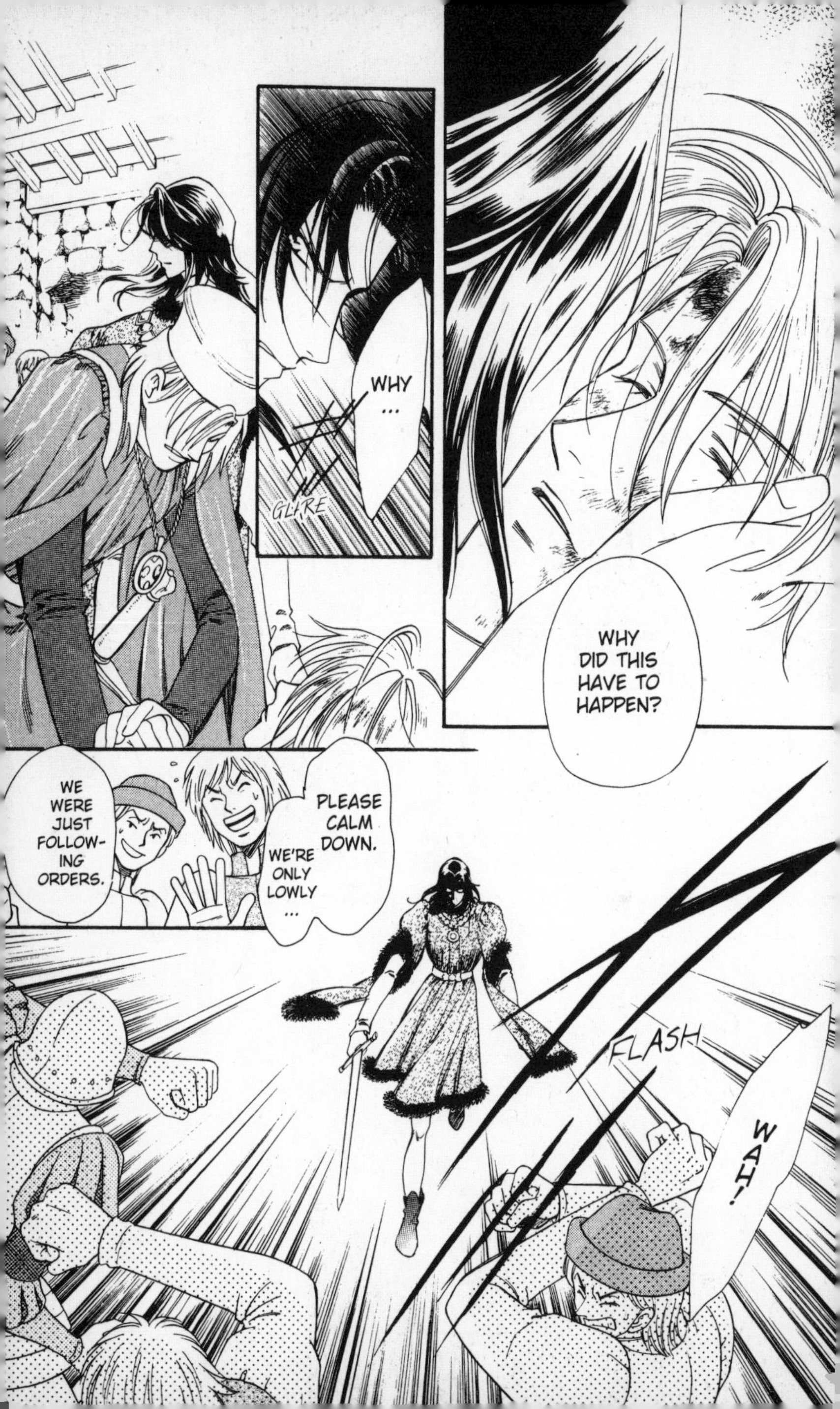
WHY DID THIS HAVE TO HAPPEN?
WHY ...
GLARE
PLEASE CALM DOWN.
WE'RE ONLY LOWLY ...
WE WERE JUST FOLLOW-ING ORDERS.
FLASH
WAH!

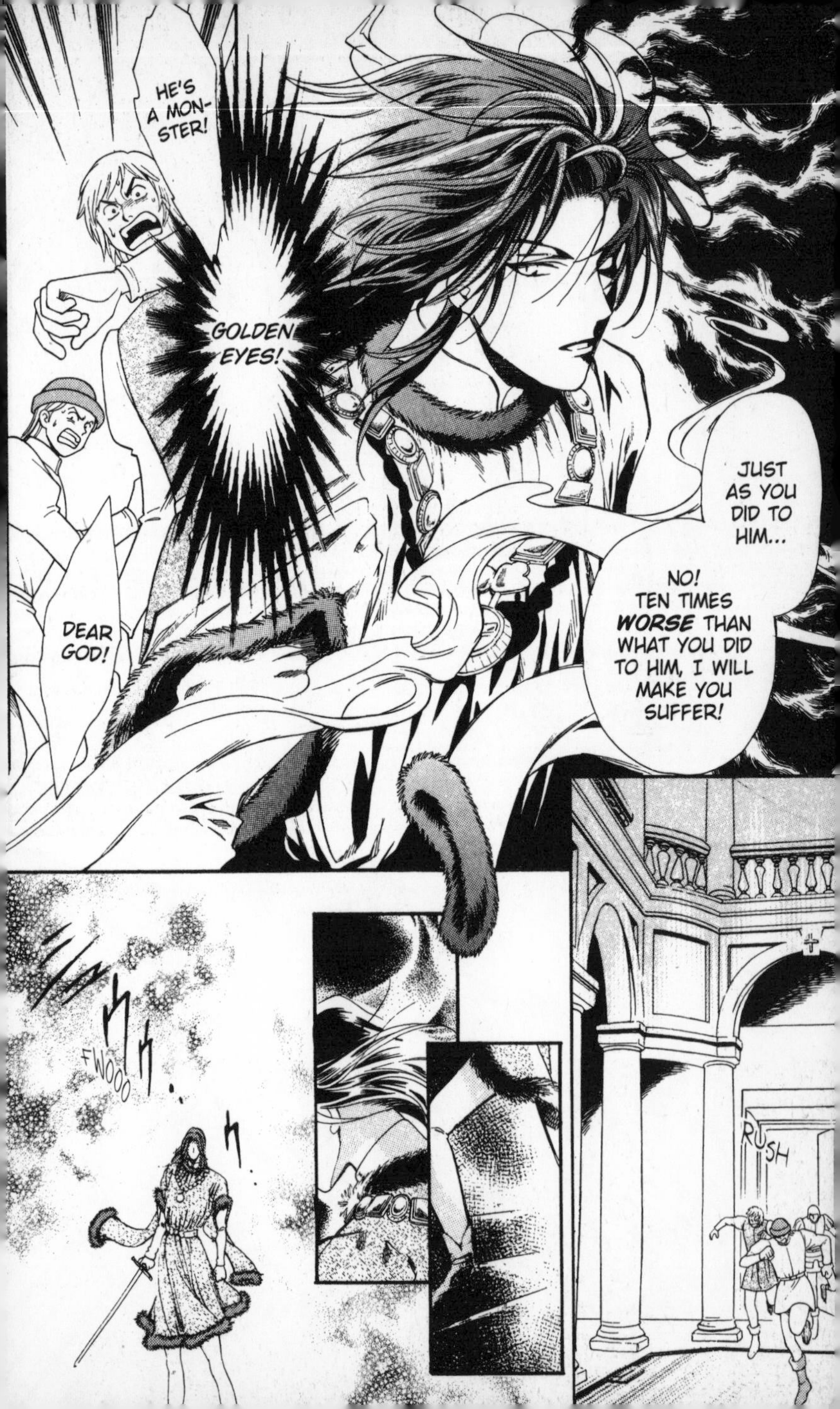
HE'S A MON-STER!
GOLDEN EYES!
JUST AS YOU DID TO HIM...
NO! TEN TIMES **WORSE** THAN WHAT YOU DID TO HIM, I WILL MAKE YOU SUFFER!
DEAR GOD!
RUSH
FWOOO

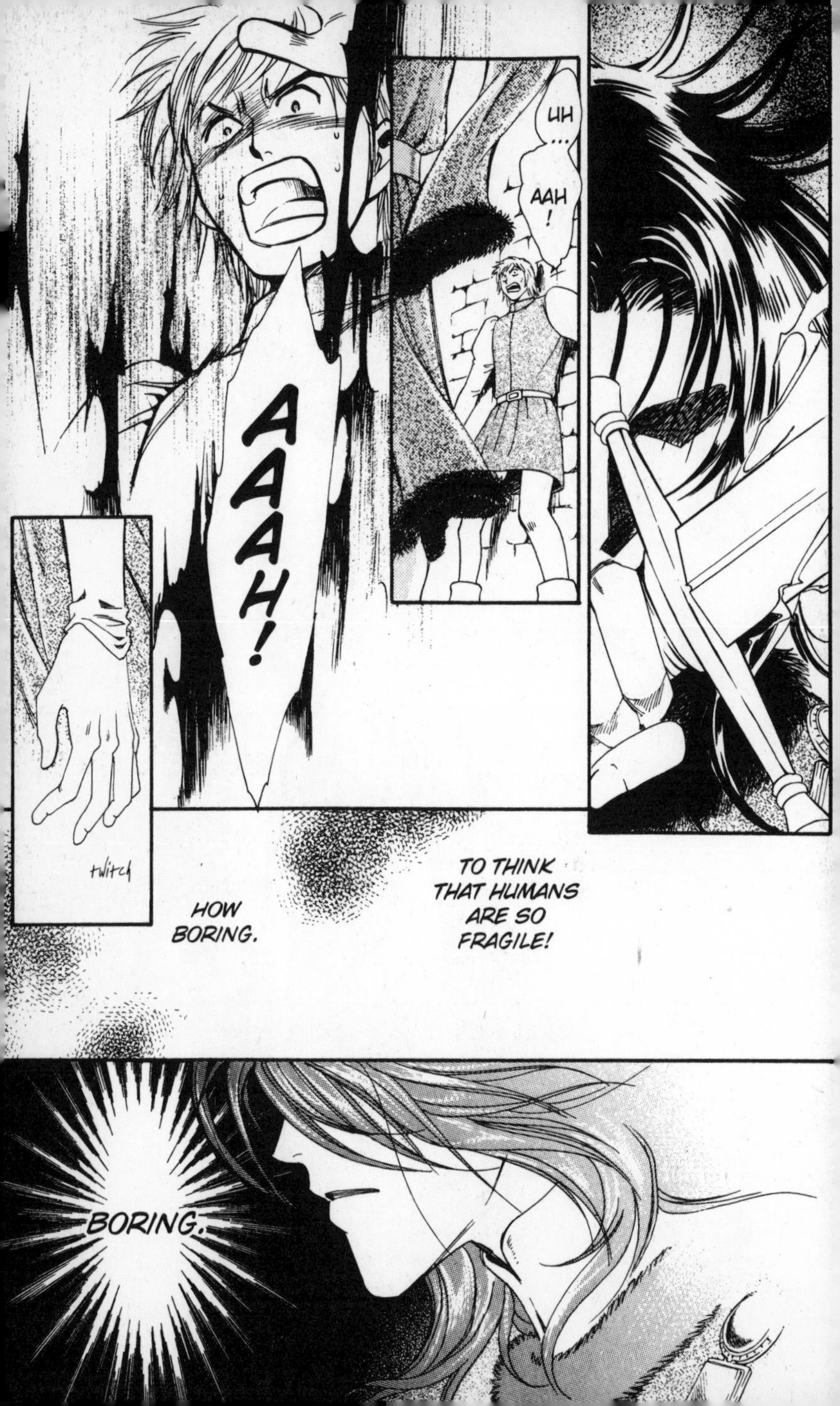
UH ... AAH!
AAAAH!
twitch
TO THINK THAT HUMANS ARE SO FRAGILE!
HOW BORING.
BORING.

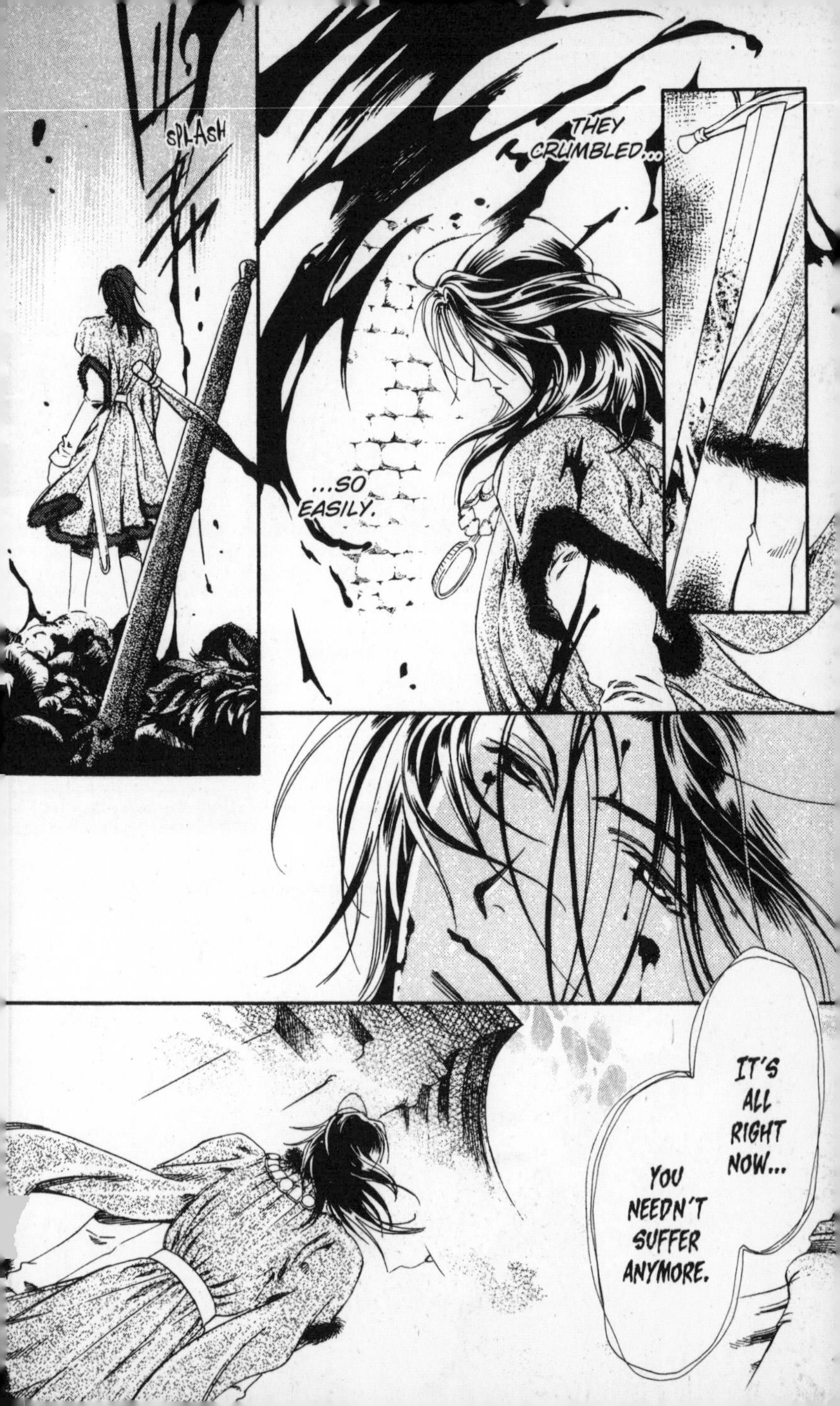
THEY CRUMBLED...
...SO EASILY.
SPLASH
IT'S ALL RIGHT NOW...
YOU NEEDN'T SUFFER ANYMORE.

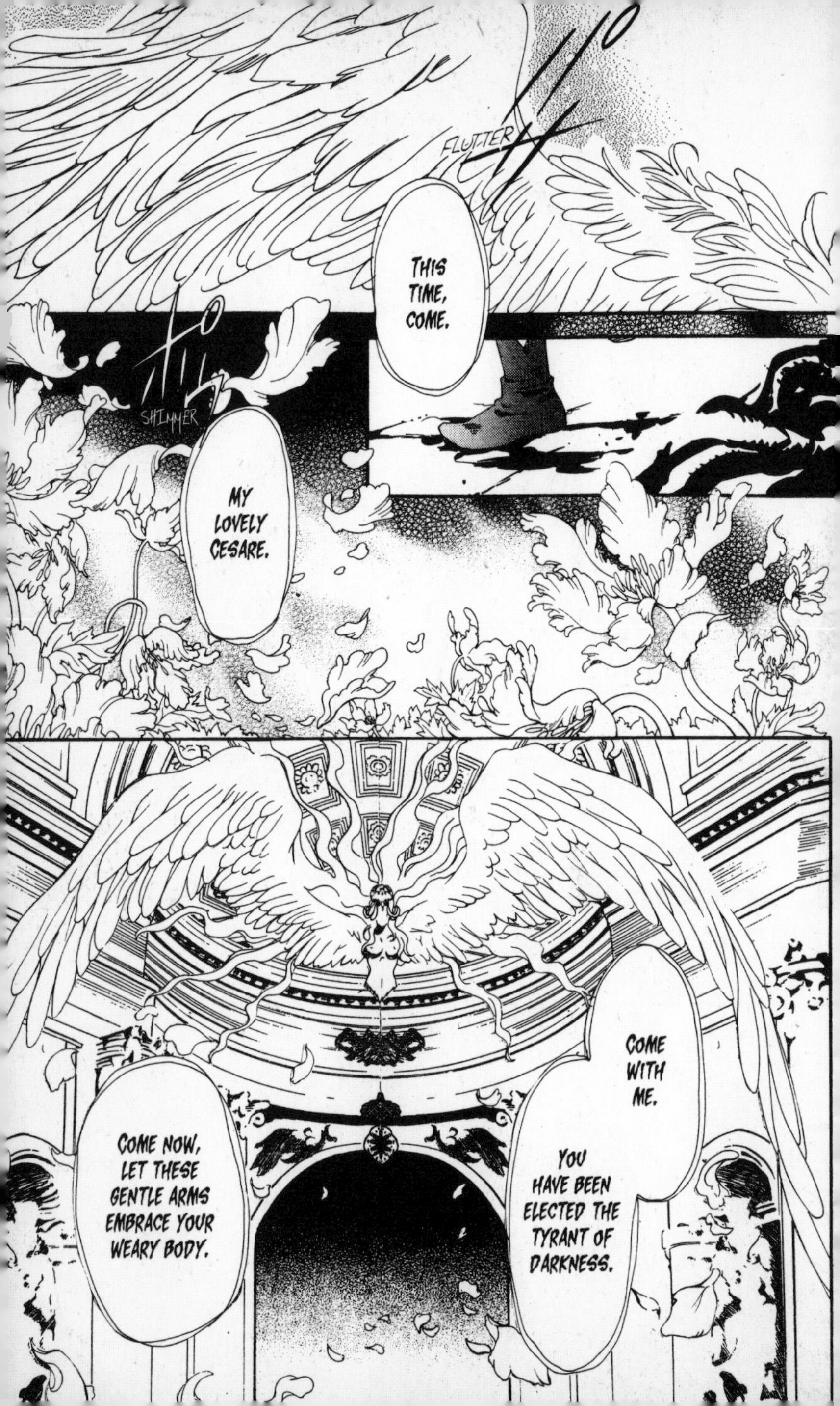
FLUTTER
THIS TIME, COME.
SHIMMER
MY LOVELY CESARE.
COME WITH ME.
YOU HAVE BEEN ELECTED THE TYRANT OF DARKNESS.
COME NOW, LET THESE GENTLE ARMS EMBRACE YOUR WEARY BODY.

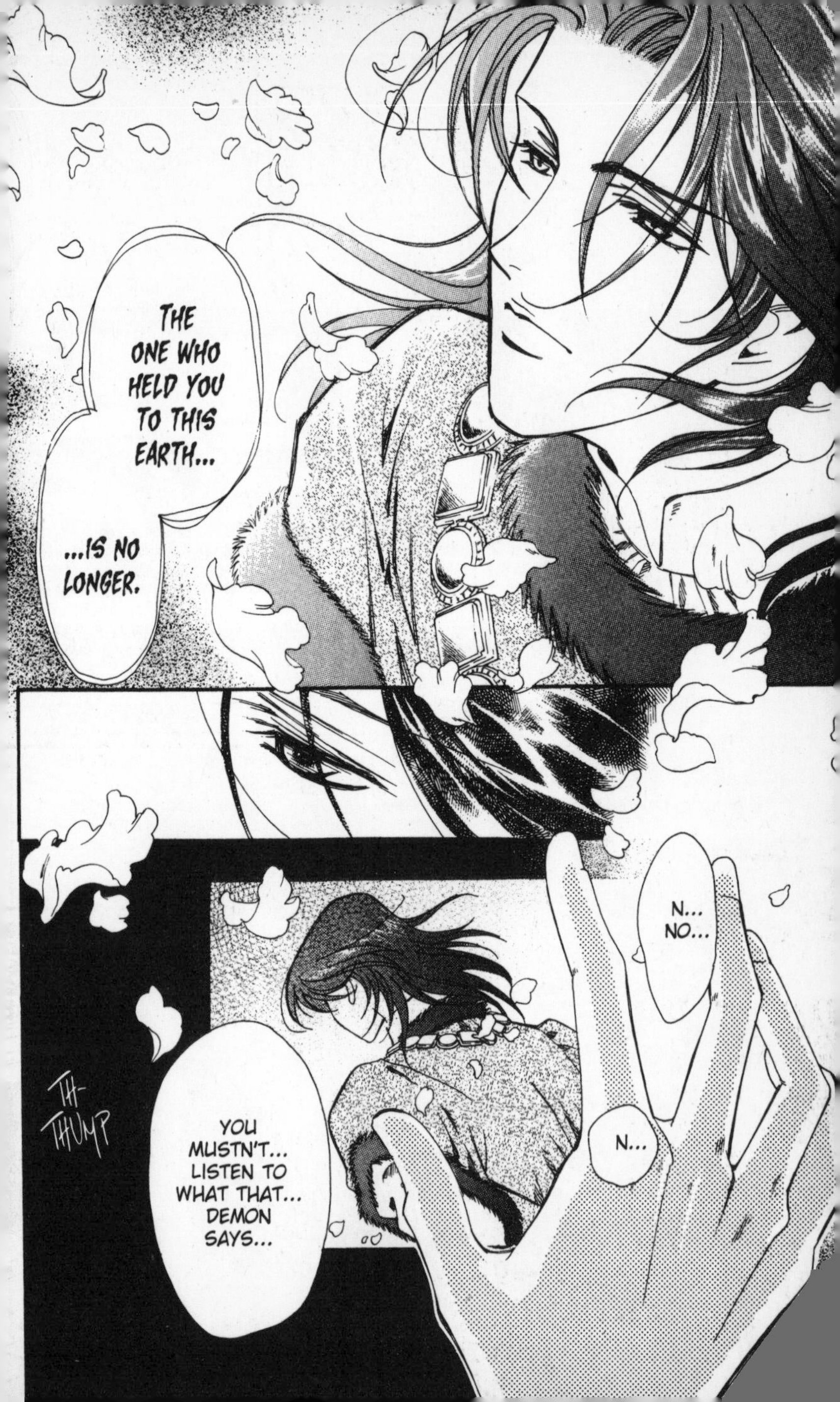
THE ONE WHO HELD YOU TO THIS EARTH...
...IS NO LONGER.
N... NO...
N...
YOU MUSTN'T... LISTEN TO WHAT THAT... DEMON SAYS...
TH-THUMP

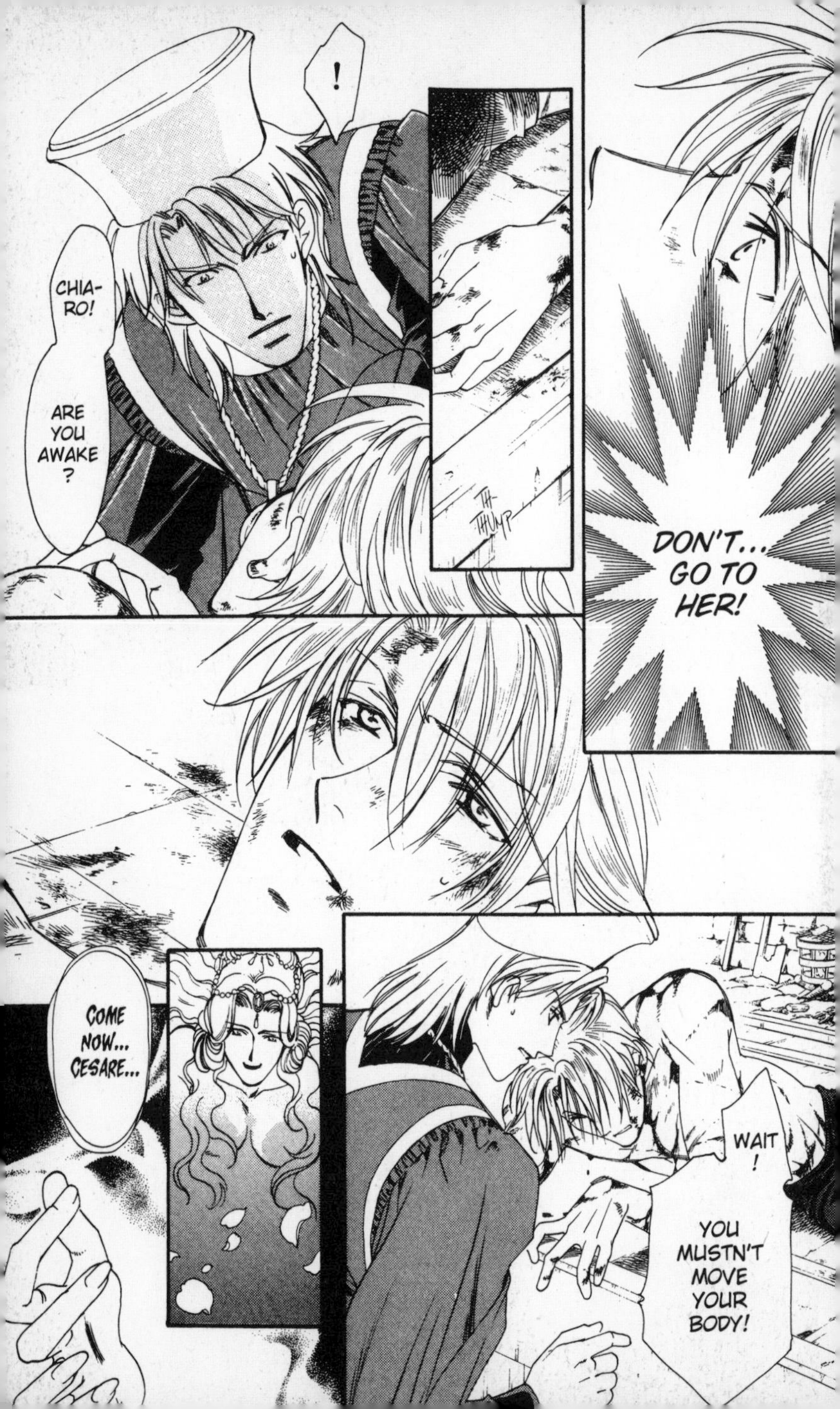
DON'T... GO TO HER!
TH THUMP
!
CHIA-RO!
ARE YOU AWAKE?
WAIT!
YOU MUSTN'T MOVE YOUR BODY!
COME NOW... CESARE...

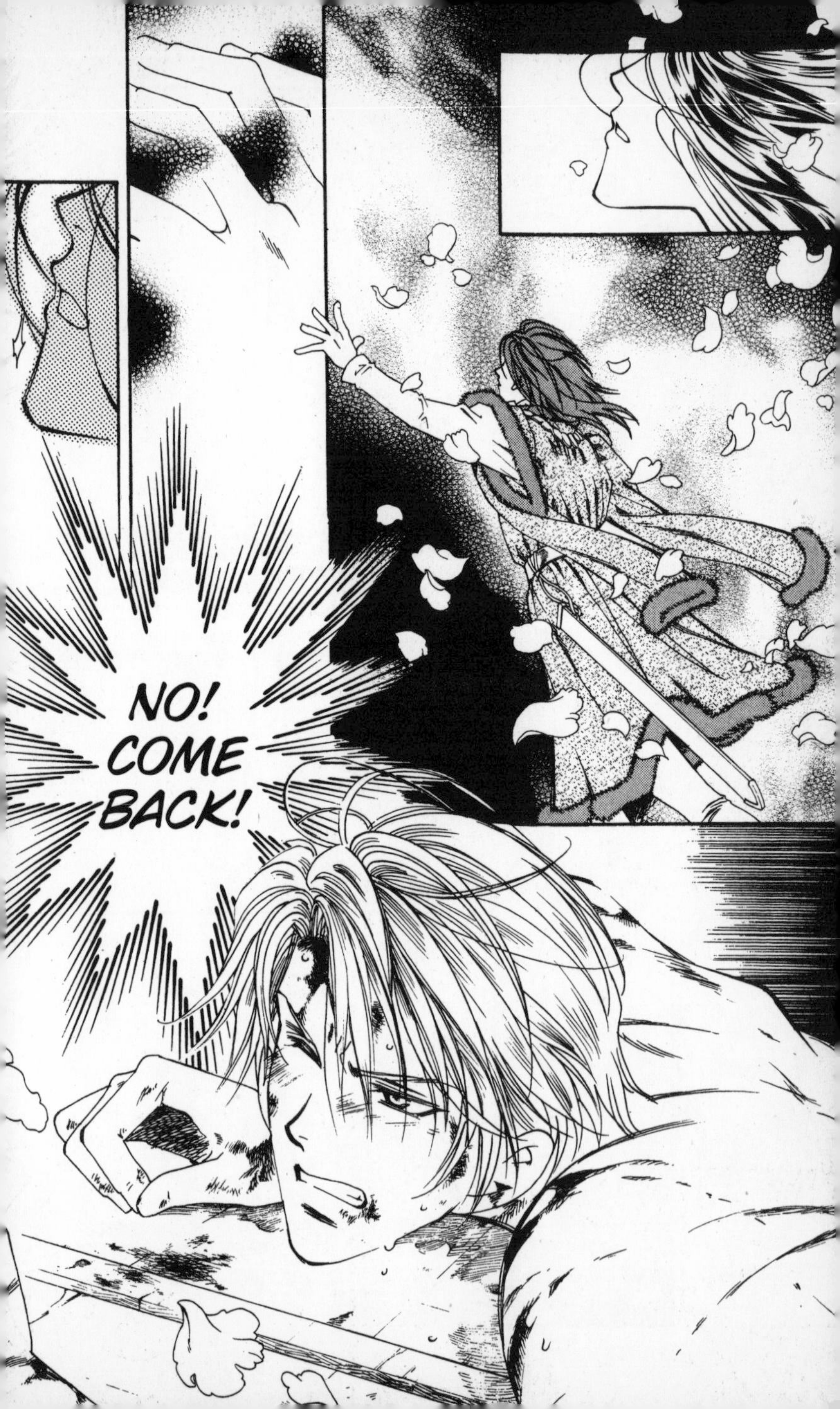
NO! COME BACK!

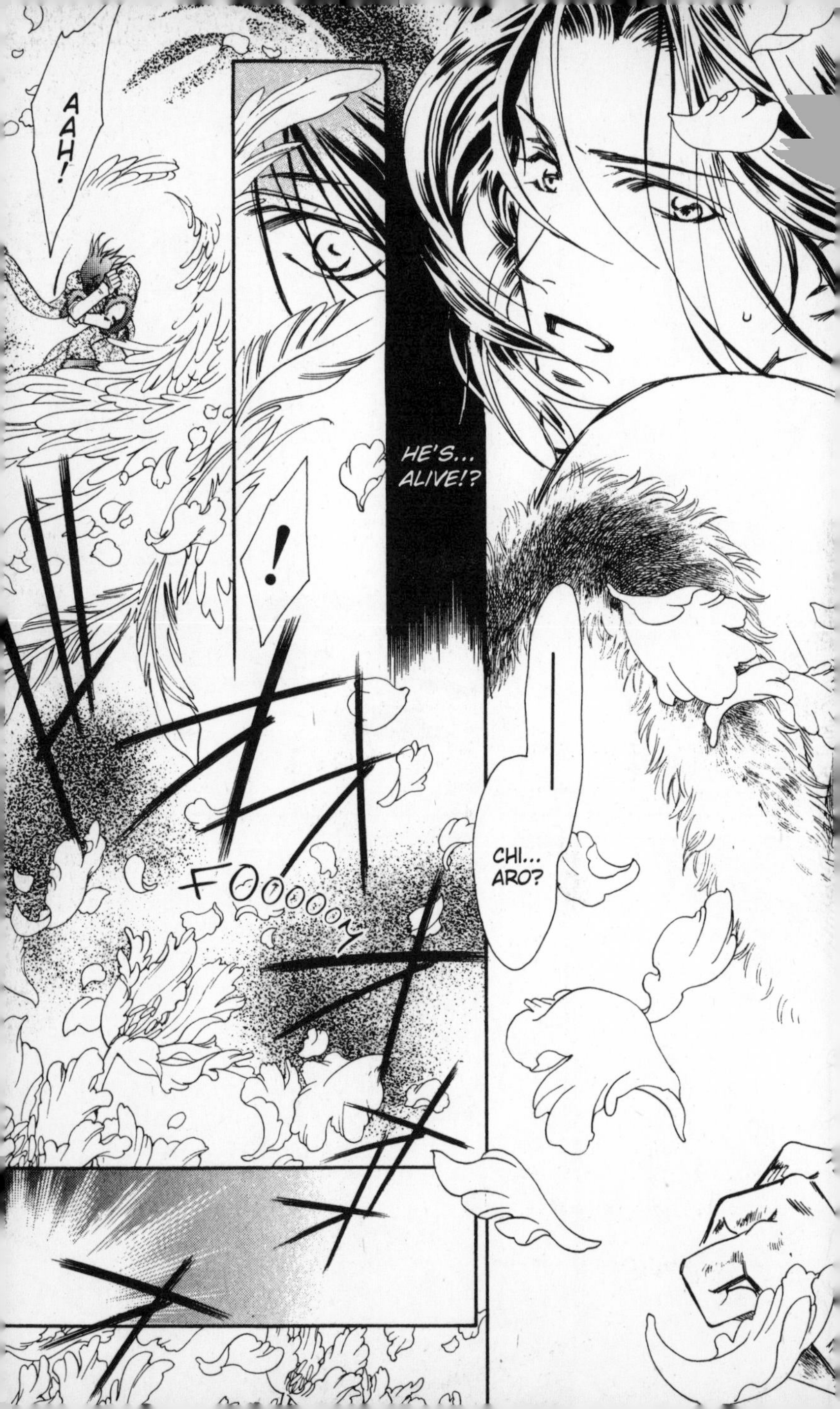
HE'S... ALIVE!?
CHI... ARO?
!
AAH!
FOOOOOOM

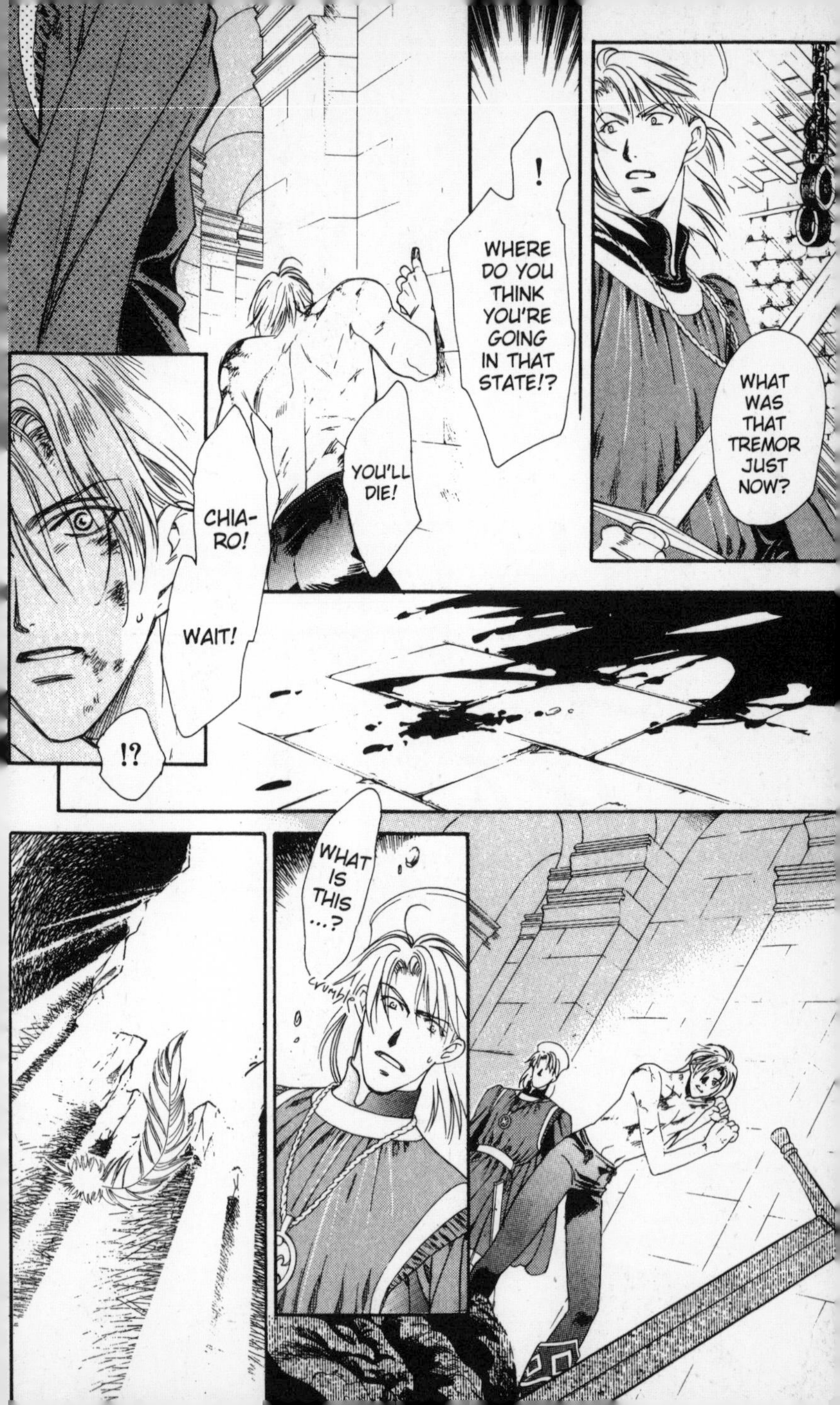
WHAT WAS THAT TREMOR JUST NOW?
!
WHERE DO YOU THINK YOU'RE GOING IN THAT STATE!?
YOU'LL DIE!
CHIA-RO!
WAIT!
!?
WHAT IS THIS ...?
crumble

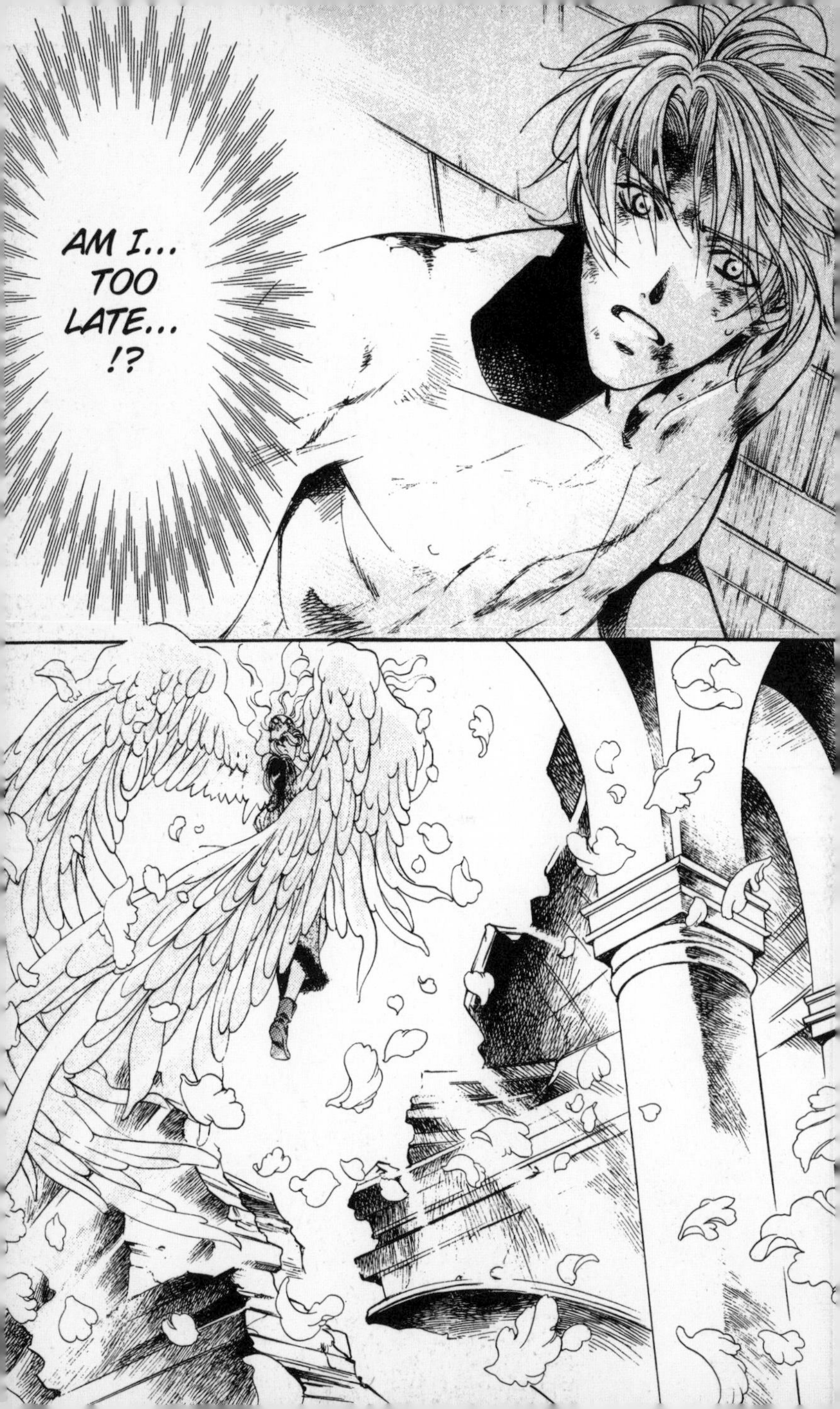
AM I... TOO LATE... !?

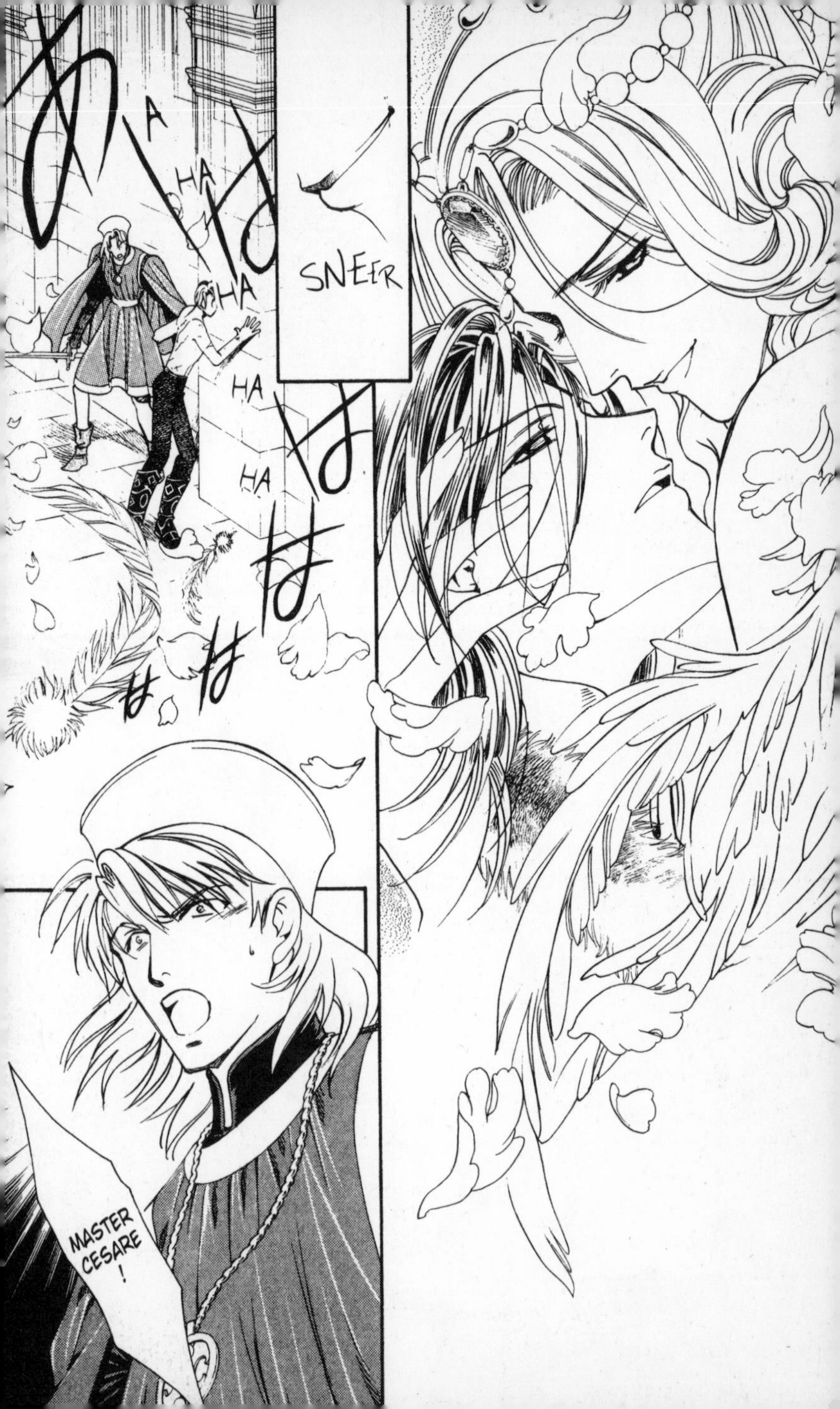

SNEER
A HA HA HA HA
MASTER CESARE!

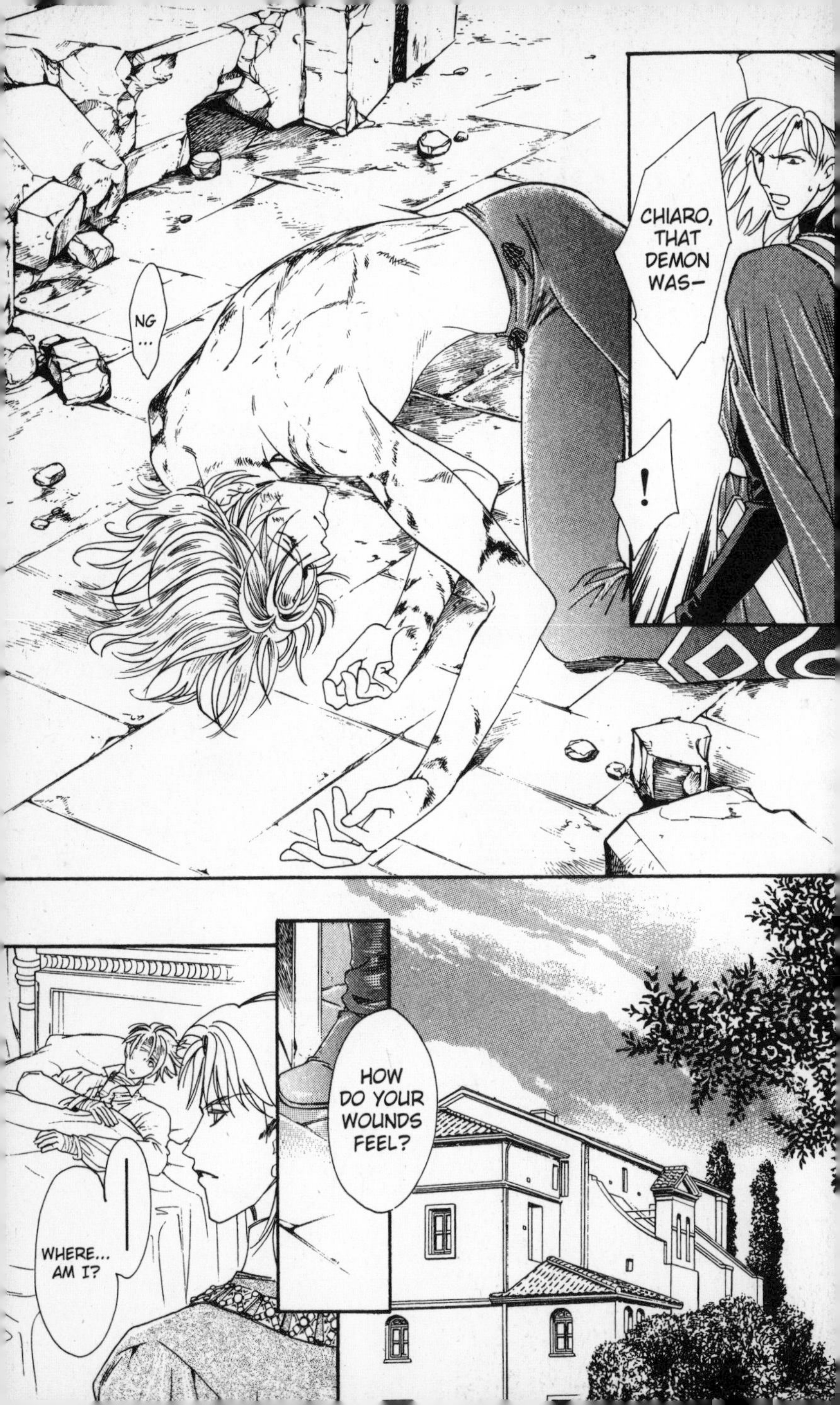
CHIARO, THAT DEMON WAS—
!
NG ...
HOW DO YOUR WOUNDS FEEL?
WHERE... AM I?

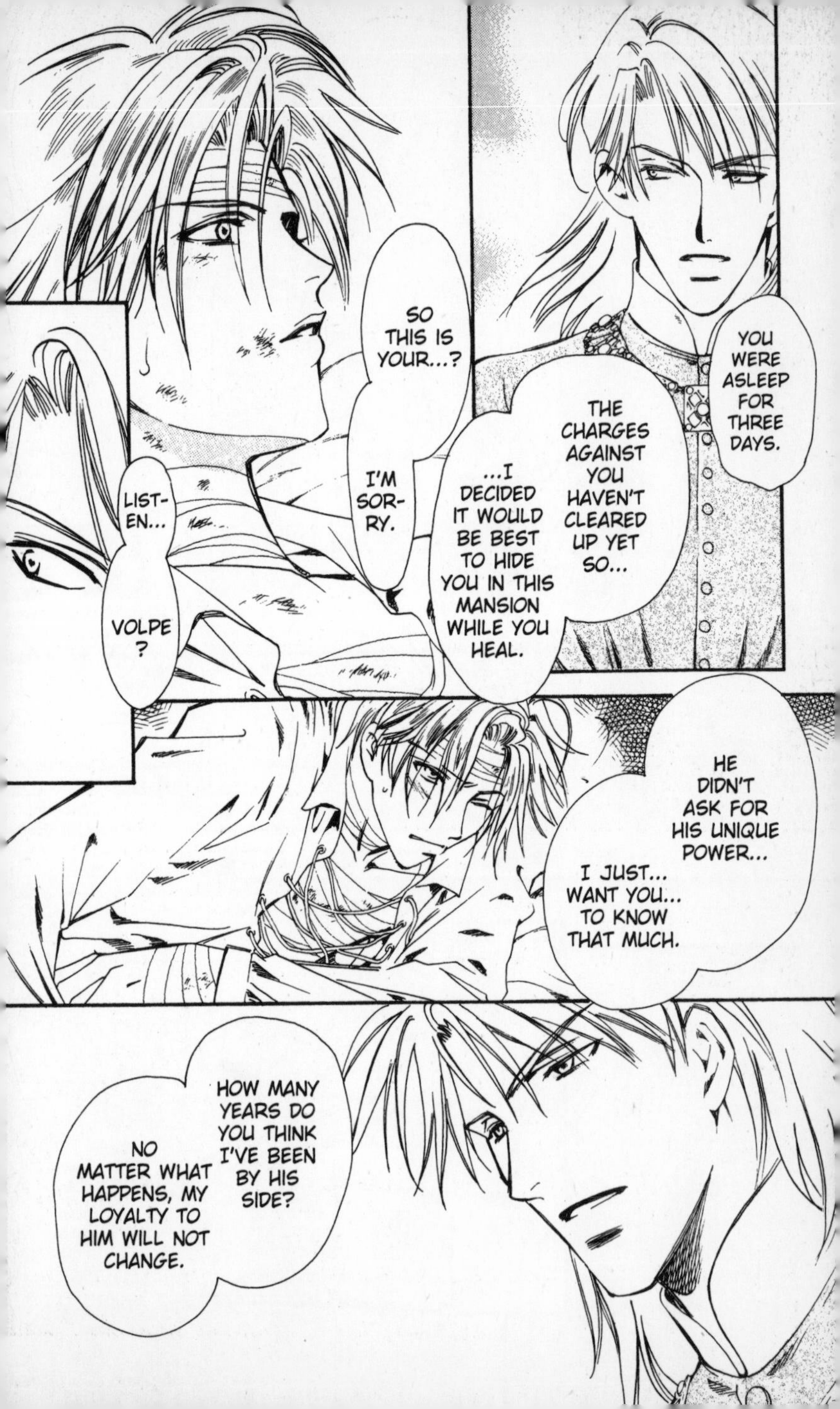
YOU WERE ASLEEP FOR THREE DAYS.
THE CHARGES AGAINST YOU HAVEN'T CLEARED UP YET SO...
...I DECIDED IT WOULD BE BEST TO HIDE YOU IN THIS MANSION WHILE YOU HEAL.
SO THIS IS YOUR...?
I'M SOR-RY.
LIST-EN...
VOLPE?
HE DIDN'T ASK FOR HIS UNIQUE POWER...
I JUST... WANT YOU... TO KNOW THAT MUCH.
HOW MANY YEARS DO YOU THINK I'VE BEEN BY HIS SIDE?
NO MATTER WHAT HAPPENS, MY LOYALTY TO HIM WILL NOT CHANGE.

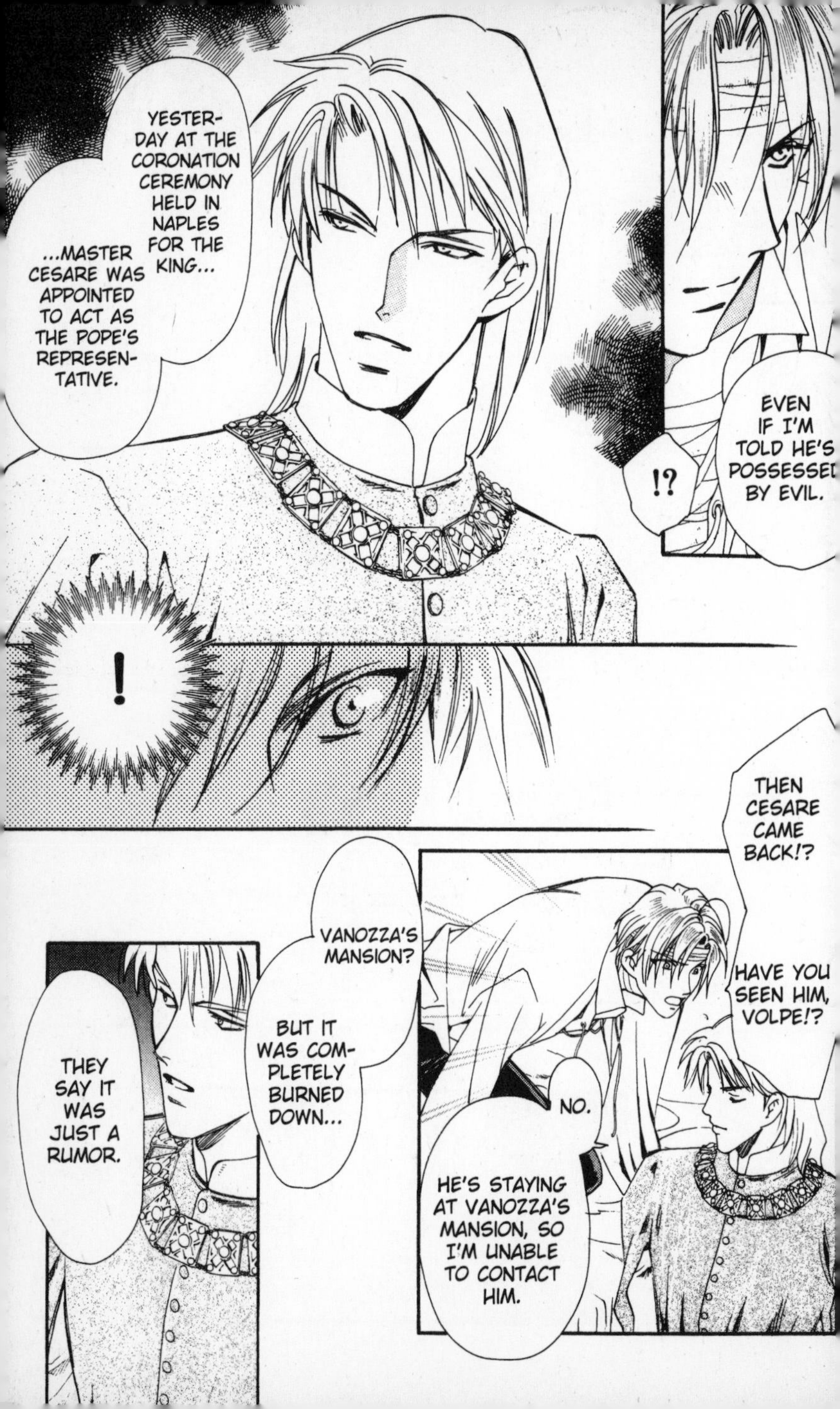
EVEN IF I'M TOLD HE'S POSSESSED BY EVIL.
!?
YESTERDAY AT THE CORONATION CEREMONY HELD IN NAPLES FOR THE KING...
...MASTER CESARE WAS APPOINTED TO ACT AS THE POPE'S REPRESENTATIVE.
!
THEN CESARE CAME BACK!?
HAVE YOU SEEN HIM, VOLPE!?
NO.
HE'S STAYING AT VANOZZA'S MANSION, SO I'M UNABLE TO CONTACT HIM.
VANOZZA'S MANSION?
BUT IT WAS COMPLETELY BURNED DOWN...
THEY SAY IT WAS JUST A RUMOR.

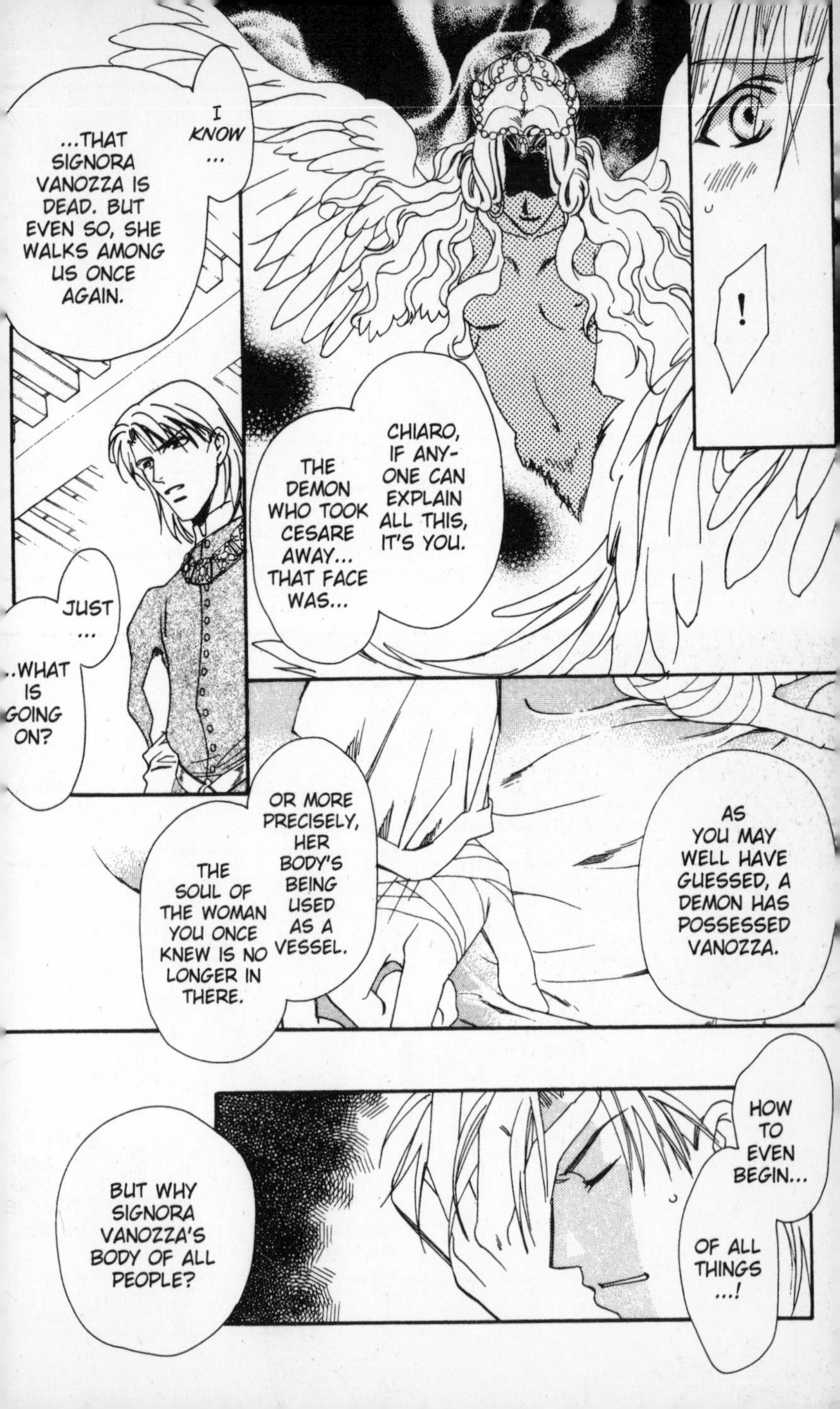
!
CHIARO, IF ANY-ONE CAN EXPLAIN ALL THIS, IT'S YOU.
THE DEMON WHO TOOK CESARE AWAY... THAT FACE WAS...
I KNOW...
...THAT SIGNORA VANOZZA IS DEAD. BUT EVEN SO, SHE WALKS AMONG US ONCE AGAIN.
JUST...
...WHAT IS GOING ON?
AS YOU MAY WELL HAVE GUESSED, A DEMON HAS POSSESSED VANOZZA.
THE SOUL OF THE WOMAN YOU ONCE KNEW IS NO LONGER IN THERE.
OR MORE PRECISELY, HER BODY'S BEING USED AS A VESSEL.
HOW TO EVEN BEGIN...
OF ALL THINGS...!
BUT WHY SIGNORA VANOZZA'S BODY OF ALL PEOPLE?

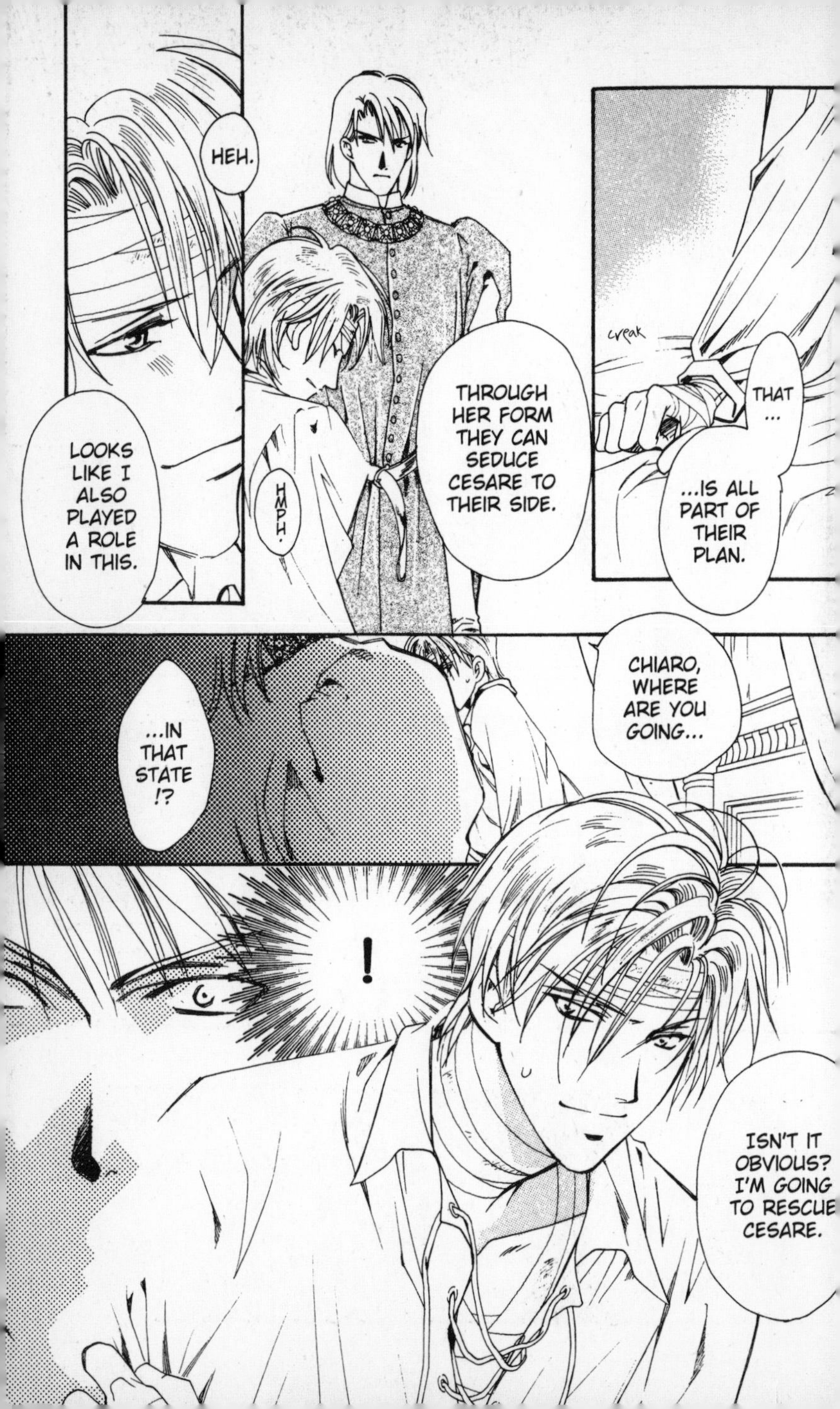
creak
THAT...
...IS ALL PART OF THEIR PLAN.
THROUGH HER FORM THEY CAN SEDUCE CESARE TO THEIR SIDE.
HMPH.
HEH.
LOOKS LIKE I ALSO PLAYED A ROLE IN THIS.
CHIARO, WHERE ARE YOU GOING...
...IN THAT STATE!?
!
ISN'T IT OBVIOUS? I'M GOING TO RESCUE CESARE.

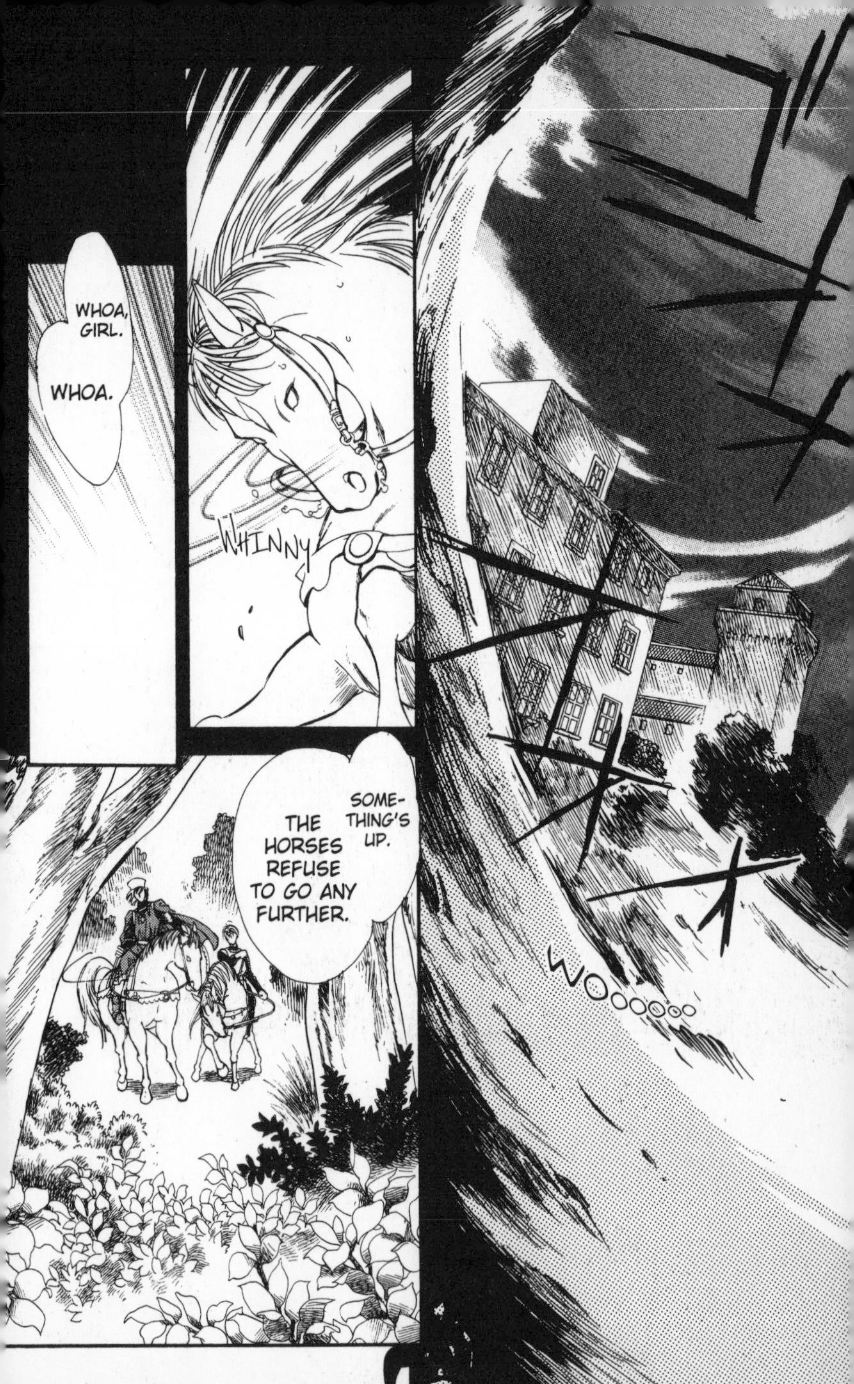
ゴ
WOOOOOO
WHINNY
WHOA, GIRL.
WHOA.
SOMETHING'S UP.
THE HORSES REFUSE TO GO ANY FURTHER.

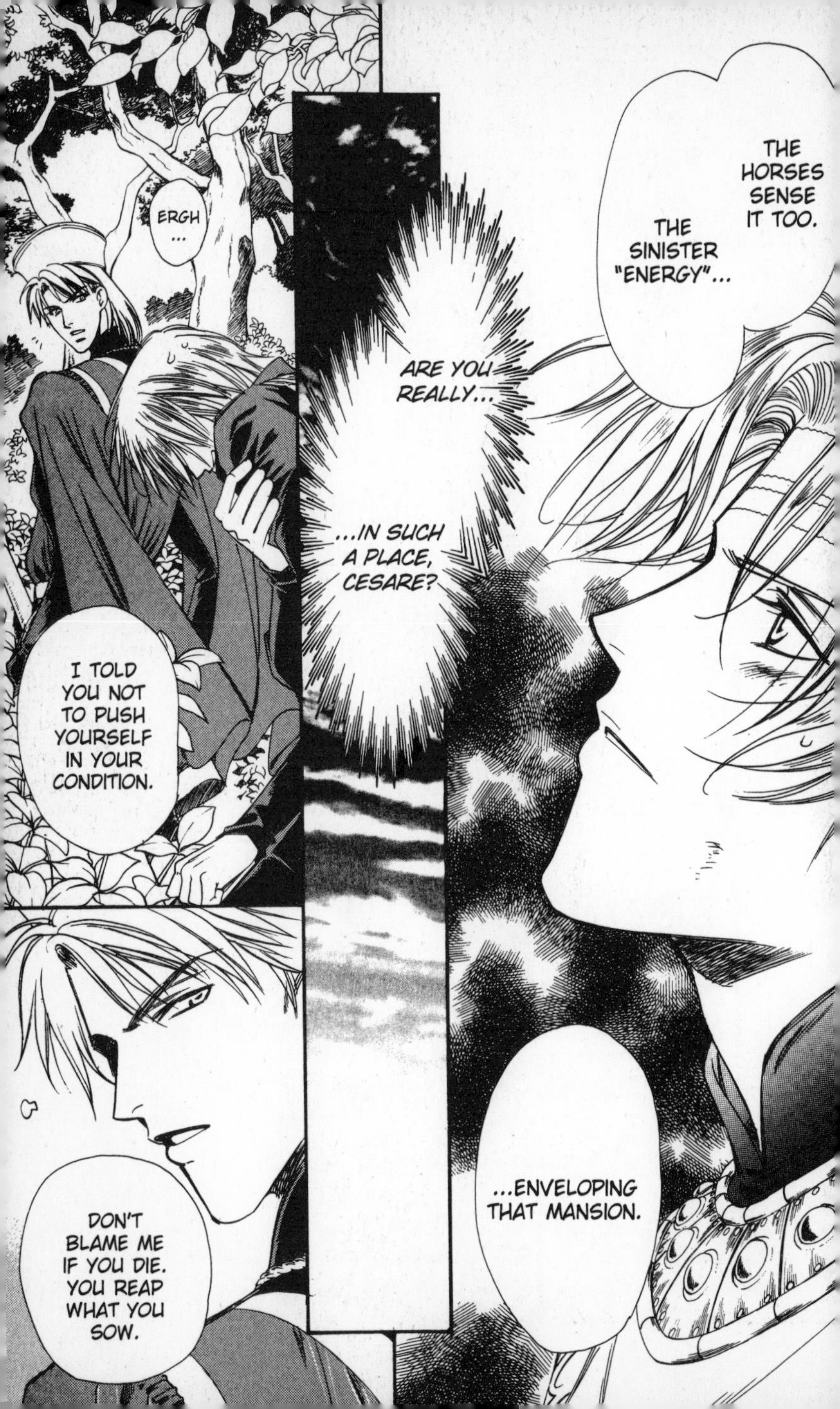
THE HORSES SENSE IT TOO.
THE SINISTER "ENERGY"...
...ENVELOPING THAT MANSION.
ARE YOU REALLY...
...IN SUCH A PLACE, CESARE?
ERGH...
I TOLD YOU NOT TO PUSH YOURSELF IN YOUR CONDITION.
DON'T BLAME ME IF YOU DIE. YOU REAP WHAT YOU SOW.

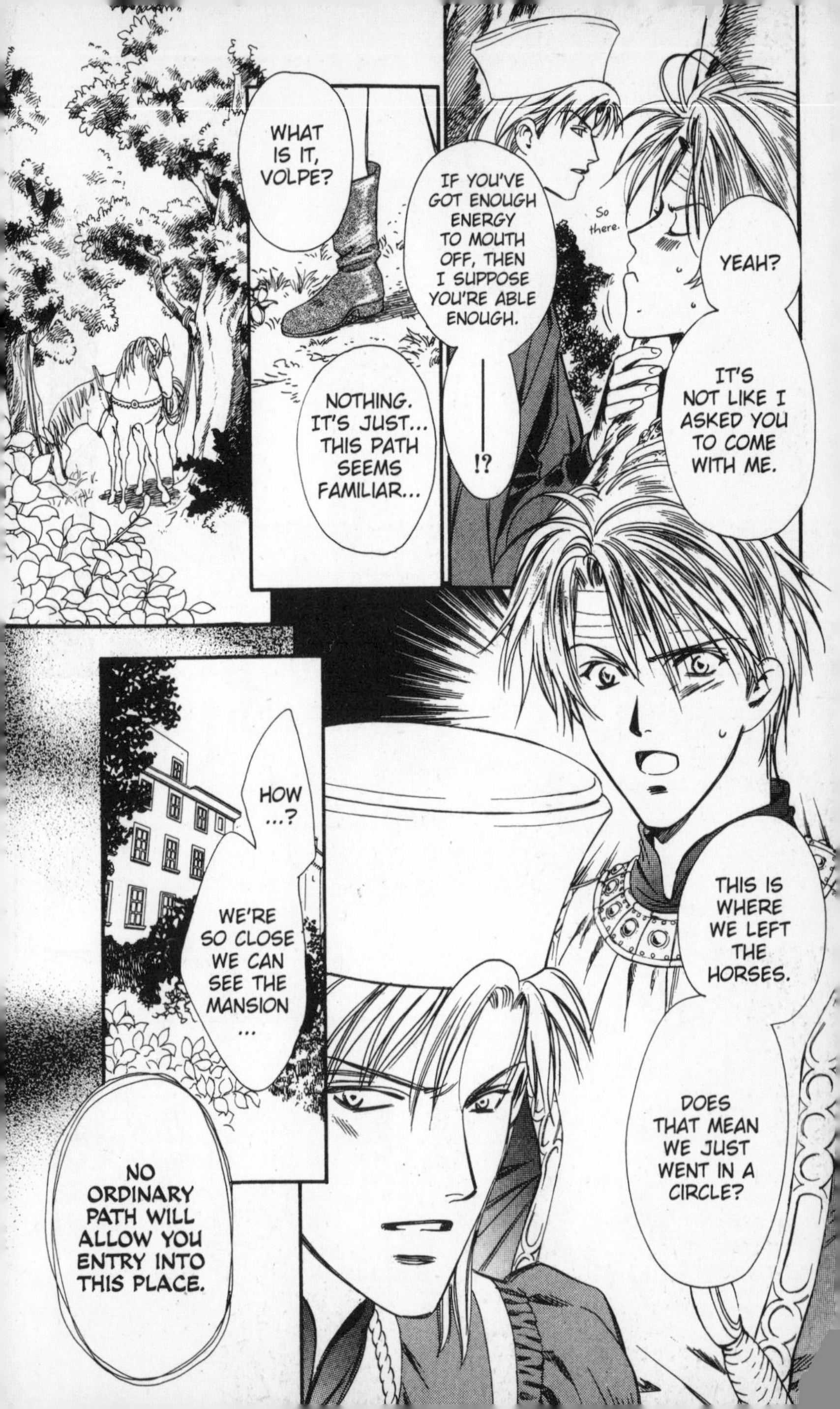
YEAH?
IT'S NOT LIKE I ASKED YOU TO COME WITH ME.
So there.
IF YOU'VE GOT ENOUGH ENERGY TO MOUTH OFF, THEN I SUPPOSE YOU'RE ABLE ENOUGH.
!?
WHAT IS IT, VOLPE?
NOTHING. IT'S JUST... THIS PATH SEEMS FAMILIAR...
THIS IS WHERE WE LEFT THE HORSES.
DOES THAT MEAN WE JUST WENT IN A CIRCLE?
HOW ...?
WE'RE SO CLOSE WE CAN SEE THE MANSION ...
NO ORDINARY PATH WILL ALLOW YOU ENTRY INTO THIS PLACE.

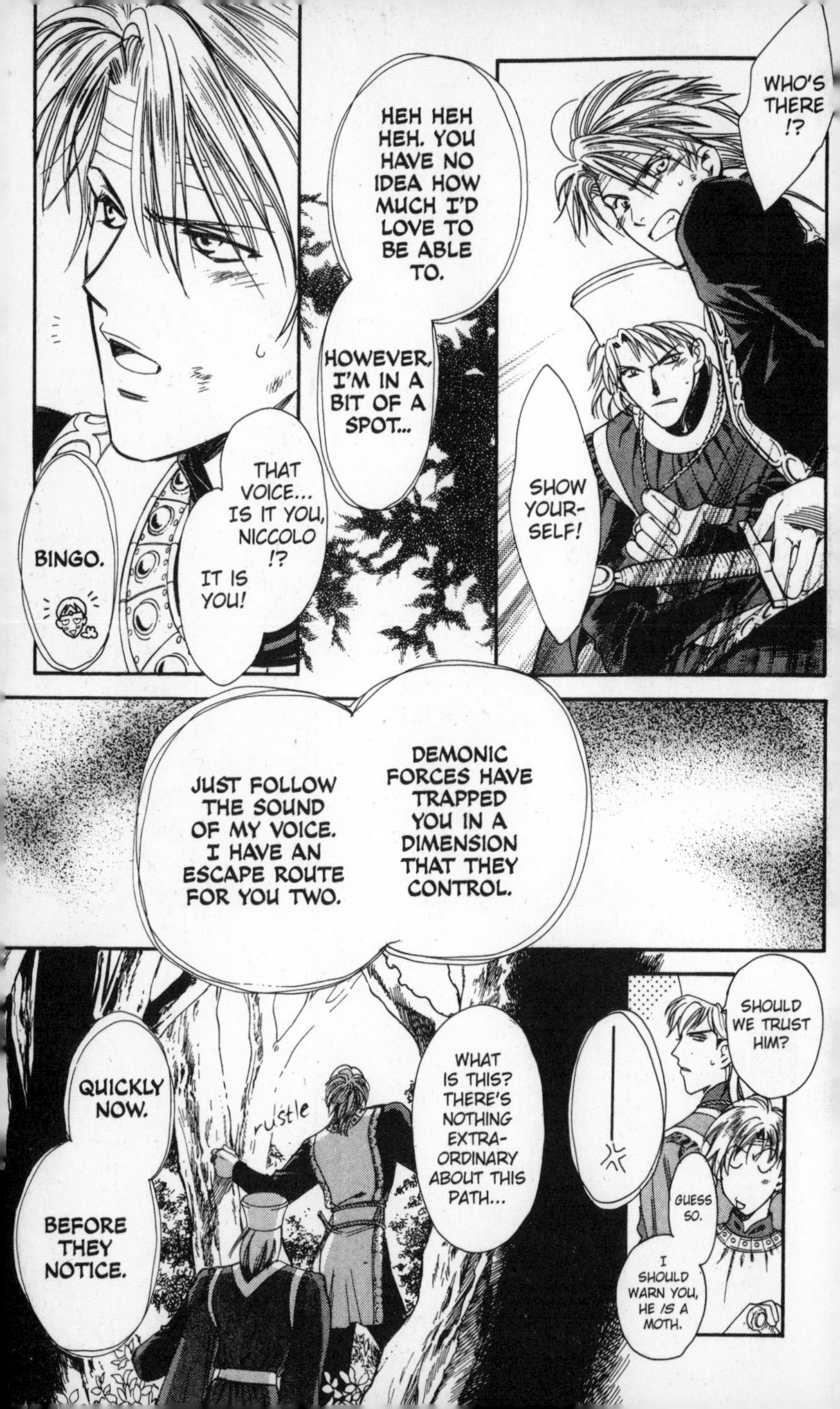
WHO'S THERE !?
SHOW YOURSELF!
HEH HEH HEH. YOU HAVE NO IDEA HOW MUCH I'D LOVE TO BE ABLE TO.
HOWEVER, I'M IN A BIT OF A SPOT...
THAT VOICE... IS IT YOU, NICCOLO !?
IT IS YOU!
BINGO.
DEMONIC FORCES HAVE TRAPPED YOU IN A DIMENSION THAT THEY CONTROL.
JUST FOLLOW THE SOUND OF MY VOICE. I HAVE AN ESCAPE ROUTE FOR YOU TWO.
SHOULD WE TRUST HIM?
GUESS SO.
I SHOULD WARN YOU, HE IS A MOTH.
WHAT IS THIS? THERE'S NOTHING EXTRA-ORDINARY ABOUT THIS PATH...
rustle
QUICKLY NOW.
BEFORE THEY NOTICE.

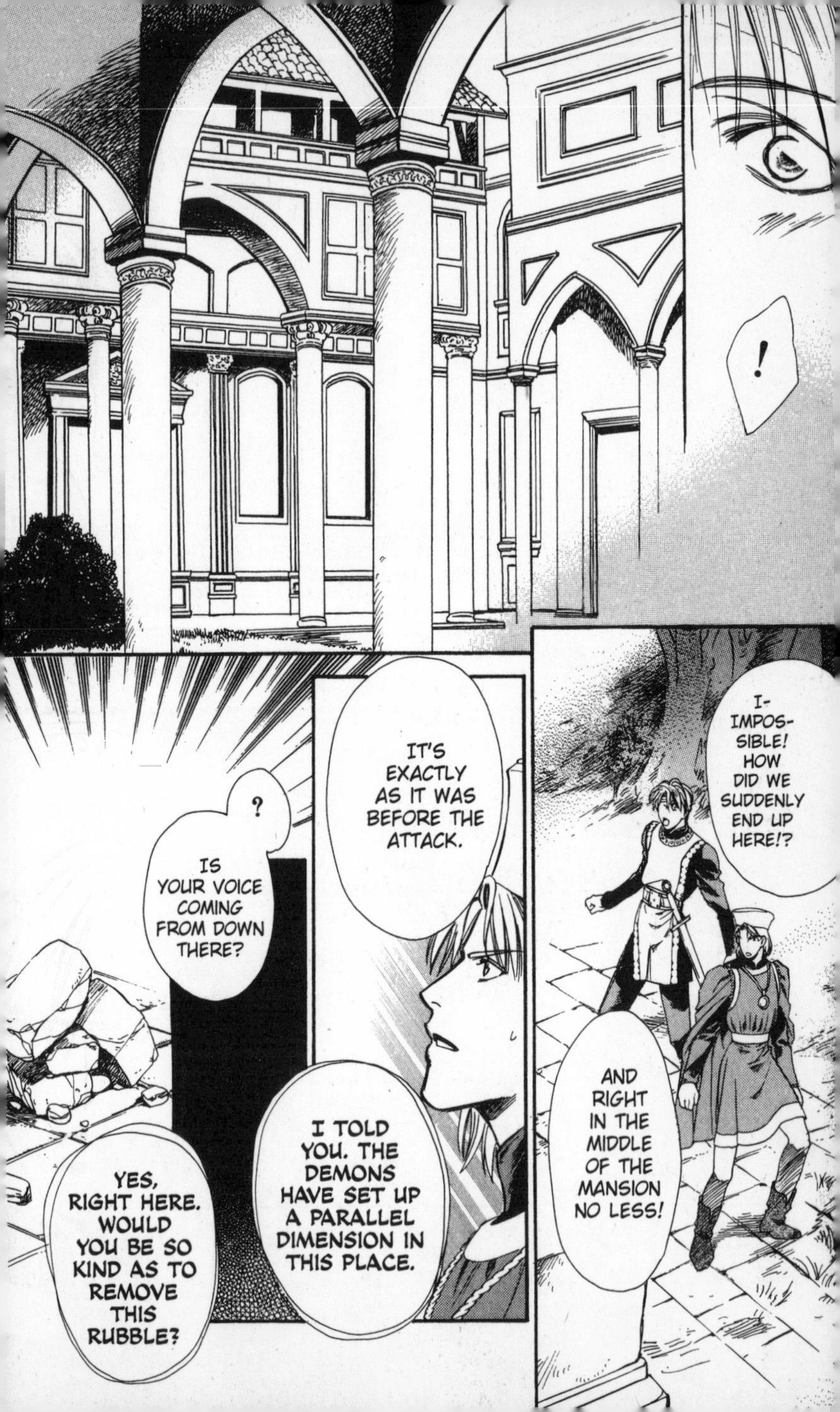
!
I- IMPOSSIBLE! HOW DID WE SUDDENLY END UP HERE!?
AND RIGHT IN THE MIDDLE OF THE MANSION NO LESS!
IT'S EXACTLY AS IT WAS BEFORE THE ATTACK.
I TOLD YOU. THE DEMONS HAVE SET UP A PARALLEL DIMENSION IN THIS PLACE.
?
IS YOUR VOICE COMING FROM DOWN THERE?
YES, RIGHT HERE. WOULD YOU BE SO KIND AS TO REMOVE THIS RUBBLE?

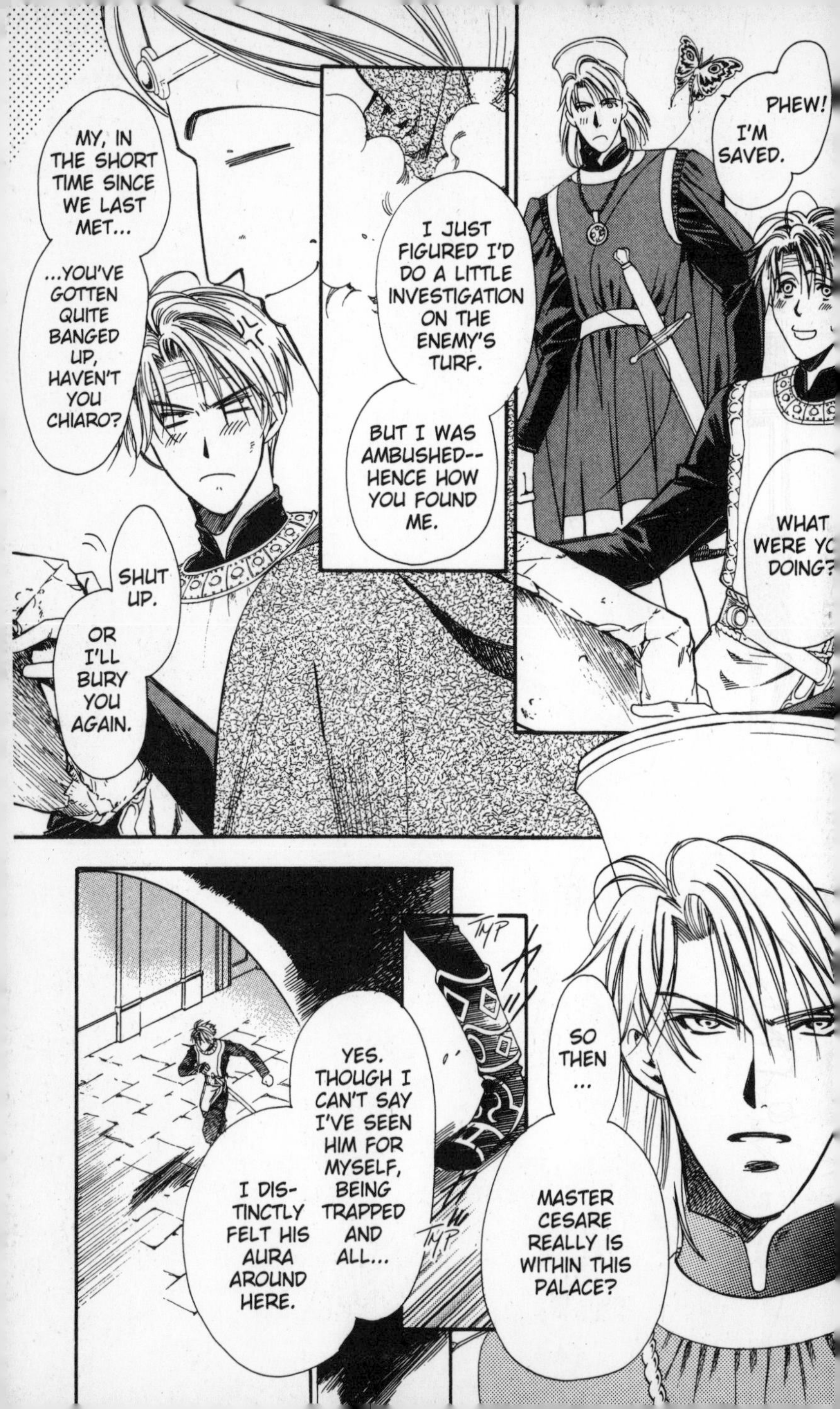
PHEW! I'M SAVED.
WHAT WERE YO DOING?
I JUST FIGURED I'D DO A LITTLE INVESTIGATION ON THE ENEMY'S TURF.
BUT I WAS AMBUSHED-- HENCE HOW YOU FOUND ME.
MY, IN THE SHORT TIME SINCE WE LAST MET...
...YOU'VE GOTTEN QUITE BANGED UP, HAVEN'T YOU CHIARO?
SHUT UP.
OR I'LL BURY YOU AGAIN.
SO THEN...
MASTER CESARE REALLY IS WITHIN THIS PALACE?
YES. THOUGH I CAN'T SAY I'VE SEEN HIM FOR MYSELF, BEING TRAPPED AND ALL...
I DIS-TINCTLY FELT HIS AURA AROUND HERE.
TMP
TMP

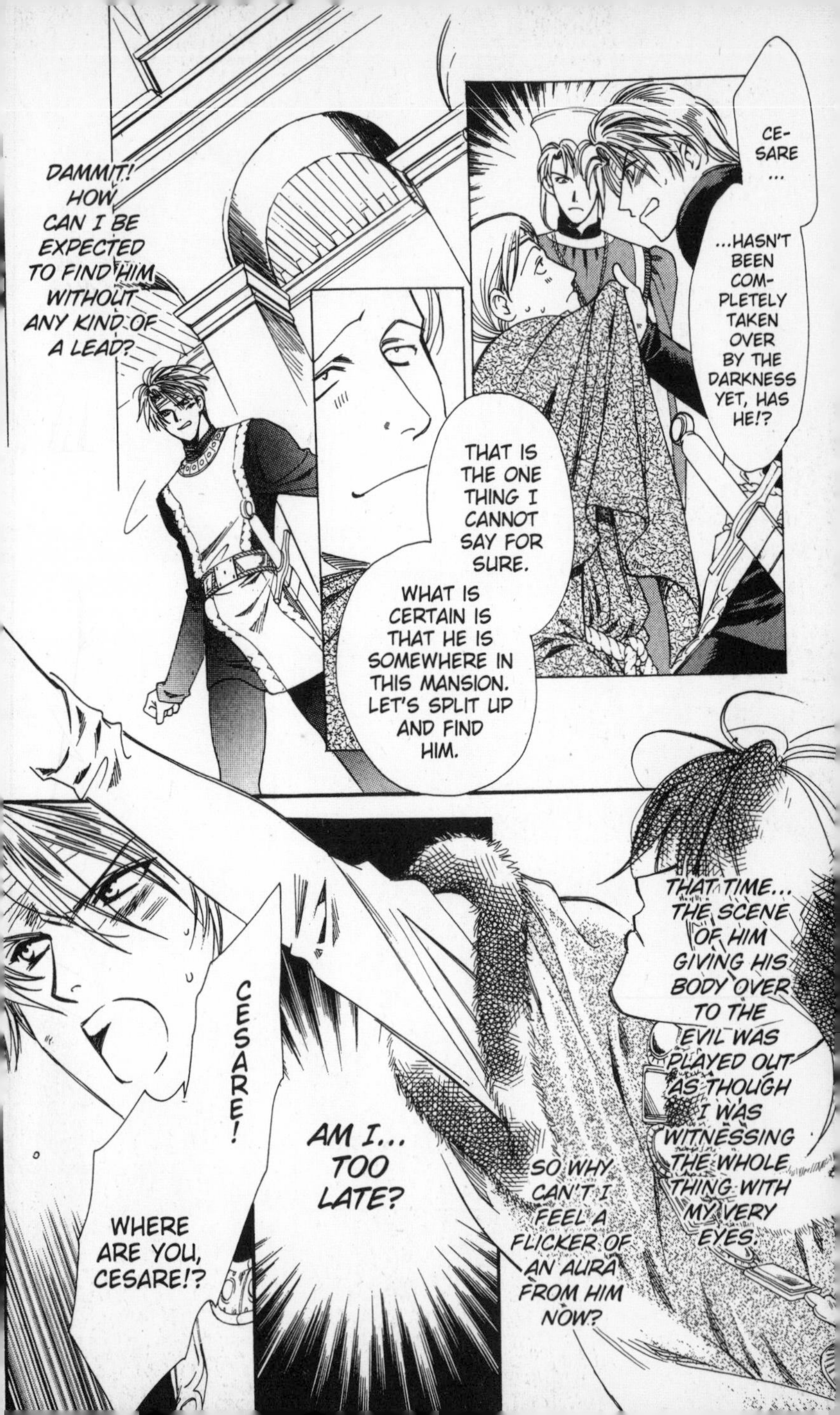
CE-SARE ...
...HASN'T BEEN COM-PLETELY TAKEN OVER BY THE DARKNESS YET, HAS HE!?
THAT IS THE ONE THING I CANNOT SAY FOR SURE.
WHAT IS CERTAIN IS THAT HE IS SOMEWHERE IN THIS MANSION. LET'S SPLIT UP AND FIND HIM.
DAMMIT! HOW CAN I BE EXPECTED TO FIND HIM WITHOUT ANY KIND OF A LEAD?
THAT TIME... THE SCENE OF HIM GIVING HIS BODY OVER TO THE EVIL WAS PLAYED OUT AS THOUGH I WAS WITNESSING THE WHOLE THING WITH MY VERY EYES.
SO WHY CAN'T I FEEL A FLICKER OF AN AURA FROM HIM NOW?
AM I... TOO LATE?
CESARE!
WHERE ARE YOU, CESARE!?

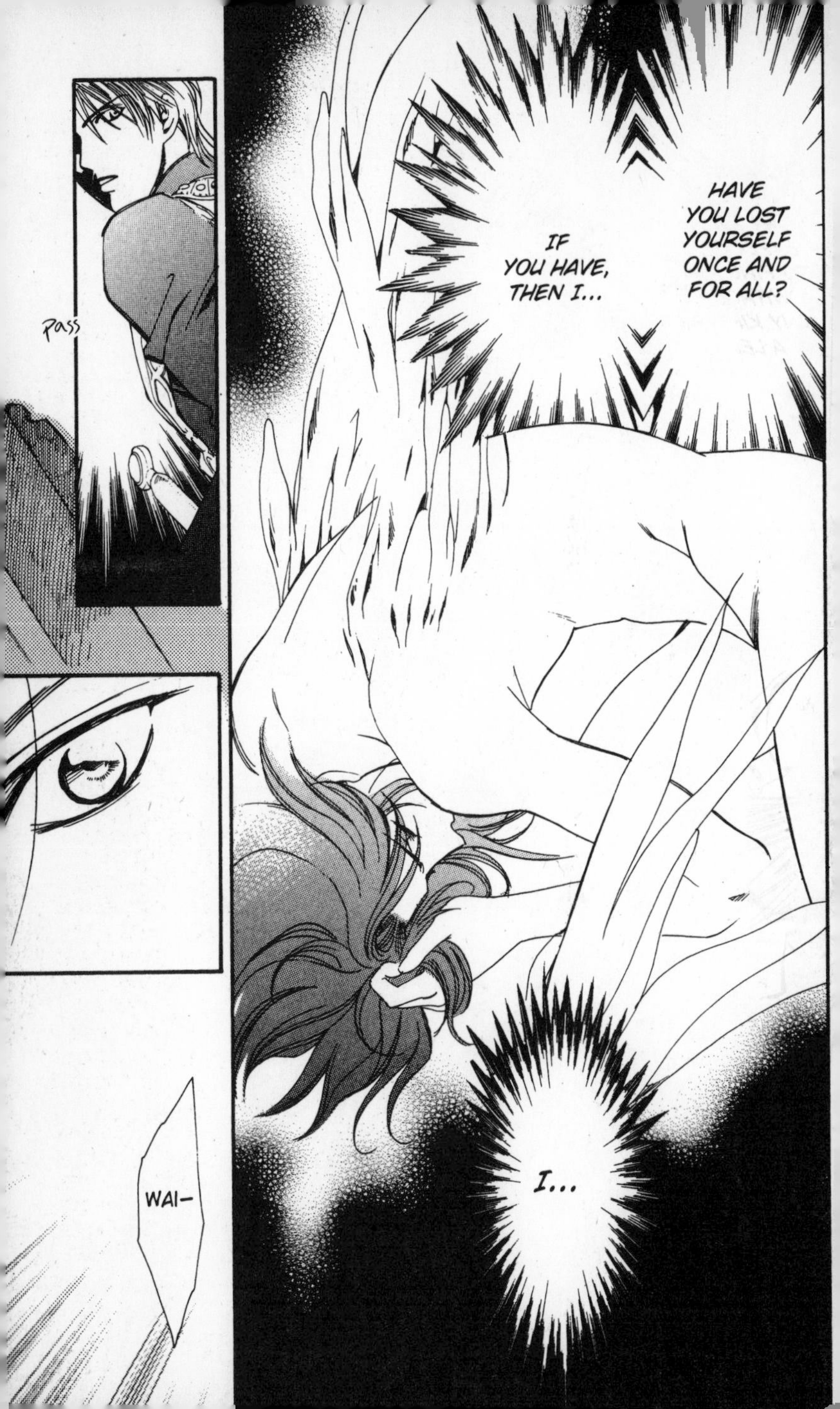
HAVE YOU LOST YOURSELF ONCE AND FOR ALL?
IF YOU HAVE, THEN I...
I...
Pass
WAI-

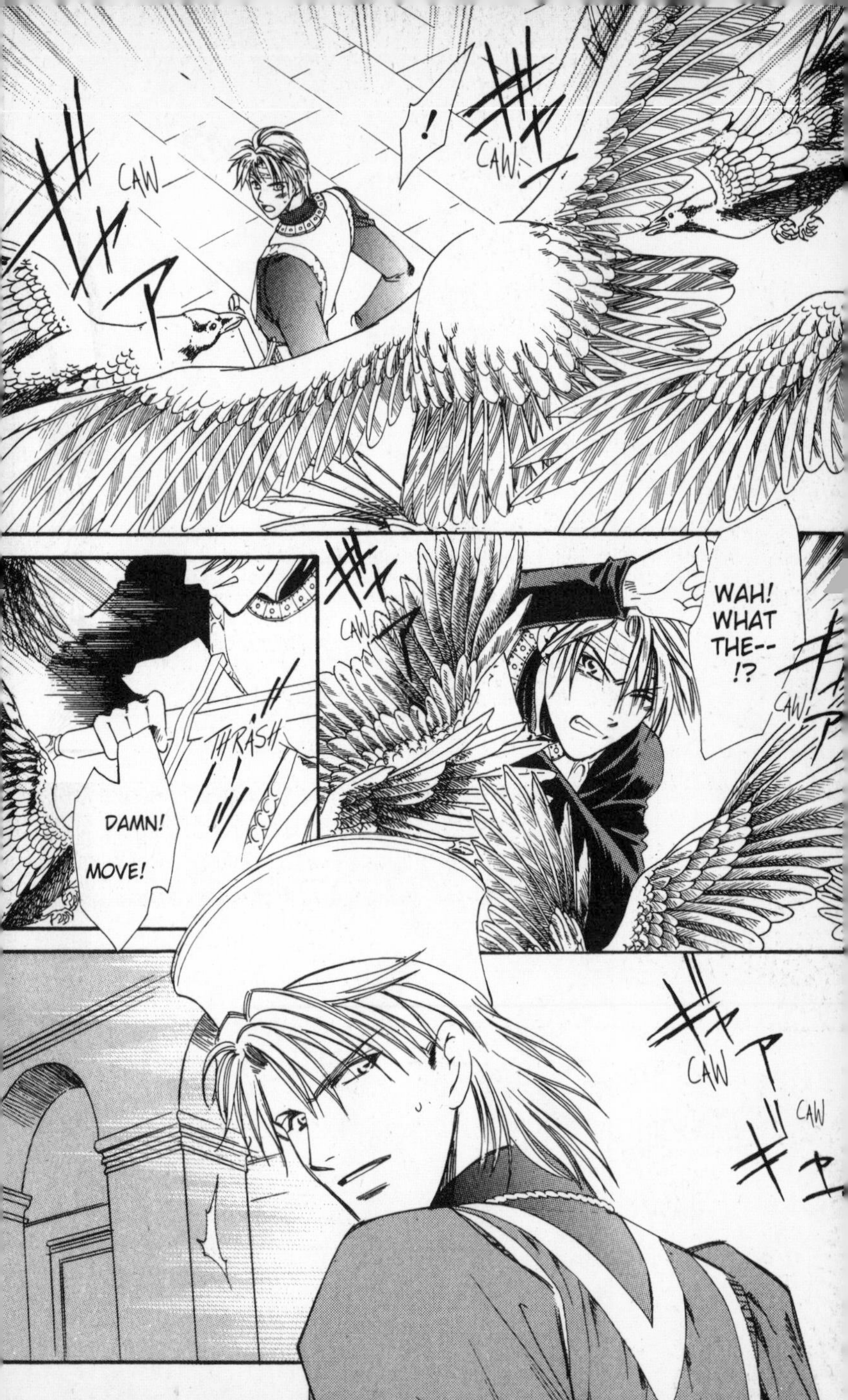

CAW
!
CAW
WAH! WHAT THE-- !?
CAW
CAW
THRASH
DAMN!
MOVE!
CAW
CAW

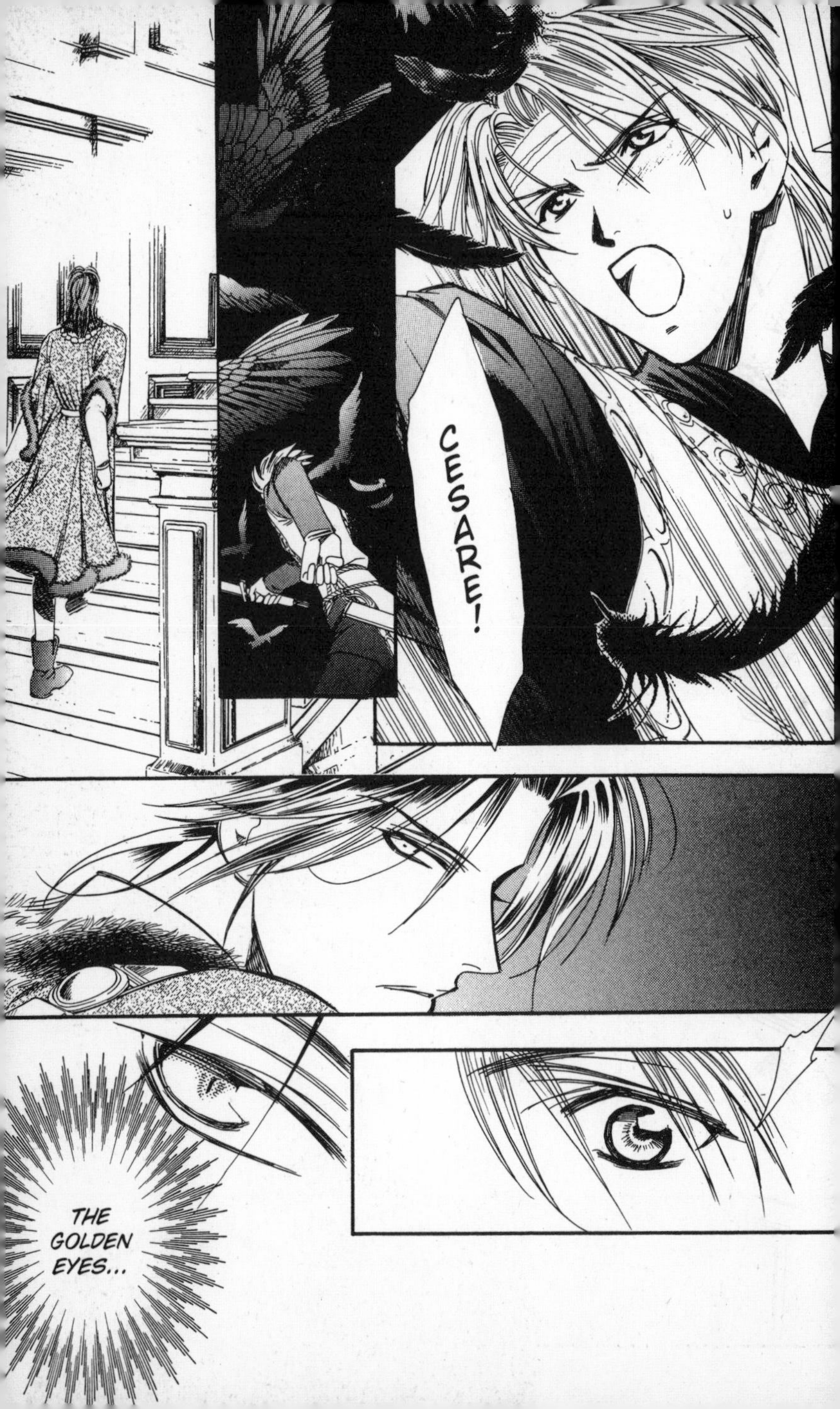
CESARE!
THE GOLDEN EYES...

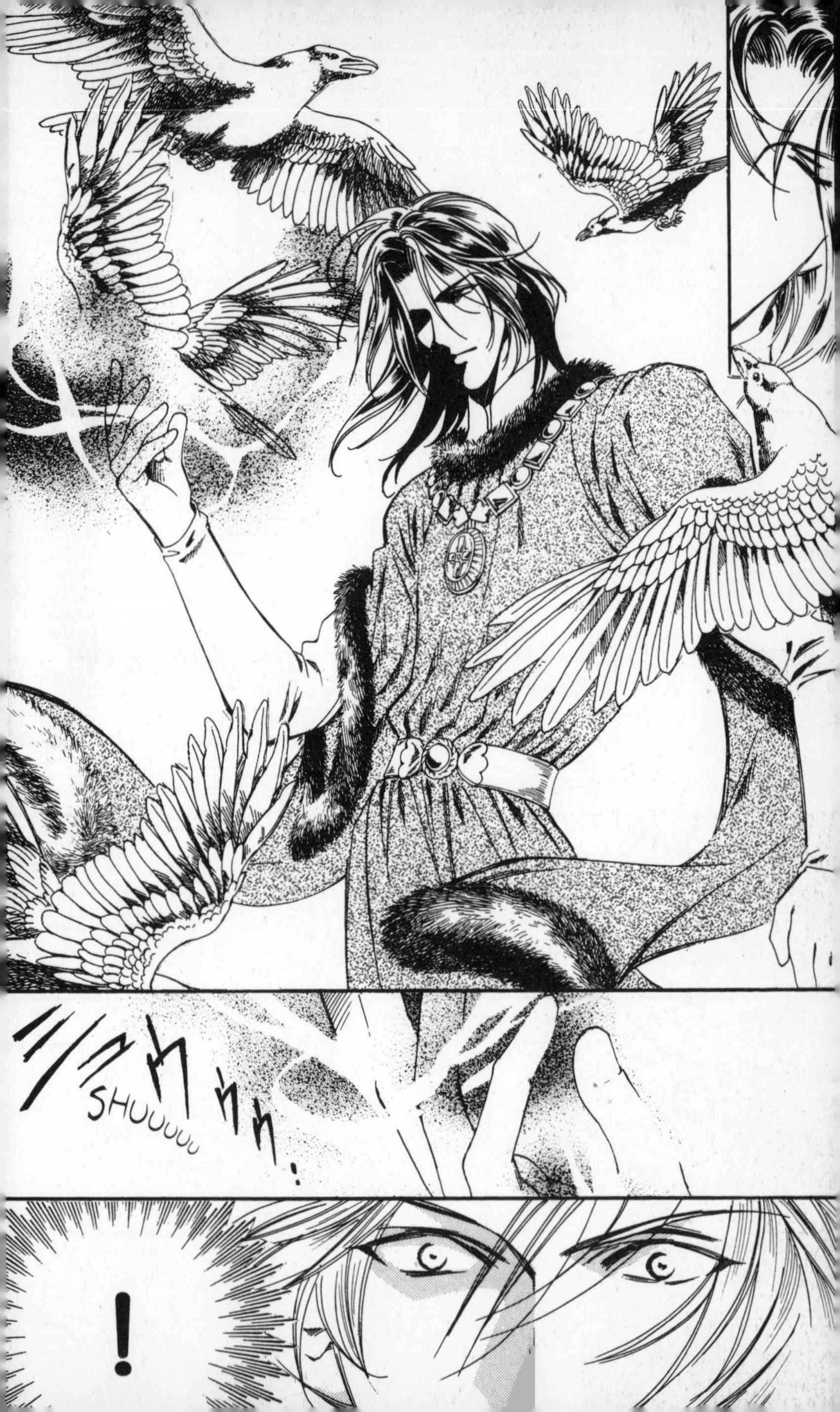
シュウゥゥ
SHUUUUU
!

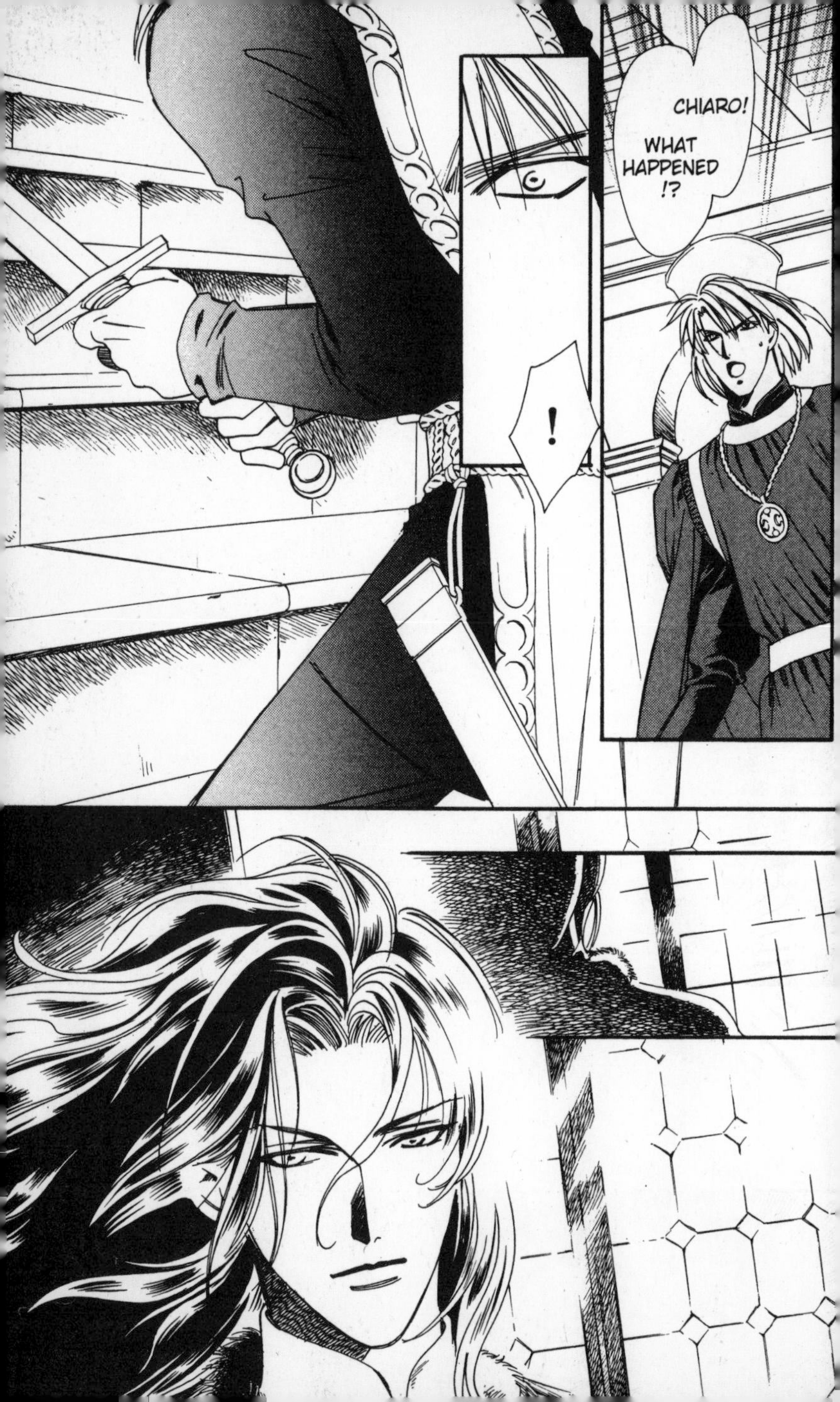
CHIARO!
WHAT HAPPENED !?
!

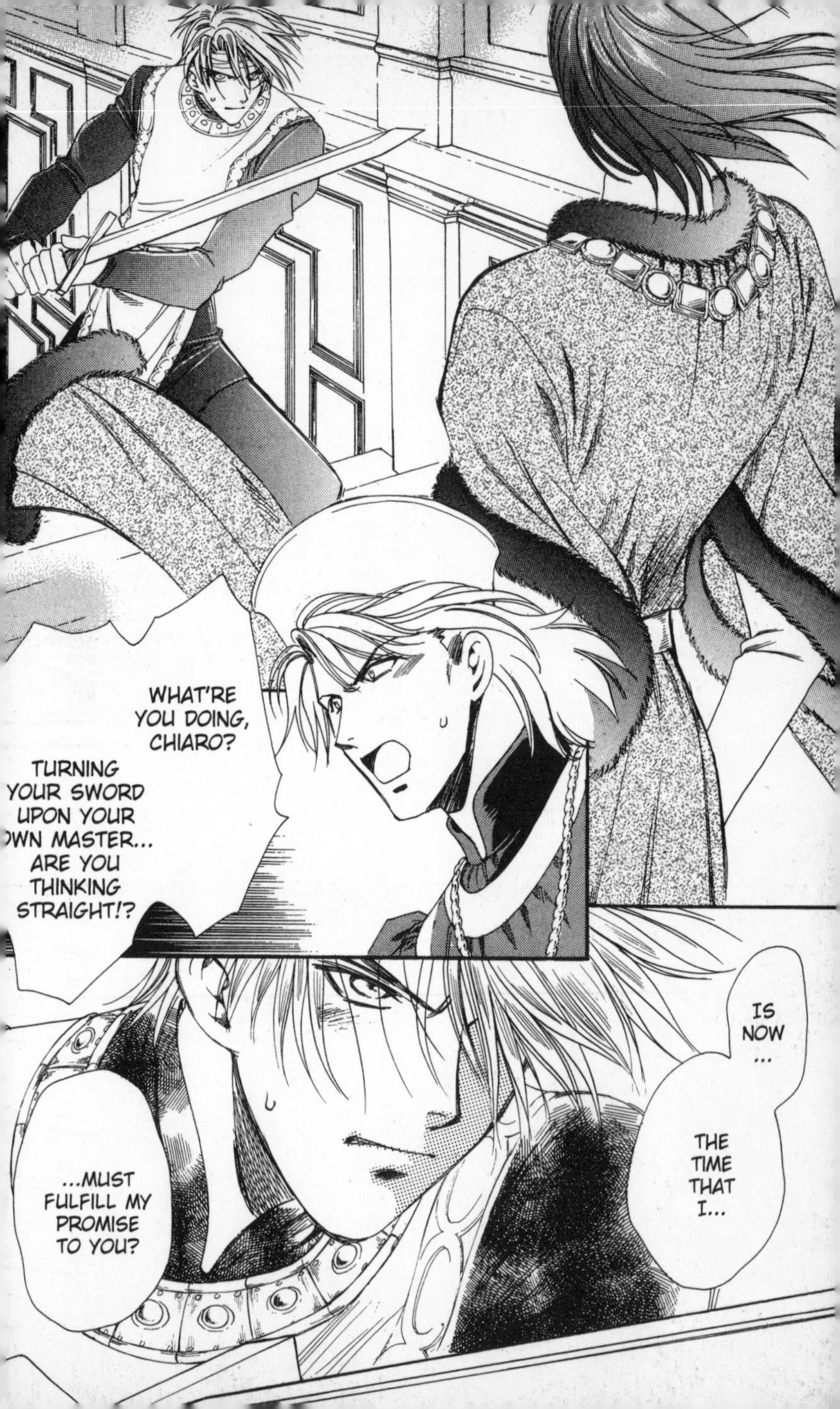

WHAT'RE YOU DOING, CHIARO?
TURNING YOUR SWORD UPON YOUR WN MASTER... ARE YOU THINKING STRAIGHT!?
IS NOW ...
THE TIME THAT I...
...MUST FULFILL MY PROMISE TO YOU?

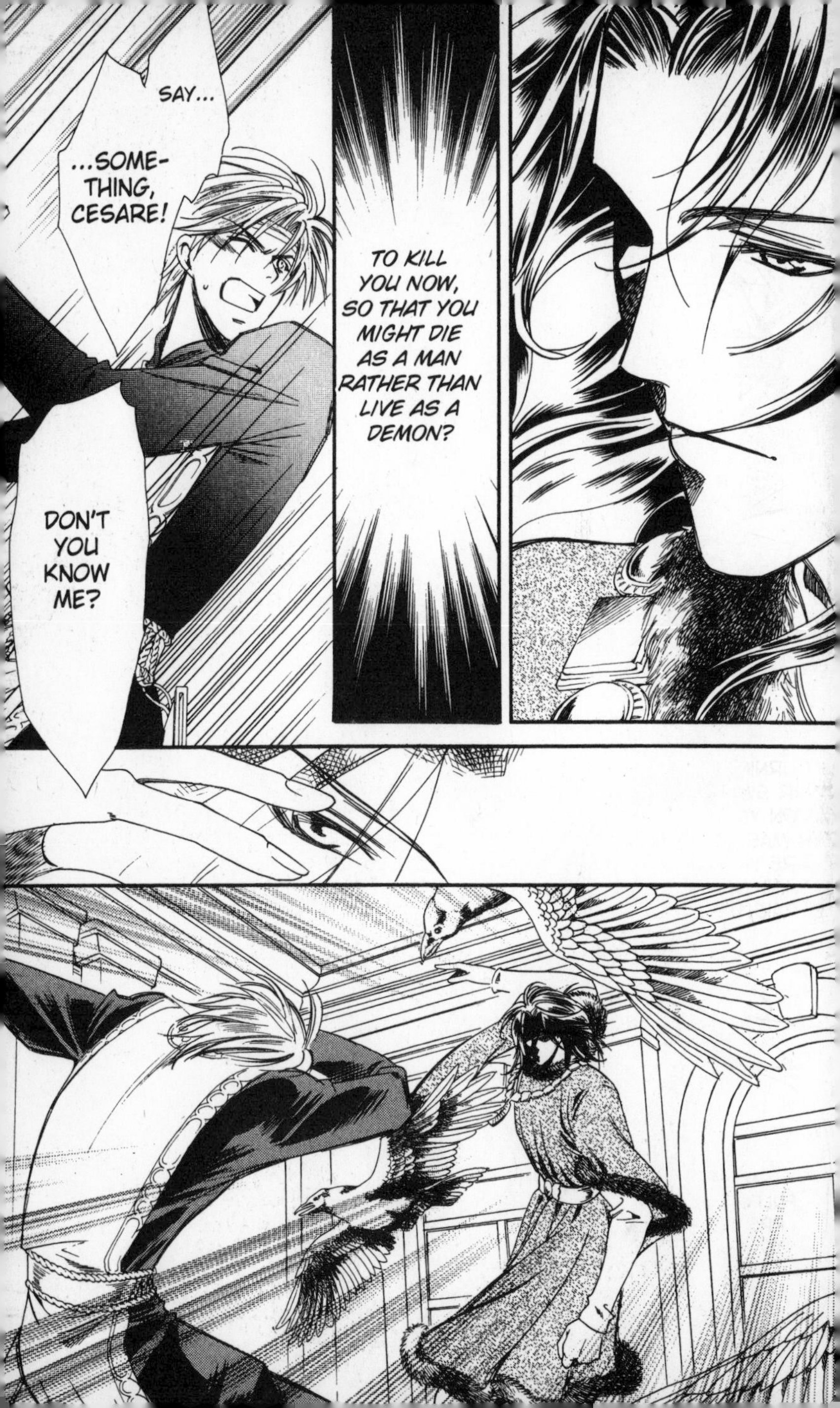
TO KILL YOU NOW, SO THAT YOU MIGHT DIE AS A MAN RATHER THAN LIVE AS A DEMON?
SAY...
...SOME-THING, CESARE!
DON'T YOU KNOW ME?

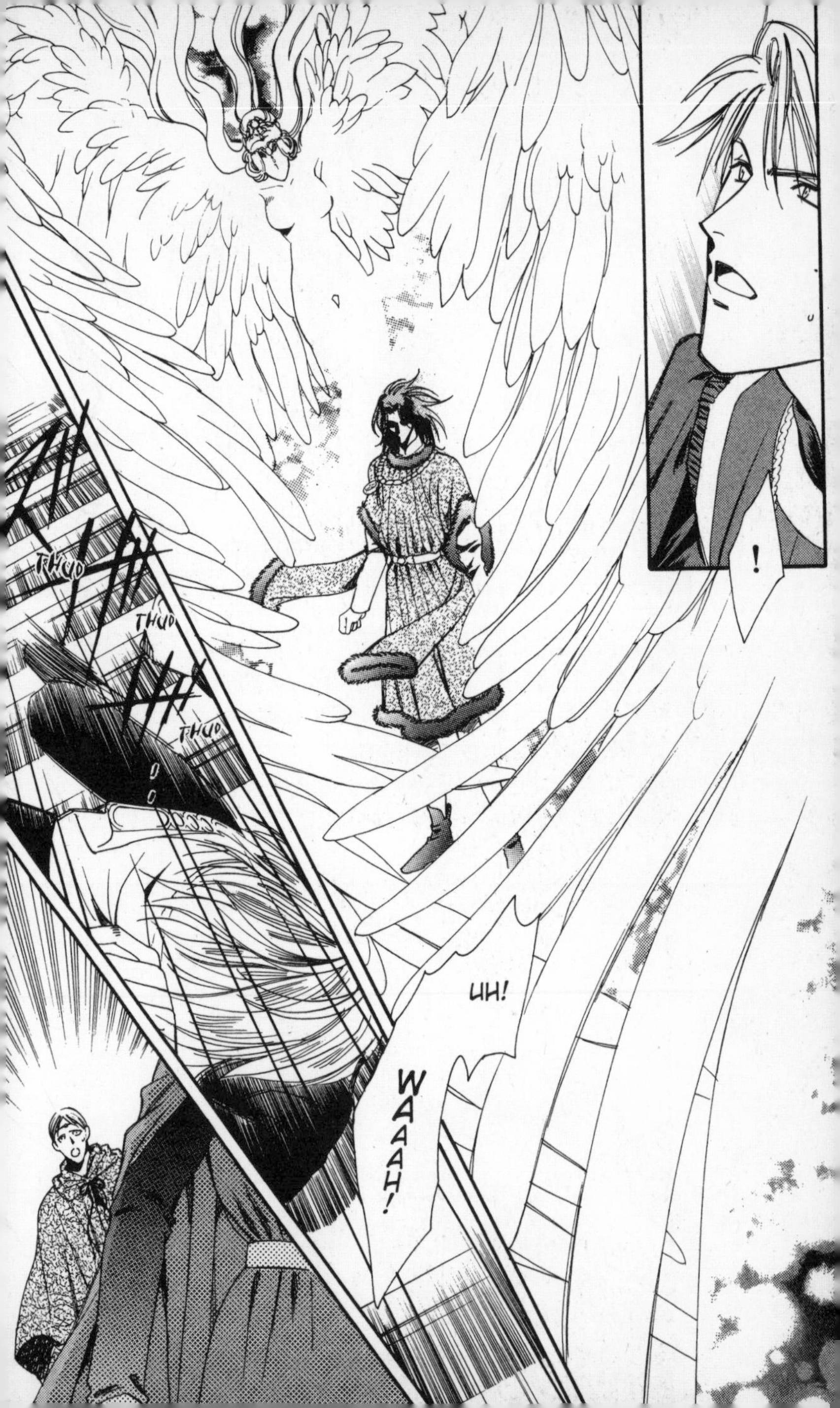
!
THUD
THUD
THUD
UH!
WAAAH!

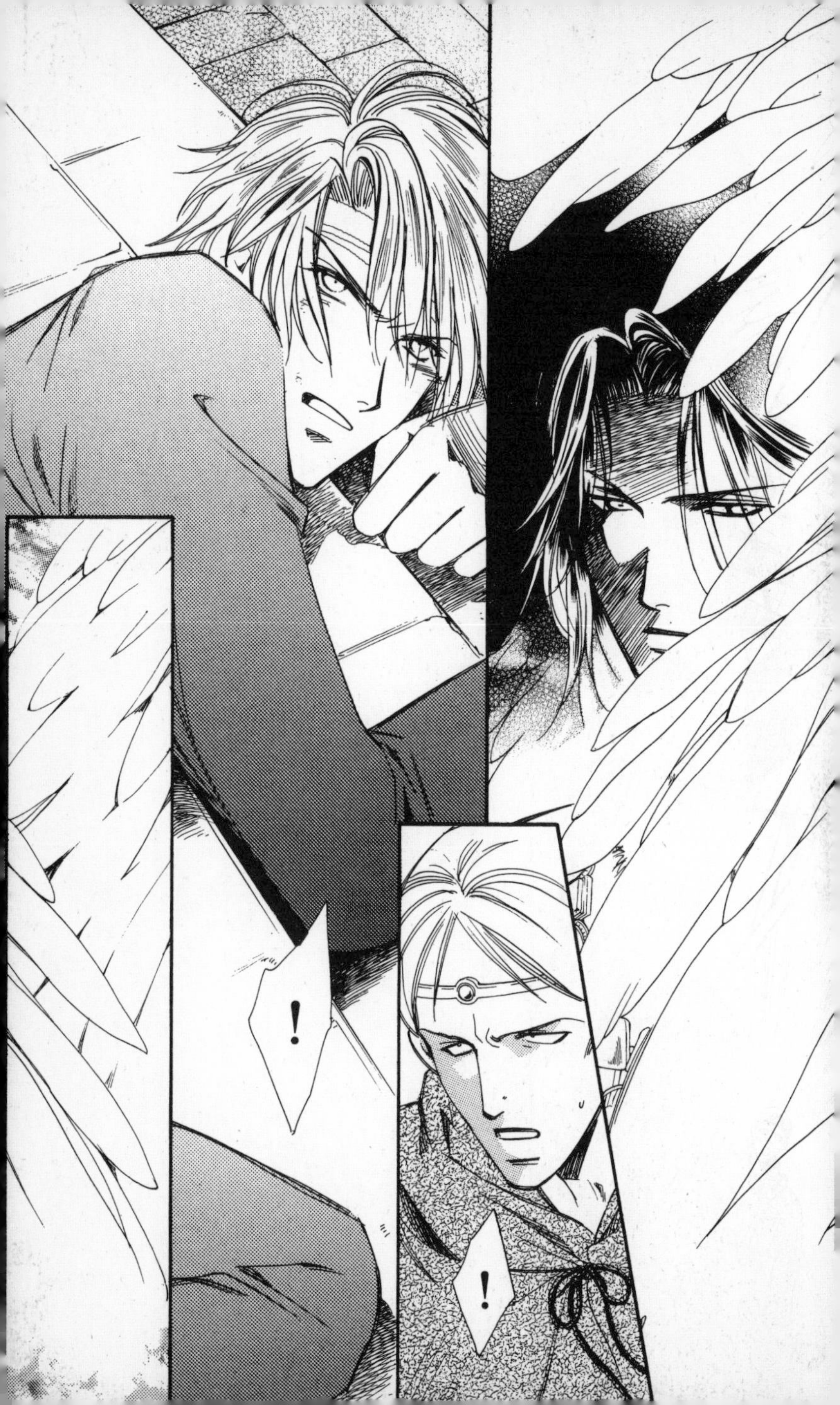
!
!

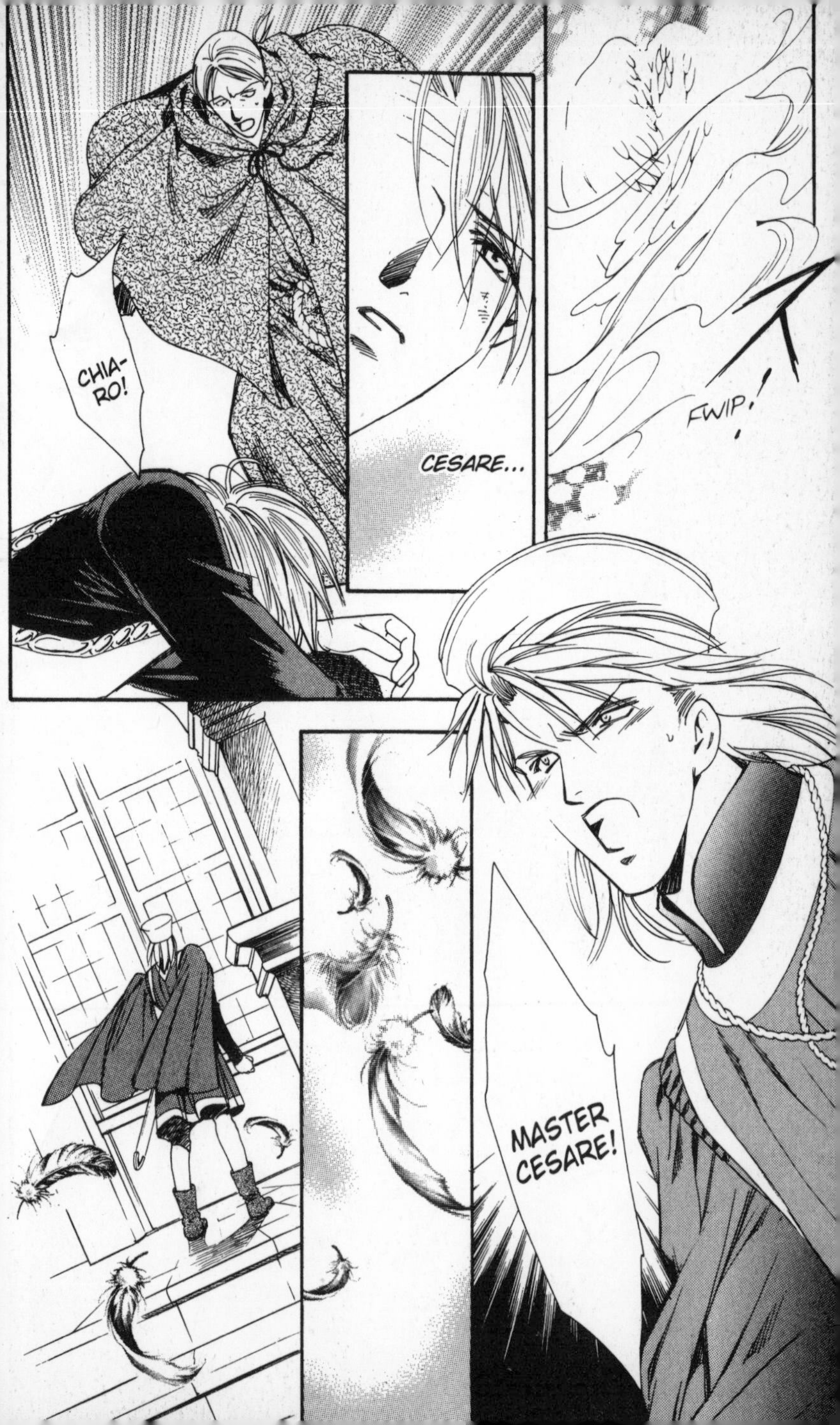
FWIP!
CESARE...
CHIA-RO!
MASTER CESARE!

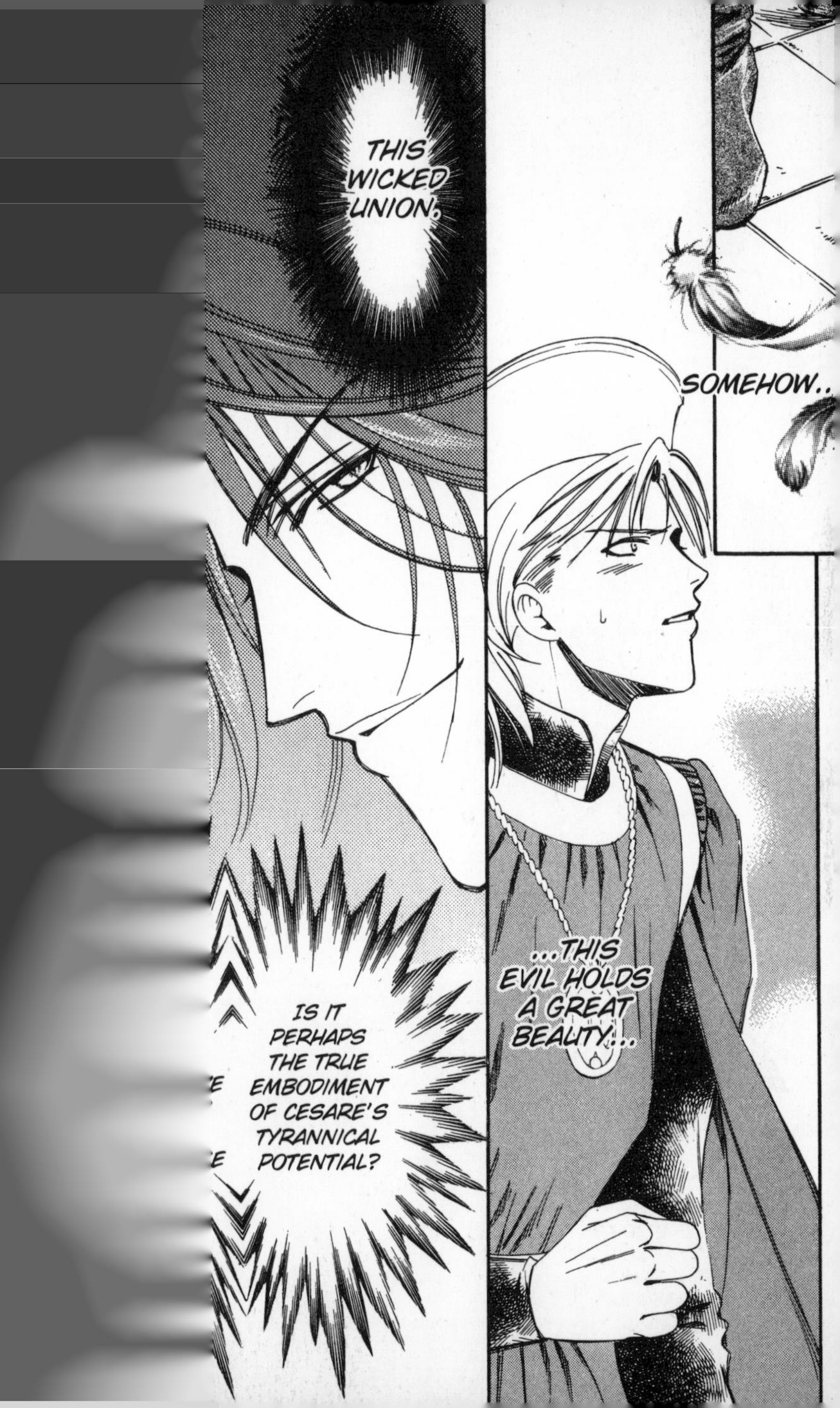
SOMEHOW..
...THIS EVIL HOLDS A GREAT BEAUTY...
THIS WICKED UNION,
IS IT PERHAPS THE TRUE EMBODIMENT OF CESARE'S TYRANNICAL POTENTIAL?

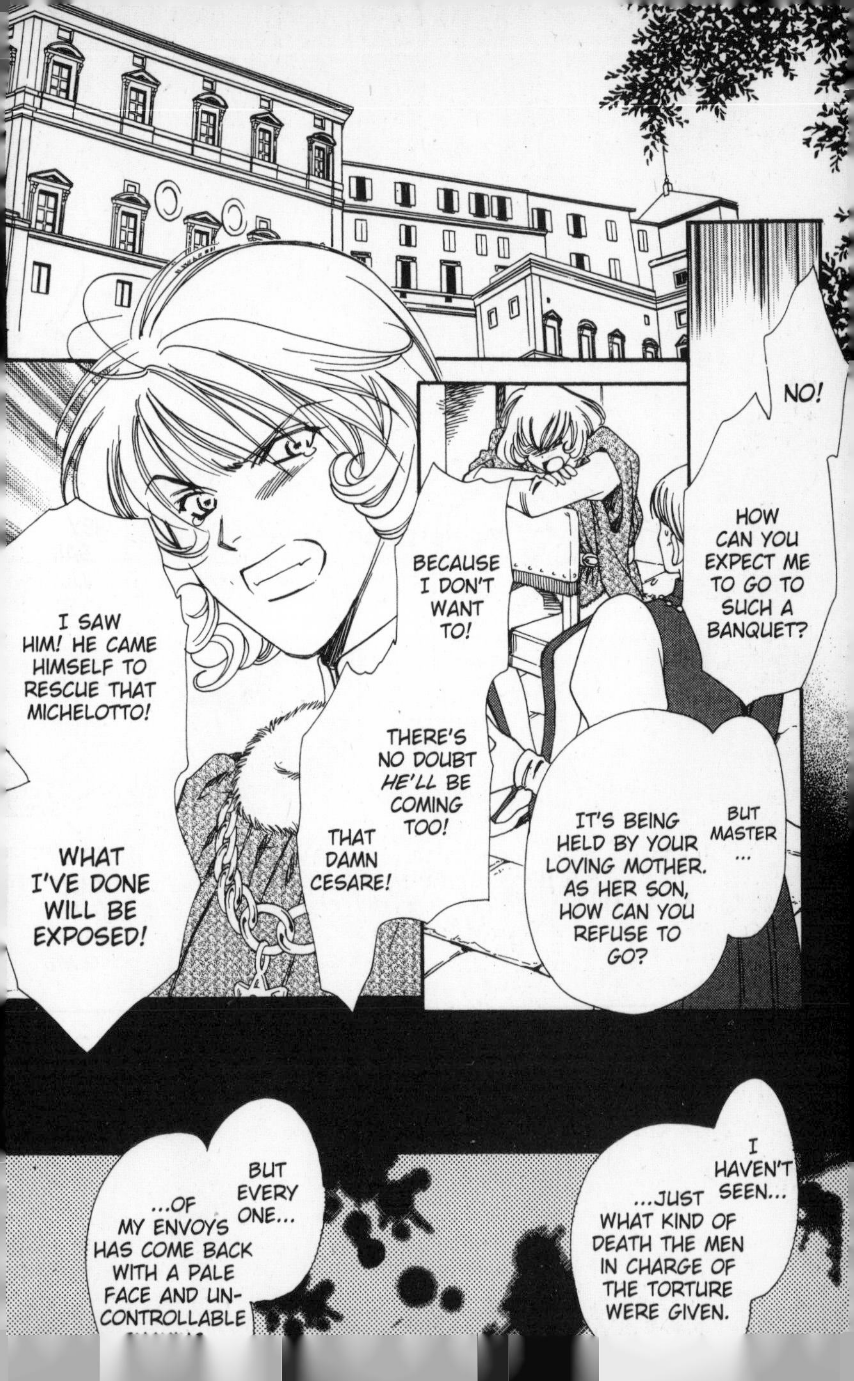
NO!
HOW CAN YOU EXPECT ME TO GO TO SUCH A BANQUET?
BUT MASTER...
IT'S BEING HELD BY YOUR LOVING MOTHER. AS HER SON, HOW CAN YOU REFUSE TO GO?
BECAUSE I DON'T WANT TO!
THERE'S NO DOUBT *HE'LL* BE COMING TOO!
THAT DAMN CESARE!
I SAW HIM! HE CAME HIMSELF TO RESCUE THAT MICHELOTTO!
WHAT I'VE DONE WILL BE EXPOSED!
I HAVEN'T SEEN...
...JUST WHAT KIND OF DEATH THE MEN IN CHARGE OF THE TORTURE WERE GIVEN.
BUT EVERY ONE...
...OF MY ENVOYS HAS COME BACK WITH A PALE FACE AND UN-CONTROLLABLE

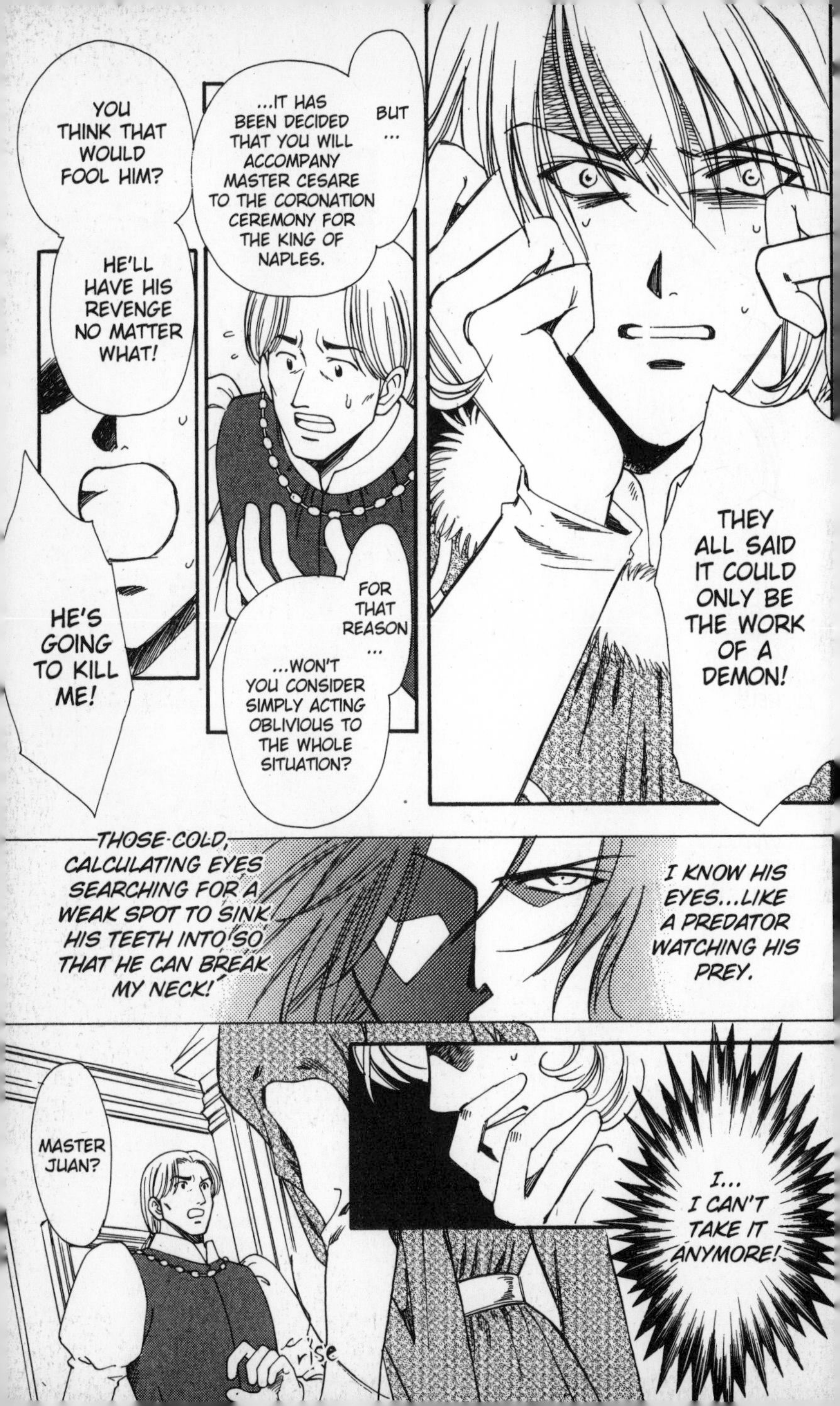
THEY ALL SAID IT COULD ONLY BE THE WORK OF A DEMON!
BUT...
...IT HAS BEEN DECIDED THAT YOU WILL ACCOMPANY MASTER CESARE TO THE CORONATION CEREMONY FOR THE KING OF NAPLES.
FOR THAT REASON...
...WON'T YOU CONSIDER SIMPLY ACTING OBLIVIOUS TO THE WHOLE SITUATION?
YOU THINK THAT WOULD FOOL HIM?
HE'LL HAVE HIS REVENGE NO MATTER WHAT!
HE'S GOING TO KILL ME!
I KNOW HIS EYES...LIKE A PREDATOR WATCHING HIS PREY.
THOSE COLD, CALCULATING EYES SEARCHING FOR A WEAK SPOT TO SINK HIS TEETH INTO SO THAT HE CAN BREAK MY NECK!
I... I CAN'T TAKE IT ANYMORE!
rise
MASTER JUAN?

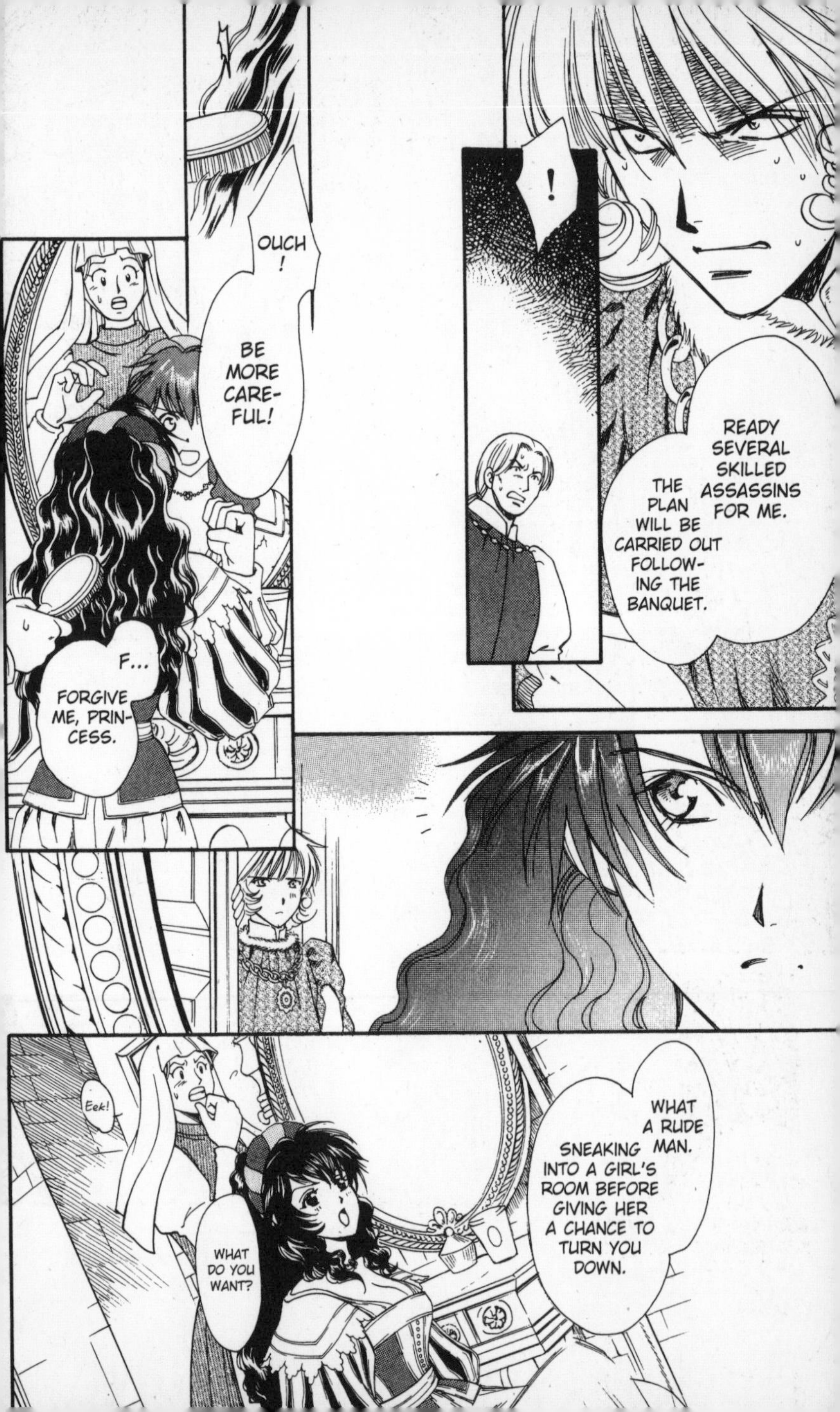
READY SEVERAL SKILLED ASSASSINS FOR ME.
THE PLAN WILL BE CARRIED OUT FOLLOWING THE BANQUET.
!
OUCH!
BE MORE CARE-FUL!
F...
FORGIVE ME, PRIN-CESS.
WHAT A RUDE MAN.
SNEAKING INTO A GIRL'S ROOM BEFORE GIVING HER A CHANCE TO TURN YOU DOWN.
Eek!
WHAT DO YOU WANT?

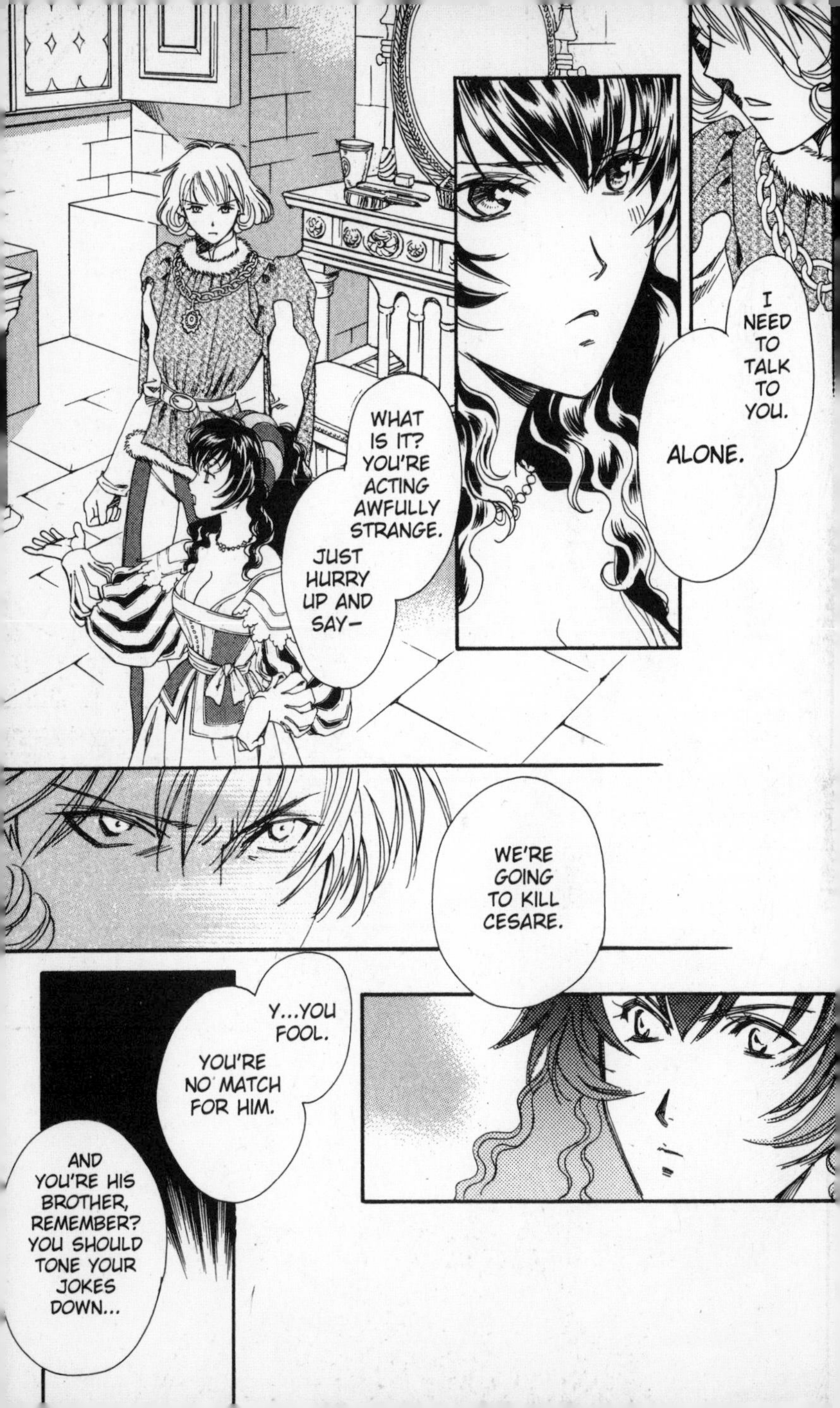
I NEED TO TALK TO YOU.
ALONE.
WHAT IS IT? YOU'RE ACTING AWFULLY STRANGE.
JUST HURRY UP AND SAY–
WE'RE GOING TO KILL CESARE.
Y...YOU FOOL.
YOU'RE NO MATCH FOR HIM.
AND YOU'RE HIS BROTHER, REMEMBER? YOU SHOULD TONE YOUR JOKES DOWN...

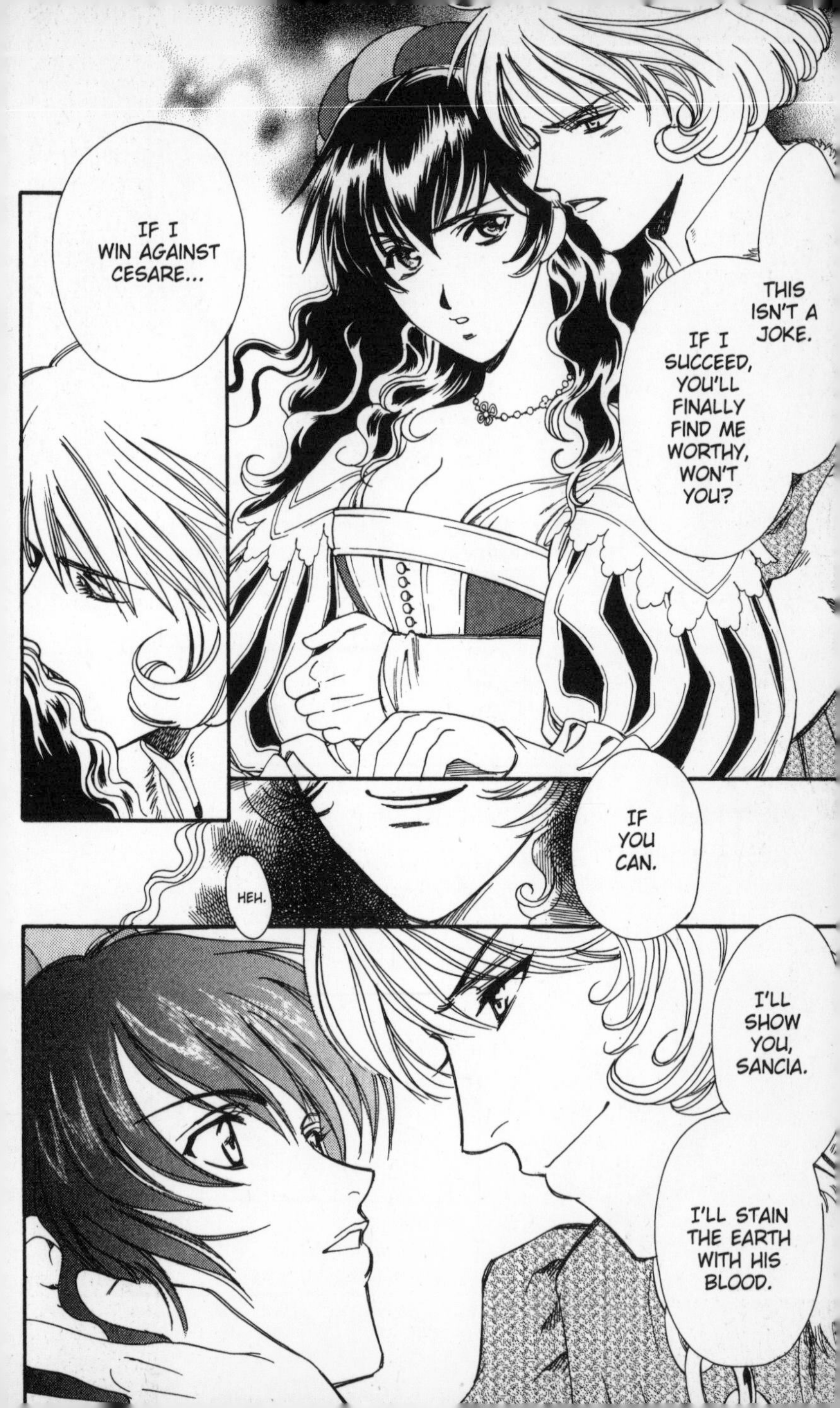
THIS ISN'T A JOKE.
IF I SUCCEED, YOU'LL FINALLY FIND ME WORTHY, WON'T YOU?
IF I WIN AGAINST CESARE...
IF YOU CAN.
HEH.
I'LL SHOW YOU, SANCIA.
I'LL STAIN THE EARTH WITH HIS BLOOD.

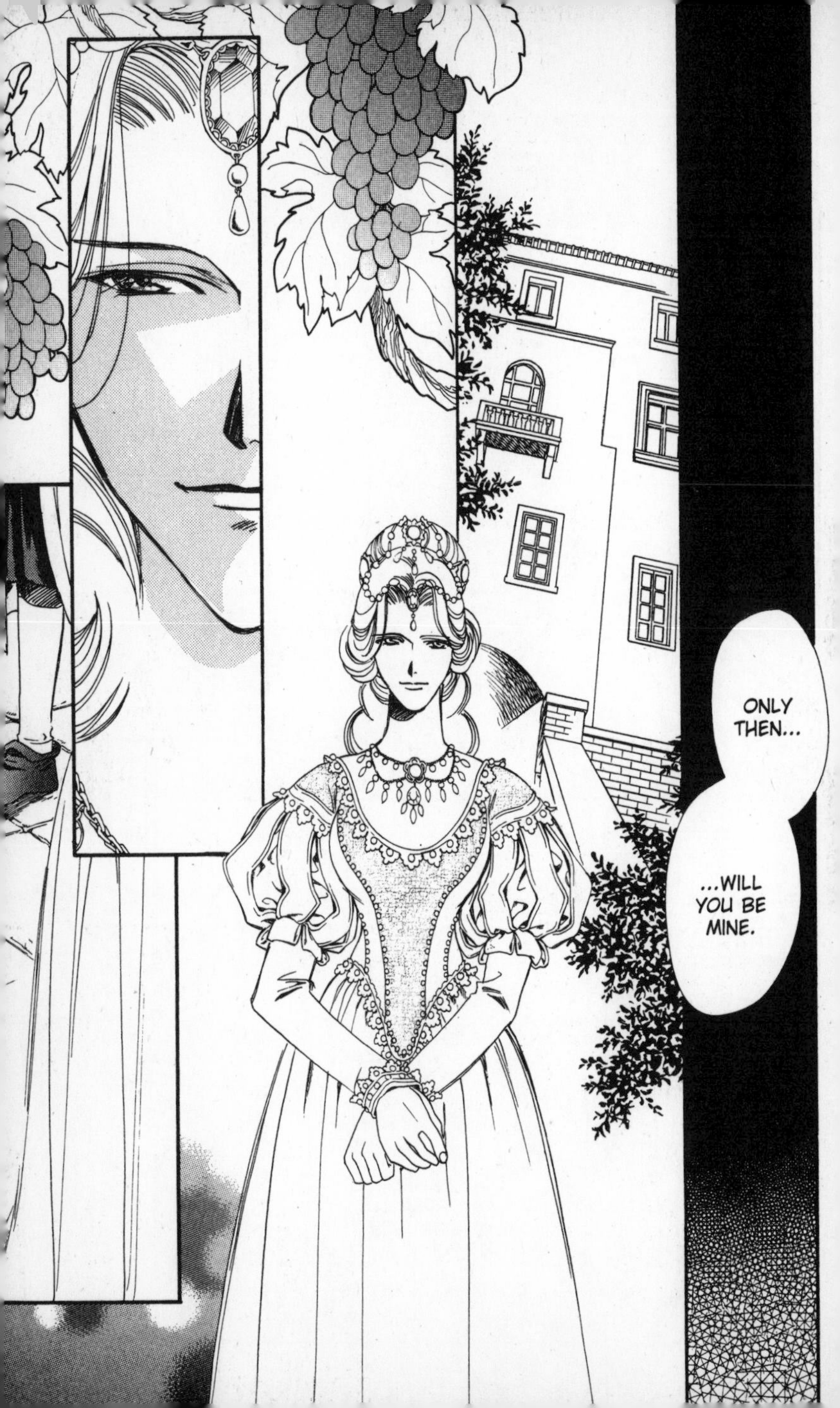
ONLY THEN...
...WILL YOU BE MINE.

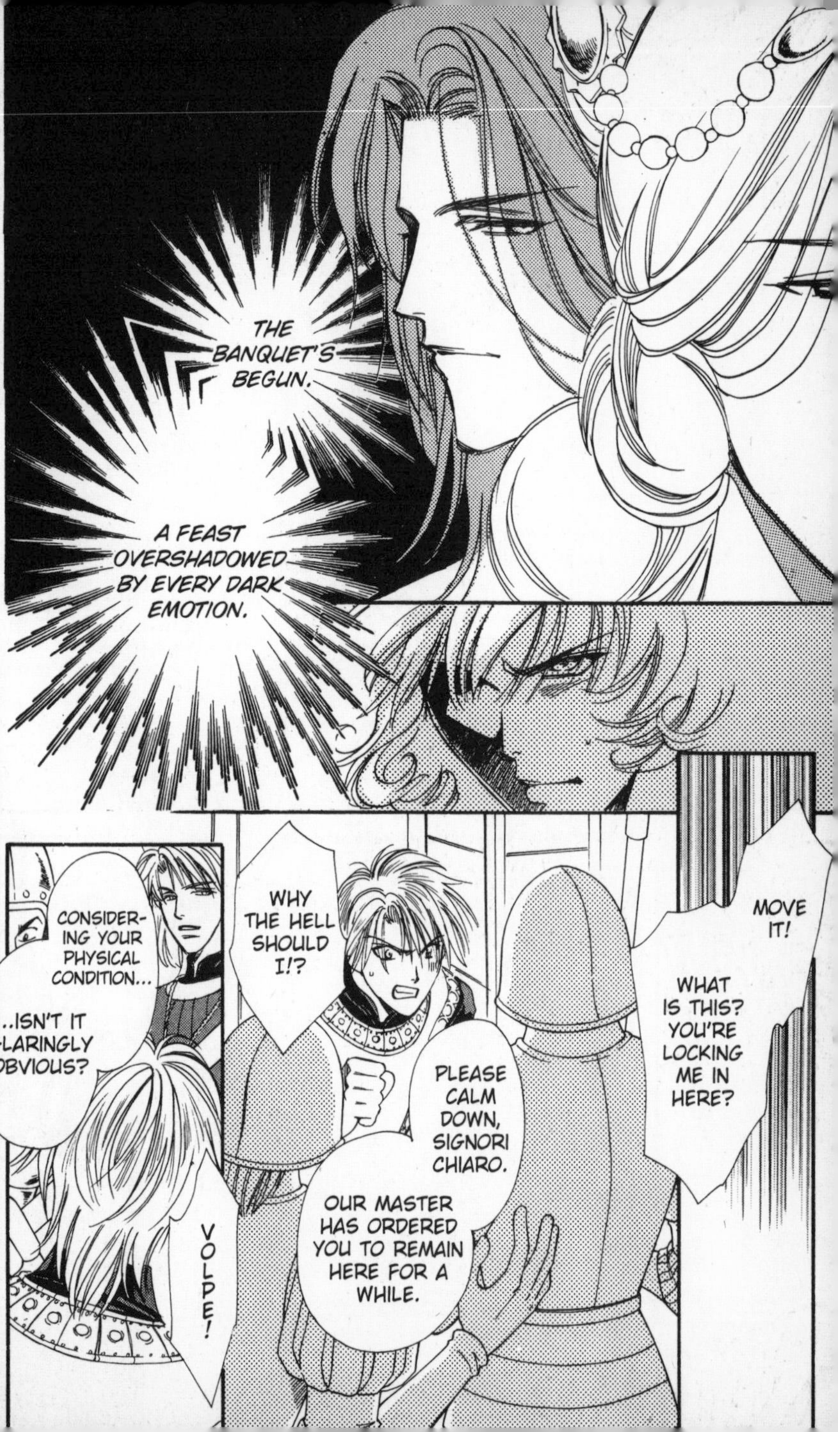
THE BANQUET'S BEGUN.
A FEAST OVERSHADOWED BY EVERY DARK EMOTION.
MOVE IT!
WHAT IS THIS? YOU'RE LOCKING ME IN HERE?
PLEASE CALM DOWN, SIGNORI CHIARO.
OUR MASTER HAS ORDERED YOU TO REMAIN HERE FOR A WHILE.
WHY THE HELL SHOULD I!?
VOLPE!
CONSIDER-ING YOUR PHYSICAL CONDITION...
...ISN'T IT GLARINGLY OBVIOUS?

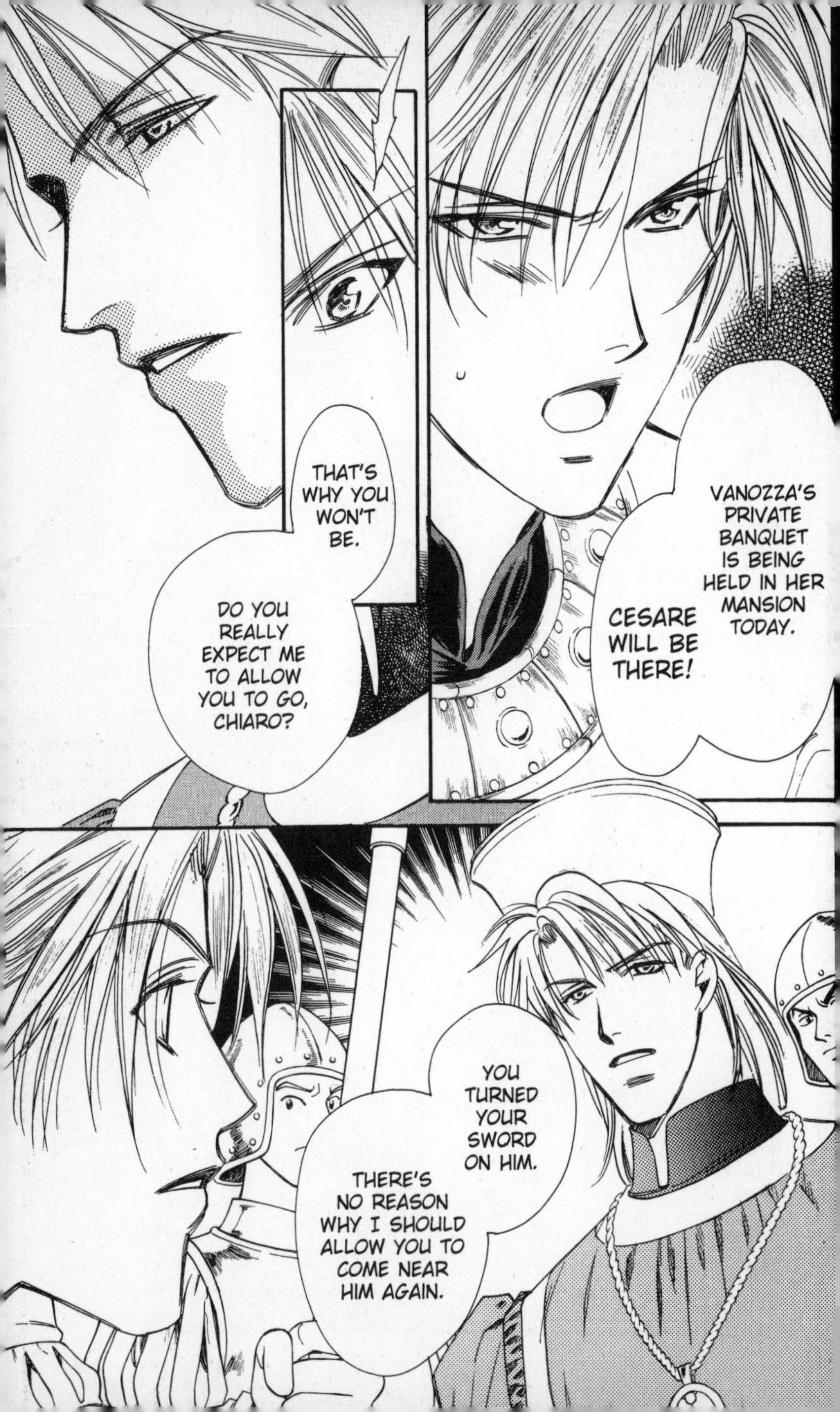
VANOZZA'S PRIVATE BANQUET IS BEING HELD IN HER MANSION TODAY.
CESARE WILL BE THERE!
THAT'S WHY YOU WON'T BE.
DO YOU REALLY EXPECT ME TO ALLOW YOU TO GO, CHIARO?
YOU TURNED YOUR SWORD ON HIM.
THERE'S NO REASON WHY I SHOULD ALLOW YOU TO COME NEAR HIM AGAIN.

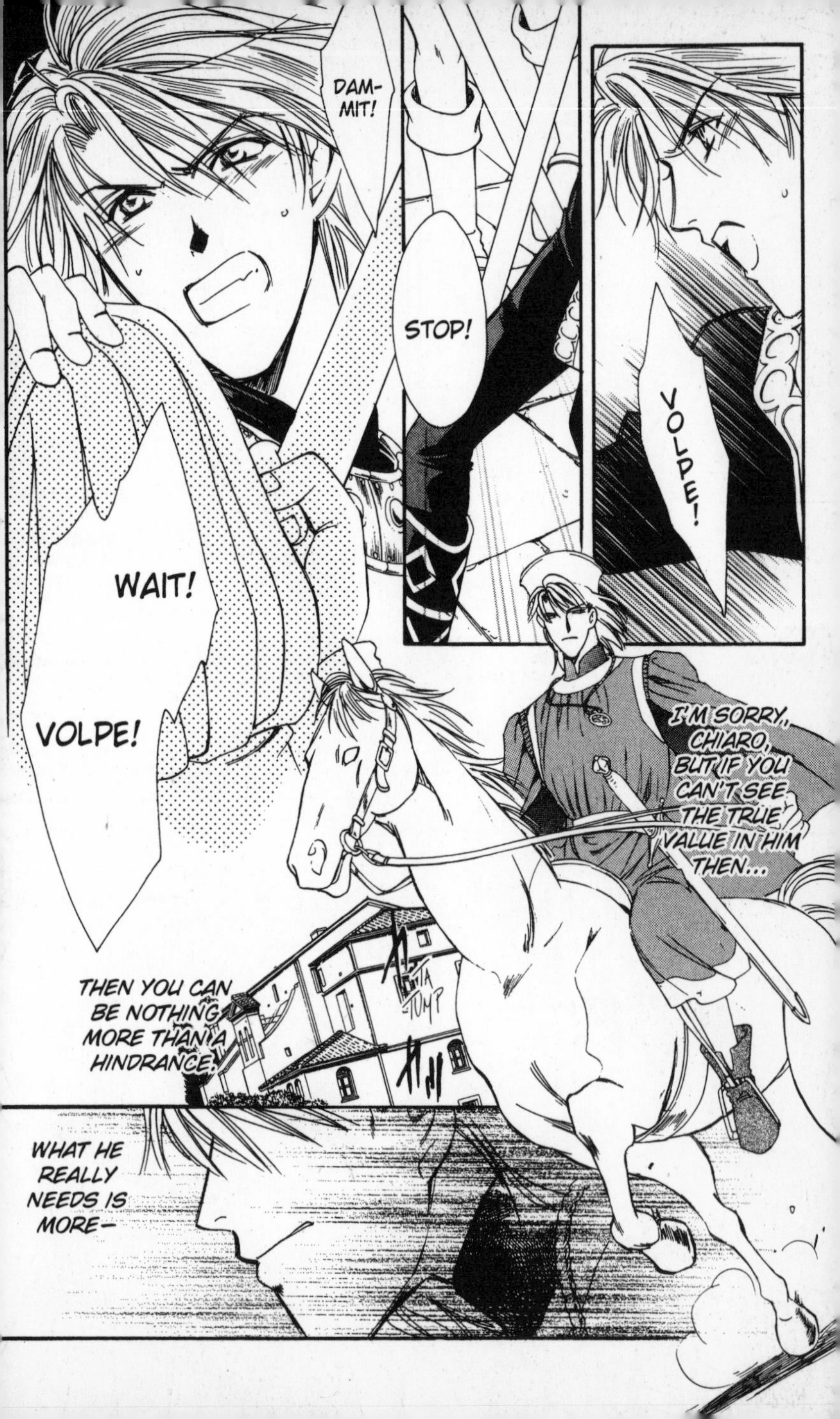
VOLPE!
STOP!
DAM-MIT!
WAIT! VOLPE!
I'M SORRY, CHIARO, BUT IF YOU CAN'T SEE THE TRUE VALUE IN HIM THEN...
THEN YOU CAN BE NOTHING MORE THAN A HINDRANCE.
TA TUMP
WHAT HE REALLY NEEDS IS MORE—

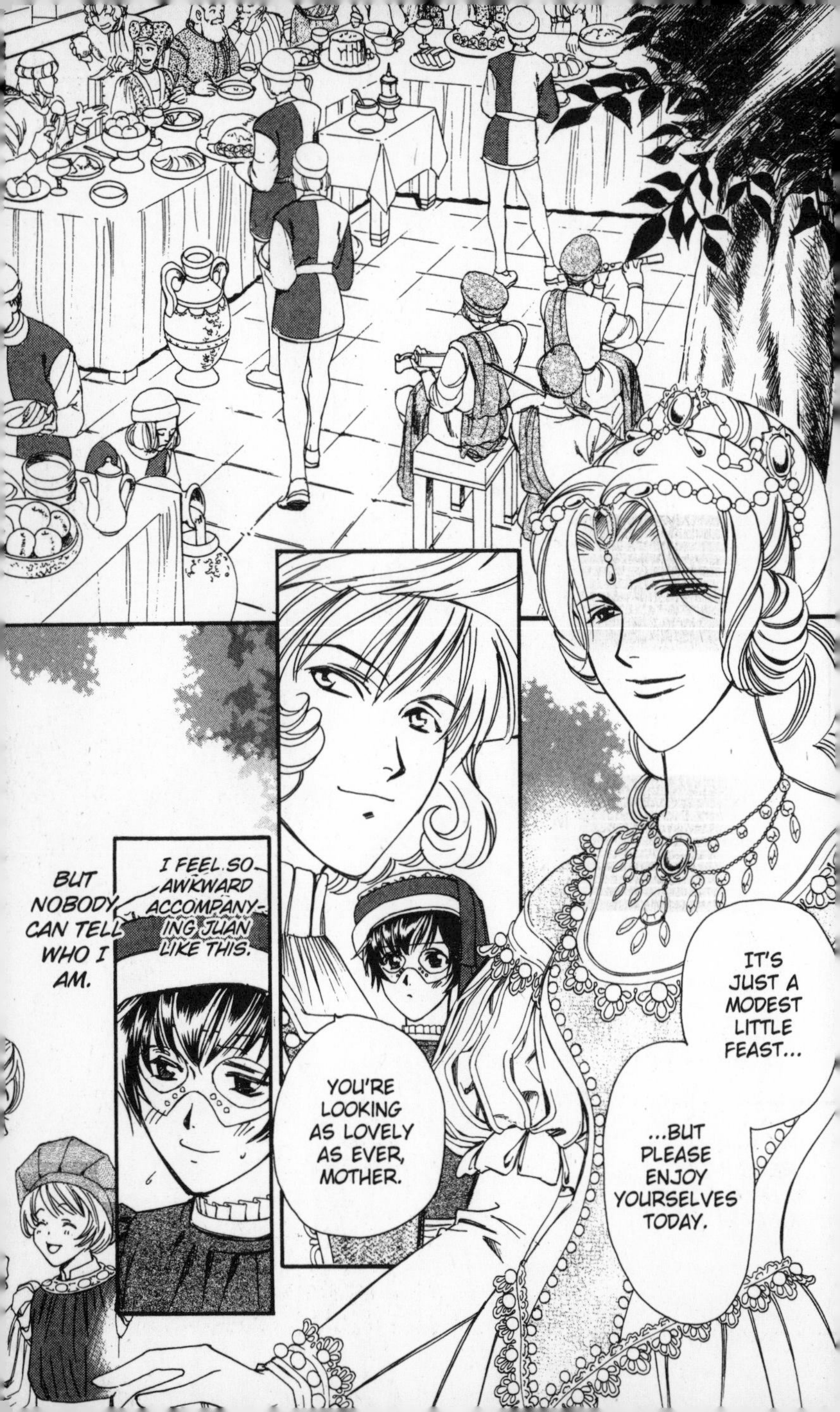
IT'S JUST A MODEST LITTLE FEAST...
...BUT PLEASE ENJOY YOURSELVES TODAY.
YOU'RE LOOKING AS LOVELY AS EVER, MOTHER.
I FEEL SO AWKWARD ACCOMPANYING JUAN LIKE THIS.
BUT NOBODY CAN TELL WHO I AM.

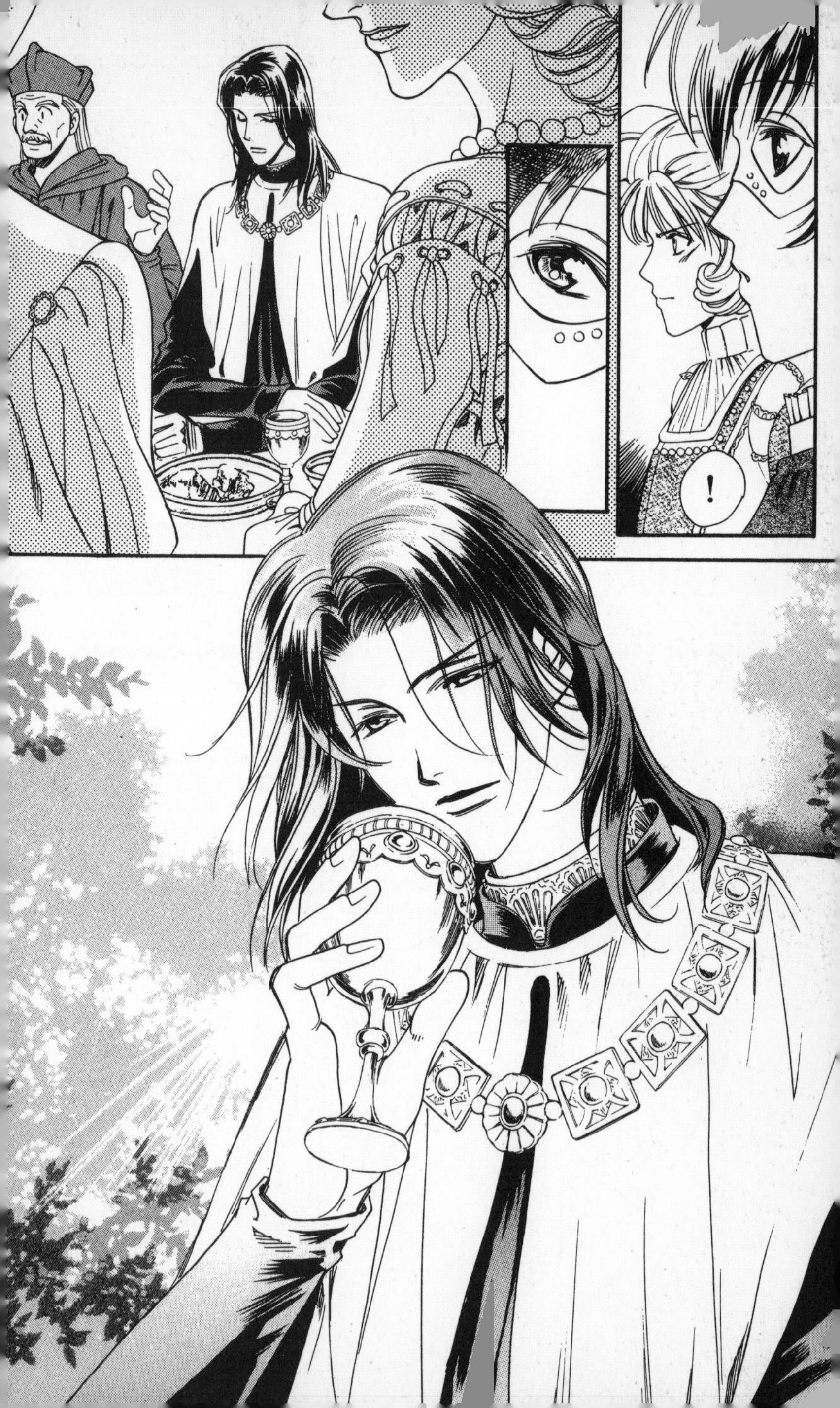
!

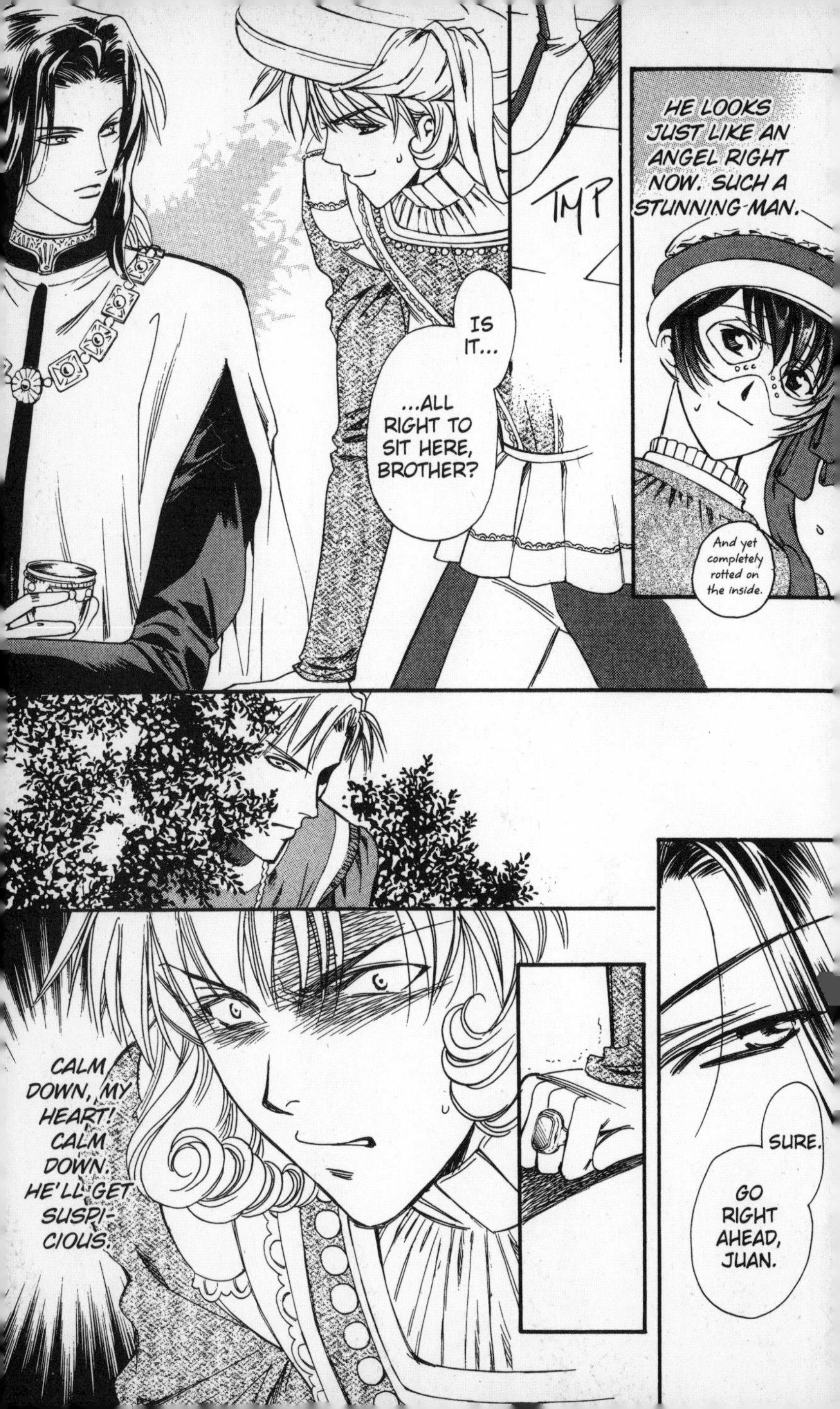
HE LOOKS JUST LIKE AN ANGEL RIGHT NOW. SUCH A STUNNING MAN.
And yet completely rotted on the inside.
TMP
IS IT...
...ALL RIGHT TO SIT HERE, BROTHER?
SURE.
GO RIGHT AHEAD, JUAN.
CALM DOWN, MY HEART! CALM DOWN. HE'LL GET SUSPI-CIOUS.

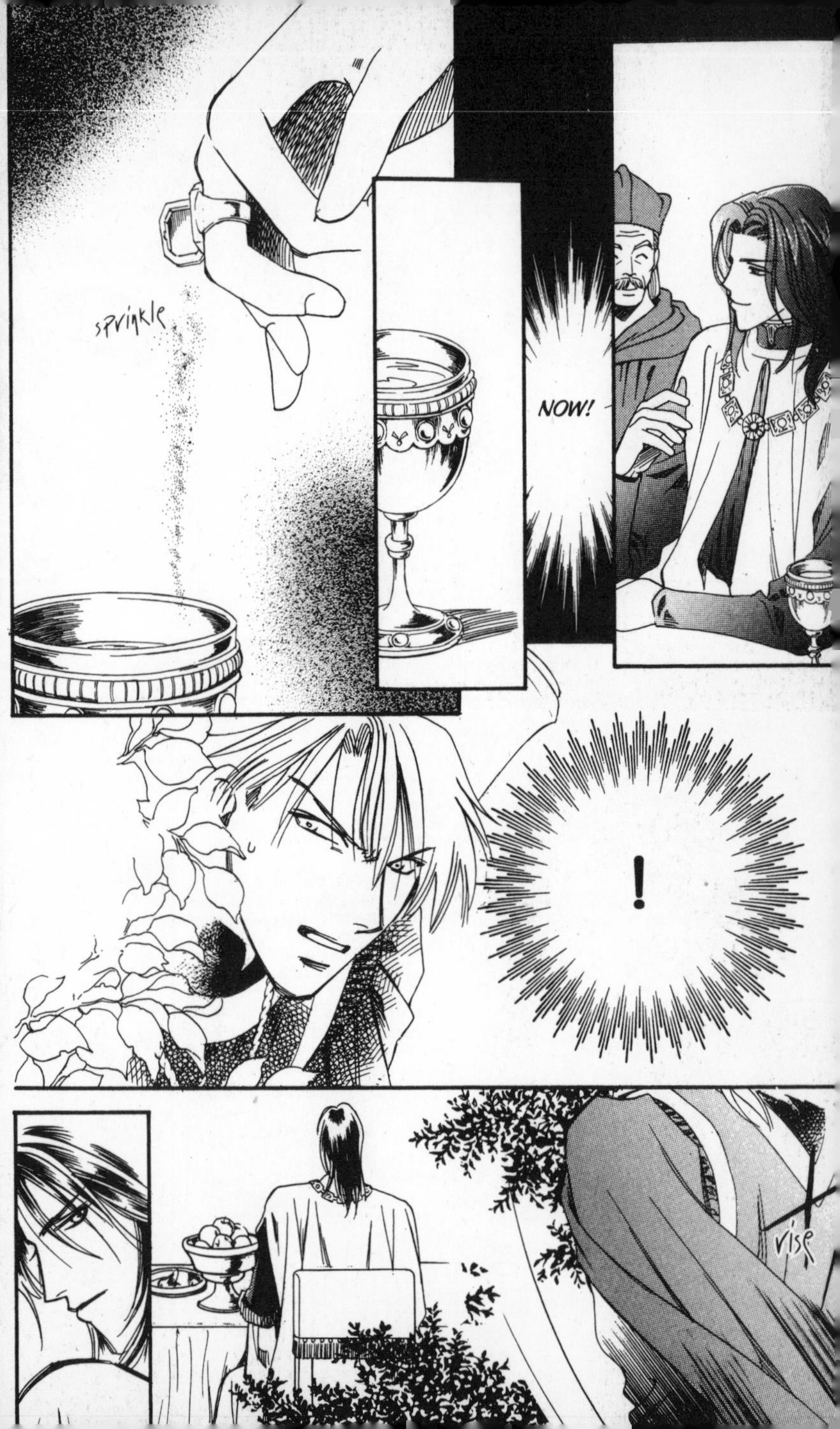
NOW!
sprinkle
!
rise

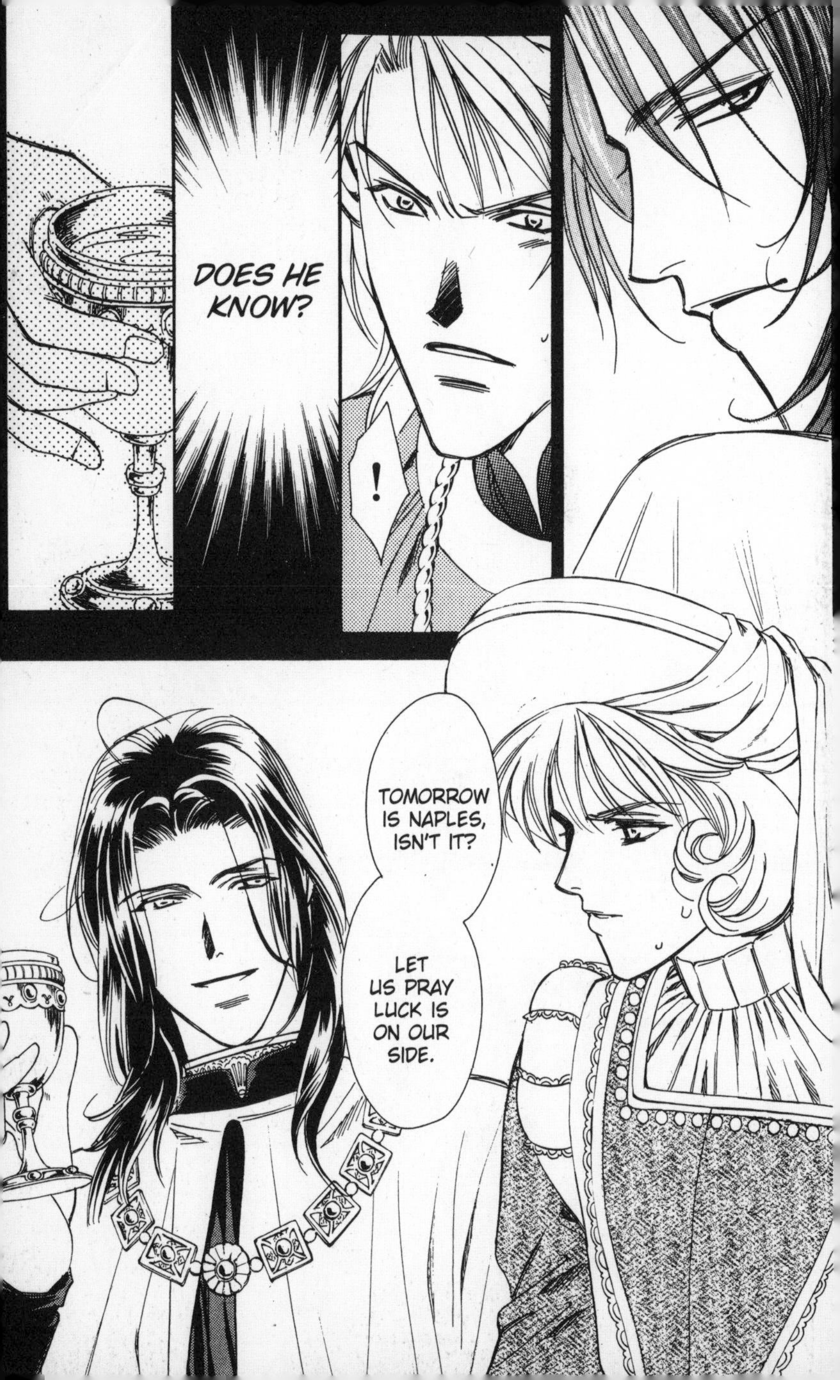
!
DOES HE KNOW?
TOMORROW IS NAPLES, ISN'T IT?
LET US PRAY LUCK IS ON OUR SIDE.

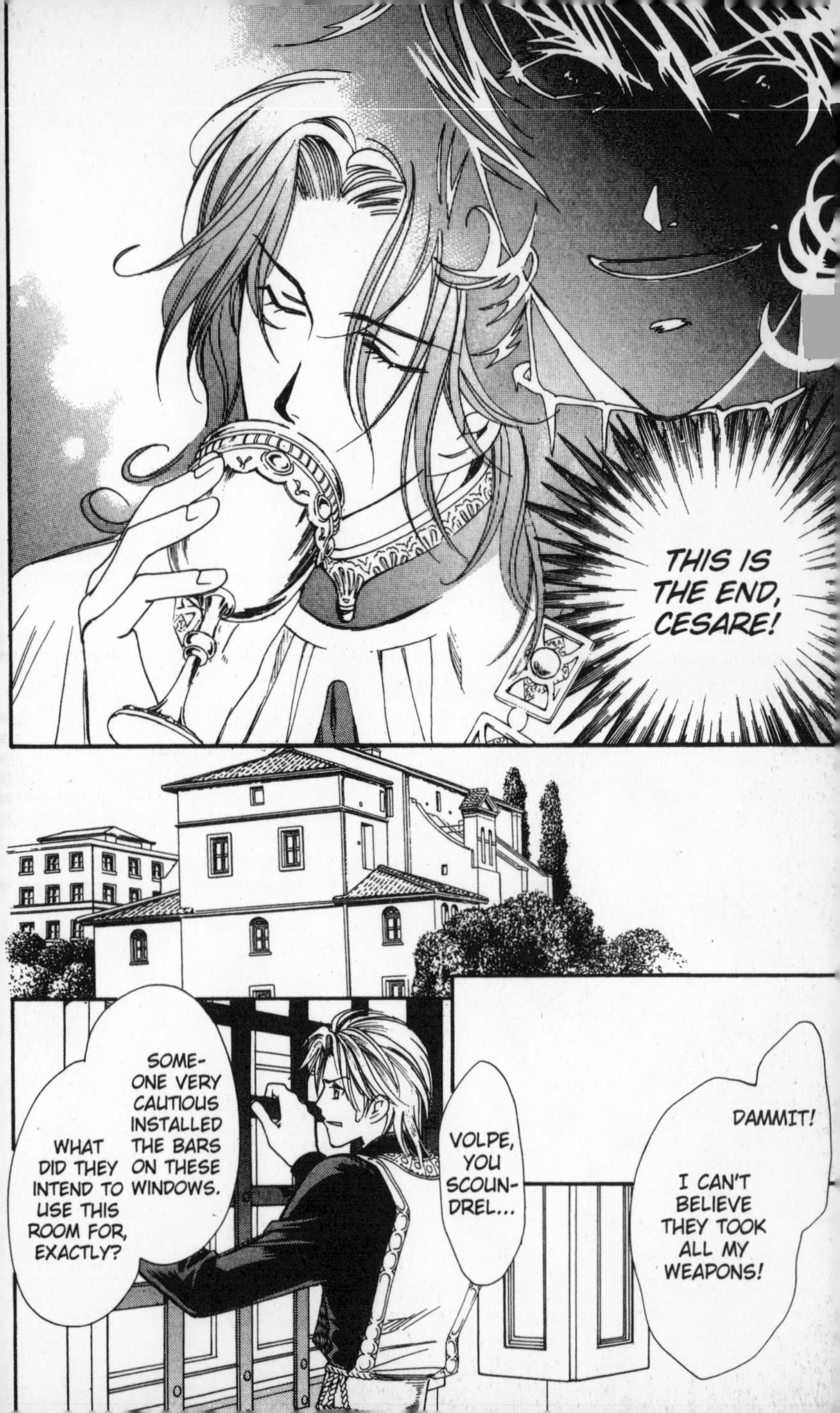
THIS IS THE END, CESARE!
DAMMIT!
I CAN'T BELIEVE THEY TOOK ALL MY WEAPONS!
VOLPE, YOU SCOUNDREL...
SOME-ONE VERY CAUTIOUS INSTALLED THE BARS ON THESE WINDOWS.
WHAT DID THEY INTEND TO USE THIS ROOM FOR, EXACTLY?

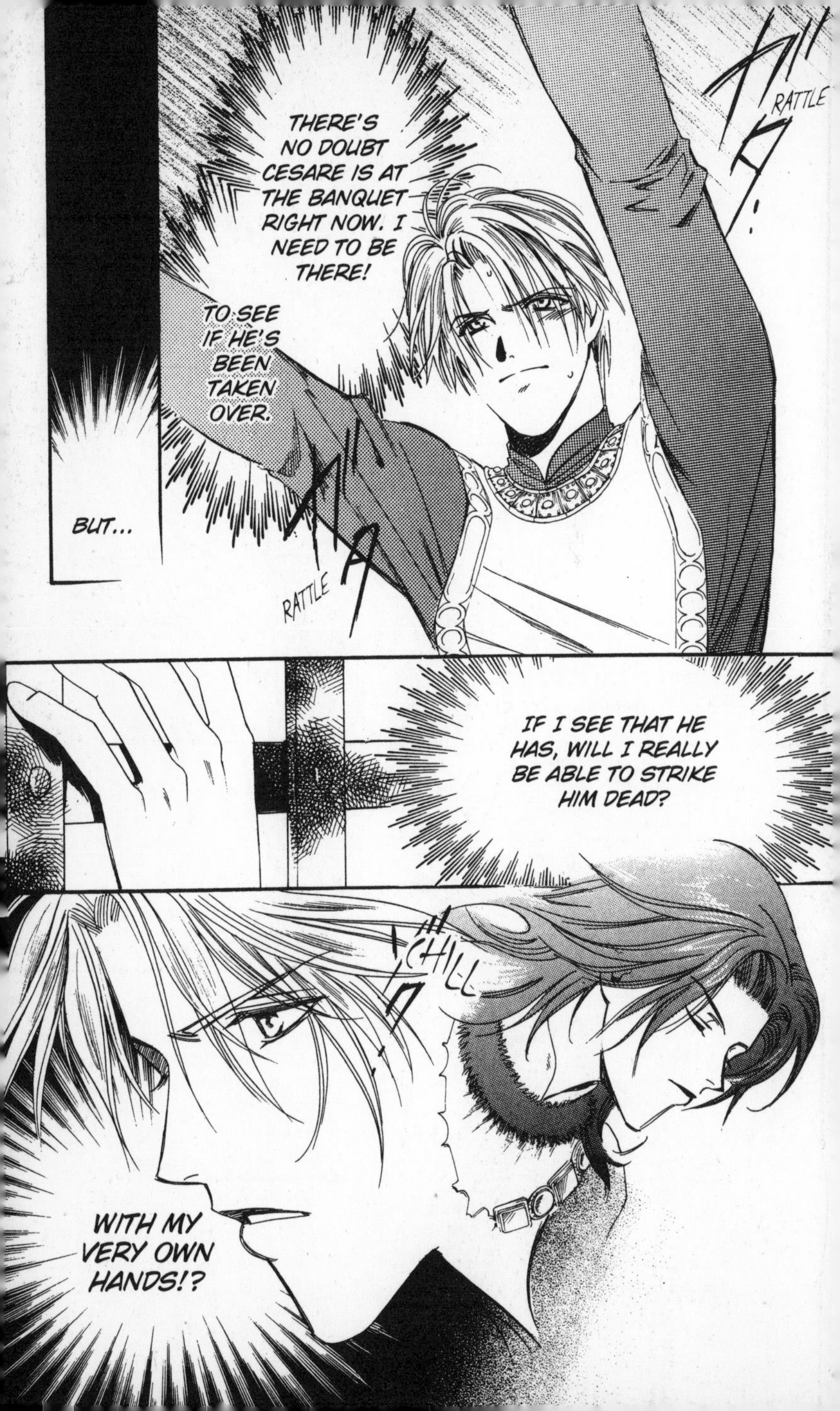
RATTLE
THERE'S NO DOUBT CESARE IS AT THE BANQUET RIGHT NOW. I NEED TO BE THERE!
TO SEE IF HE'S BEEN TAKEN OVER.
BUT...
RATTLE
IF I SEE THAT HE HAS, WILL I REALLY BE ABLE TO STRIKE HIM DEAD?
CHILL
WITH MY VERY OWN HANDS!?

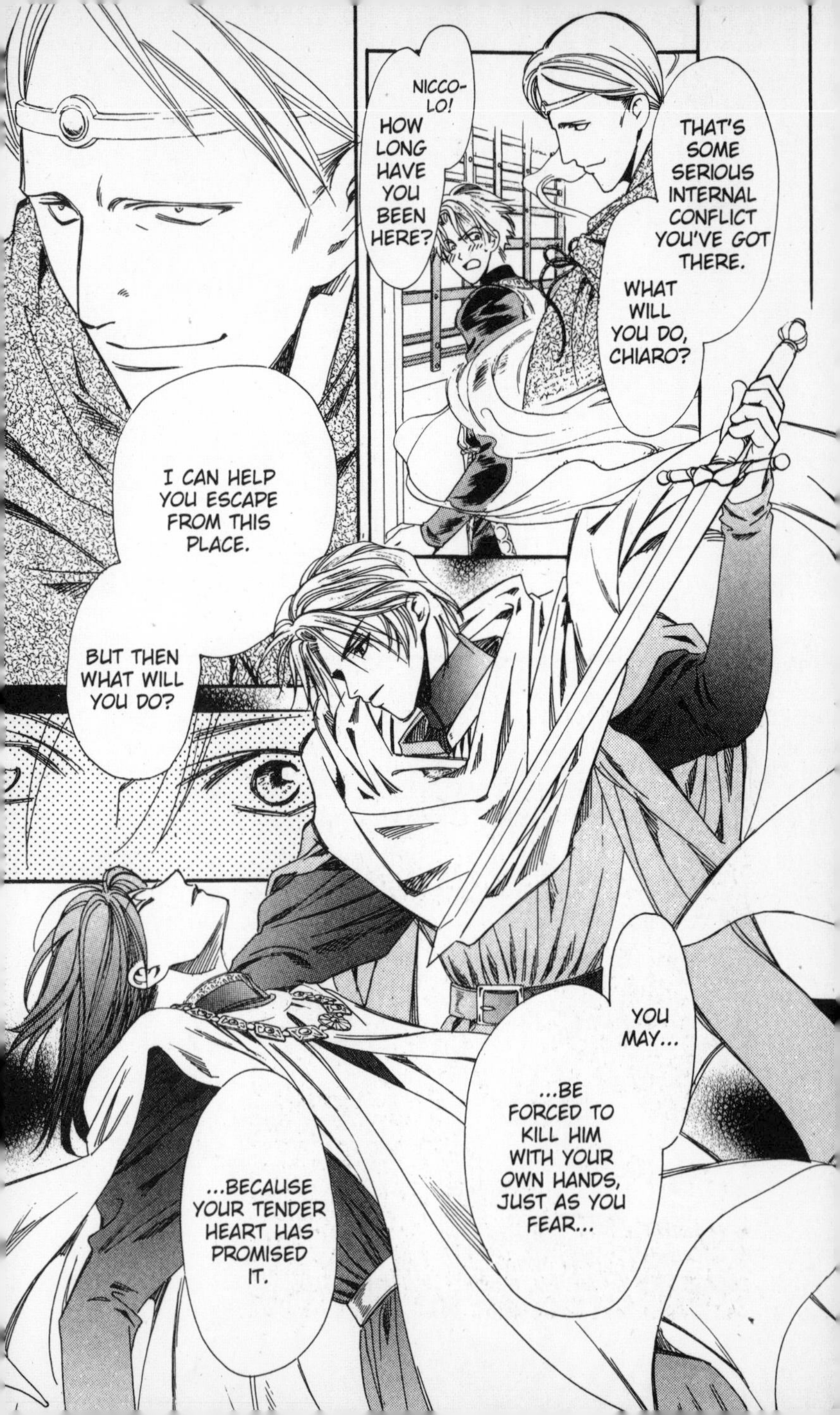
THAT'S SOME SERIOUS INTERNAL CONFLICT YOU'VE GOT THERE.
NICCO-LO! HOW LONG HAVE YOU BEEN HERE?
WHAT WILL YOU DO, CHIARO?
I CAN HELP YOU ESCAPE FROM THIS PLACE.
BUT THEN WHAT WILL YOU DO?
YOU MAY...
...BE FORCED TO KILL HIM WITH YOUR OWN HANDS, JUST AS YOU FEAR...
...BECAUSE YOUR TENDER HEART HAS PROMISED IT.

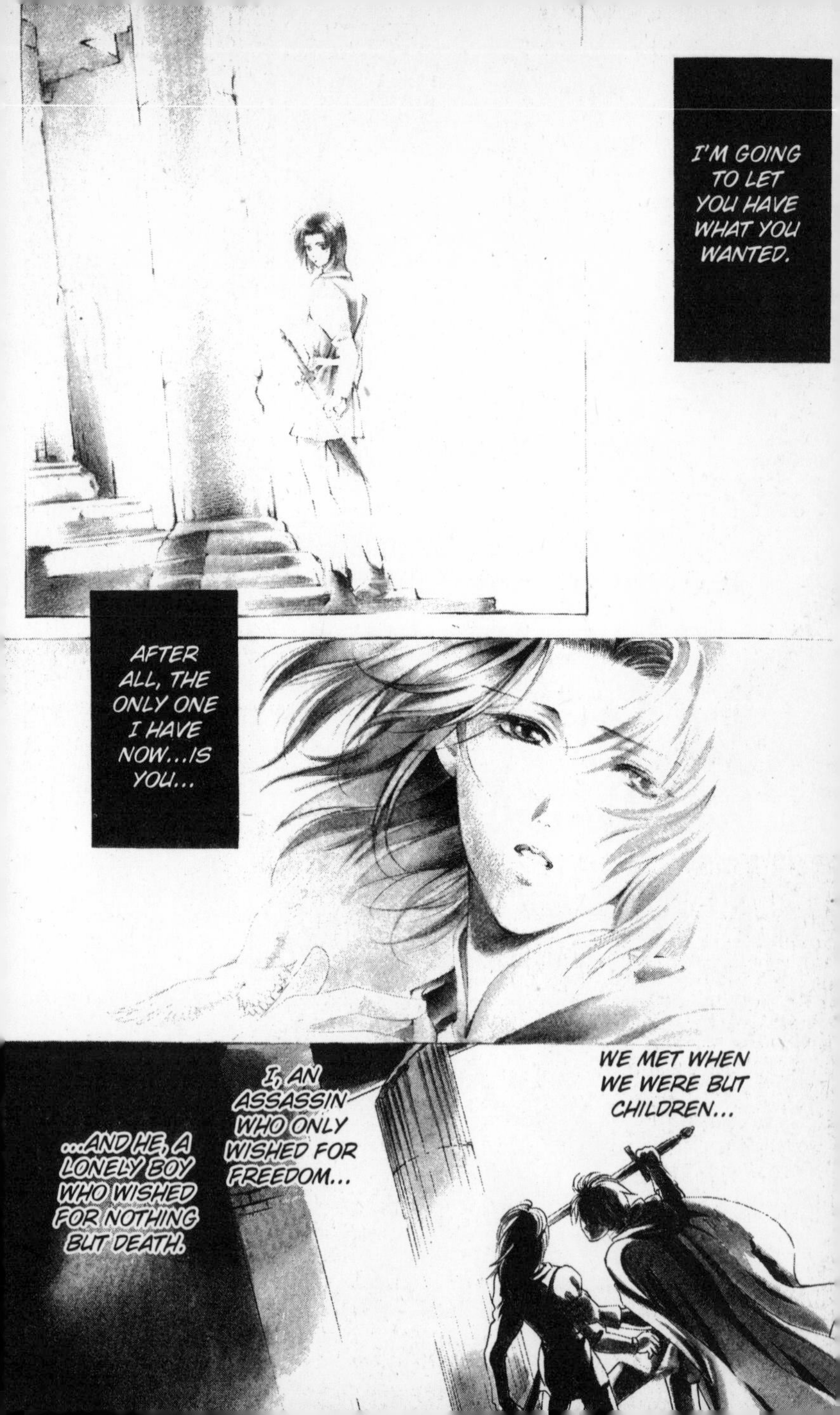
I'M GOING TO LET YOU HAVE WHAT YOU WANTED.
AFTER ALL, THE ONLY ONE I HAVE NOW...IS YOU...
WE MET WHEN WE WERE BUT CHILDREN...
I, AN ASSASSIN WHO ONLY WISHED FOR FREEDOM...
...AND HE, A LONELY BOY WHO WISHED FOR NOTHING BUT DEATH.

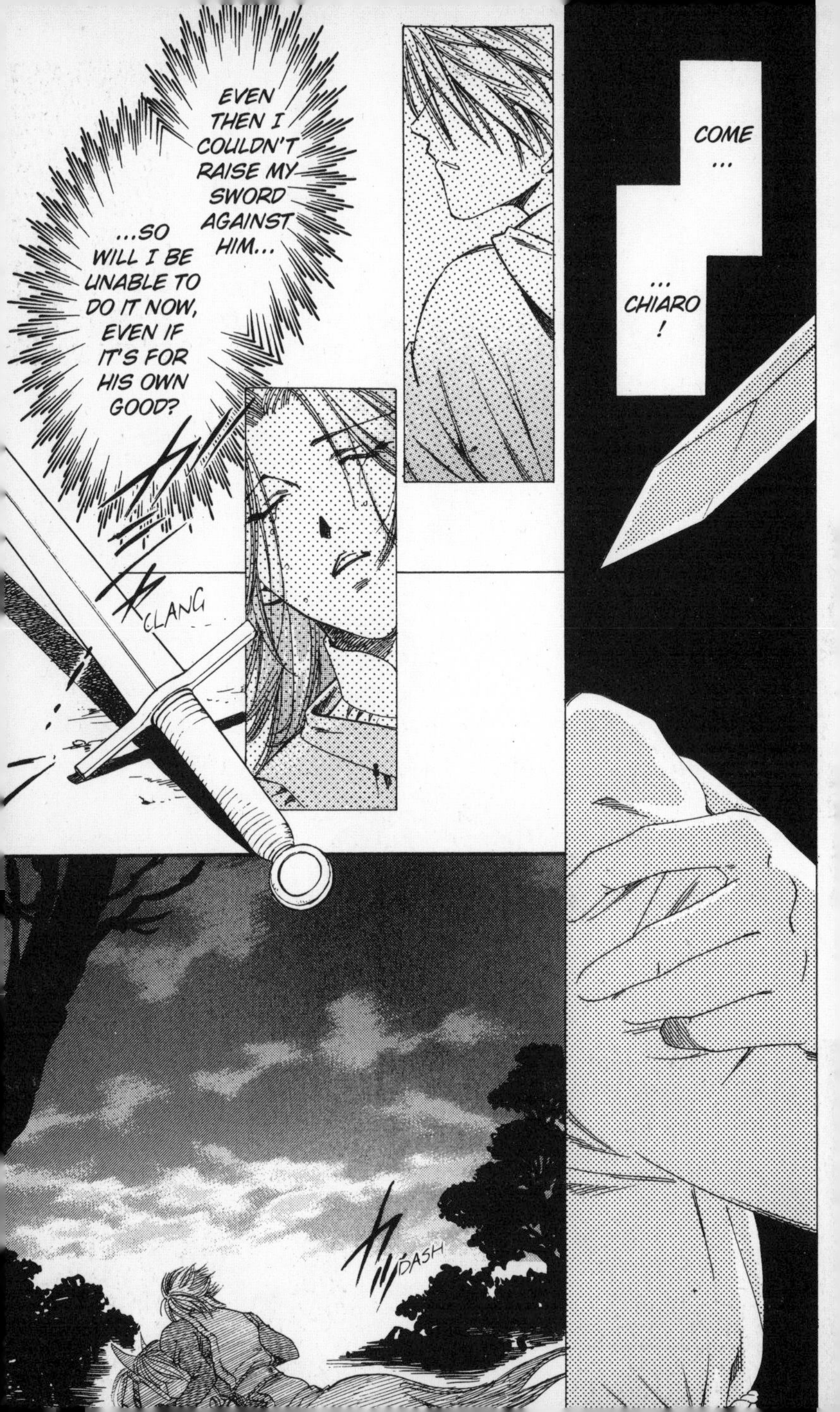
COME ...
... CHIARO!
EVEN THEN I COULDN'T RAISE MY SWORD AGAINST HIM...
...SO WILL I BE UNABLE TO DO IT NOW, EVEN IF IT'S FOR HIS OWN GOOD?
CLANG
DASH

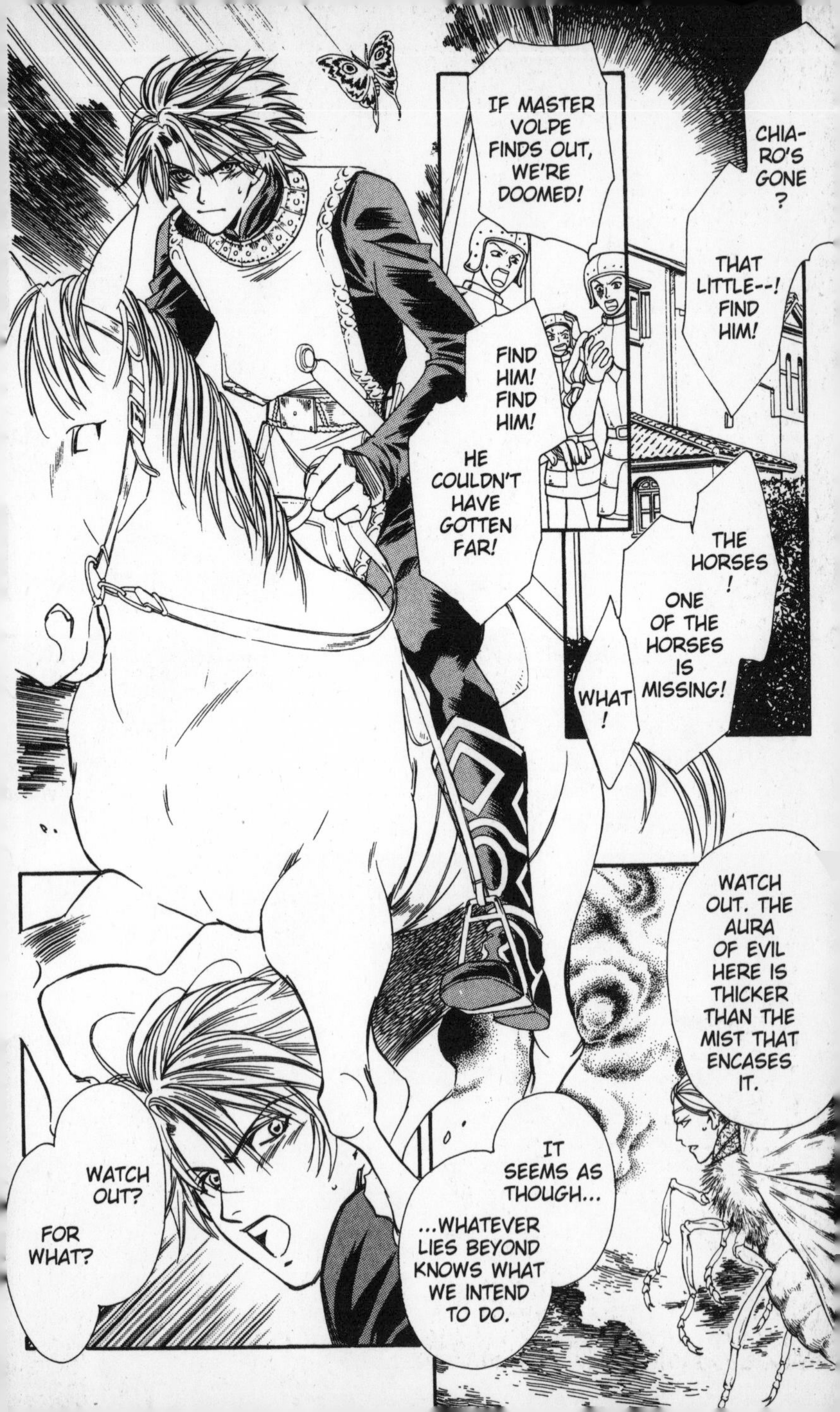
CHIARO'S GONE?
THAT LITTLE--! FIND HIM!
IF MASTER VOLPE FINDS OUT, WE'RE DOOMED!
FIND HIM! FIND HIM!
HE COULDN'T HAVE GOTTEN FAR!
THE HORSES!
ONE OF THE HORSES IS MISSING!
WHAT!
WATCH OUT. THE AURA OF EVIL HERE IS THICKER THAN THE MIST THAT ENCASES IT.
IT SEEMS AS THOUGH...
...WHATEVER LIES BEYOND KNOWS WHAT WE INTEND TO DO.
WATCH OUT?
FOR WHAT?

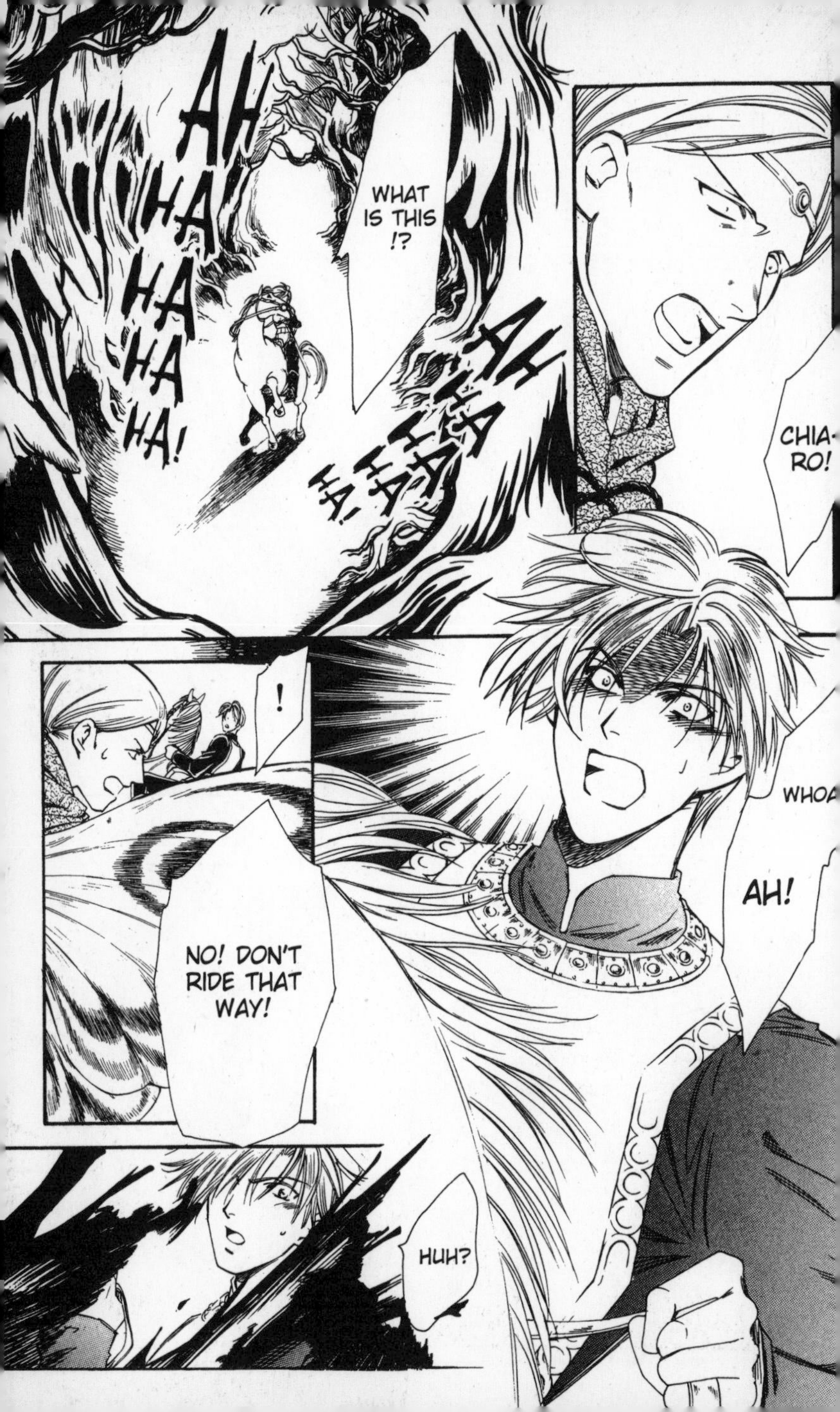
CHIA-RO!
WHAT IS THIS !?
AH HA HA HA HA!
AH HA HA HA HA HA!
WHOA
AH!
!
NO! DON'T RIDE THAT WAY!
HUH?

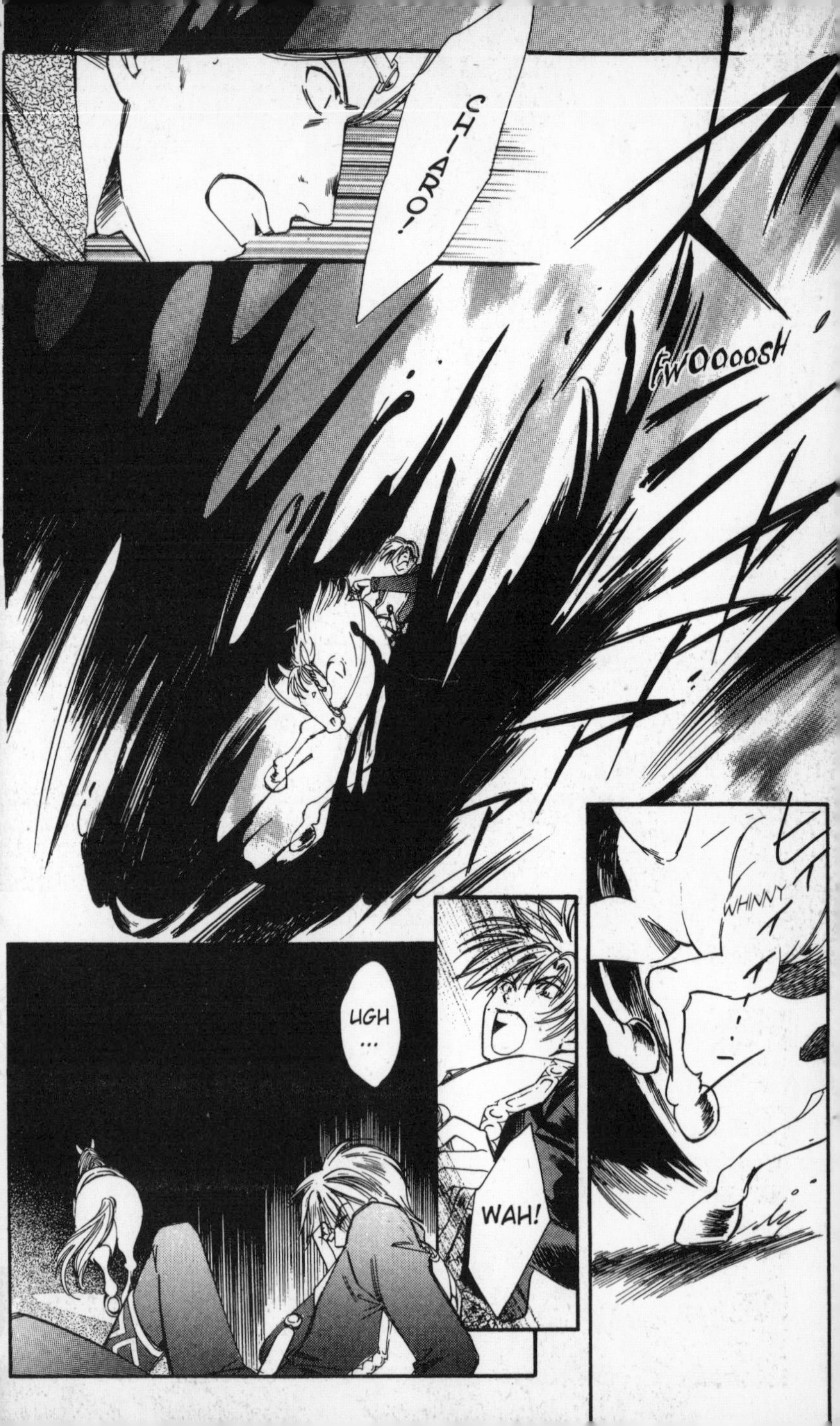
CHIARO!
TWOOOOSH
WHINNY
WAH!
UGH ...

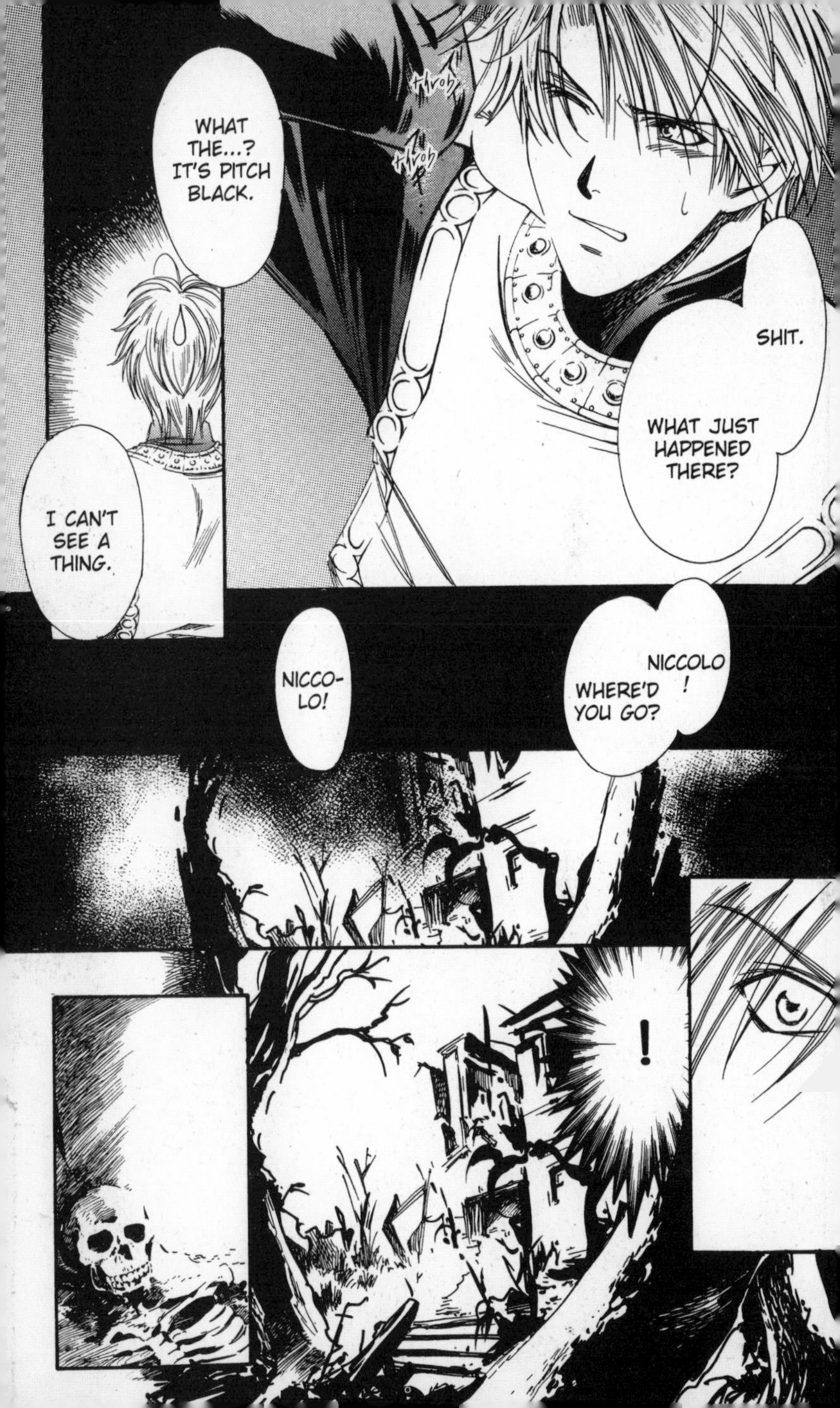
throb
throb
WHAT THE...? IT'S PITCH BLACK.
SHIT.
WHAT JUST HAPPENED THERE?
I CAN'T SEE A THING.
NICCOLO! WHERE'D YOU GO?
NICCO-LO!
!

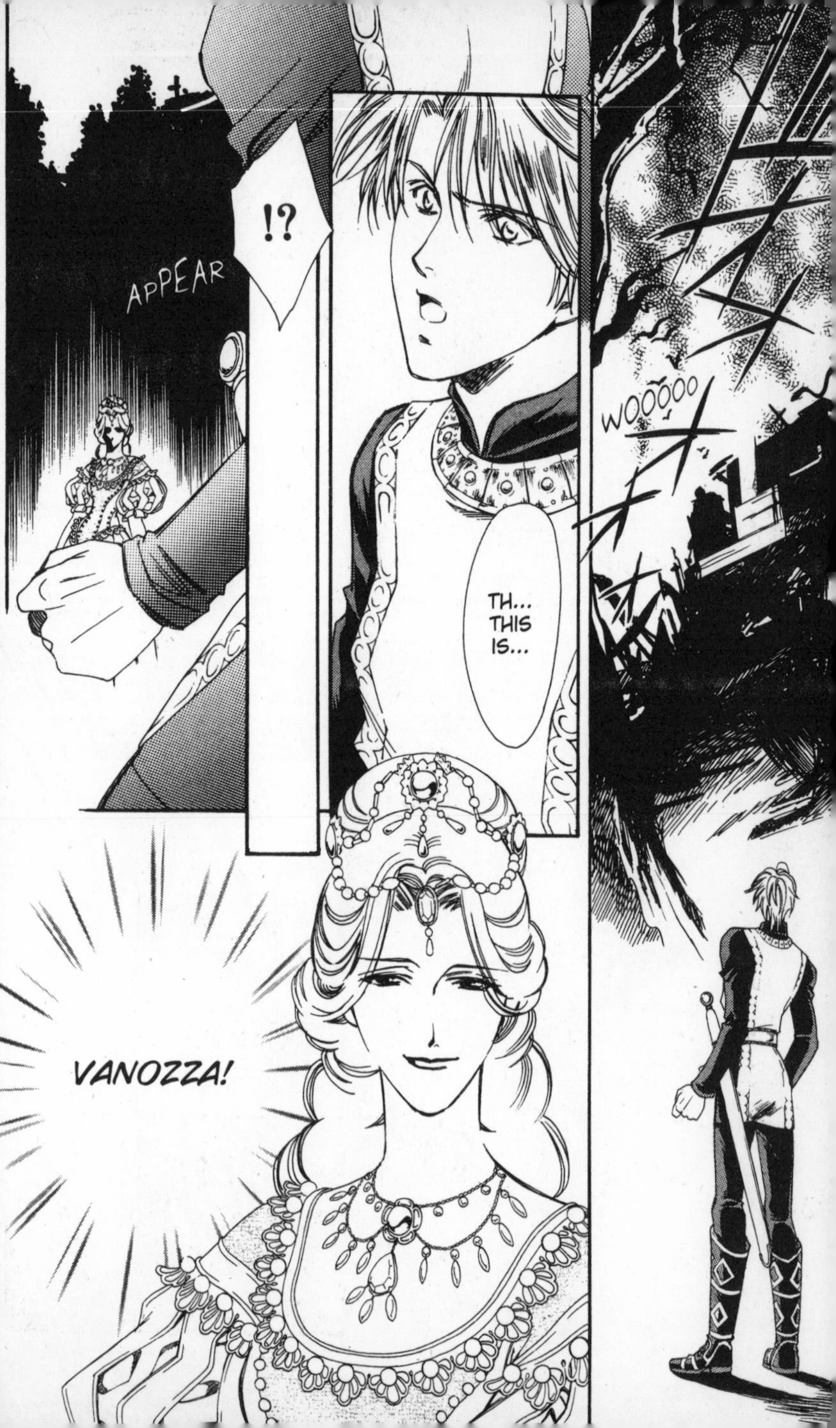
WOOOOO
!?
TH... THIS IS...
APPEAR
VANOZZA!

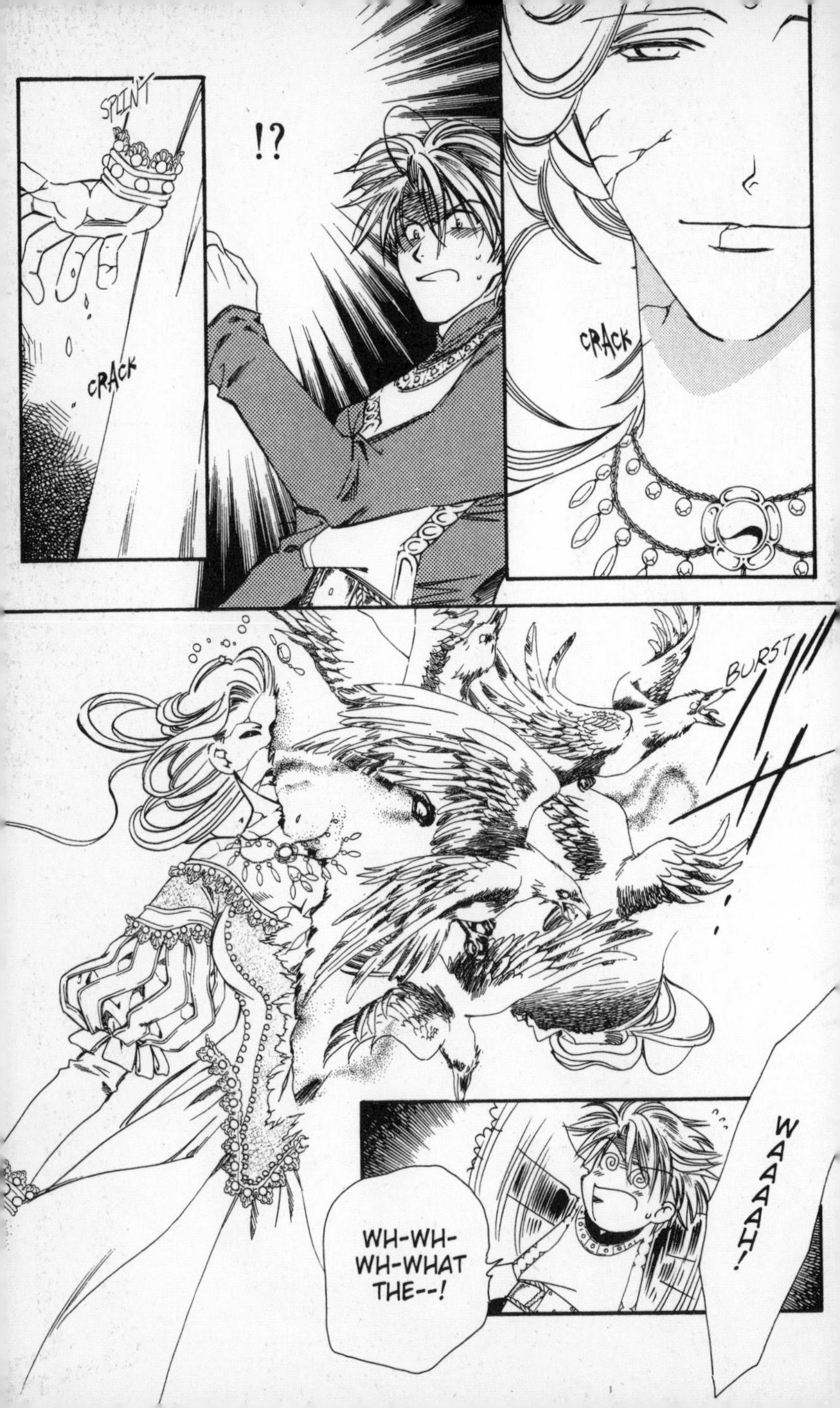
CRACK
!?
SPLINT
CRACK
BURST
WAAAAAH!
WH-WH-WH-WHAT THE--!

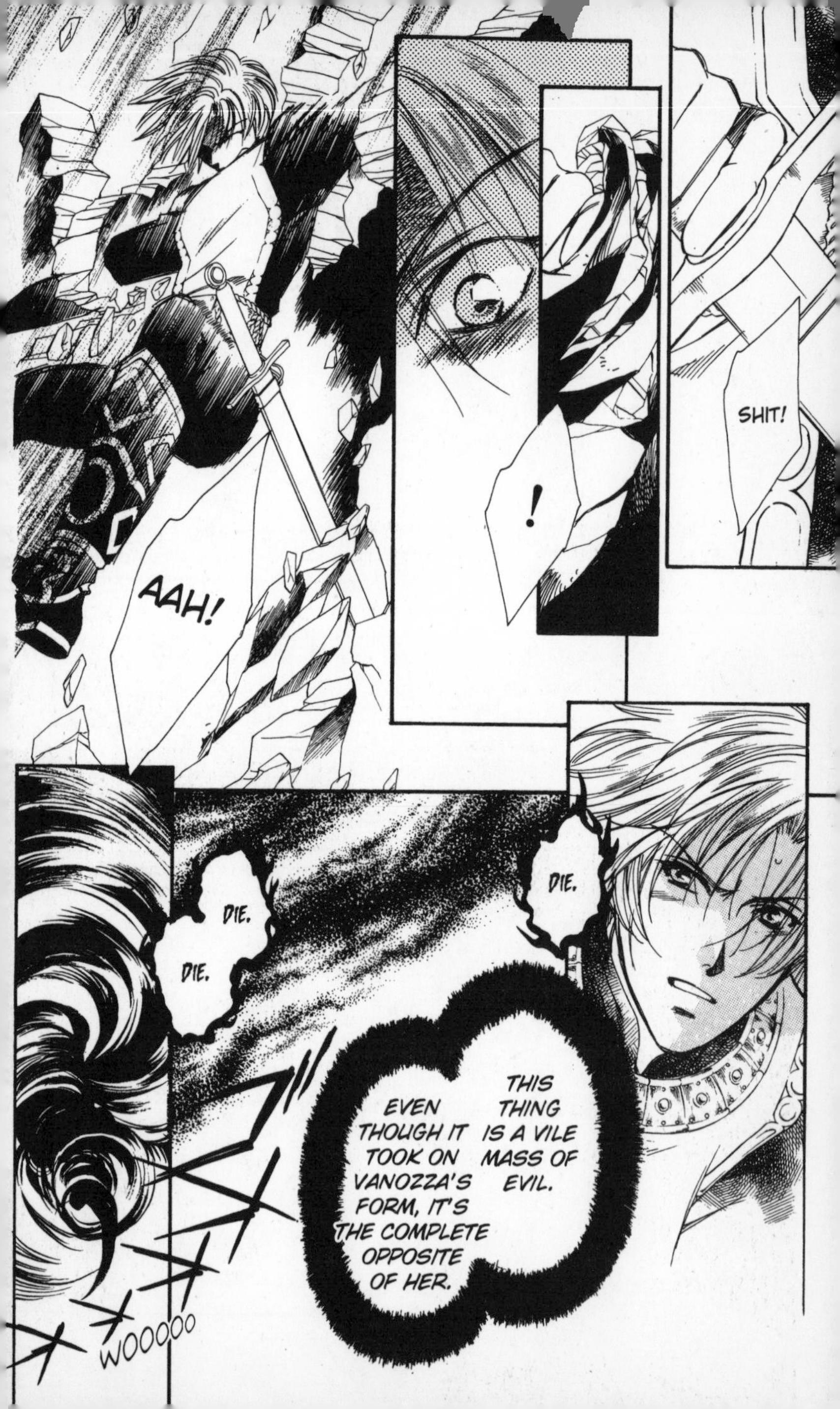
SHIT!
!
AAH!
DIE.
DIE.
DIE.
THIS THING IS A VILE MASS OF EVIL.
EVEN THOUGH IT TOOK ON VANOZZA'S FORM, IT'S THE COMPLETE OPPOSITE OF HER.
WOOOOO

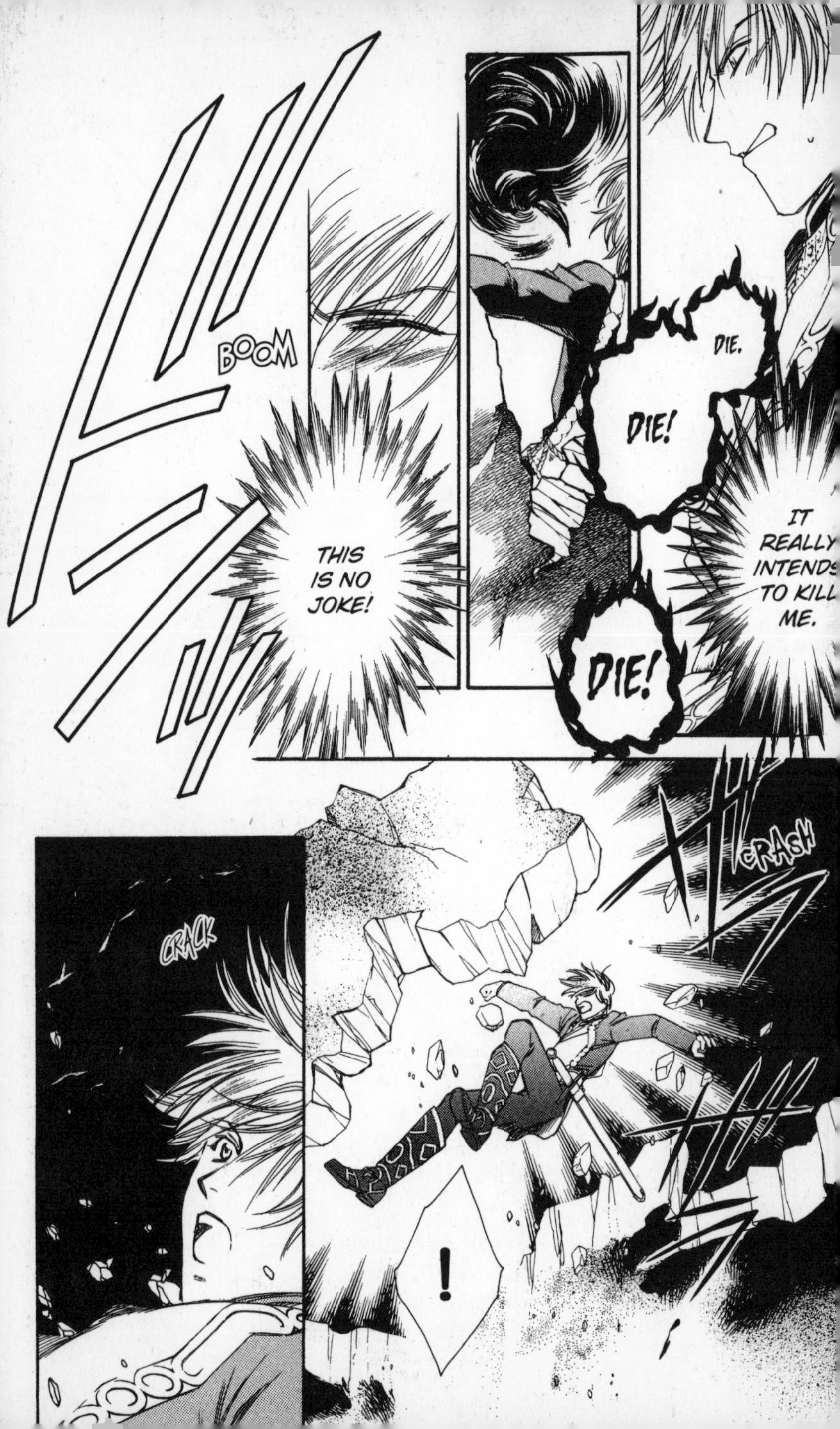
DIE.
DIE!
DIE!
IT REALLY INTENDS TO KILL ME.
BOOM
THIS IS NO JOKE!
CRASH
!
CRACK

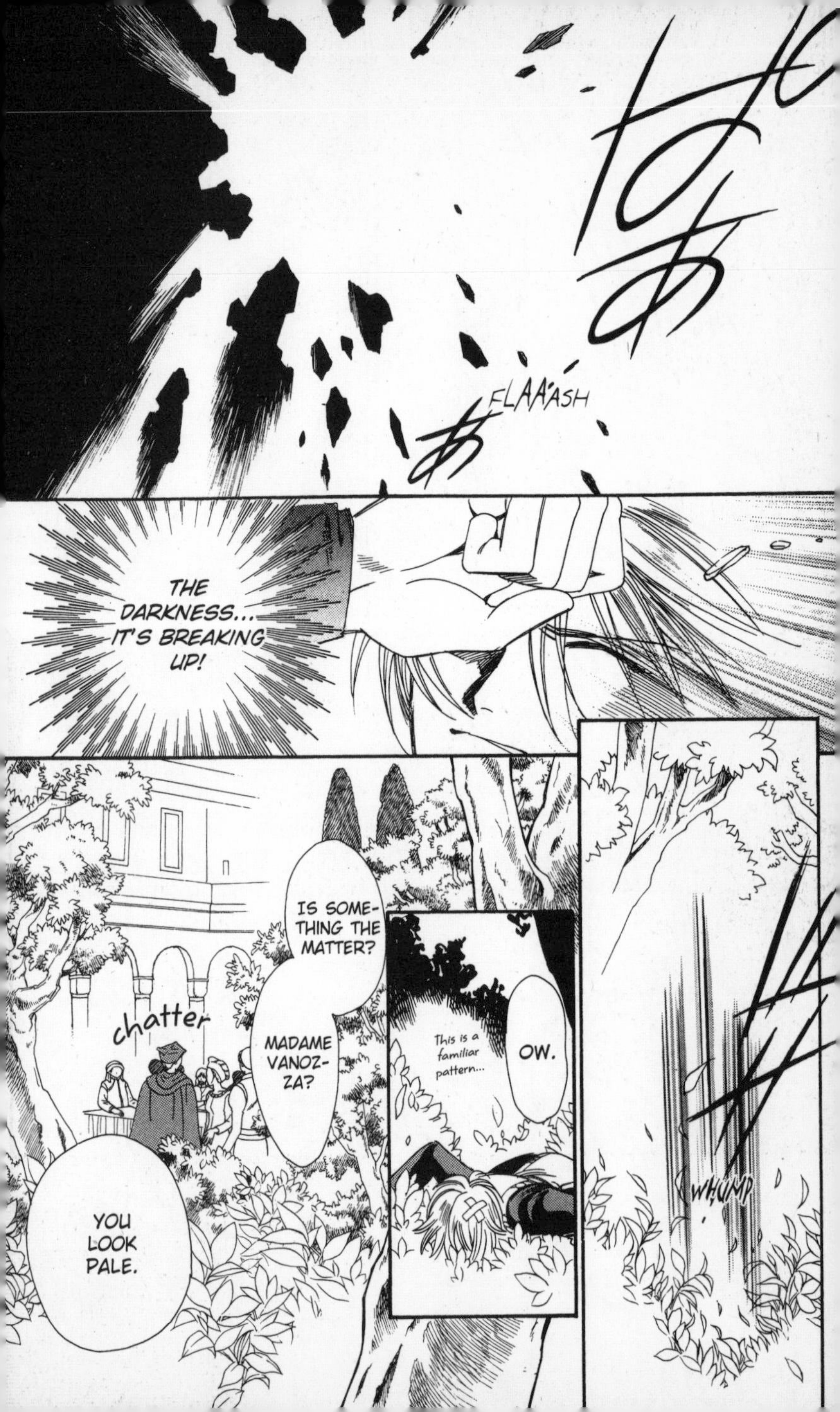
FLAAASH
THE DARKNESS... IT'S BREAKING UP!
WHUMP
OW.
This is a familiar pattern...
IS SOME-THING THE MATTER?
MADAME VANOZ-ZA?
chatter
YOU LOOK PALE.

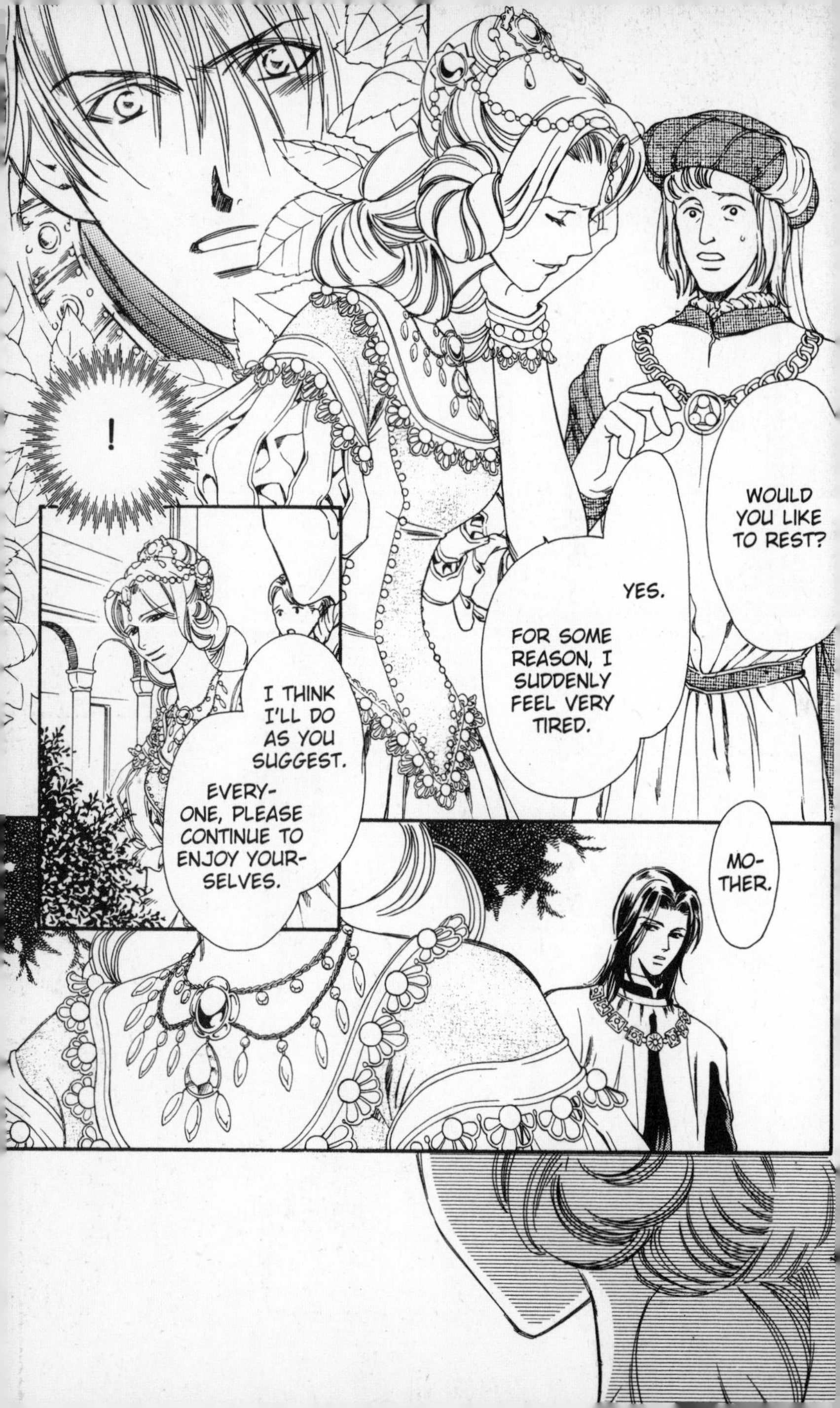
WOULD YOU LIKE TO REST?
YES.
FOR SOME REASON, I SUDDENLY FEEL VERY TIRED.
!
I THINK I'LL DO AS YOU SUGGEST.
EVERY-ONE, PLEASE CONTINUE TO ENJOY YOUR-SELVES.
MO-THER.

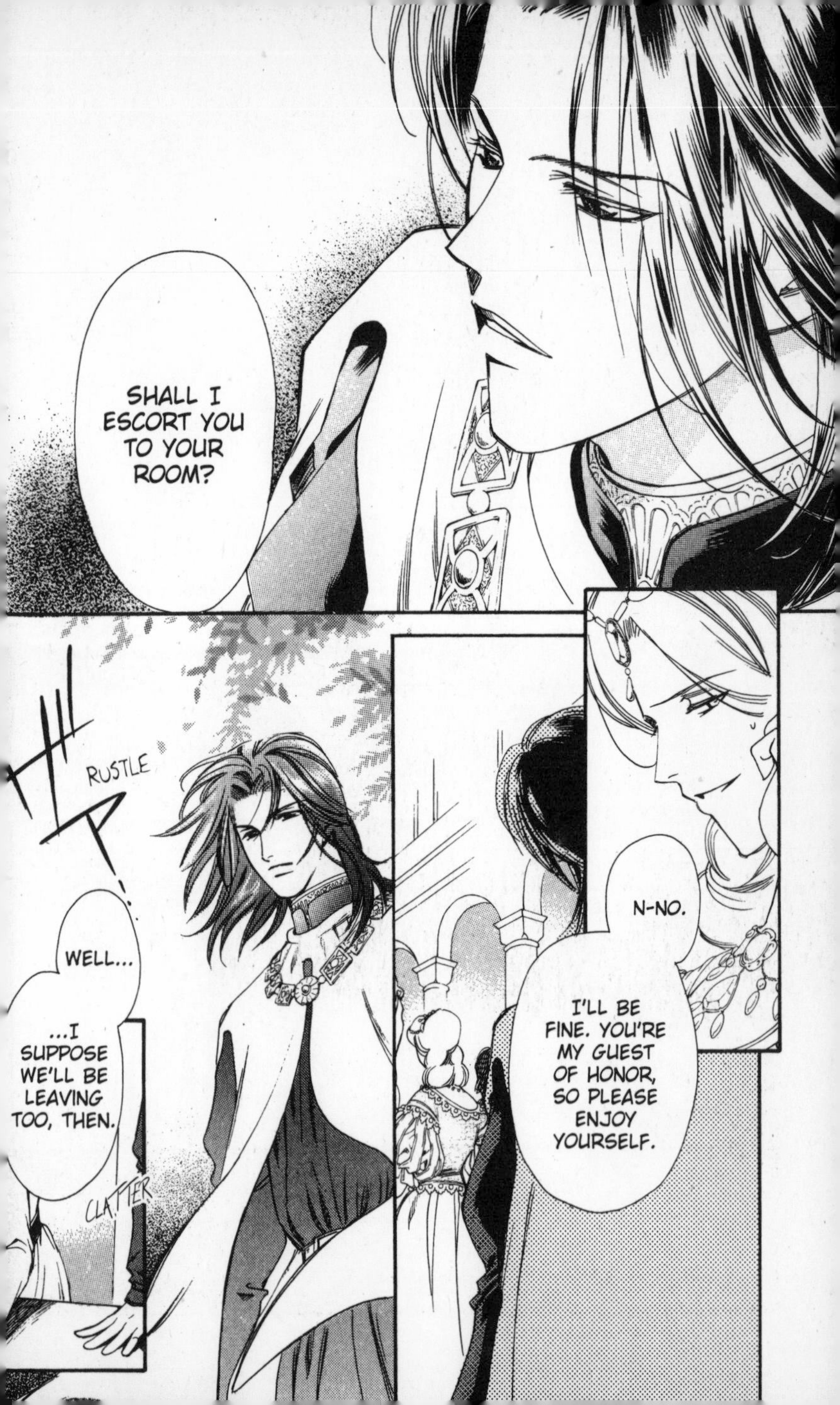
SHALL I ESCORT YOU TO YOUR ROOM?
N-NO.
I'LL BE FINE. YOU'RE MY GUEST OF HONOR, SO PLEASE ENJOY YOURSELF.
RUSTLE
WELL...
...I SUPPOSE WE'LL BE LEAVING TOO, THEN.
CLATTER

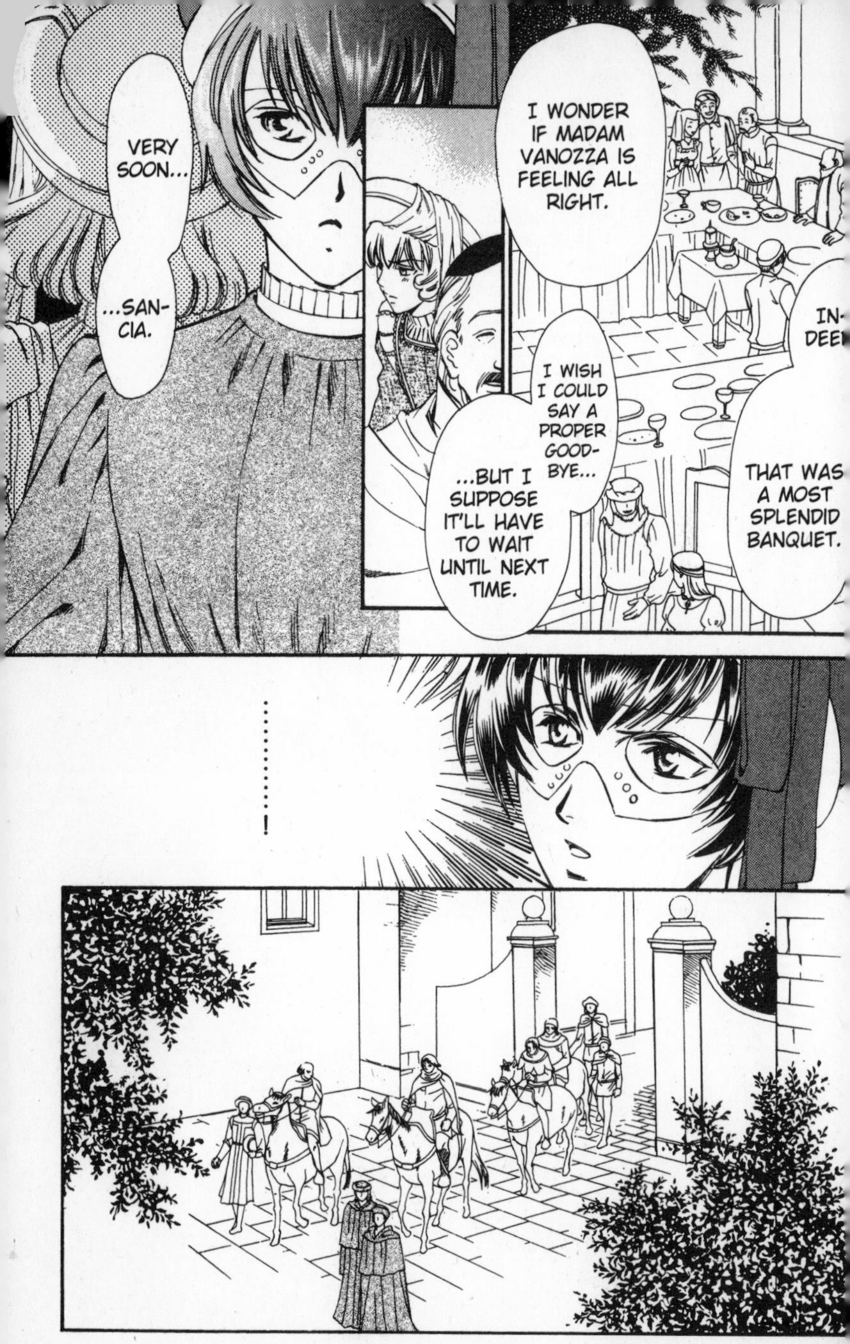
I WONDER IF MADAM VANOZZA IS FEELING ALL RIGHT.
IN-DEE
THAT WAS A MOST SPLENDID BANQUET.
I WISH I COULD SAY A PROPER GOOD-BYE...
...BUT I SUPPOSE IT'LL HAVE TO WAIT UNTIL NEXT TIME.
VERY SOON...
...SAN-CIA.
......!

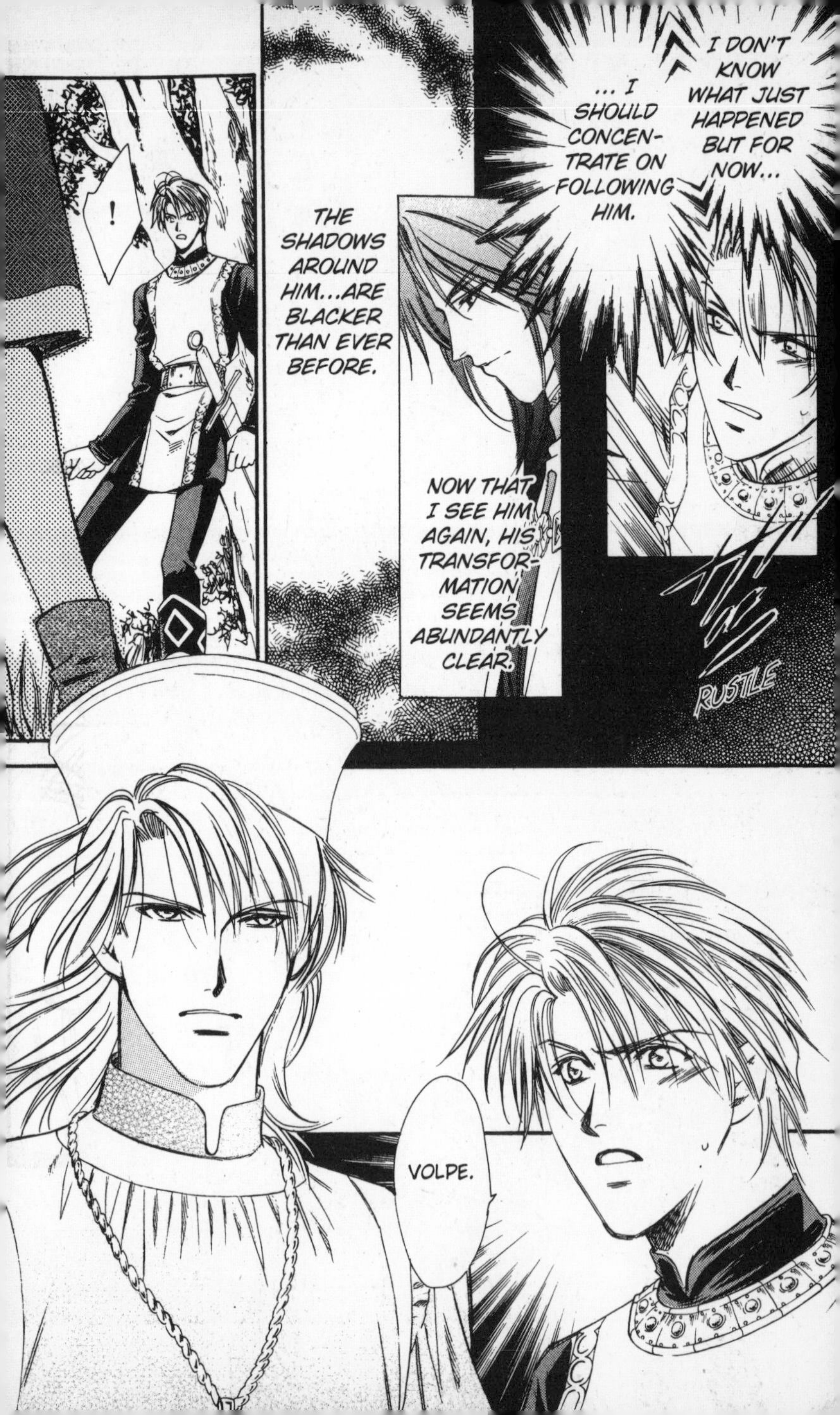

I DON'T KNOW WHAT JUST HAPPENED BUT FOR NOW...
... I SHOULD CONCENTRATE ON FOLLOWING HIM.
RUSTLE
NOW THAT I SEE HIM AGAIN, HIS TRANSFORMATION SEEMS ABUNDANTLY CLEAR.
THE SHADOWS AROUND HIM...ARE BLACKER THAN EVER BEFORE.
!
VOLPE.

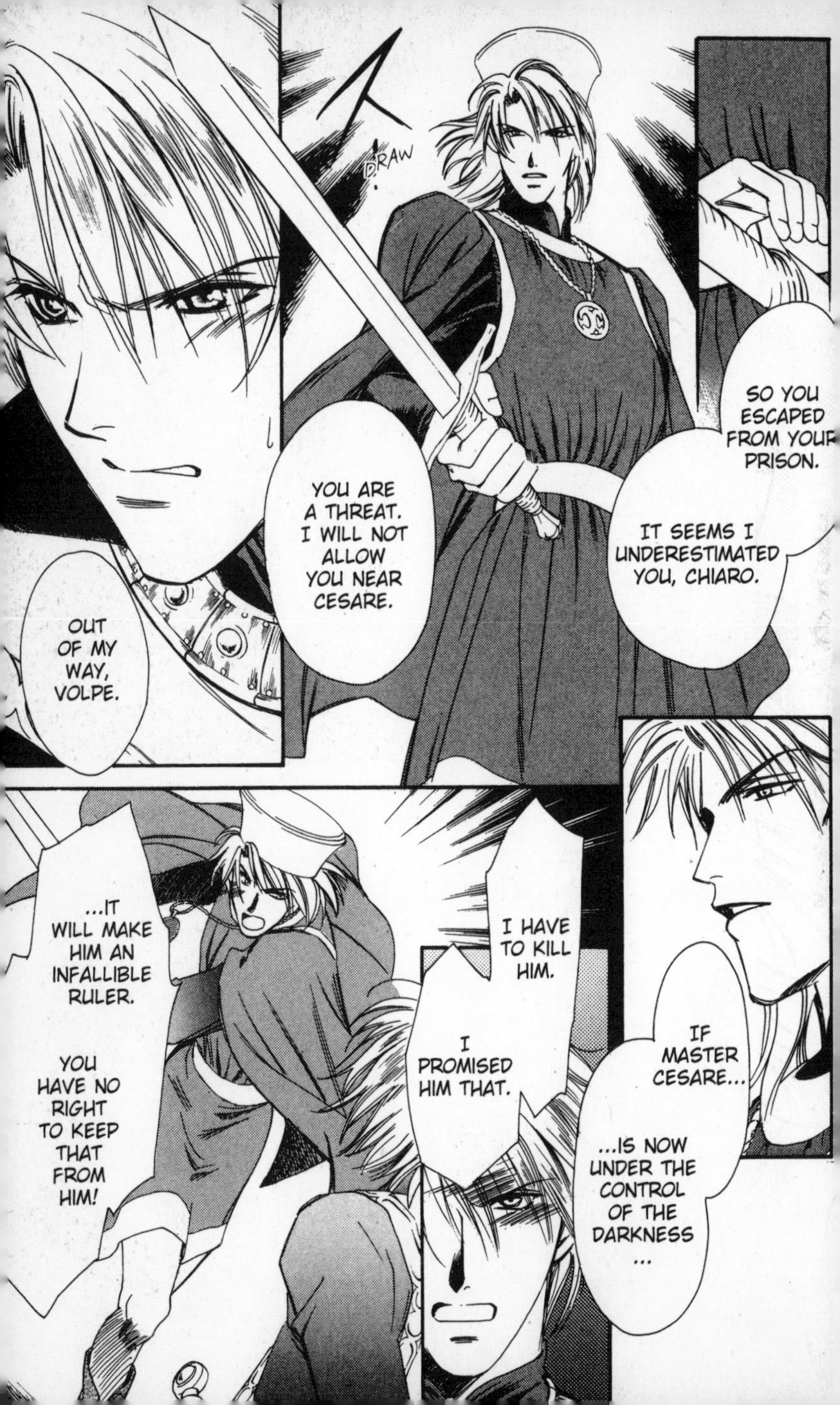
DRAW
SO YOU ESCAPED FROM YOUR PRISON.
IT SEEMS I UNDERESTIMATED YOU, CHIARO.
YOU ARE A THREAT. I WILL NOT ALLOW YOU NEAR CESARE.
OUT OF MY WAY, VOLPE.
IF MASTER CESARE...
...IS NOW UNDER THE CONTROL OF THE DARKNESS ...
I HAVE TO KILL HIM.
I PROMISED HIM THAT.
...IT WILL MAKE HIM AN INFALLIBLE RULER.
YOU HAVE NO RIGHT TO KEEP THAT FROM HIM!

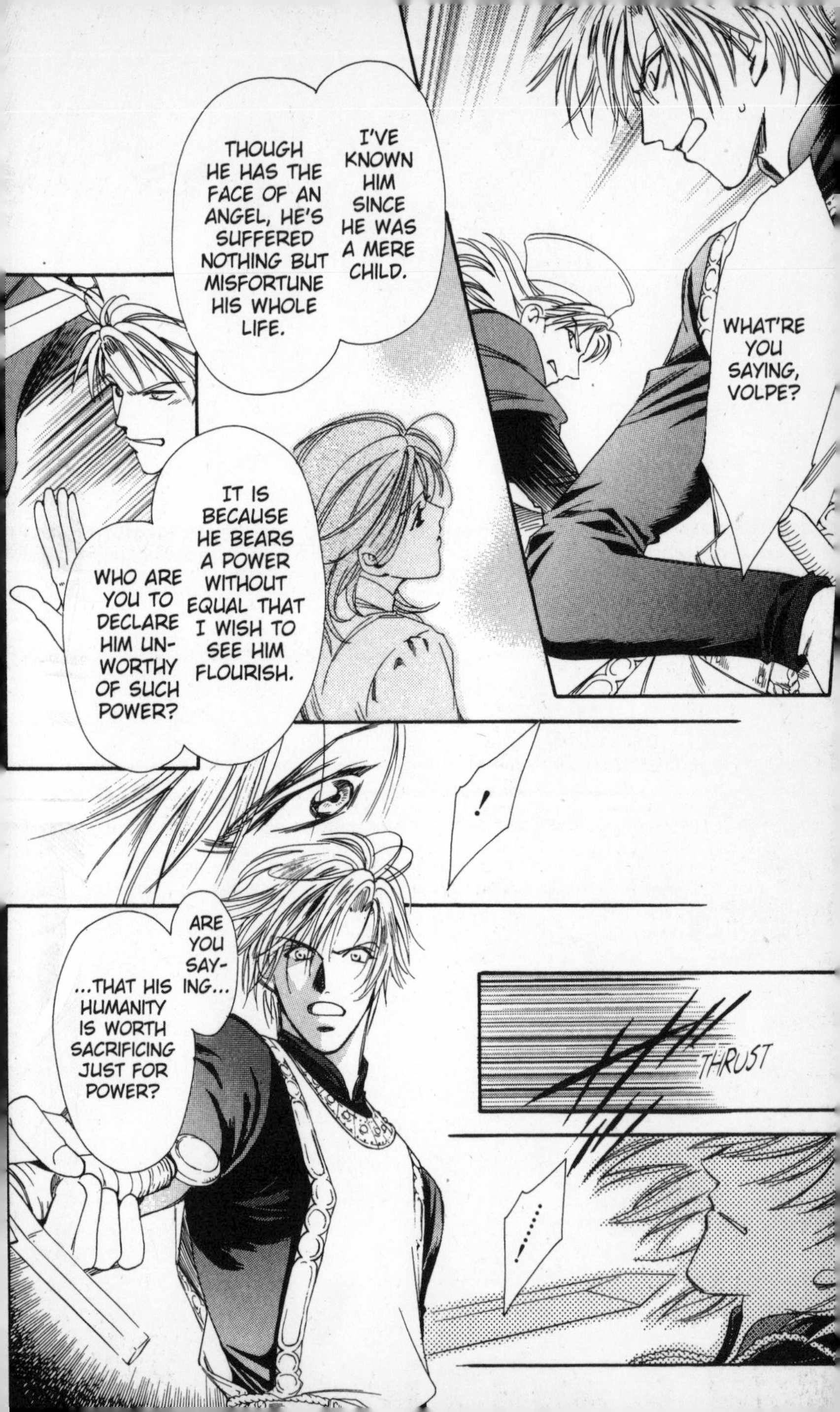
I'VE KNOWN HIM SINCE HE WAS A MERE CHILD.
THOUGH HE HAS THE FACE OF AN ANGEL, HE'S SUFFERED NOTHING BUT MISFORTUNE HIS WHOLE LIFE.
WHAT'RE YOU SAYING, VOLPE?
IT IS BECAUSE HE BEARS A POWER WITHOUT EQUAL THAT I WISH TO SEE HIM FLOURISH.
WHO ARE YOU TO DECLARE HIM UN-WORTHY OF SUCH POWER?
!
THRUST
......!
ARE YOU SAY-ING...
...THAT HIS HUMANITY IS WORTH SACRIFICING JUST FOR POWER?

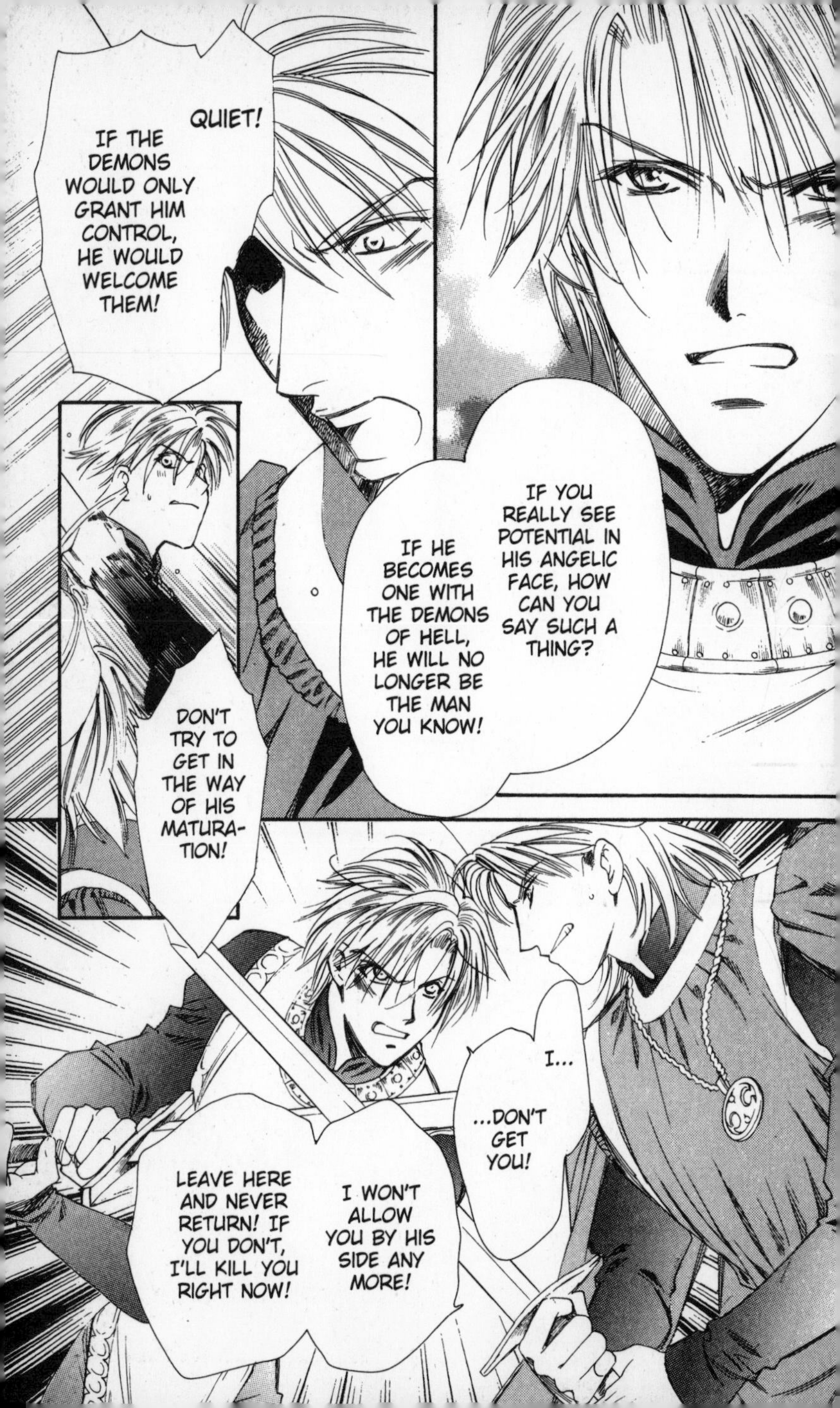
IF YOU REALLY SEE POTENTIAL IN HIS ANGELIC FACE, HOW CAN YOU SAY SUCH A THING?
IF HE BECOMES ONE WITH THE DEMONS OF HELL, HE WILL NO LONGER BE THE MAN YOU KNOW!
QUIET!
IF THE DEMONS WOULD ONLY GRANT HIM CONTROL, HE WOULD WELCOME THEM!
DON'T TRY TO GET IN THE WAY OF HIS MATURA-TION!
I...
...DON'T GET YOU!
I WON'T ALLOW YOU BY HIS SIDE ANY MORE!
LEAVE HERE AND NEVER RETURN! IF YOU DON'T, I'LL KILL YOU RIGHT NOW!

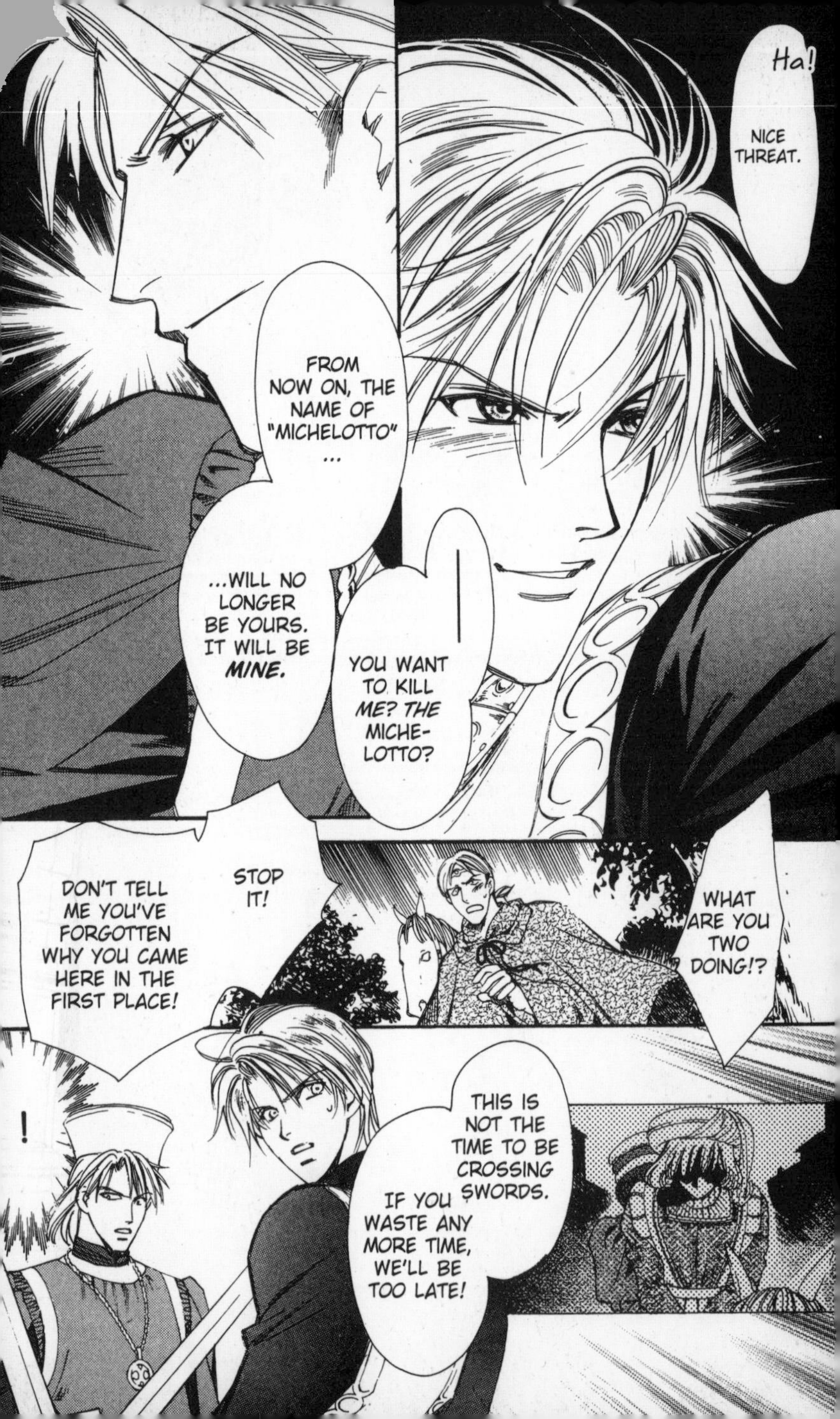
Ha!
NICE THREAT.
|
YOU WANT TO KILL ME? THE MICHE-LOTTO?
FROM NOW ON, THE NAME OF "MICHELOTTO" ...
...WILL NO LONGER BE YOURS. IT WILL BE MINE.
WHAT ARE YOU TWO DOING!?
STOP IT!
DON'T TELL ME YOU'VE FORGOTTEN WHY YOU CAME HERE IN THE FIRST PLACE!
THIS IS NOT THE TIME TO BE CROSSING SWORDS.
IF YOU WASTE ANY MORE TIME, WE'LL BE TOO LATE!
!

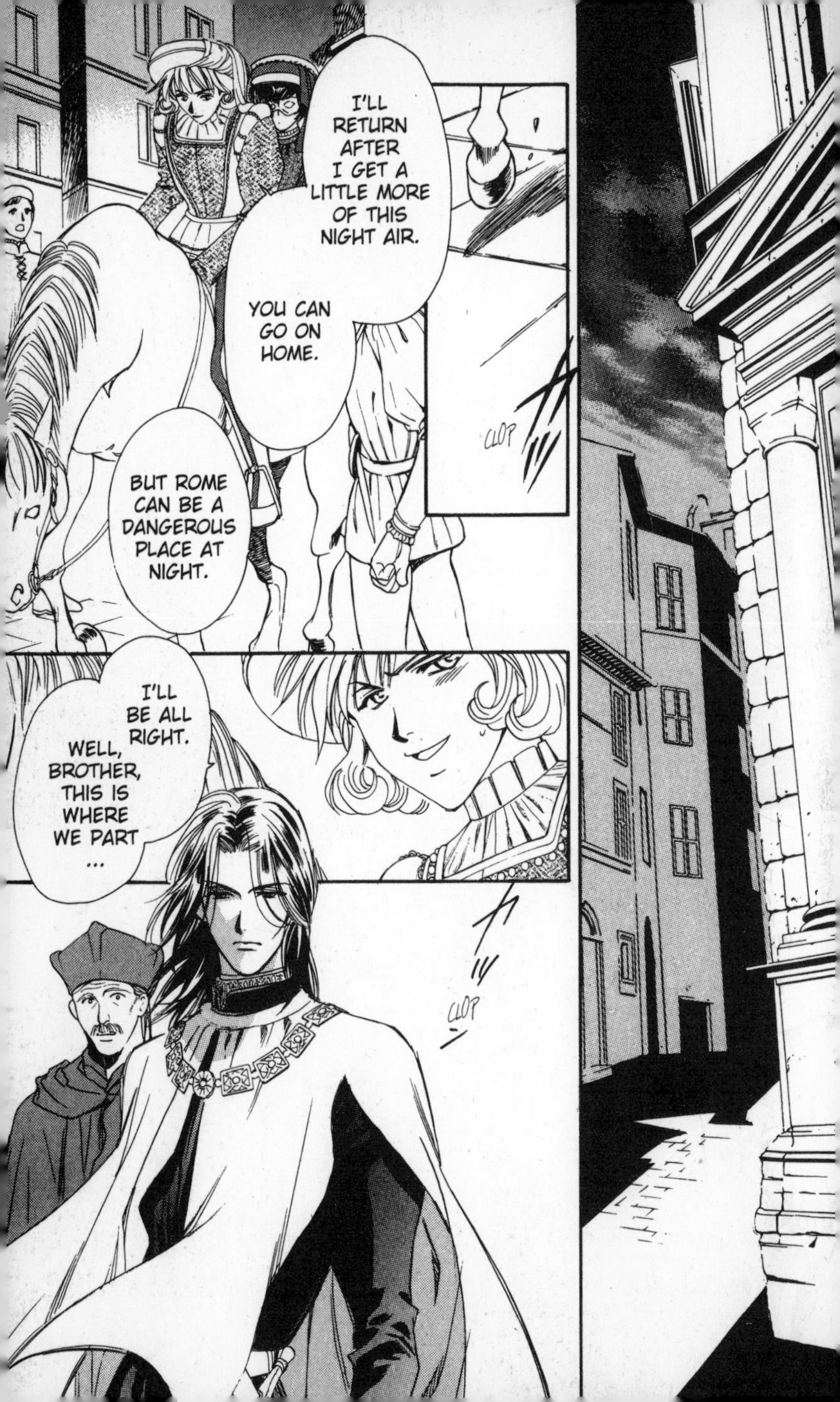
I'LL RETURN AFTER I GET A LITTLE MORE OF THIS NIGHT AIR.
YOU CAN GO ON HOME.
CLOP
BUT ROME CAN BE A DANGEROUS PLACE AT NIGHT.
I'LL BE ALL RIGHT.
WELL, BROTHER, THIS IS WHERE WE PART ...
CLOP

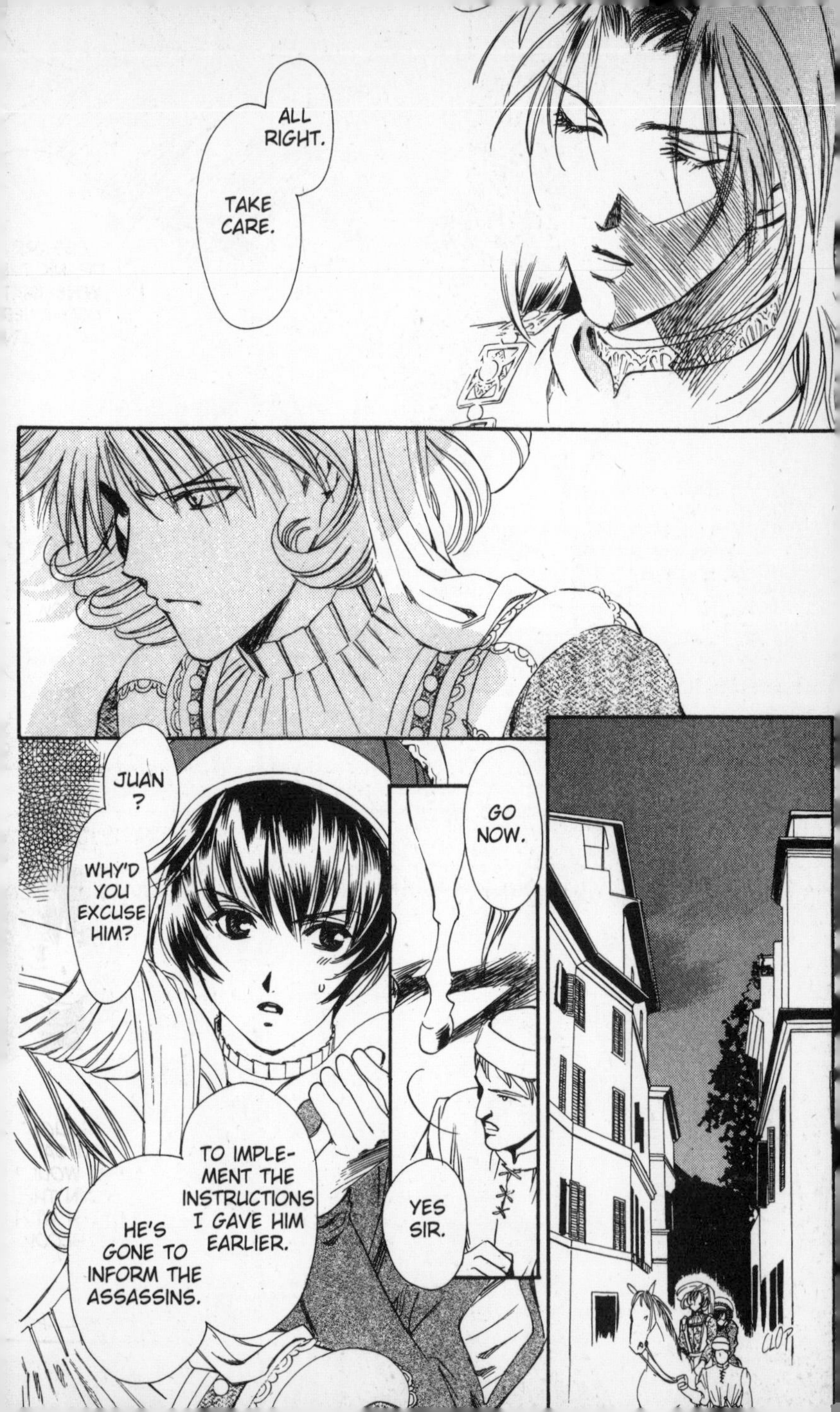
ALL RIGHT.
TAKE CARE.
CLOP
GO NOW.
YES SIR.
JUAN ?
WHY'D YOU EXCUSE HIM?
TO IMPLEMENT THE INSTRUCTIONS I GAVE HIM EARLIER.
HE'S GONE TO INFORM THE ASSASSINS.

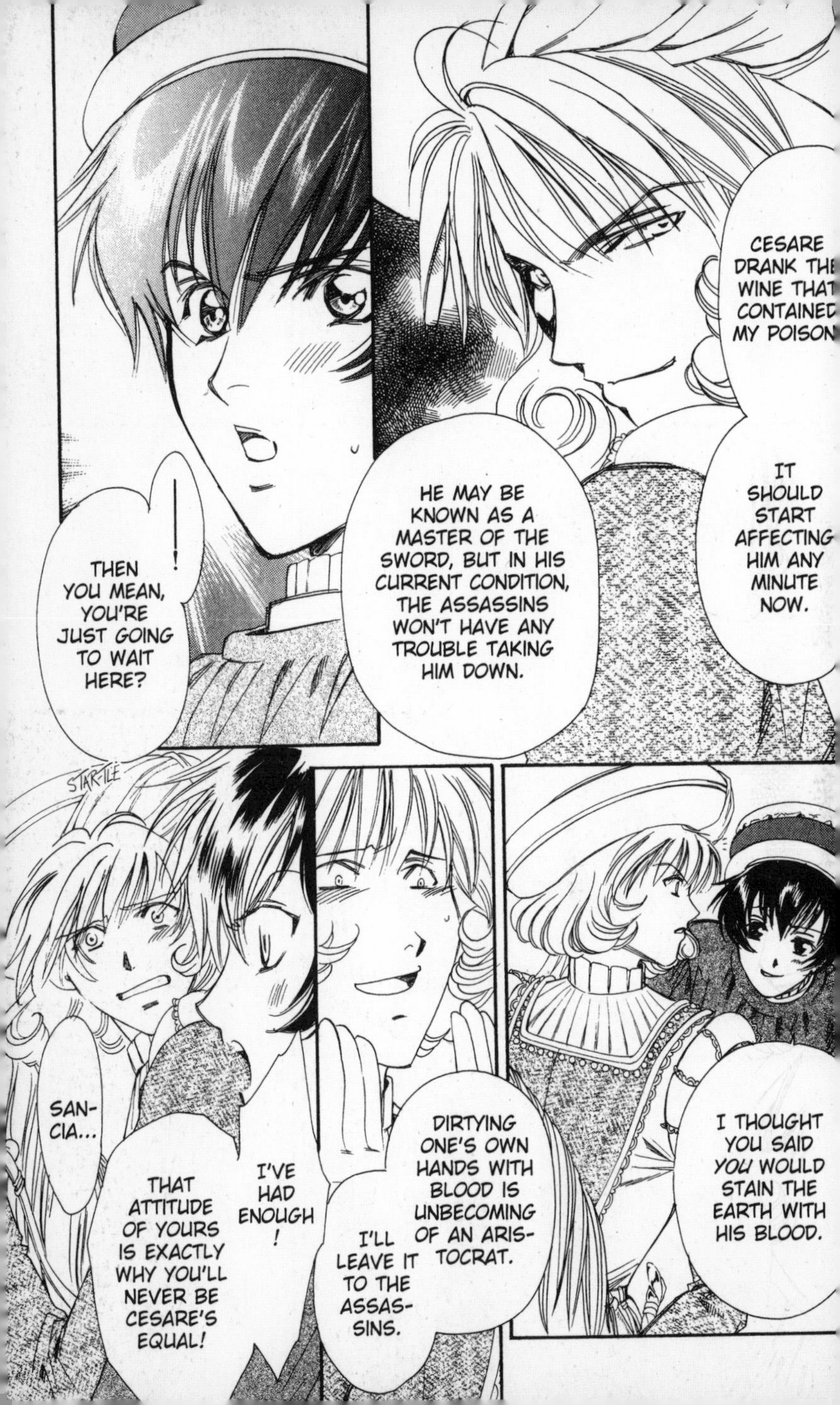
CESARE DRANK THE WINE THAT CONTAINED MY POISON
IT SHOULD START AFFECTING HIM ANY MINUTE NOW.
HE MAY BE KNOWN AS A MASTER OF THE SWORD, BUT IN HIS CURRENT CONDITION, THE ASSASSINS WON'T HAVE ANY TROUBLE TAKING HIM DOWN.
!
THEN YOU MEAN, YOU'RE JUST GOING TO WAIT HERE?
I THOUGHT YOU SAID *YOU* WOULD STAIN THE EARTH WITH HIS BLOOD.
DIRTYING ONE'S OWN HANDS WITH BLOOD IS UNBECOMING OF AN ARIS-TOCRAT.
I'LL LEAVE IT TO THE ASSAS-SINS.
STAR-TLE
I'VE HAD ENOUGH!
THAT ATTITUDE OF YOURS IS EXACTLY WHY YOU'LL NEVER BE CESARE'S EQUAL!
SAN-CIA...

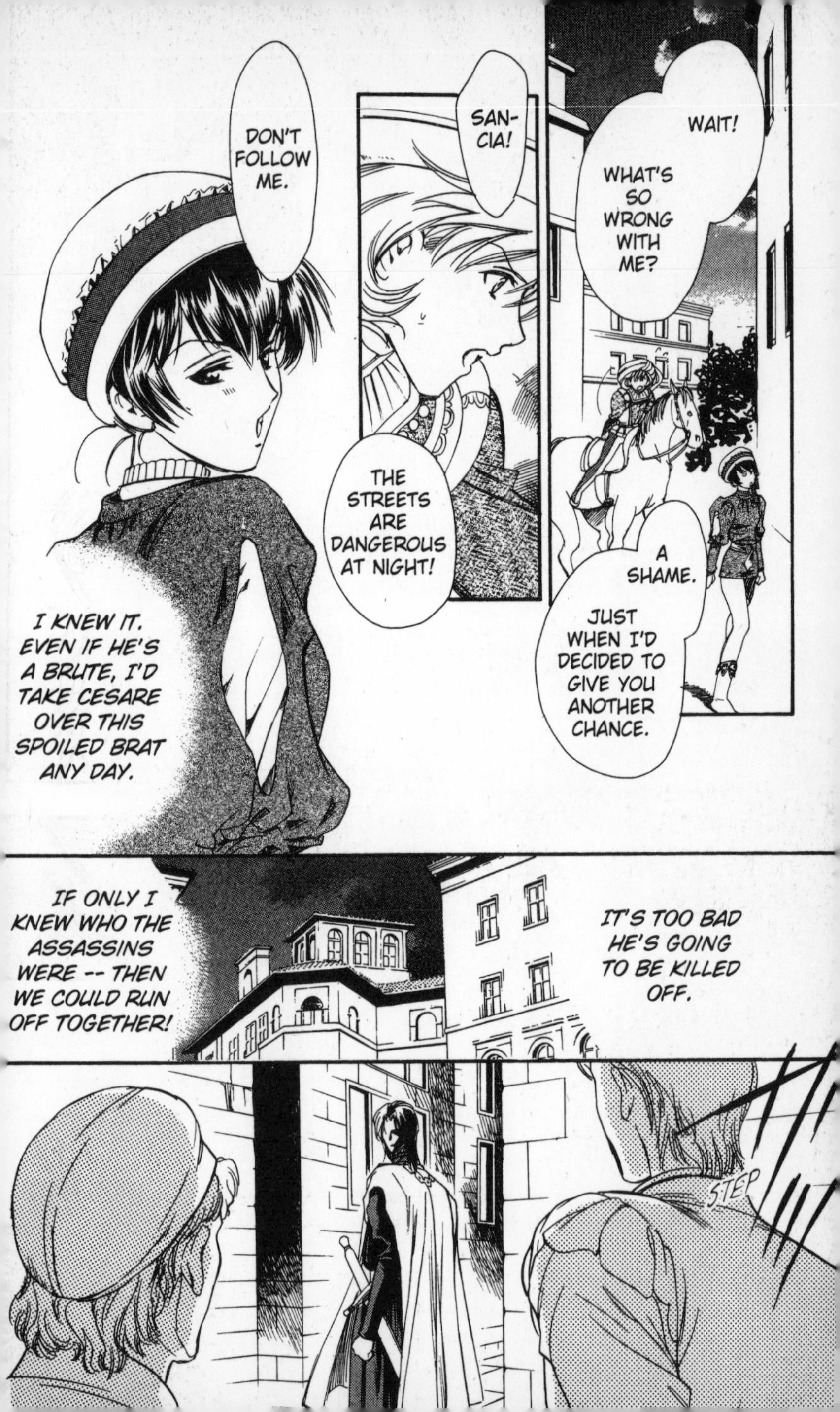
WAIT!
WHAT'S SO WRONG WITH ME?
A SHAME.
JUST WHEN I'D DECIDED TO GIVE YOU ANOTHER CHANCE.
SAN-CIA!
THE STREETS ARE DANGEROUS AT NIGHT!
DON'T FOLLOW ME.
I KNEW IT. EVEN IF HE'S A BRUTE, I'D TAKE CESARE OVER THIS SPOILED BRAT ANY DAY.
IT'S TOO BAD HE'S GOING TO BE KILLED OFF.
IF ONLY I KNEW WHO THE ASSASSINS WERE -- THEN WE COULD RUN OFF TOGETHER!
STEP

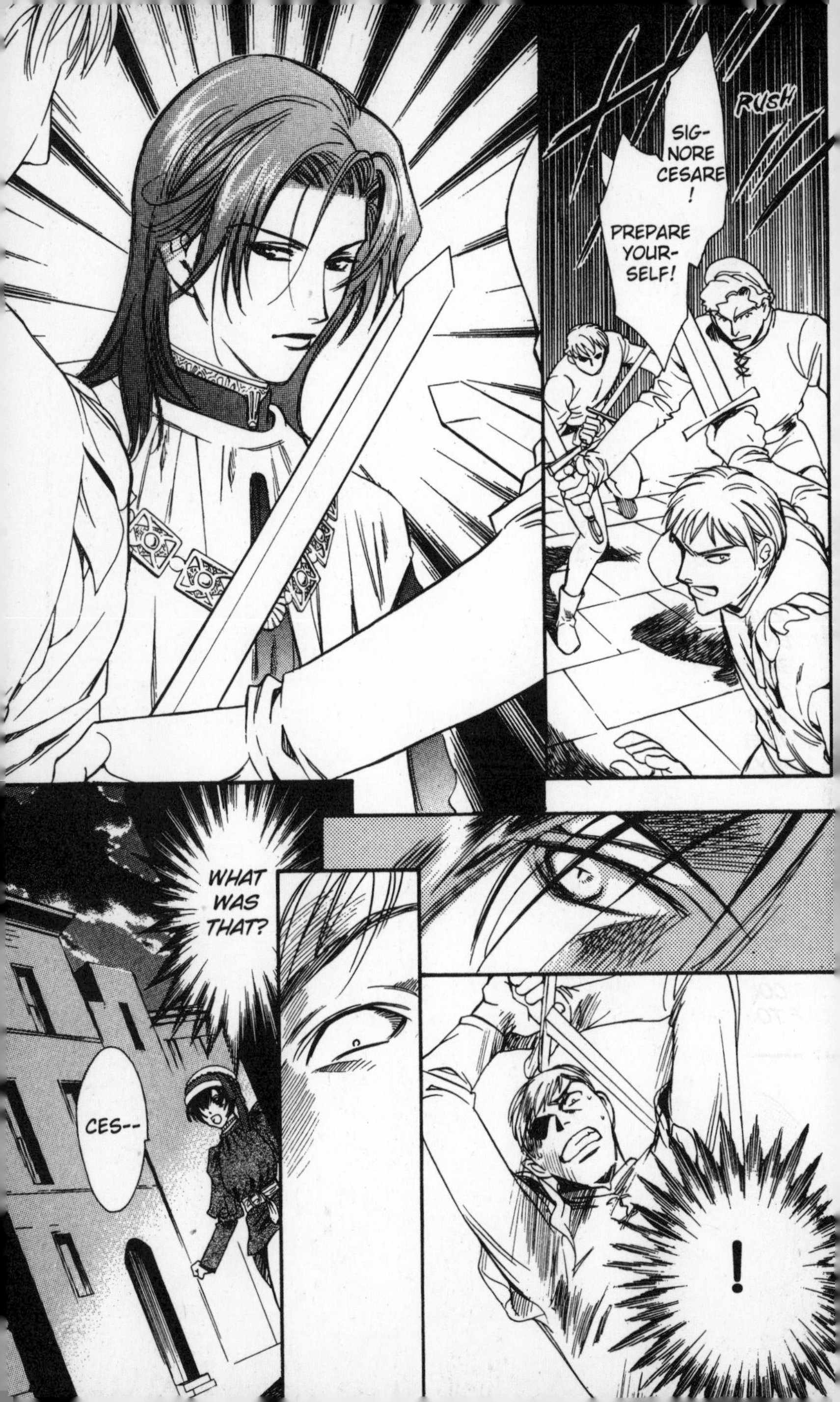
RUSH
SIG-NORE CESARE!
PREPARE YOUR-SELF!
!
WHAT WAS THAT?
CES--

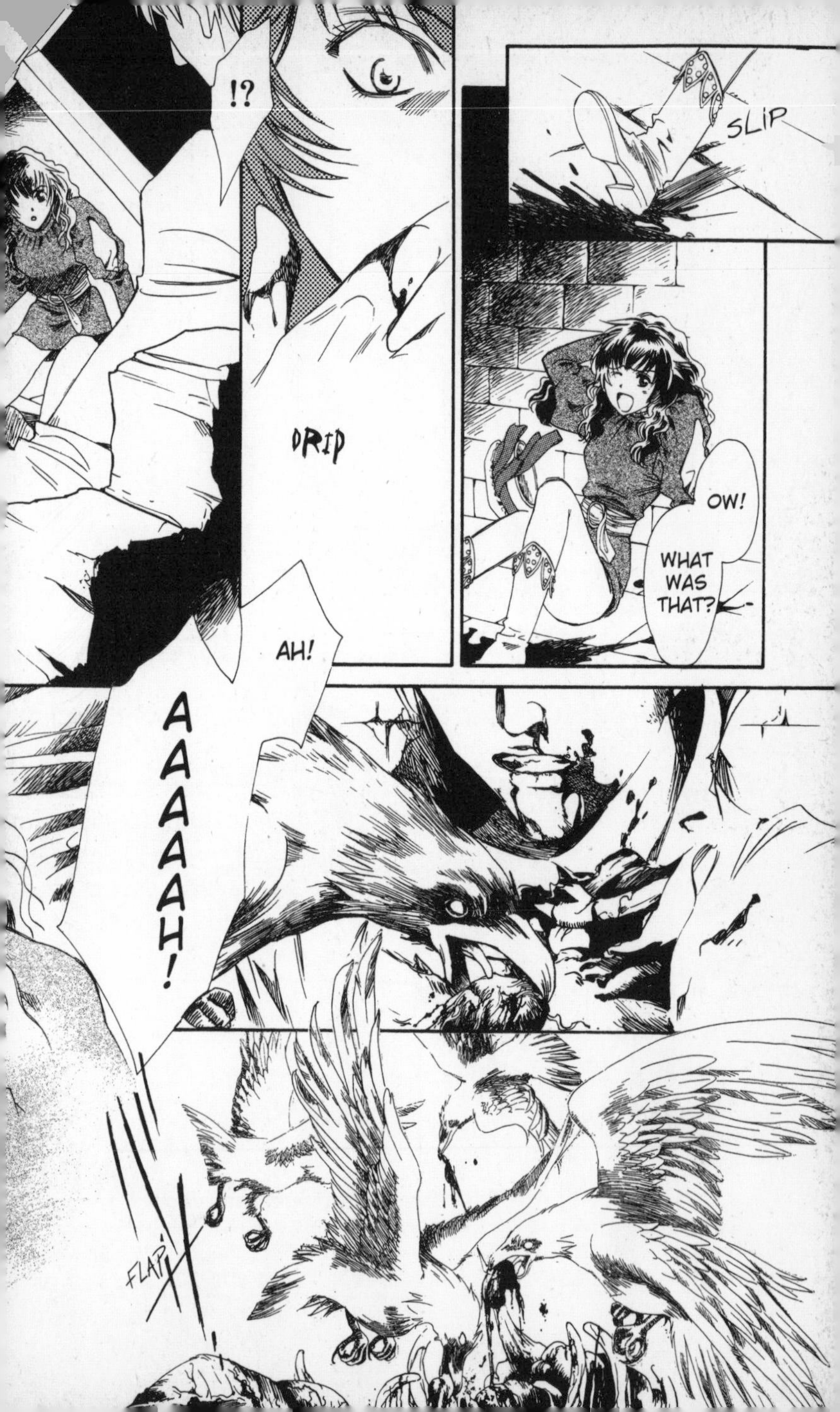
SLIP
OW!
WHAT WAS THAT?
!?
DRIP
AH!
AAAAAH!
FLAP

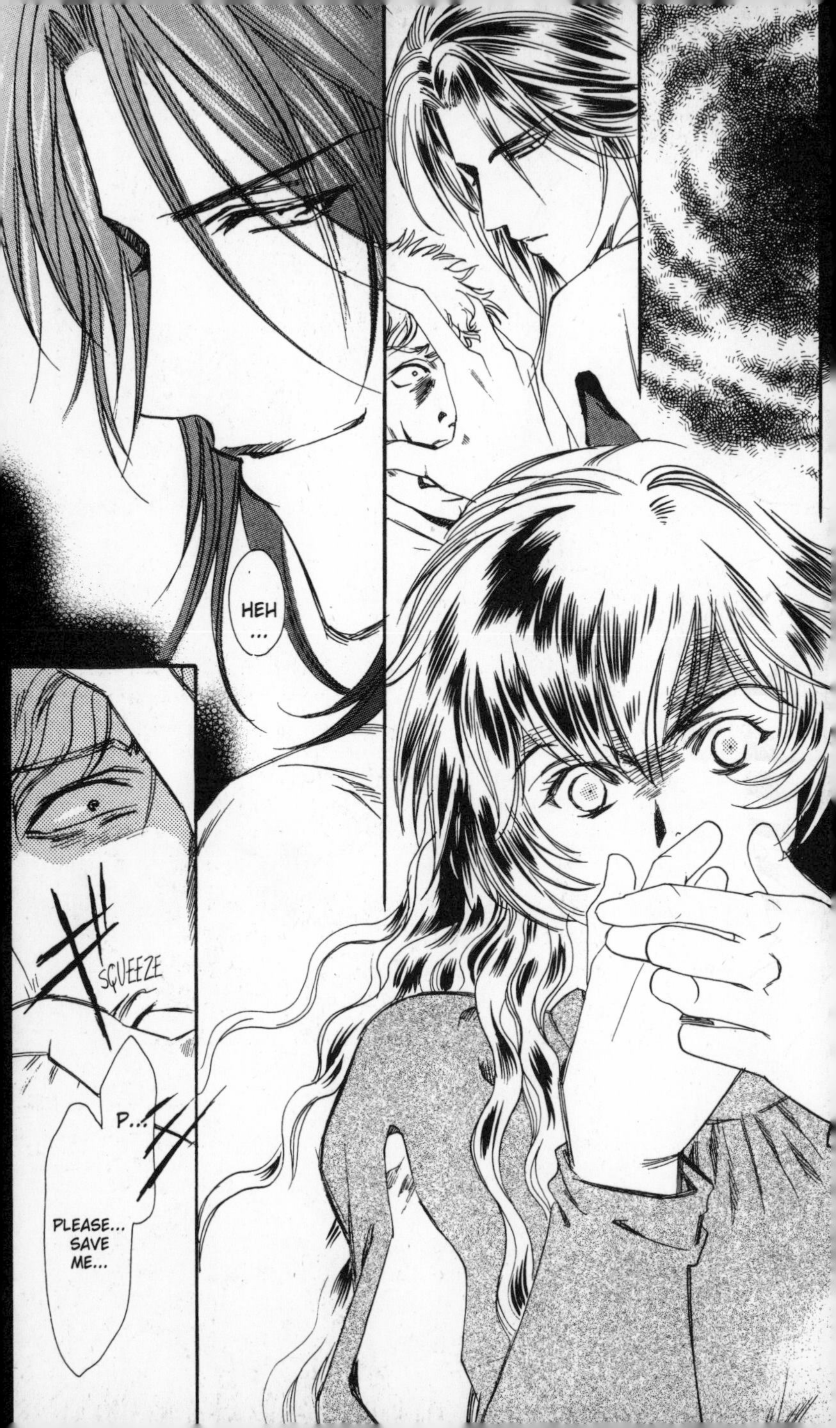
HEH ...
SQUEEZE
P...
PLEASE... SAVE ME...

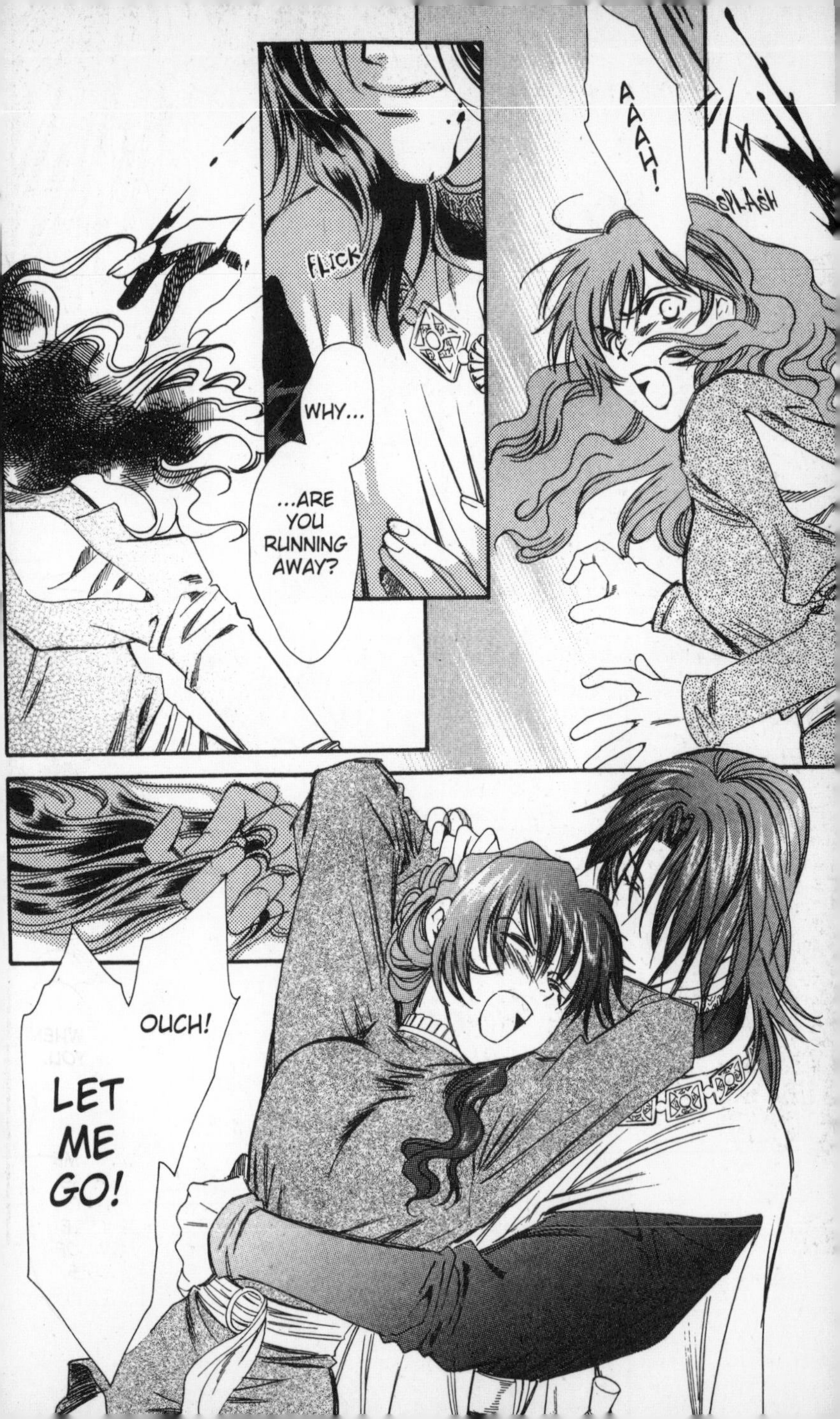
AAAH!
SPLASH
FLICK
WHY...
...ARE YOU RUNNING AWAY?
OUCH!
LET ME GO!

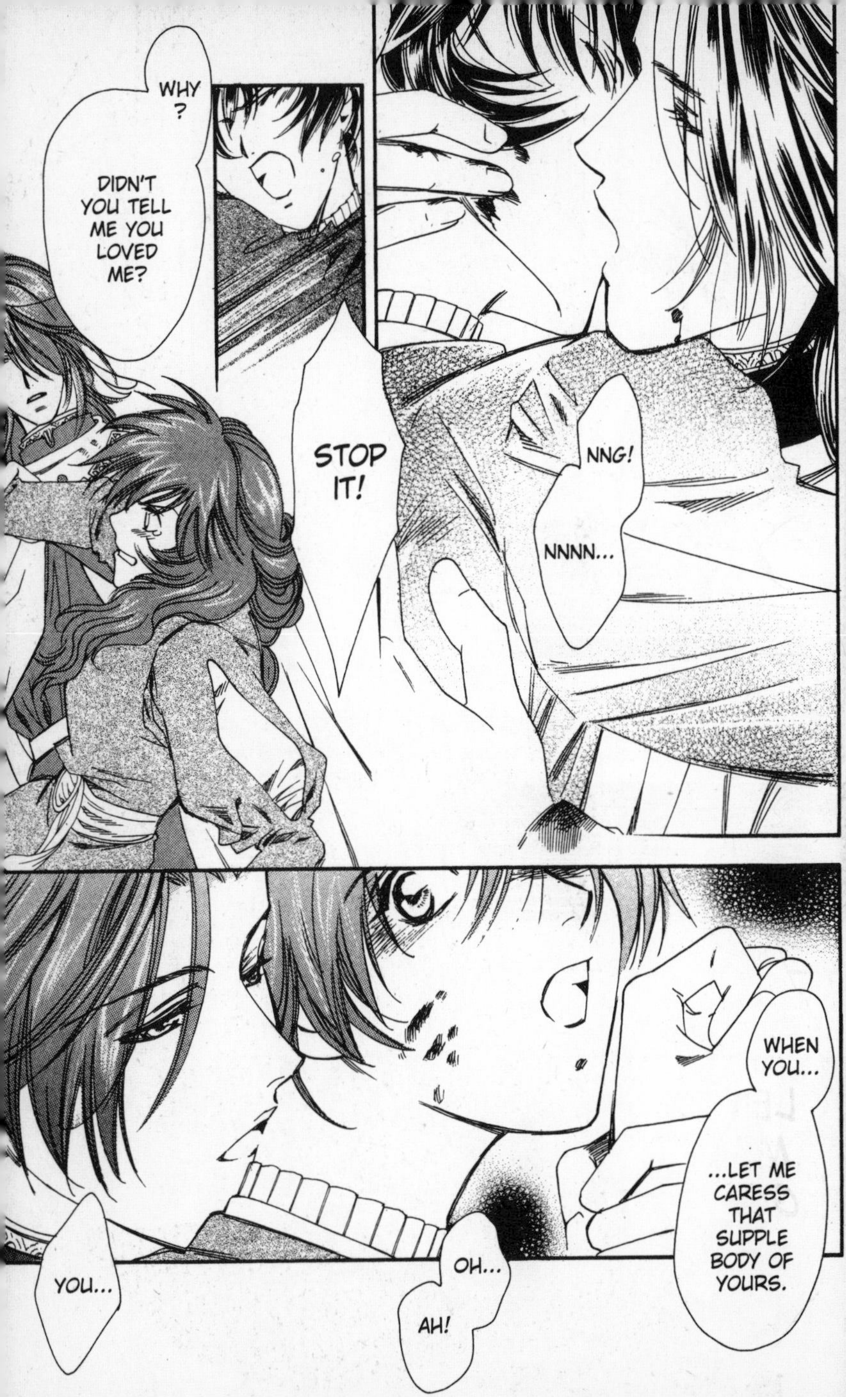
NNG!
NNNN...
STOP IT!
WHY?
DIDN'T YOU TELL ME YOU LOVED ME?
WHEN YOU...
...LET ME CARESS THAT SUPPLE BODY OF YOURS.
OH...
AH!
YOU...

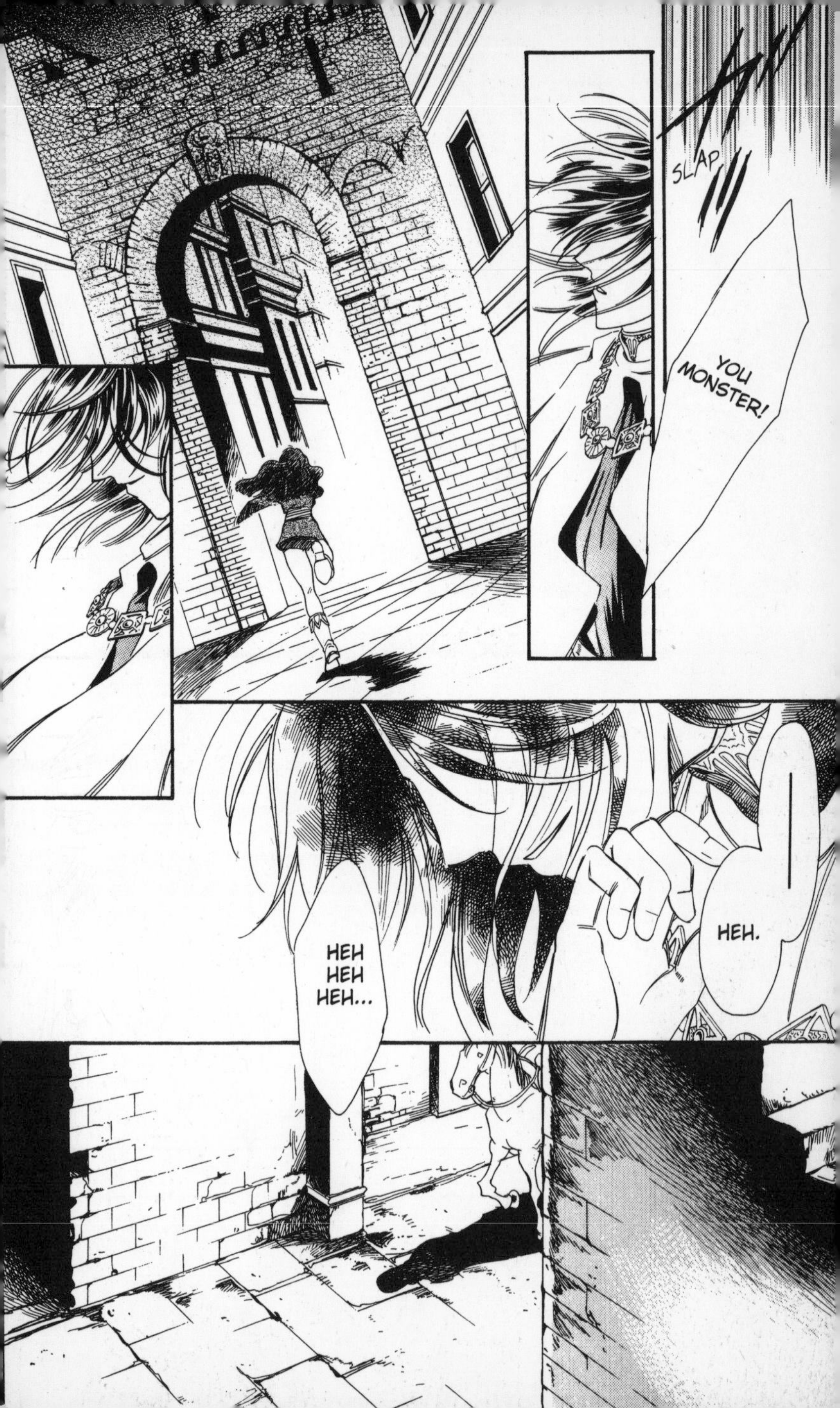
SLAP
YOU MONSTER!
HEH.
HEH HEH HEH...

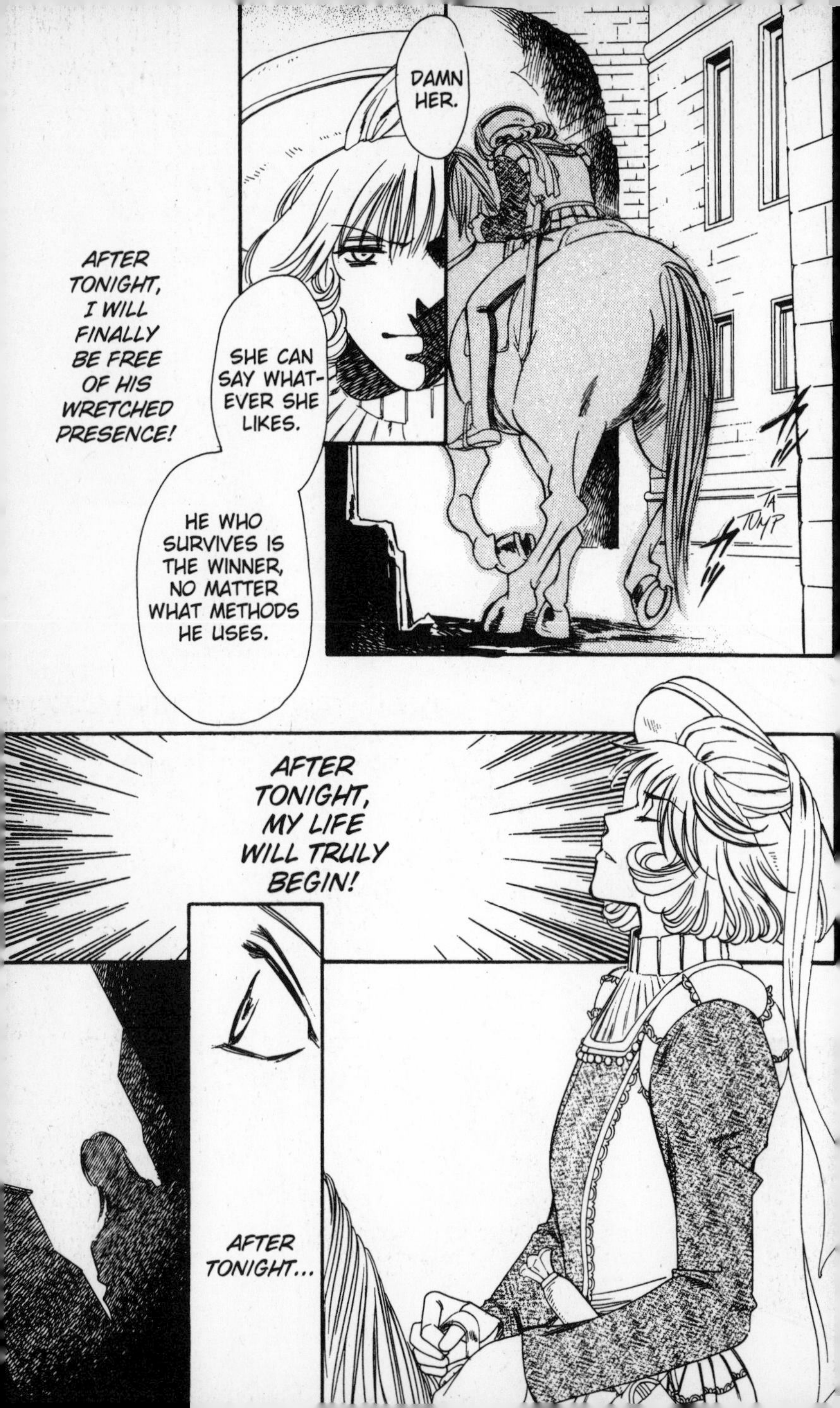
TA TUMP
DAMN HER.
SHE CAN SAY WHATEVER SHE LIKES.
HE WHO SURVIVES IS THE WINNER, NO MATTER WHAT METHODS HE USES.
AFTER TONIGHT, I WILL FINALLY BE FREE OF HIS WRETCHED PRESENCE!
AFTER TONIGHT, MY LIFE WILL TRULY BEGIN!
AFTER TONIGHT...

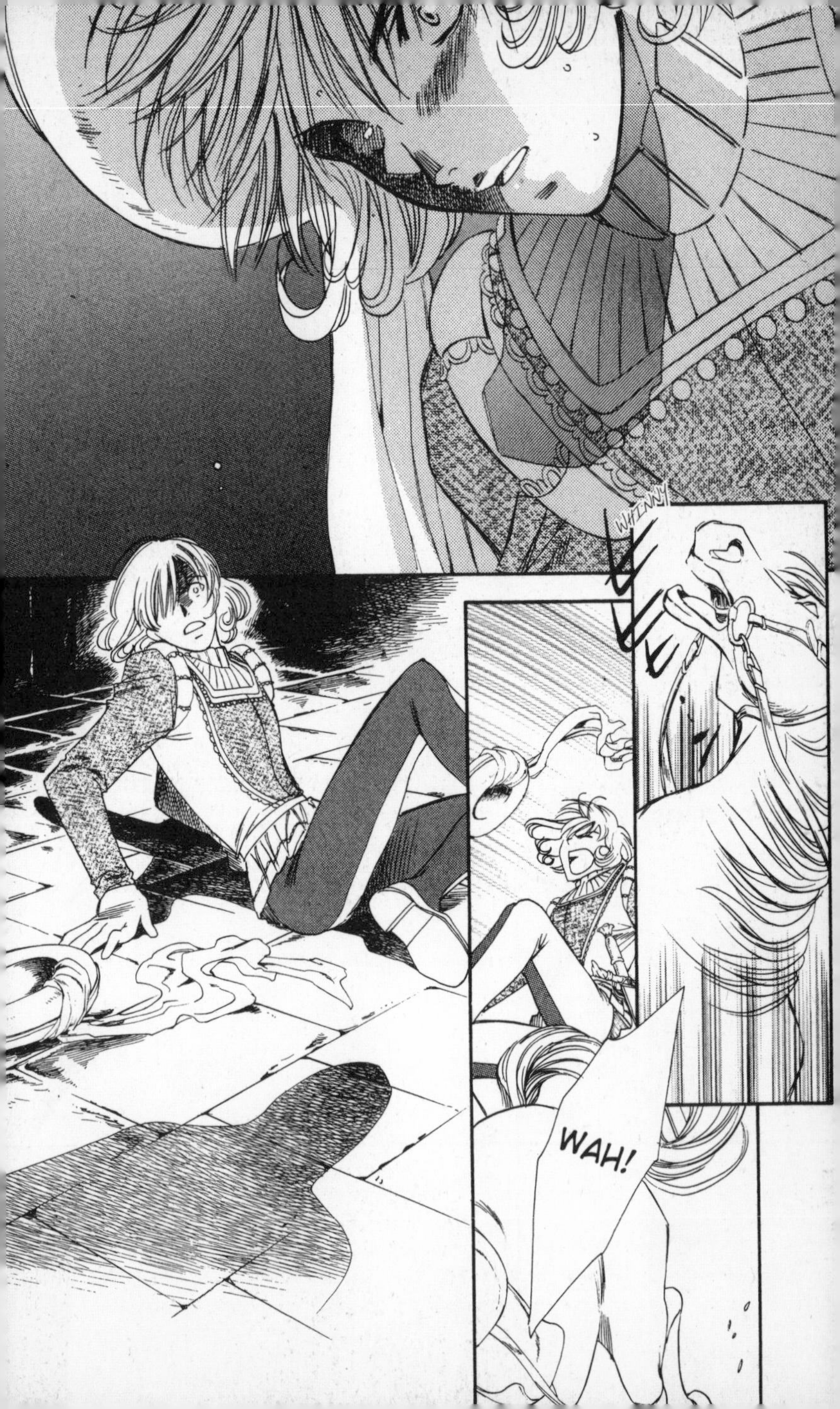
WHINNY
WAH!

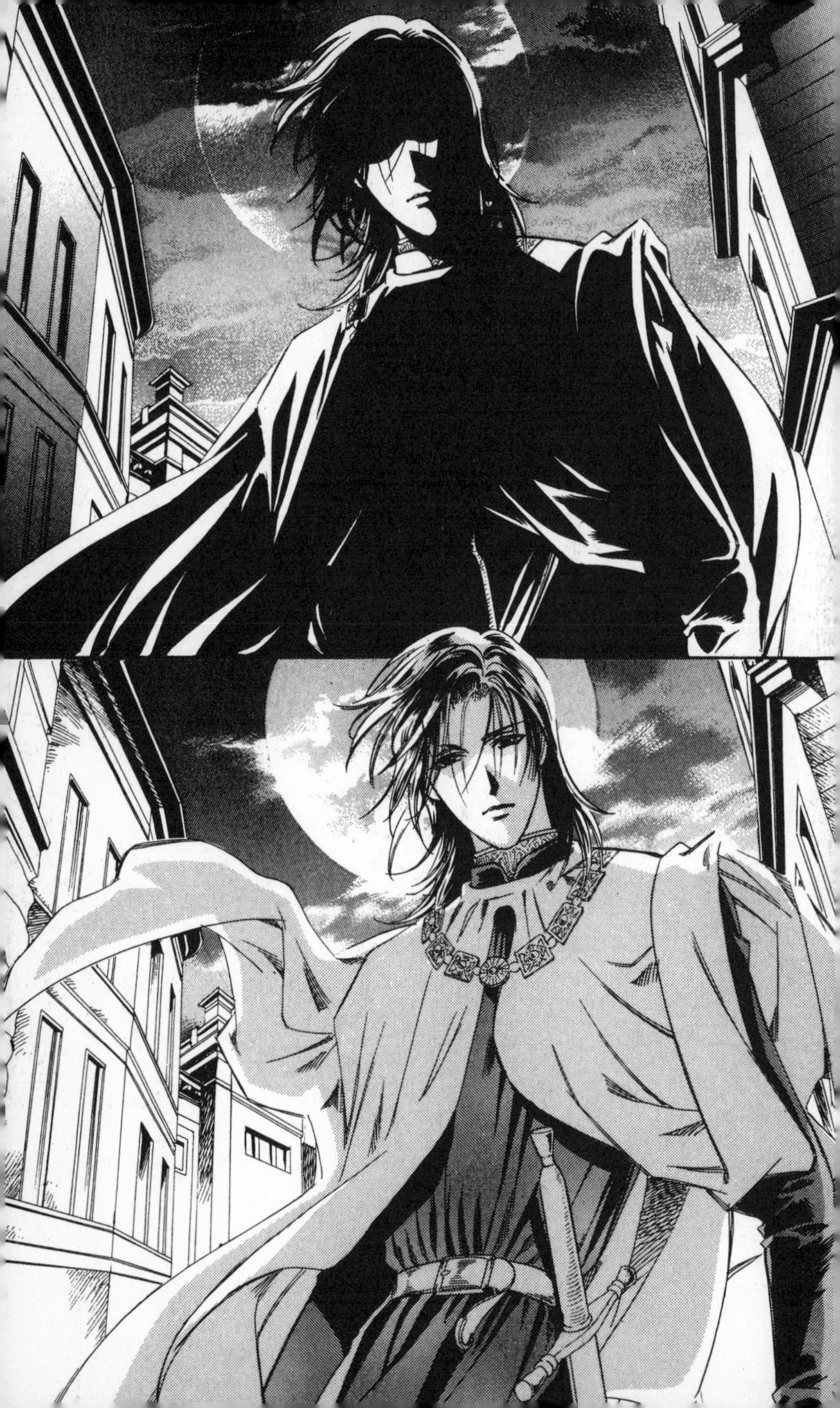

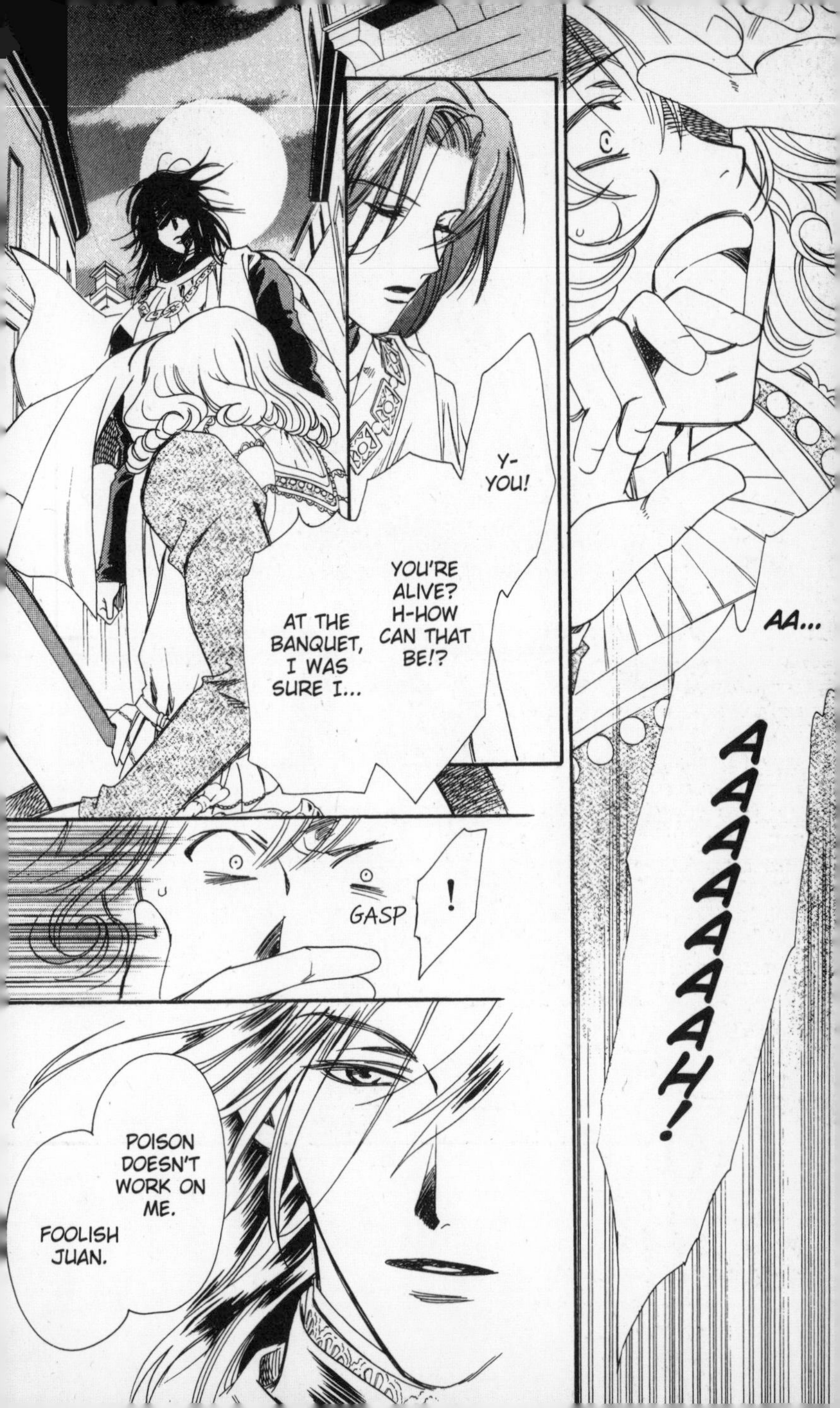
AA...
AAAAAAAAAH!
Y-
YOU!
YOU'RE ALIVE? H-HOW CAN THAT BE!?
AT THE BANQUET, I WAS SURE I...
!
GASP
POISON DOESN'T WORK ON ME.
FOOLISH JUAN.

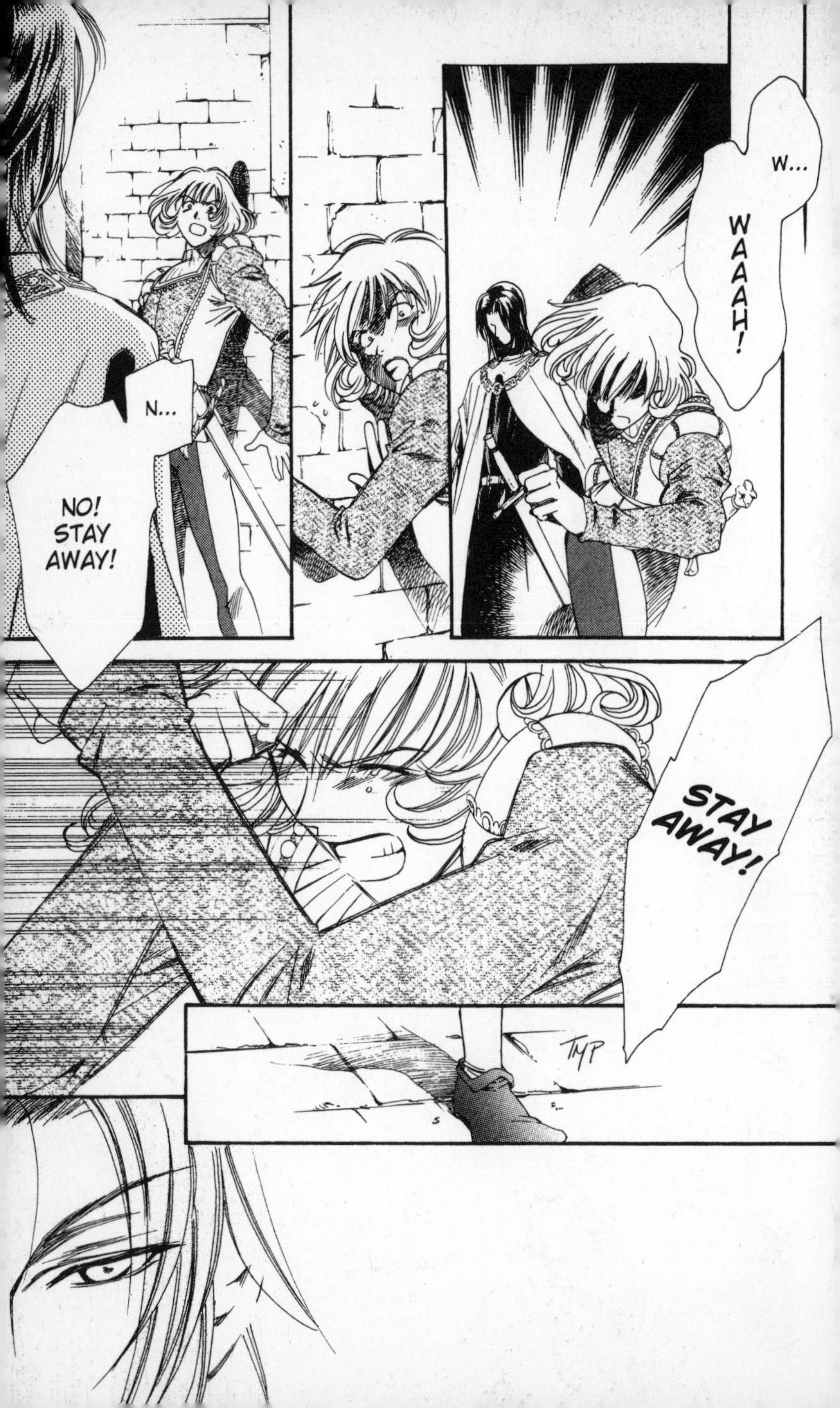
W...
WAAAAH!
N...
NO! STAY AWAY!
STAY AWAY!
TMP

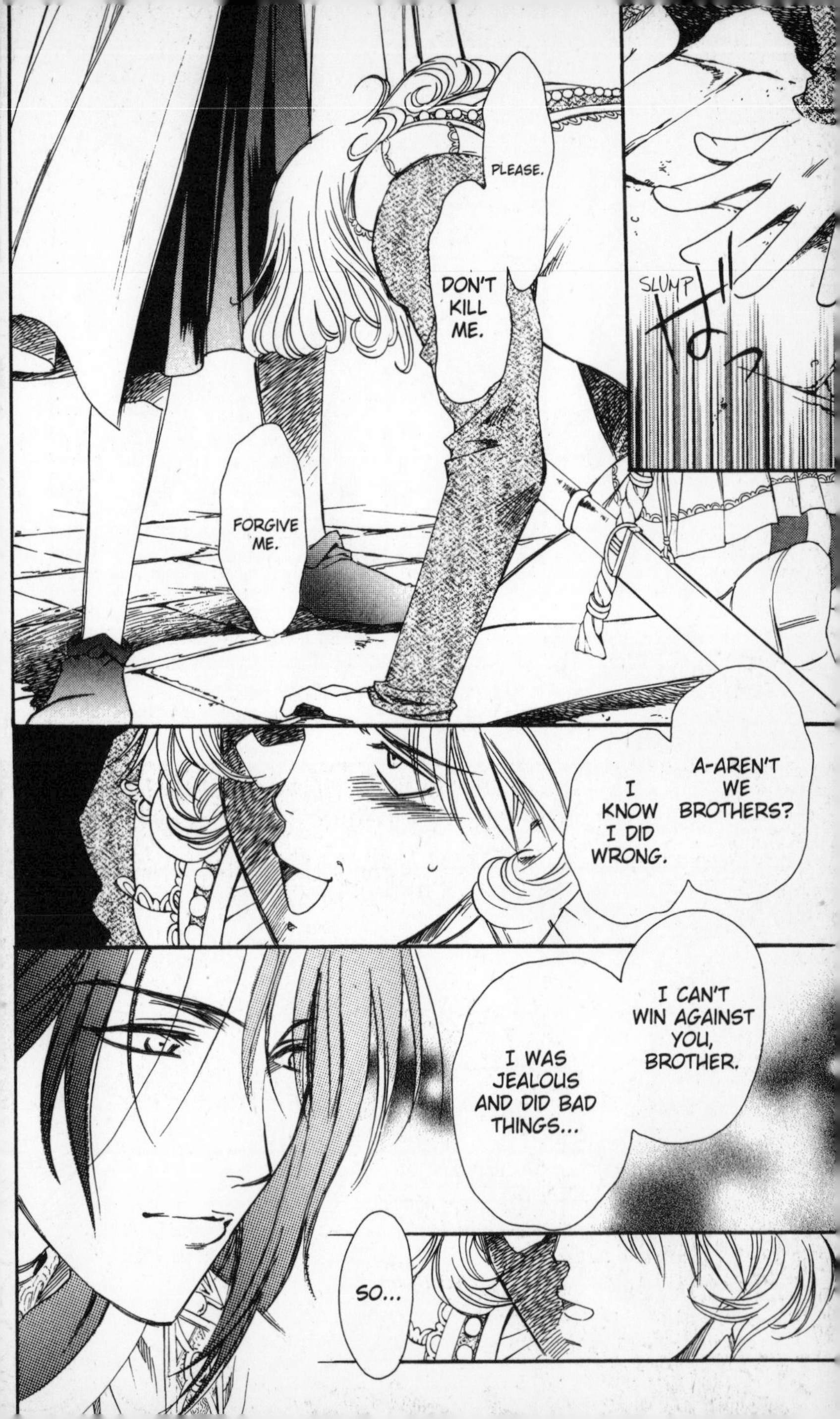
SLUMP
PLEASE.
DON'T KILL ME.
FORGIVE ME.
A-AREN'T WE BROTHERS?
I KNOW I DID WRONG.
I CAN'T WIN AGAINST YOU, BROTHER.
I WAS JEALOUS AND DID BAD THINGS...
SO...

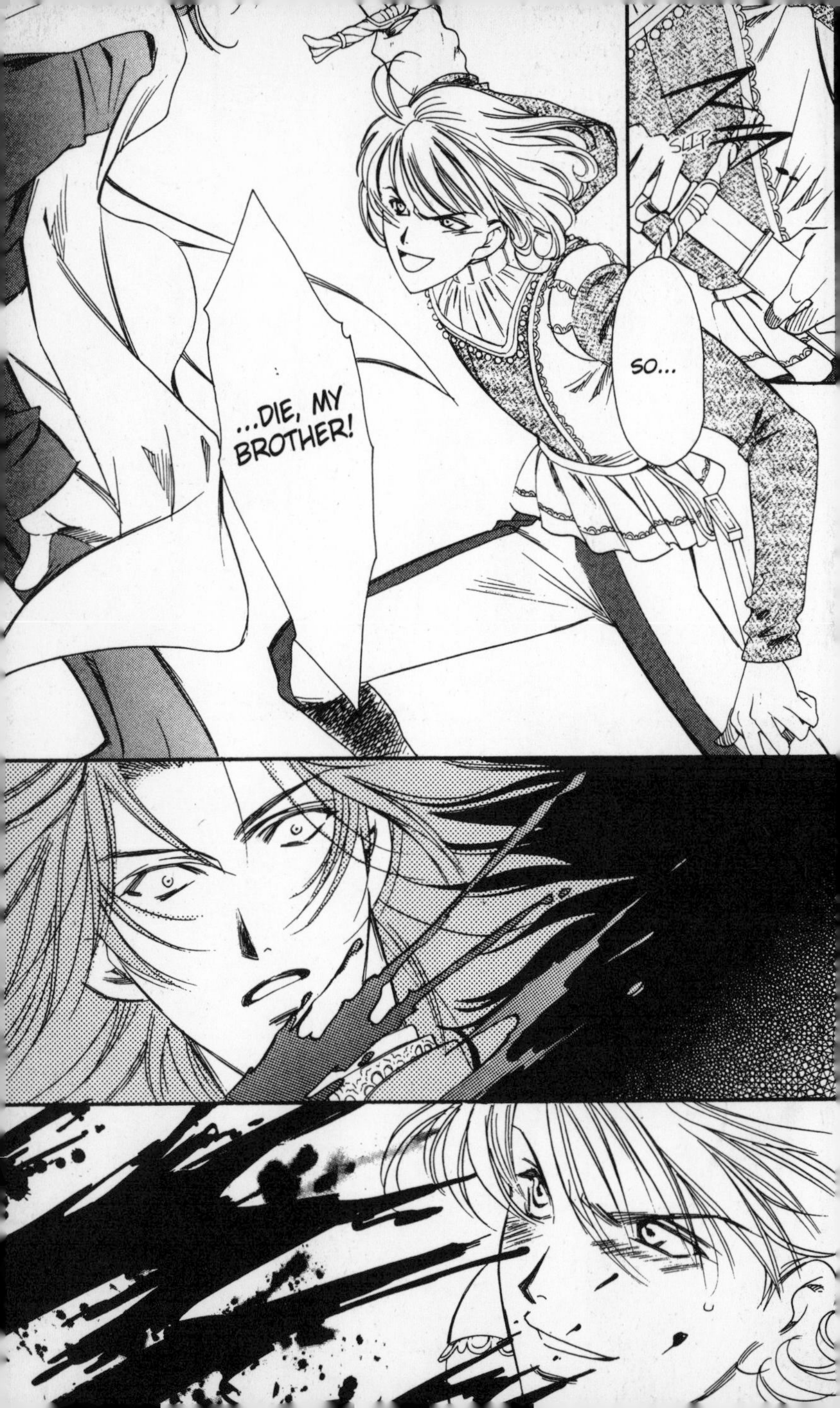
SLIP
SO...
...DIE, MY BROTHER!

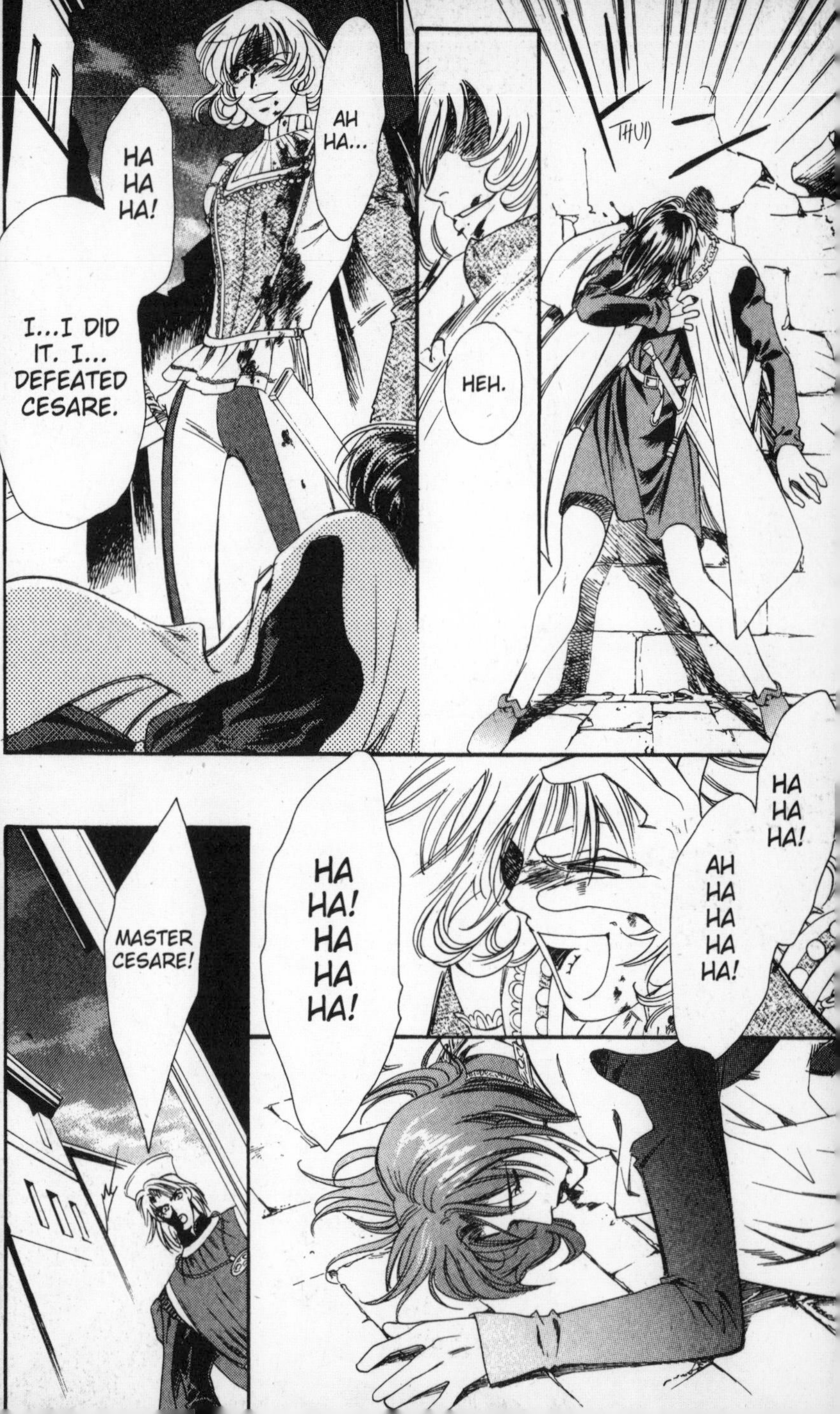
THUD
HEH.
AH HA...
HA HA HA!
I...I DID IT. I... DEFEATED CESARE.
HA HA HA!
AH HA HA HA HA HA!
HA HA! HA HA HA!
MASTER CESARE!

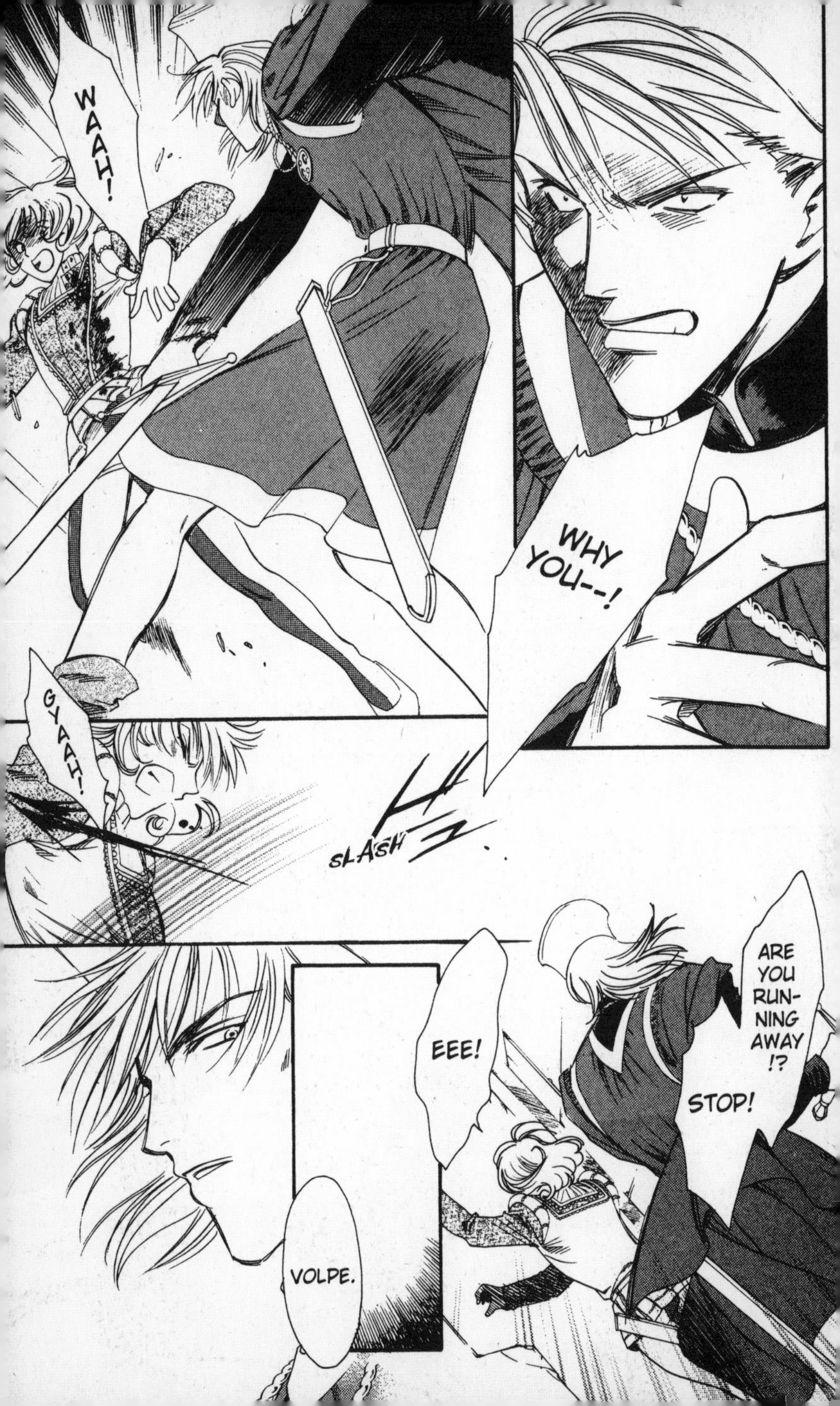
WHY YOU--!
WAAH!
GYAAH!
SLASH
ARE YOU RUNNING AWAY!?
STOP!
EEE!
VOLPE.

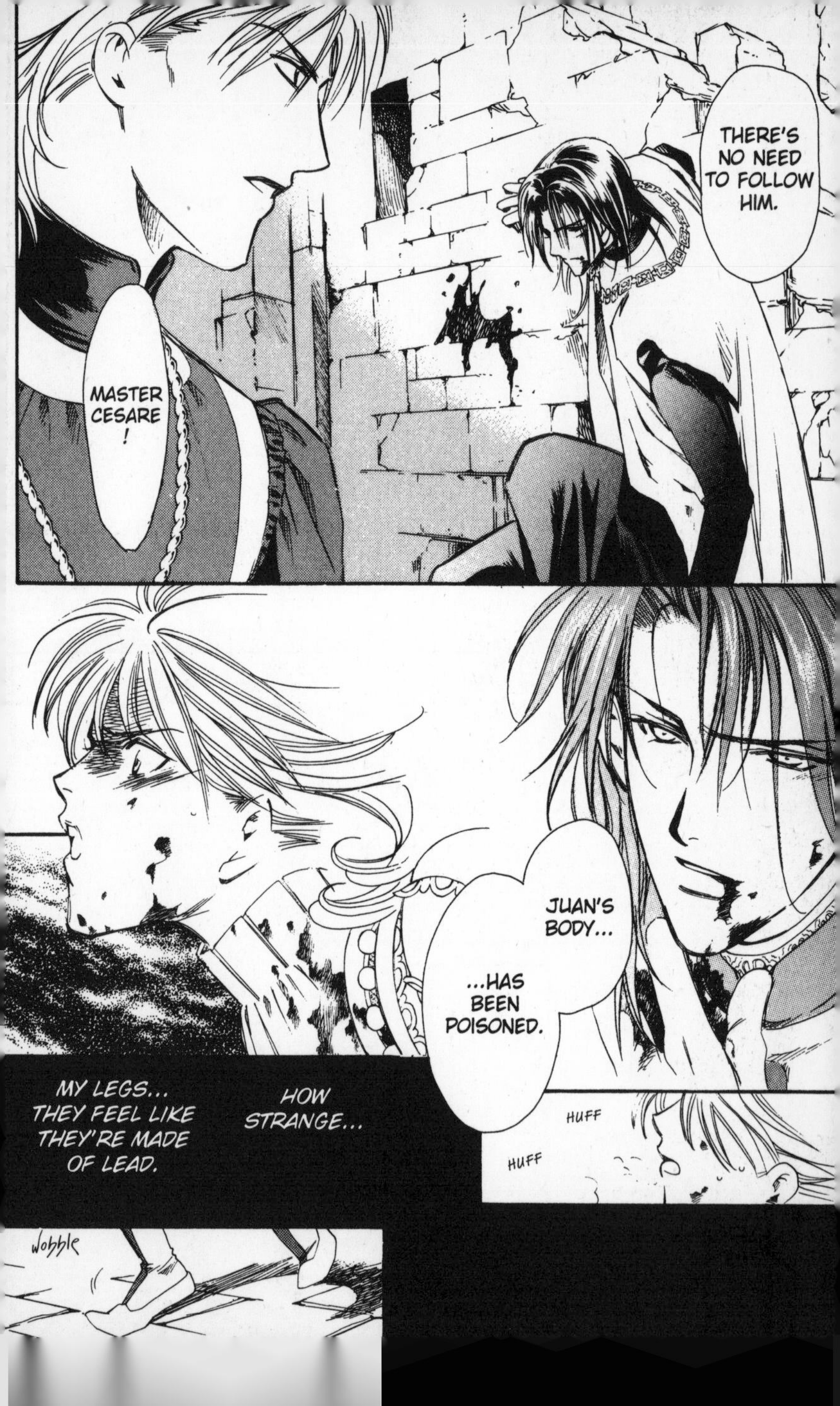
THERE'S NO NEED TO FOLLOW HIM.
MASTER CESARE!
JUAN'S BODY...
...HAS BEEN POISONED.
HUFF
HUFF
HOW STRANGE...
MY LEGS... THEY FEEL LIKE THEY'RE MADE OF LEAD.
Wobble

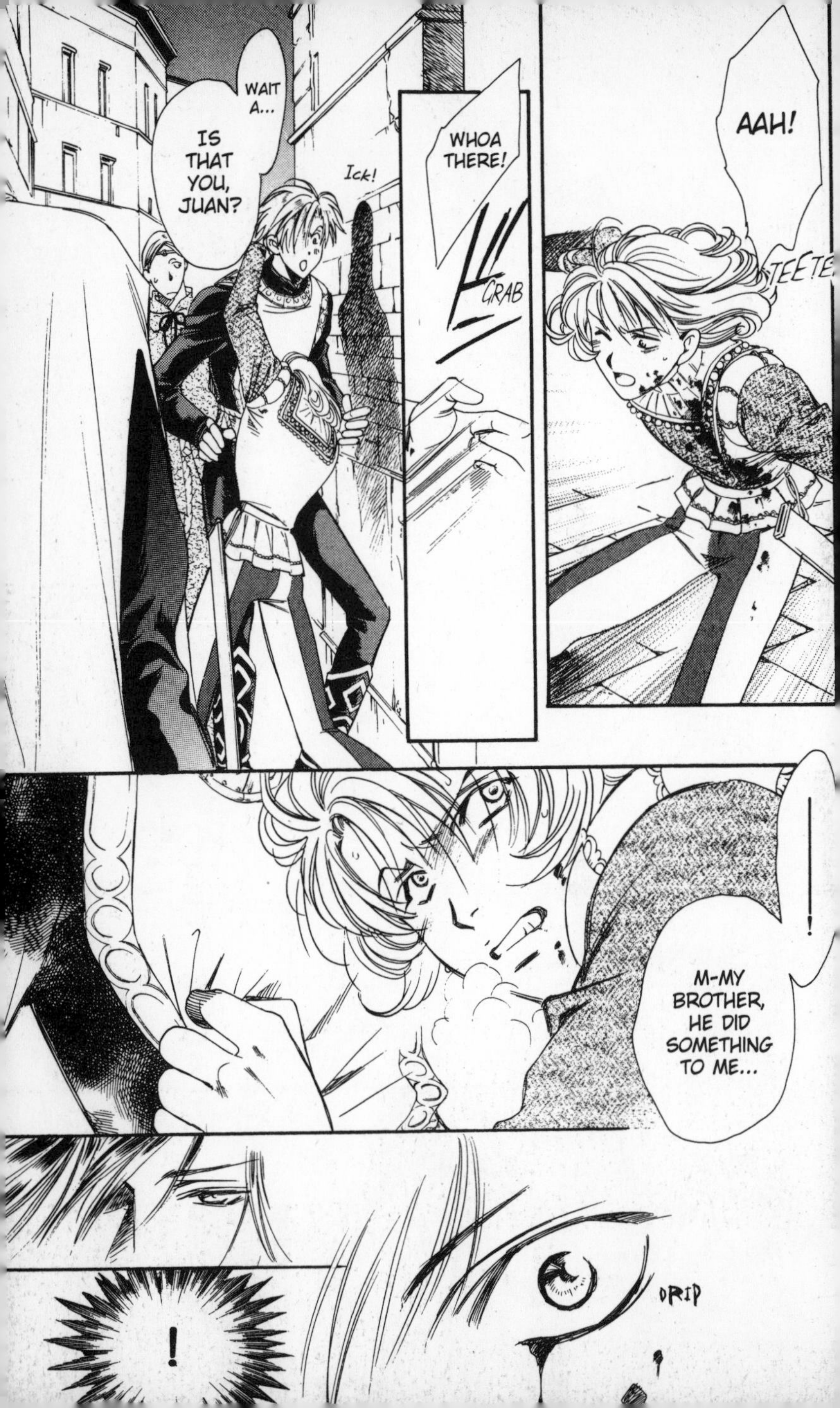
AAH!
TEETE
WHOA THERE!
GRAB
WAIT A...
IS THAT YOU, JUAN?
Ick!
!
M-MY BROTHER, HE DID SOMETHING TO ME...
DRIP
!

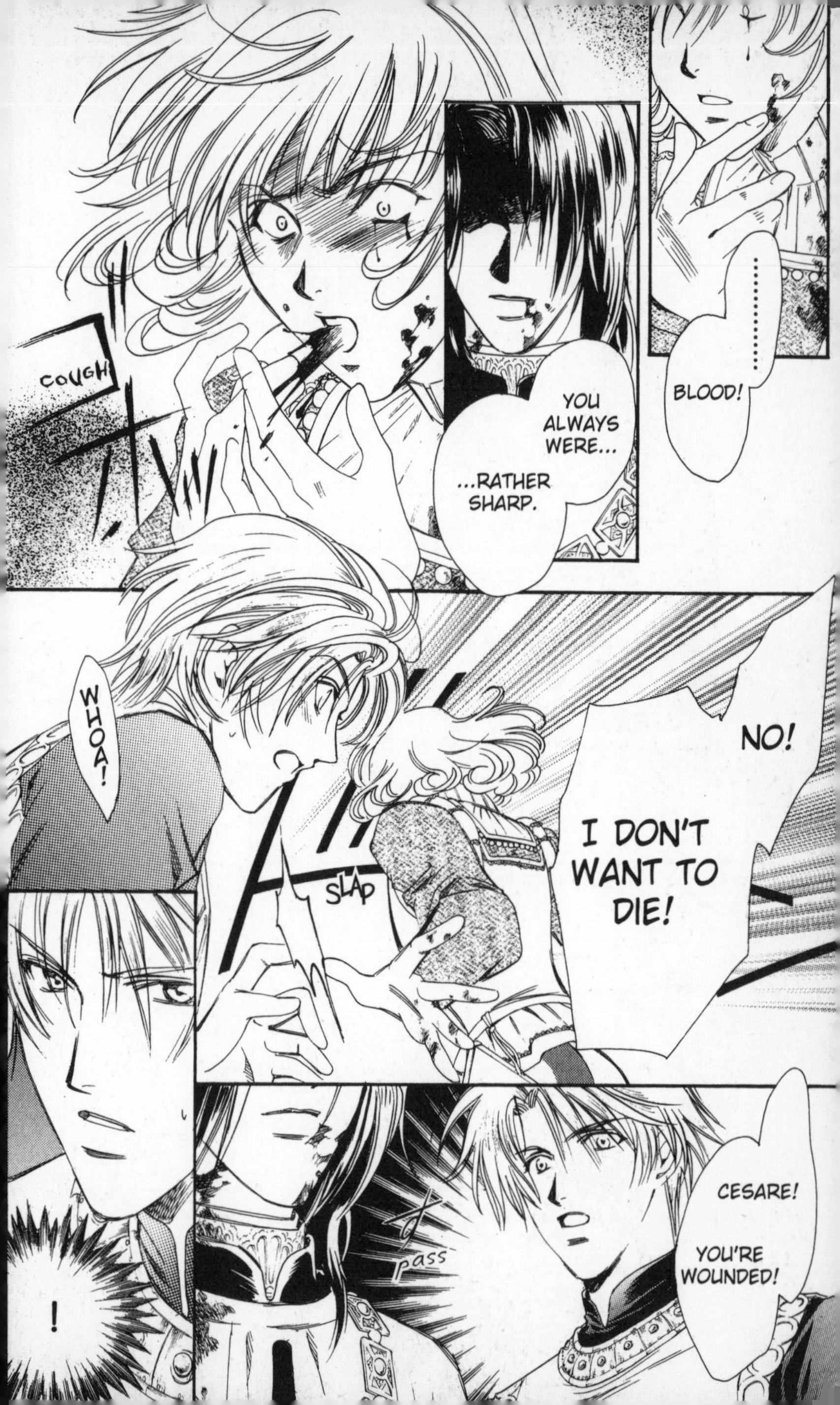
......
BLOOD!
YOU ALWAYS WERE...
...RATHER SHARP.
COUGH
NO!
I DON'T WANT TO DIE!
WHOA!
SLAP
CESARE!
YOU'RE WOUNDED!
pass
!

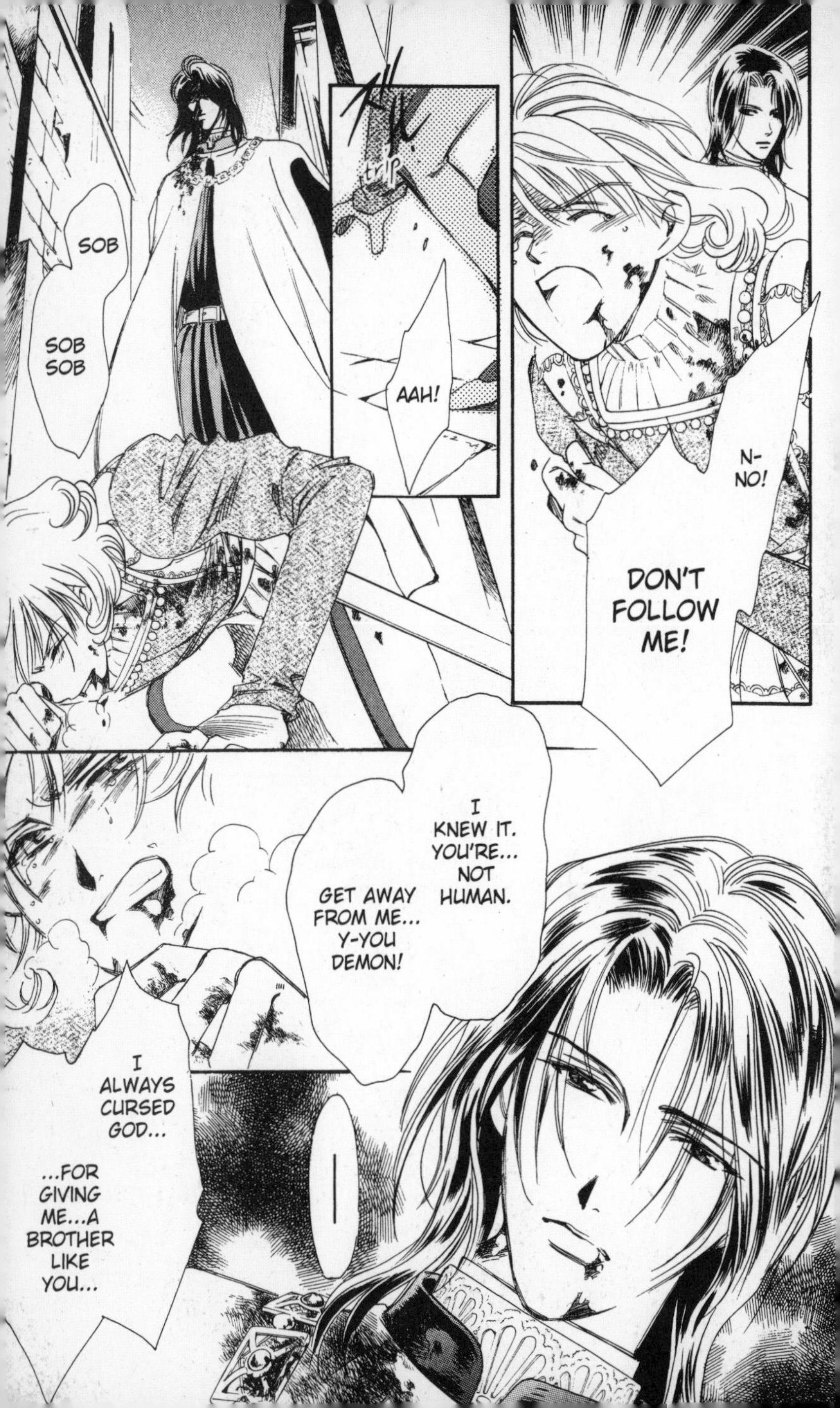
N-
NO!
DON'T FOLLOW ME!
trip
AAH!
SOB
SOB SOB
I KNEW IT. YOU'RE... NOT HUMAN.
GET AWAY FROM ME... Y-YOU DEMON!
—
I ALWAYS CURSED GOD...
...FOR GIVING ME...A BROTHER LIKE YOU...

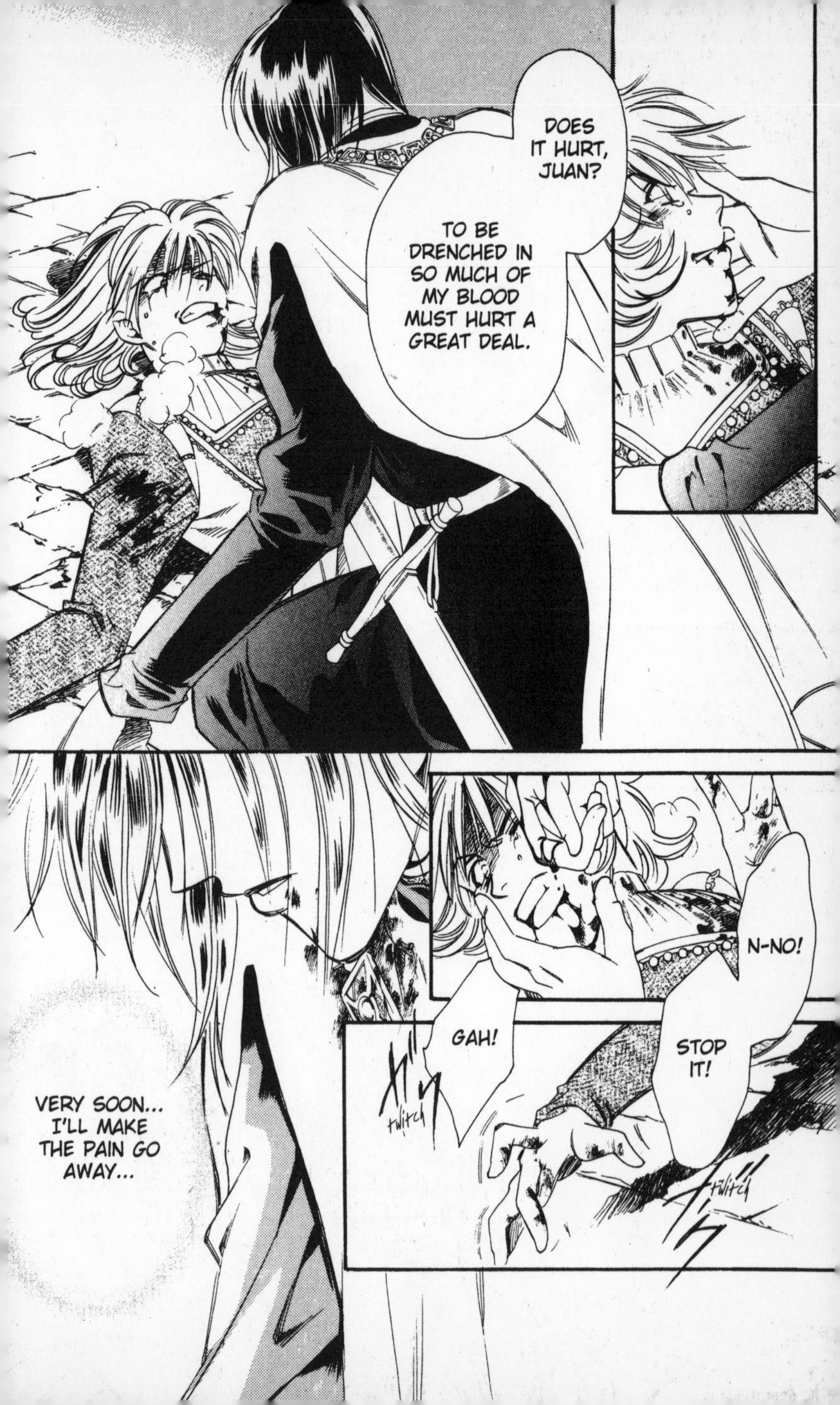
DOES IT HURT, JUAN?
TO BE DRENCHED IN SO MUCH OF MY BLOOD MUST HURT A GREAT DEAL.
N-NO!
STOP IT!
GAH!
twitch
twitch
VERY SOON... I'LL MAKE THE PAIN GO AWAY...

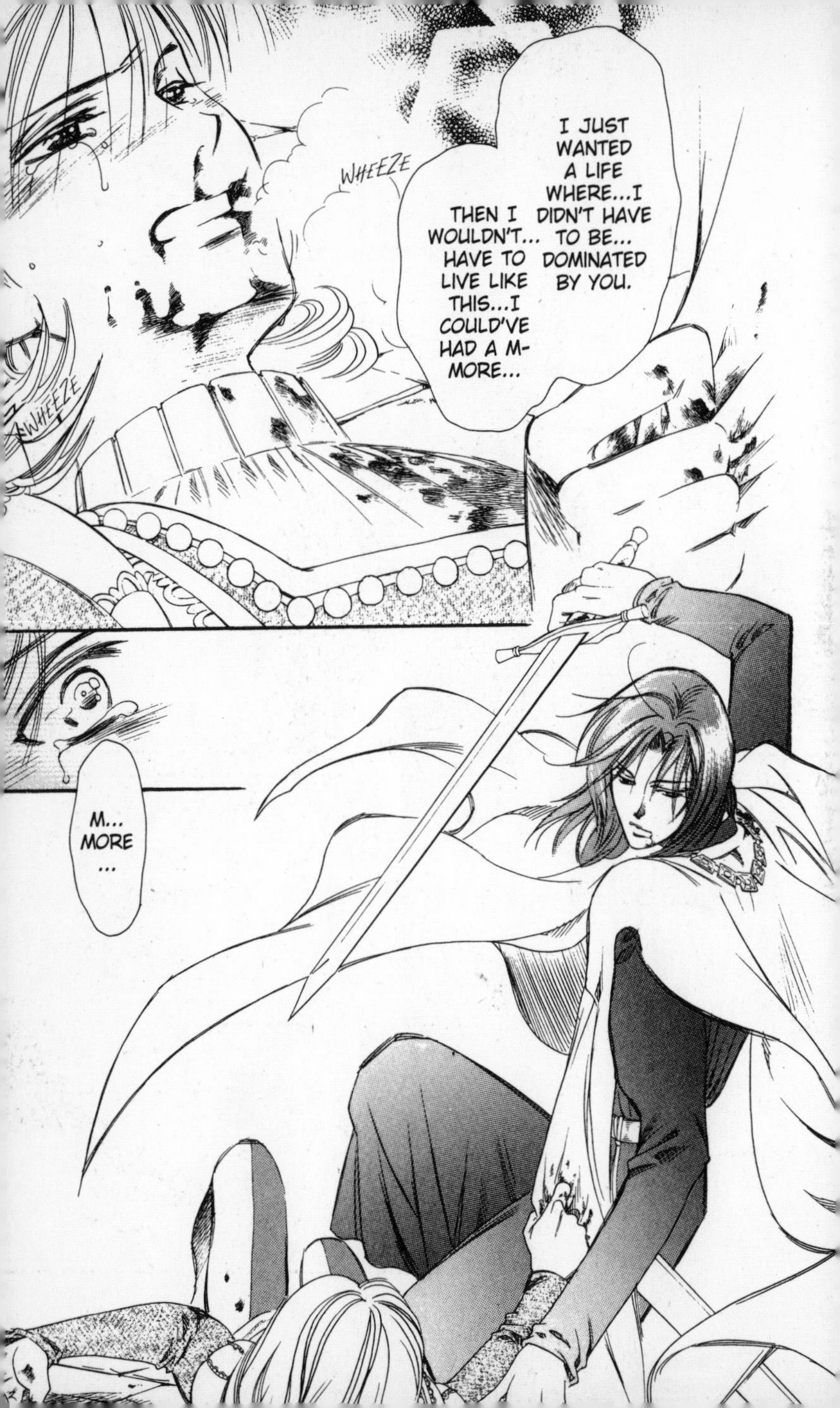
I JUST WANTED A LIFE WHERE...I DIDN'T HAVE TO BE... DOMINATED BY YOU.
THEN I WOULDN'T... HAVE TO LIVE LIKE THIS...I COULD'VE HAD A M- MORE...
WHEEZE
WHEEZE
M... MORE ...

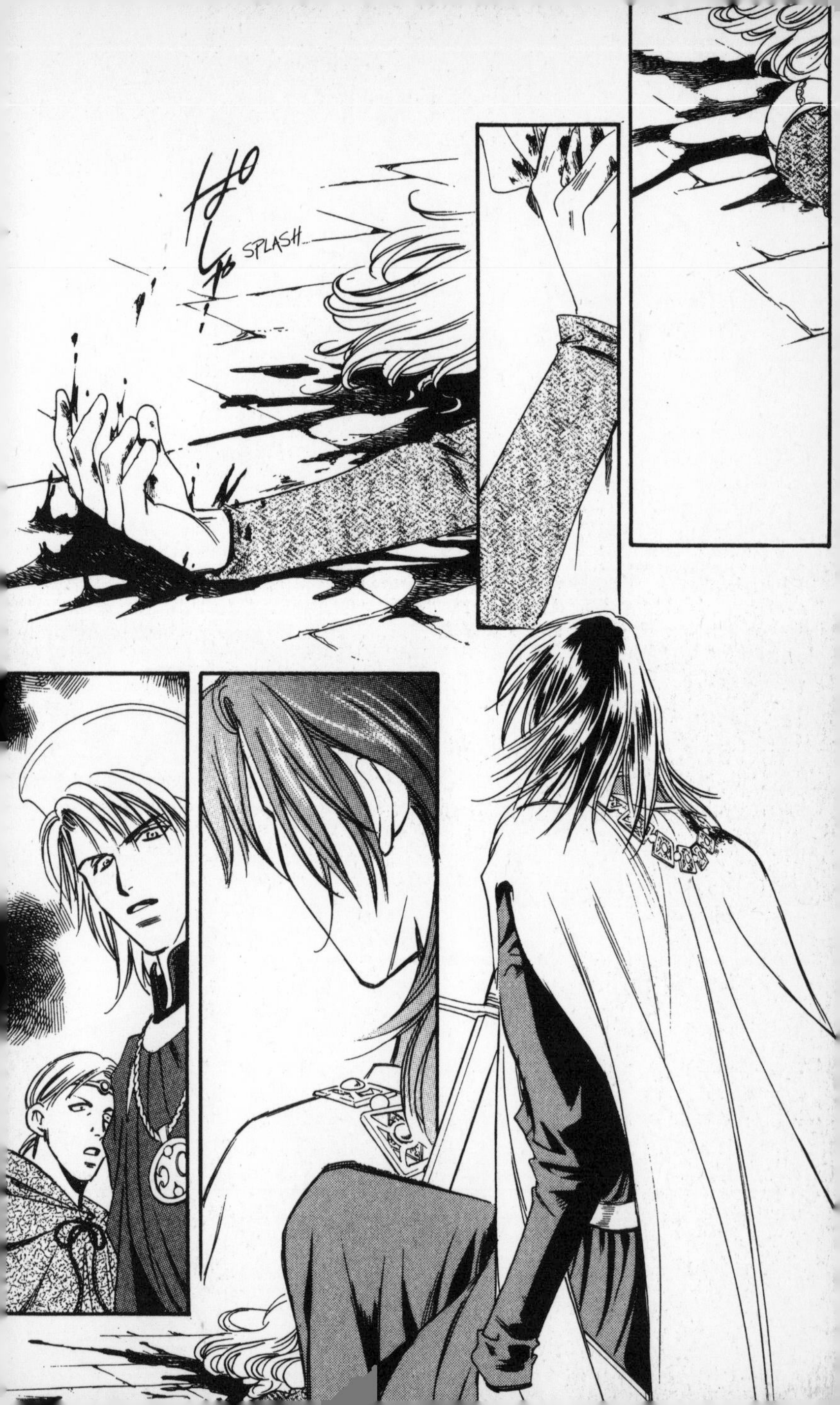
SPLASH...

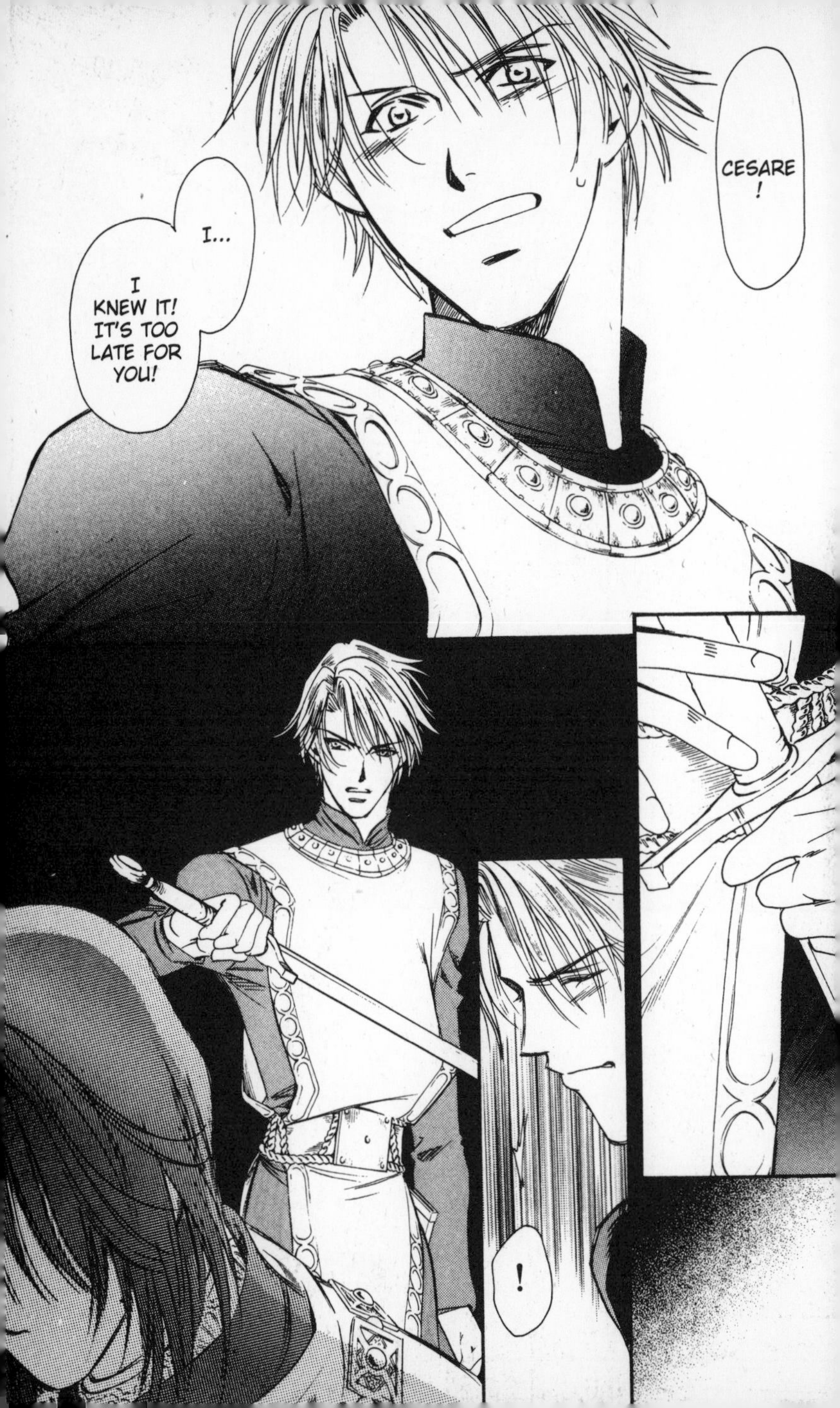
CESARE!
I...
I KNEW IT! IT'S TOO LATE FOR YOU!
!

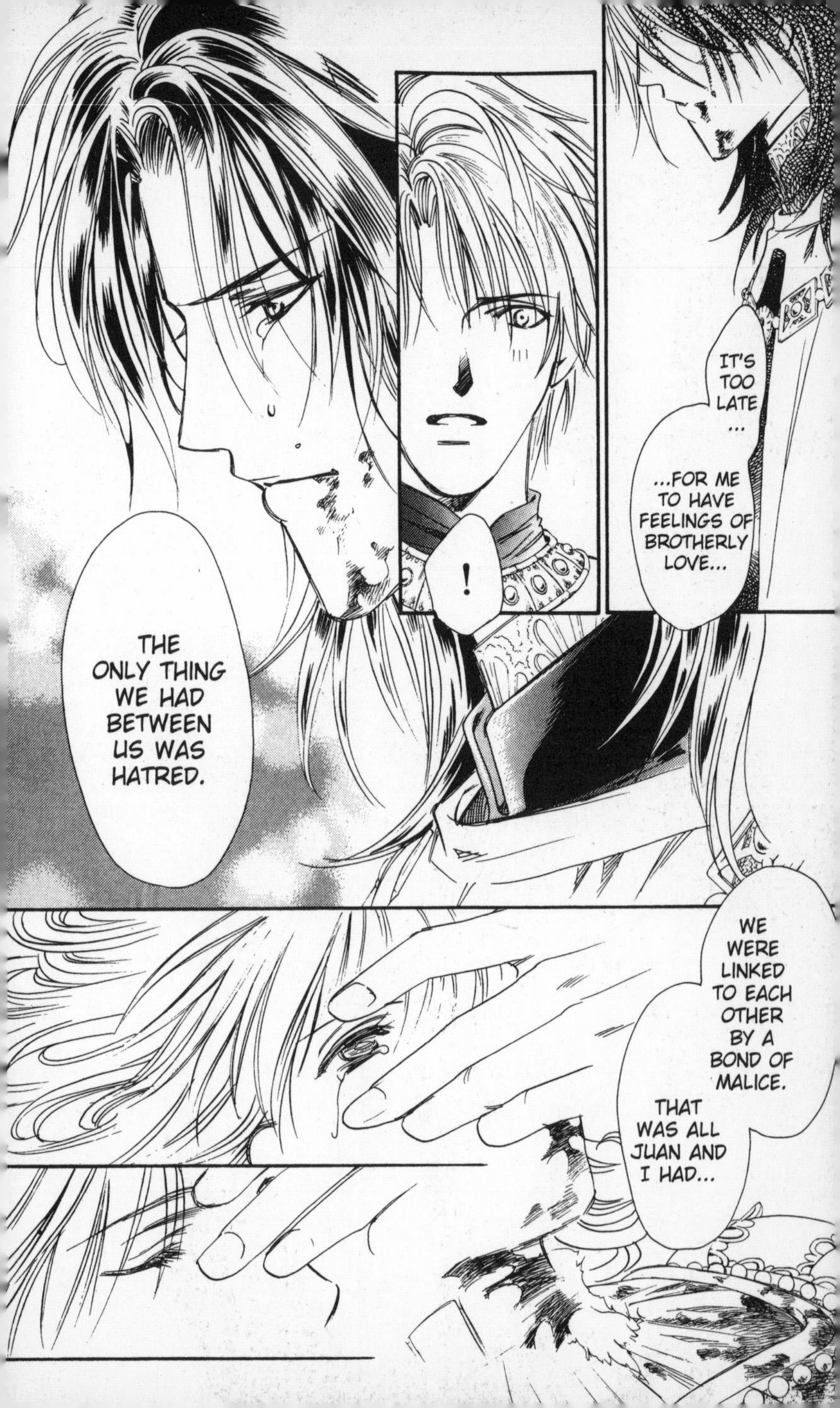
IT'S TOO LATE...
...FOR ME TO HAVE FEELINGS OF BROTHERLY LOVE...
!
THE ONLY THING WE HAD BETWEEN US WAS HATRED.
WE WERE LINKED TO EACH OTHER BY A BOND OF MALICE.
THAT WAS ALL JUAN AND I HAD...

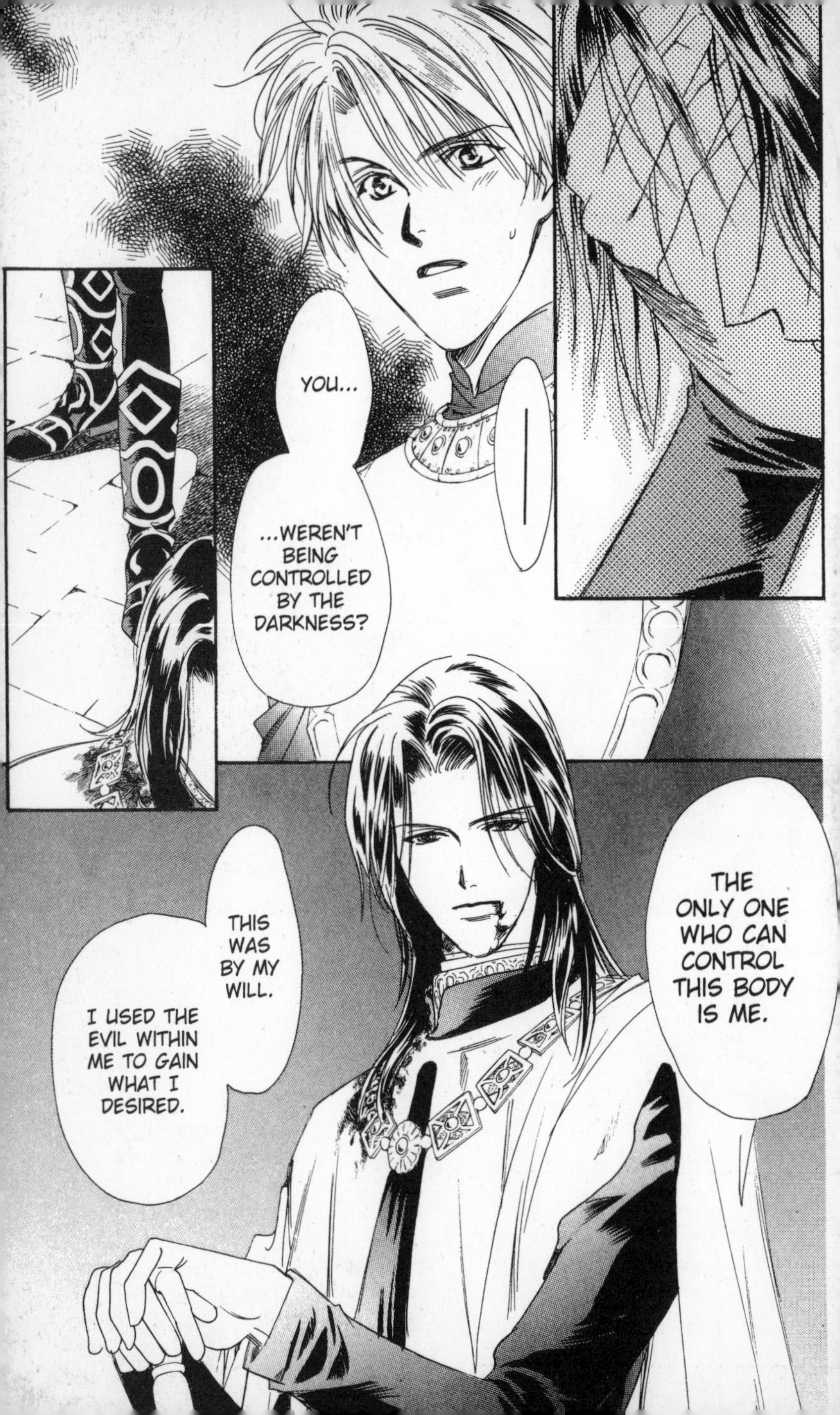
YOU...
...WEREN'T BEING CONTROLLED BY THE DARKNESS?
THE ONLY ONE WHO CAN CONTROL THIS BODY IS ME.
THIS WAS BY MY WILL.
I USED THE EVIL WITHIN ME TO GAIN WHAT I DESIRED.

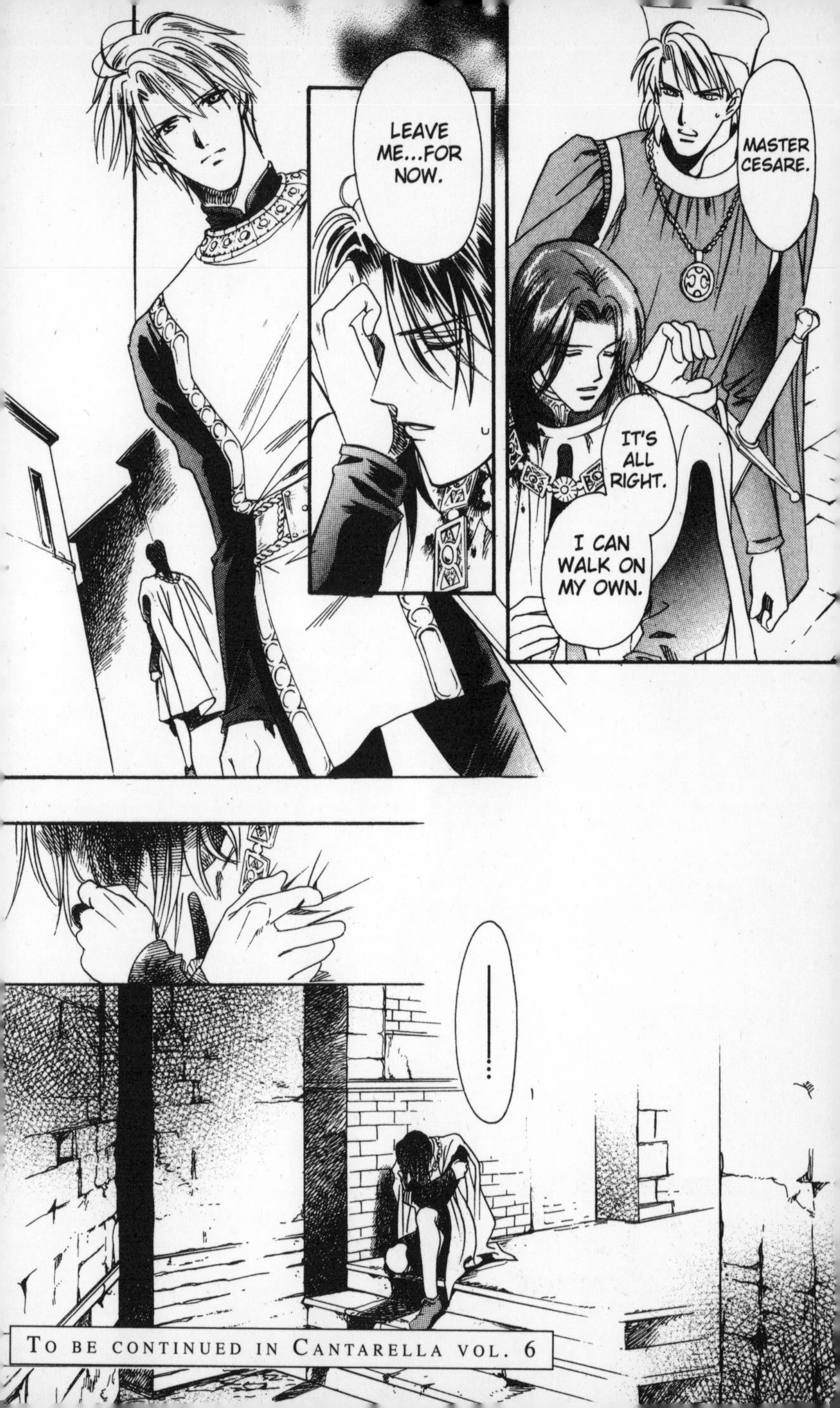
MASTER CESARE.
IT'S ALL RIGHT.
I CAN WALK ON MY OWN.
LEAVE ME...FOR NOW.
TO BE CONTINUED IN CANTARELLA VOL. 6

ファンタレラ

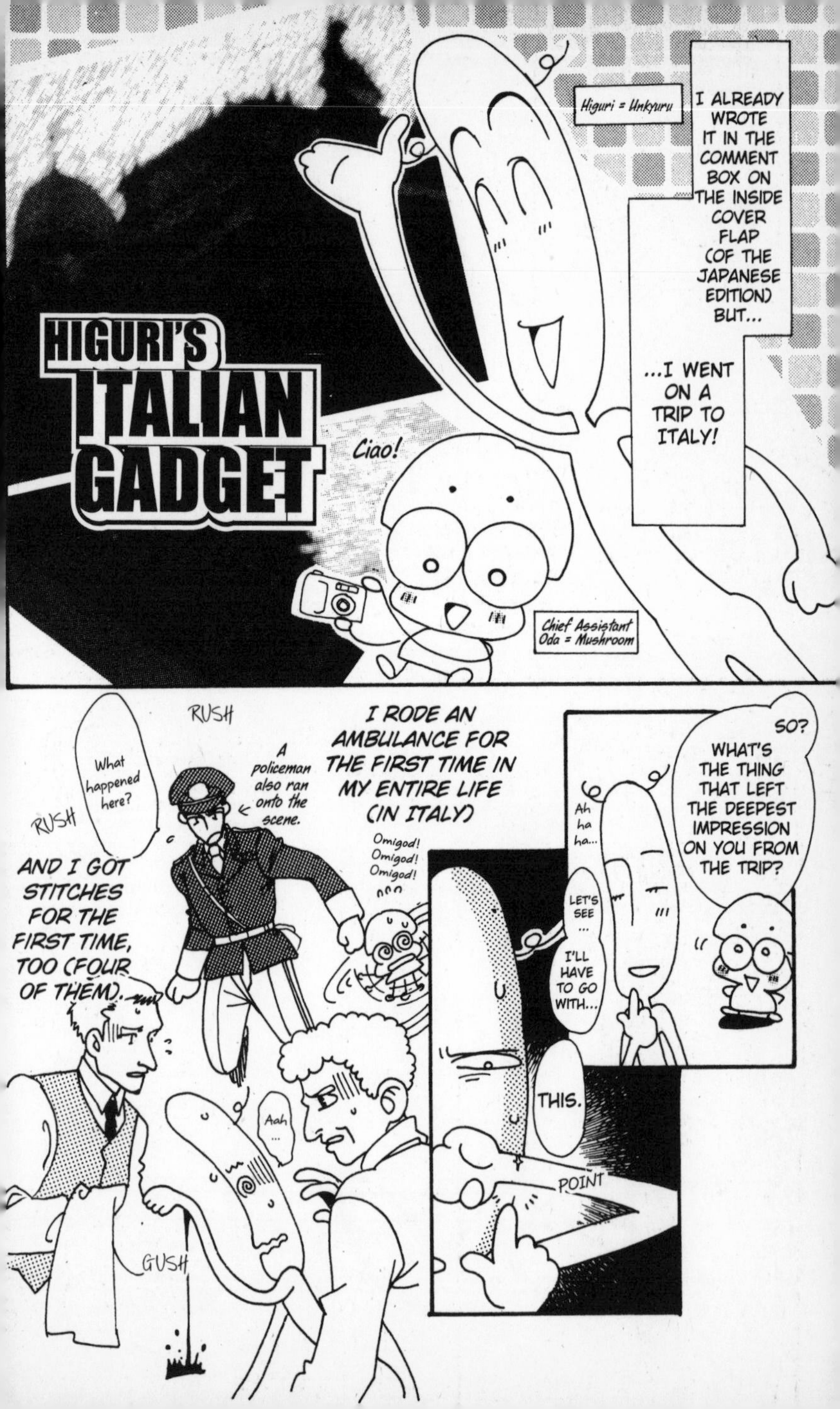
Higuri = Unkyuru
I ALREADY WROTE IT IN THE COMMENT BOX ON THE INSIDE COVER FLAP (OF THE JAPANESE EDITION) BUT...
...I WENT ON A TRIP TO ITALY!
HIGURI'S ITALIAN GADGET
Ciao!
Chief Assistant Oda = Mushroom
SO? WHAT'S THE THING THAT LEFT THE DEEPEST IMPRESSION ON YOU FROM THE TRIP?
Ah ha ha...
LET'S SEE...
I'LL HAVE TO GO WITH...
THIS.
POINT
I RODE AN AMBULANCE FOR THE FIRST TIME IN MY ENTIRE LIFE (IN ITALY)
A policeman also ran onto the scene.
RUSH
What happened here?
RUSH
Omigod! Omigod! Omigod!
AND I GOT STITCHES FOR THE FIRST TIME, TOO (FOUR OF THEM).
Aah...
GUSH

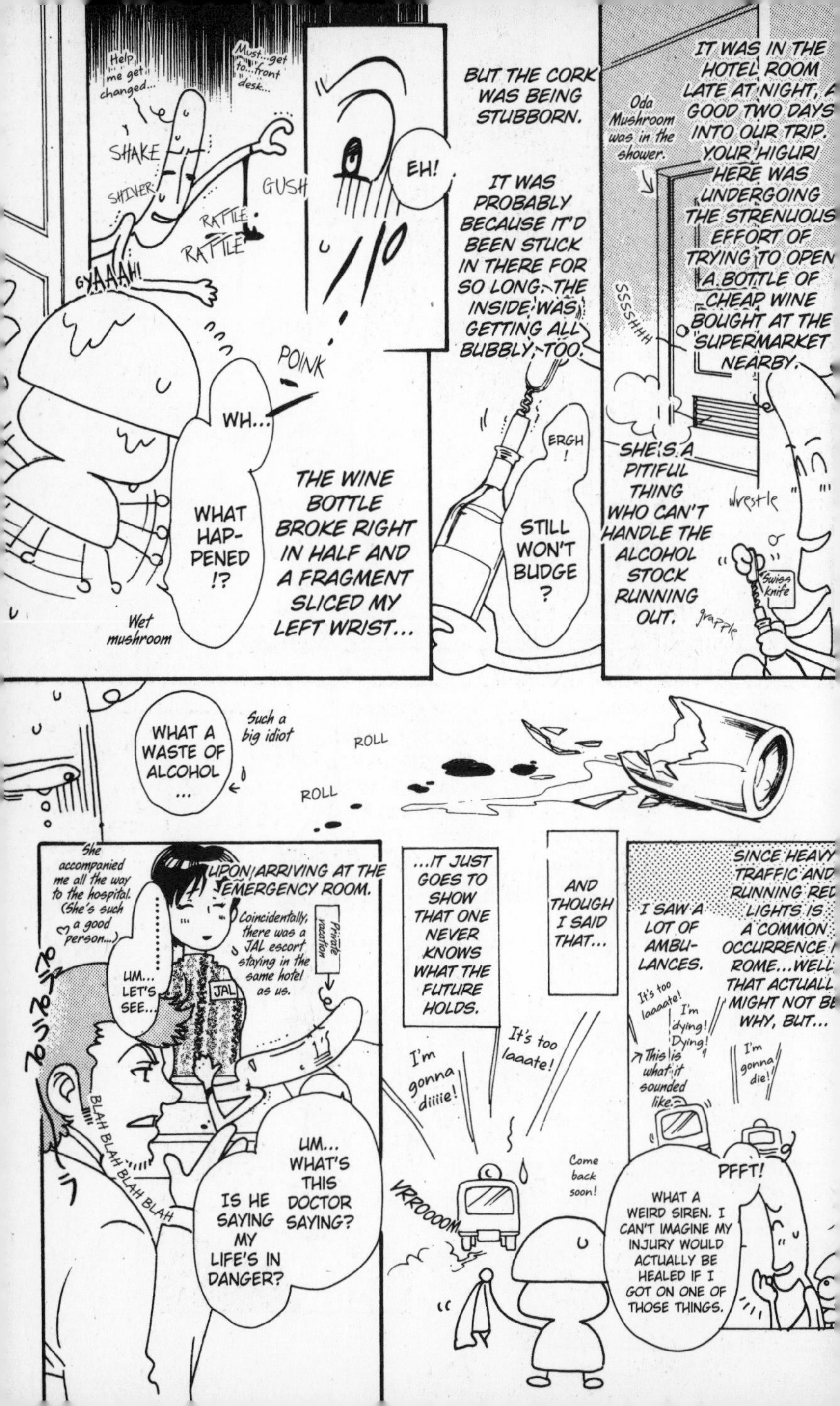

IT WAS IN THE HOTEL ROOM LATE AT NIGHT, A GOOD TWO DAYS INTO OUR TRIP. YOUR HIGURI HERE WAS UNDERGOING THE STRENUOUS EFFORT OF TRYING TO OPEN A BOTTLE OF CHEAP WINE BOUGHT AT THE SUPERMARKET NEARBY.
Oda Mushroom was in the shower.
SSSSHHHH
SHE'S A PITIFUL THING WHO CAN'T HANDLE THE ALCOHOL STOCK RUNNING OUT.
wrestle
Swiss knife
grapple
BUT THE CORK WAS BEING STUBBORN.
IT WAS PROBABLY BECAUSE IT'D BEEN STUCK IN THERE FOR SO LONG. THE INSIDE WAS GETTING ALL BUBBLY, TOO.
ERGH!
STILL WON'T BUDGE?
EH!
POINK
Must...get to...front desk...
Help me get changed...
SHAKE
SHIVER
GUSH
RATTLE RATTLE
GYAAAH!
WH...
WHAT HAPPENED!?
THE WINE BOTTLE BROKE RIGHT IN HALF AND A FRAGMENT SLICED MY LEFT WRIST...
Wet mushroom
ROLL
ROLL
WHAT A WASTE OF ALCOHOL...
Such a big idiot
SINCE HEAVY TRAFFIC AND RUNNING RED LIGHTS IS A COMMON OCCURRENCE IN ROME...WELL THAT ACTUALLY MIGHT NOT BE WHY, BUT...
I SAW A LOT OF AMBULANCES.
It's too laaaate!
I'm dying! Dying!
This is what it sounded like.
I'm gonna die!
PFFT!
WHAT A WEIRD SIREN. I CAN'T IMAGINE MY INJURY WOULD ACTUALLY BE HEALED IF I GOT ON ONE OF THOSE THINGS.
AND THOUGH I SAID THAT...
...IT JUST GOES TO SHOW THAT ONE NEVER KNOWS WHAT THE FUTURE HOLDS.
It's too laaate!
I'm gonna diiiie!
VRROOOOM
Come back soon!
UPON ARRIVING AT THE EMERGENCY ROOM.
Coincidentally, there was a JAL escort staying in the same hotel as us.
Private vacation
She accompanied me all the way to the hospital. (She's such a good person...)
JAL
UM... LET'S SEE...
BLAH BLAH BLAH BLAH
UM... WHAT'S THIS DOCTOR SAYING?
IS HE SAYING MY LIFE'S IN DANGER?

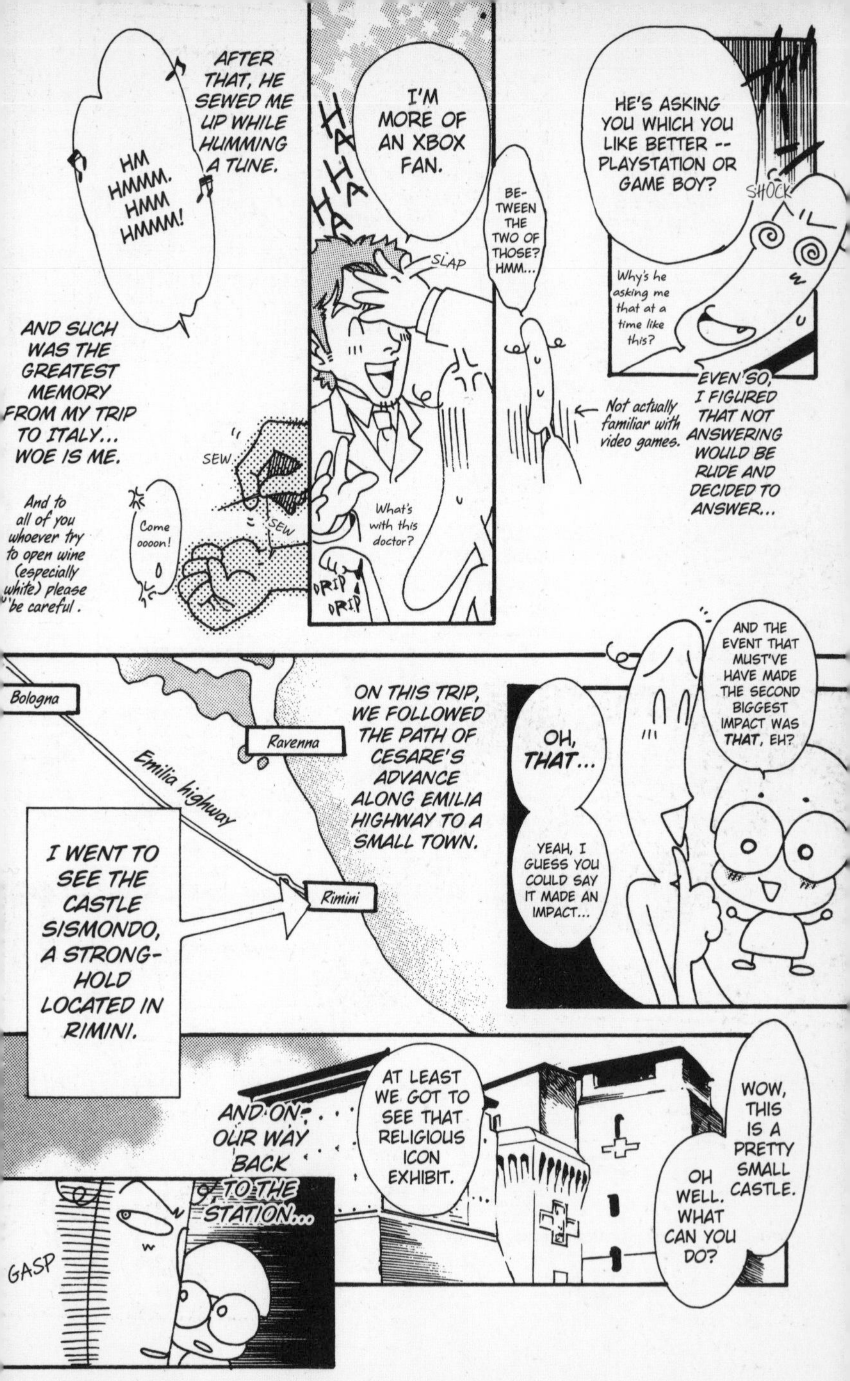
HE'S ASKING YOU WHICH YOU LIKE BETTER -- PLAYSTATION OR GAME BOY?
SHOCK
Why's he asking me that at a time like this?
EVEN SO, I FIGURED THAT NOT ANSWERING WOULD BE RUDE AND DECIDED TO ANSWER...
BE-TWEEN THE TWO OF THOSE? HMM...
Not actually familiar with video games.
HA HA HA HA
I'M MORE OF AN XBOX FAN.
SLAP
What's with this doctor?
DRIP DRIP
AFTER THAT, HE SEWED ME UP WHILE HUMMING A TUNE.
HM HMMM. HMM HMMM!
SEW
SEW
Come oooon!
AND SUCH WAS THE GREATEST MEMORY FROM MY TRIP TO ITALY... WOE IS ME.
And to all of you whoever try to open wine (especially white) please be careful.
AND THE EVENT THAT MUST'VE HAVE MADE THE SECOND BIGGEST IMPACT WAS THAT, EH?
OH, THAT...
YEAH, I GUESS YOU COULD SAY IT MADE AN IMPACT...
ON THIS TRIP, WE FOLLOWED THE PATH OF CESARE'S ADVANCE ALONG EMILIA HIGHWAY TO A SMALL TOWN.
Bologna
Ravenna
Emilia highway
Rimini
I WENT TO SEE THE CASTLE SISMONDO, A STRONG-HOLD LOCATED IN RIMINI.
WOW, THIS IS A PRETTY SMALL CASTLE.
OH WELL. WHAT CAN YOU DO?
AT LEAST WE GOT TO SEE THAT RELIGIOUS ICON EXHIBIT.
AND ON OUR WAY BACK TO THE STATION...
GASP

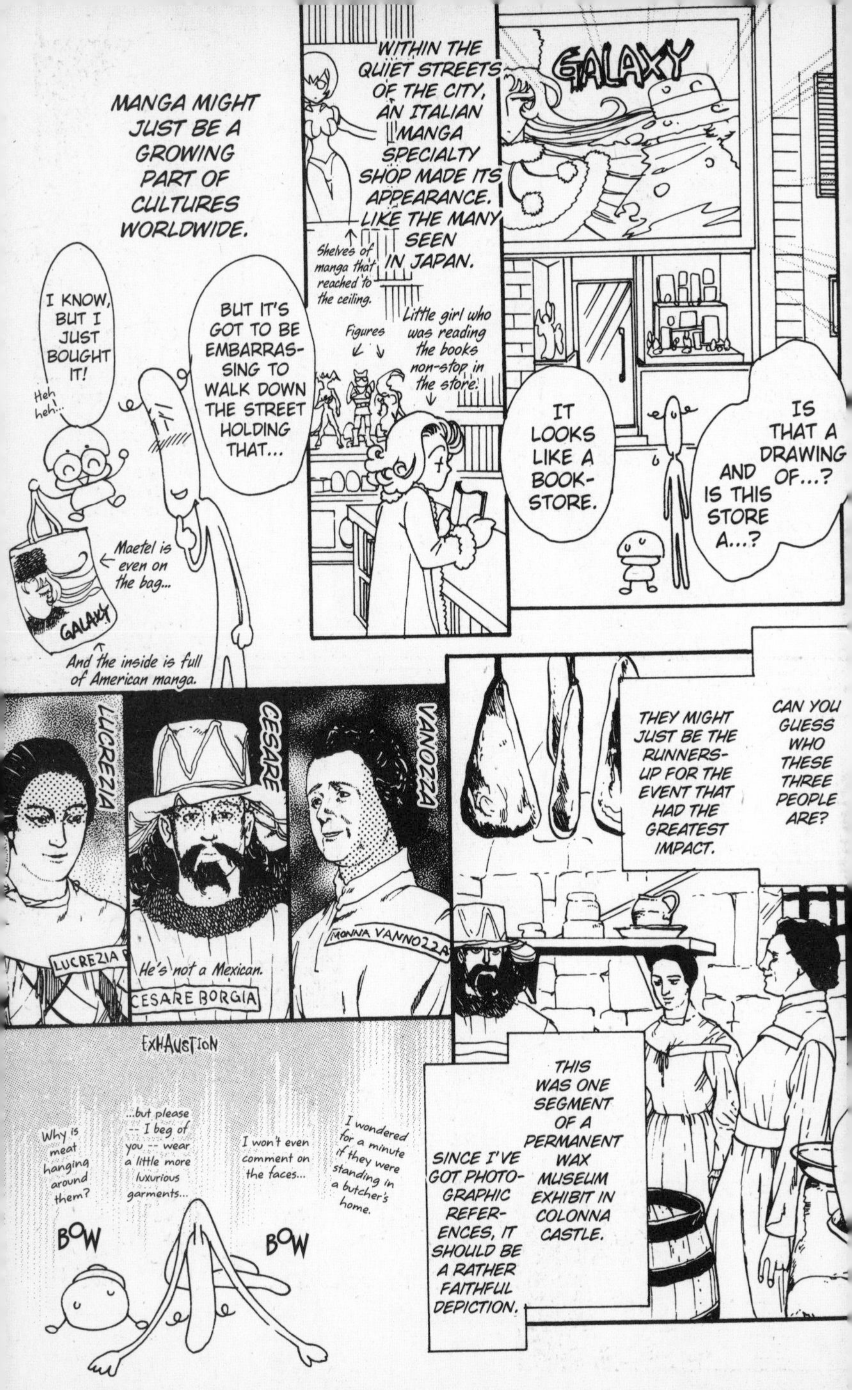

GALAXY
IS THAT A DRAWING OF...?
AND IS THIS STORE A...?
IT LOOKS LIKE A BOOKSTORE.
WITHIN THE QUIET STREETS OF THE CITY, AN ITALIAN MANGA SPECIALTY SHOP MADE ITS APPEARANCE. LIKE THE MANY SEEN IN JAPAN.
Shelves of manga that reached to the ceiling.
Little girl who was reading the books non-stop in the store.
Figures
MANGA MIGHT JUST BE A GROWING PART OF CULTURES WORLDWIDE.
BUT IT'S GOT TO BE EMBARRASSING TO WALK DOWN THE STREET HOLDING THAT...
I KNOW, BUT I JUST BOUGHT IT!
Heh heh...
Maetel is even on the bag...
GALAXY
And the inside is full of American manga.
CAN YOU GUESS WHO THESE THREE PEOPLE ARE?
THEY MIGHT JUST BE THE RUNNERS-UP FOR THE EVENT THAT HAD THE GREATEST IMPACT.
THIS WAS ONE SEGMENT OF A PERMANENT WAX MUSEUM EXHIBIT IN COLONNA CASTLE.
SINCE I'VE GOT PHOTOGRAPHIC REFERENCES, IT SHOULD BE A RATHER FAITHFUL DEPICTION.
VANOZZA
MONNA VANNOZZA
CESARE
CESARE BORGIA
He's not a Mexican.
LUCREZIA
LUCREZIA
EXHAUSTION
I wondered for a minute if they were standing in a butcher's home.
I won't even comment on the faces...
...but please -- I beg of you -- wear a little more luxurious garments...
Why is meat hanging around them?
BOW
BOW

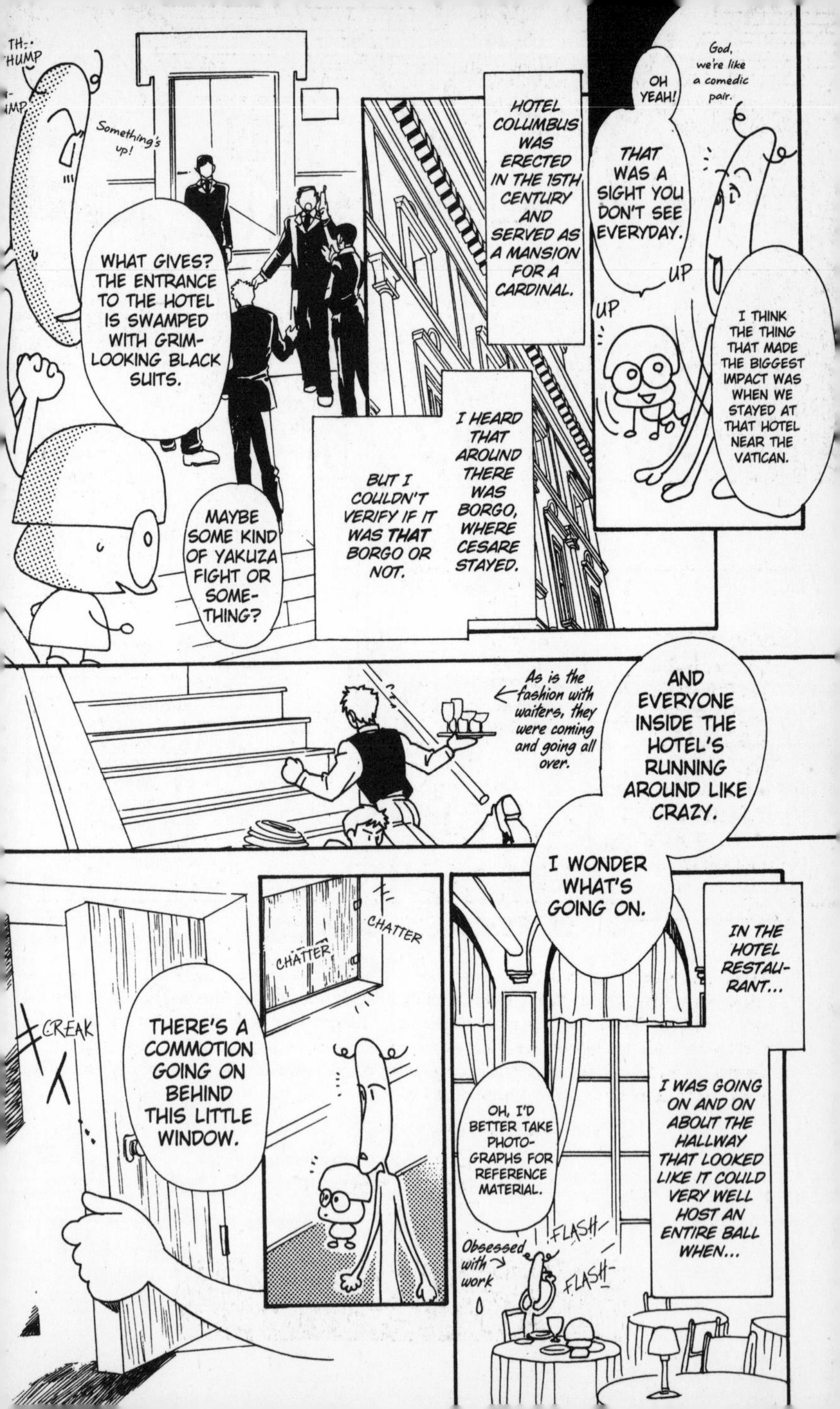
God, we're like a comedic pair.
OH YEAH!
THAT WAS A SIGHT YOU DON'T SEE EVERYDAY.
UP
UP
I THINK THE THING THAT MADE THE BIGGEST IMPACT WAS WHEN WE STAYED AT THAT HOTEL NEAR THE VATICAN.
HOTEL COLUMBUS WAS ERECTED IN THE 15TH CENTURY AND SERVED AS A MANSION FOR A CARDINAL.
I HEARD THAT AROUND THERE WAS BORGO, WHERE CESARE STAYED.
BUT I COULDN'T VERIFY IF IT WAS THAT BORGO OR NOT.
TH-HUMP
-IMP
Something's up!
WHAT GIVES? THE ENTRANCE TO THE HOTEL IS SWAMPED WITH GRIM-LOOKING BLACK SUITS.
MAYBE SOME KIND OF YAKUZA FIGHT OR SOME-THING?
AND EVERYONE INSIDE THE HOTEL'S RUNNING AROUND LIKE CRAZY.
As is the fashion with waiters, they were coming and going all over.
IN THE HOTEL RESTAU-RANT...
I WAS GOING ON AND ON ABOUT THE HALLWAY THAT LOOKED LIKE IT COULD VERY WELL HOST AN ENTIRE BALL WHEN...
OH, I'D BETTER TAKE PHOTO-GRAPHS FOR REFERENCE MATERIAL.
FLASH-
FLASH-
Obsessed with work
I WONDER WHAT'S GOING ON.
CHATTER
CHATTER
CREAK
THERE'S A COMMOTION GOING ON BEHIND THIS LITTLE WINDOW.

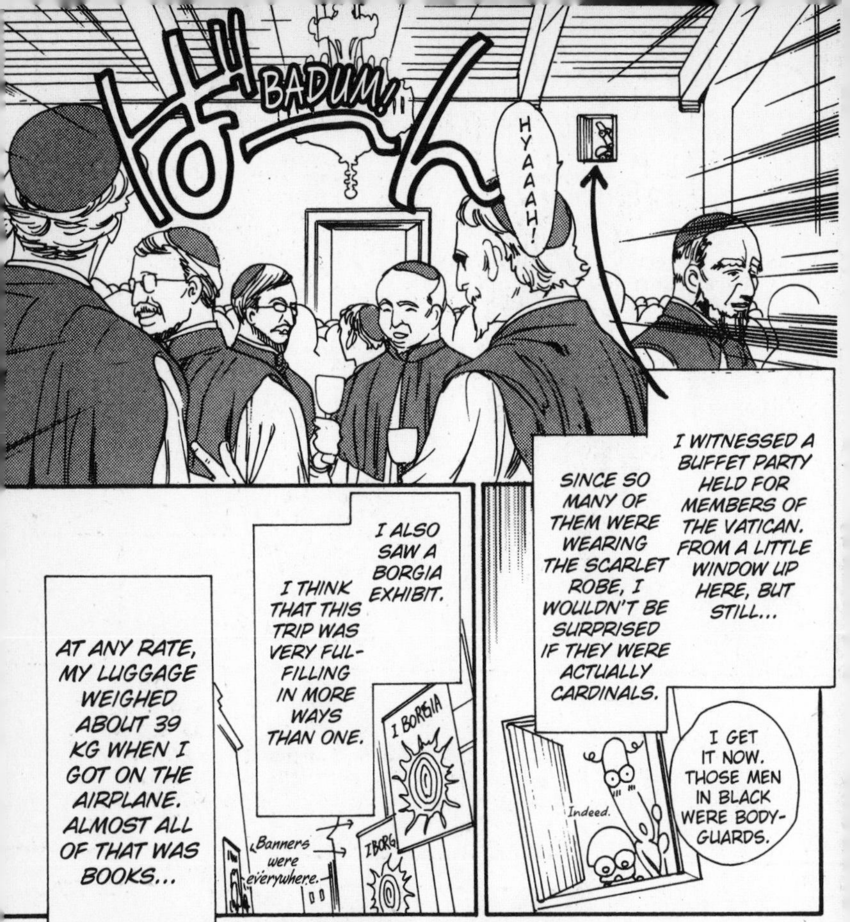
BADUM!
HYAAAH!
I WITNESSED A BUFFET PARTY HELD FOR MEMBERS OF THE VATICAN. FROM A LITTLE WINDOW UP HERE, BUT STILL...
SINCE SO MANY OF THEM WERE WEARING THE SCARLET ROBE, I WOULDN'T BE SURPRISED IF THEY WERE ACTUALLY CARDINALS.
I GET IT NOW. THOSE MEN IN BLACK WERE BODY-GUARDS.
Indeed.
I ALSO SAW A BORGIA EXHIBIT.
I THINK THAT THIS TRIP WAS VERY FUL-FILLING IN MORE WAYS THAN ONE.
I BORGIA
I BORG
Banners were everywhere.
AT ANY RATE, MY LUGGAGE WEIGHED ABOUT 39 KG WHEN I GOT ON THE AIRPLANE. ALMOST ALL OF THAT WAS BOOKS...

■SPECIAL THANKS■

Izumi Hijiri-san, Nakatsuji Naoko-san, Miyakoshi Wakusa-san, Kazuki Mari-san, Fuyutsuki Mitsuru-san, Akiyoshi-san, Igami Miki-san, Tawara Akiko-san, Hondo Makoto, Mizukara Yasuha-san, Tomonagi Hiro-san, Nakamura Ayako-san, Motoda Akira-san, Saeki Haruna-san, Udou Haruka-san, Tsukaguchi Maki-san, chief assistant Oda=Mushroom, princess in charge (sparkle) Y-sama, my editor-in-chief, everyone in the printing company and all you who read this book: a big thank you from the bottom of my heart. And I hope to see you again in the next issue!

I'll be waiting for your letters:

YOU HIGURI c/o Audry Taylor
Go! Media Entertainment, LLC
5737 Kanan Rd. #591
Agoura Hills CA 91301

Or visit her official website in English at:
http://www.youhiguri.com

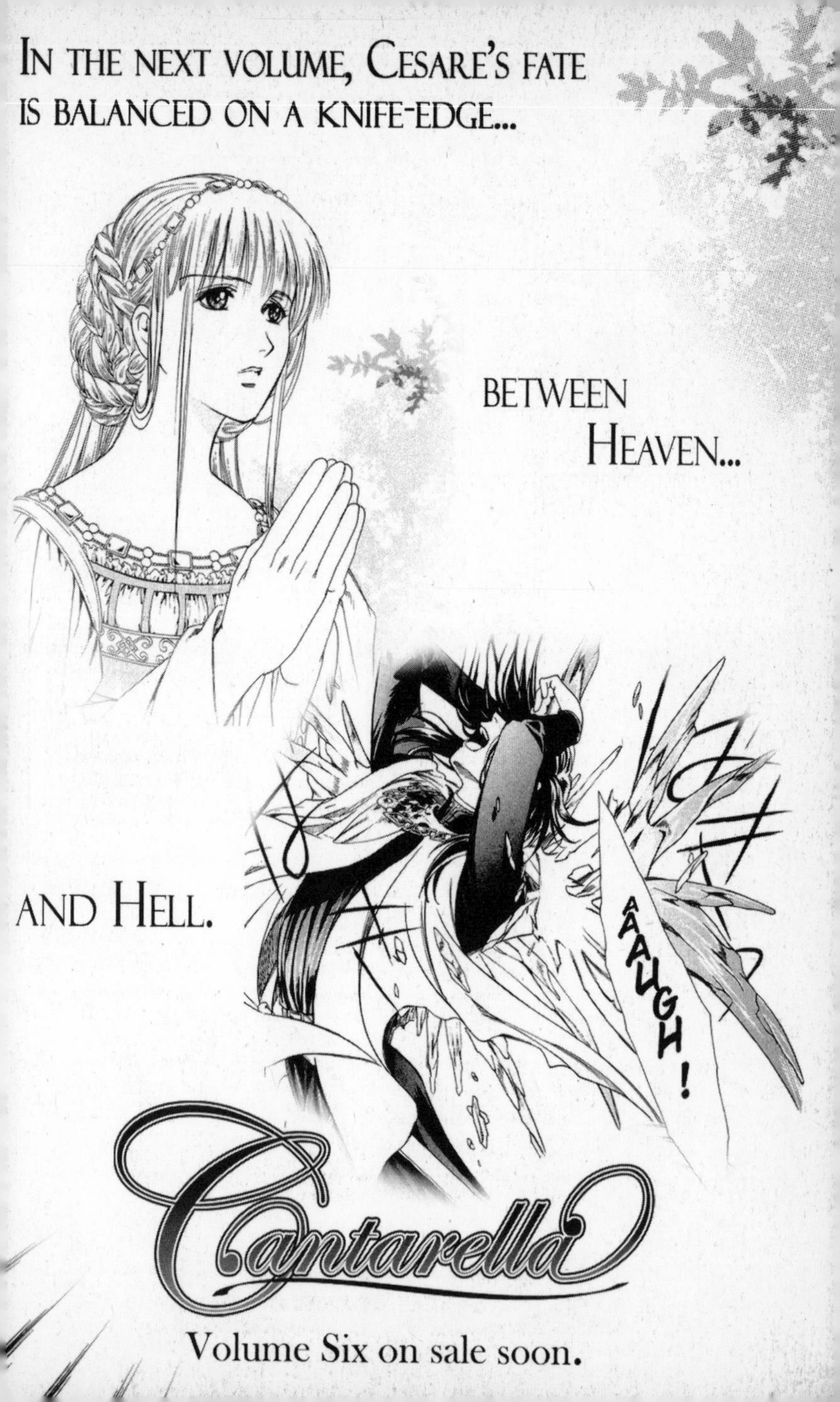
IN THE NEXT VOLUME, CESARE'S FATE IS BALANCED ON A KNIFE-EDGE...
BETWEEN HEAVEN...
AND HELL.
AAUGH!
Cantarella
Volume Six on sale soon.

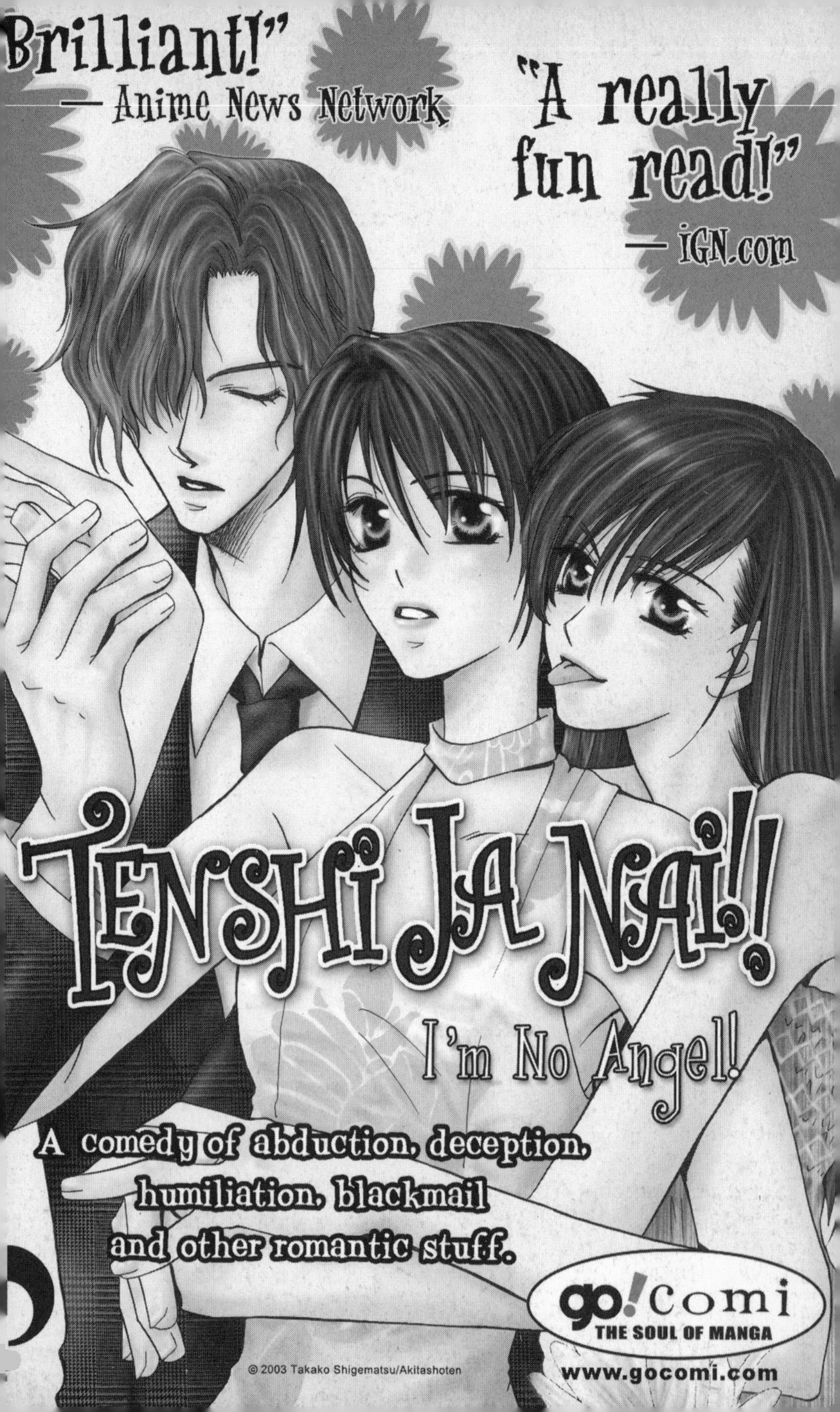
Brilliant!"
— Anime News Network
"A really fun read!"
— iGN.com
TENSHI JA NAI!
I'm No Angel!
A comedy of abduction, deception, humiliation, blackmail and other romantic stuff.
© 2003 Takako Shigematsu/Akitashoten
go!comi
THE SOUL OF MANGA
www.gocomi.com

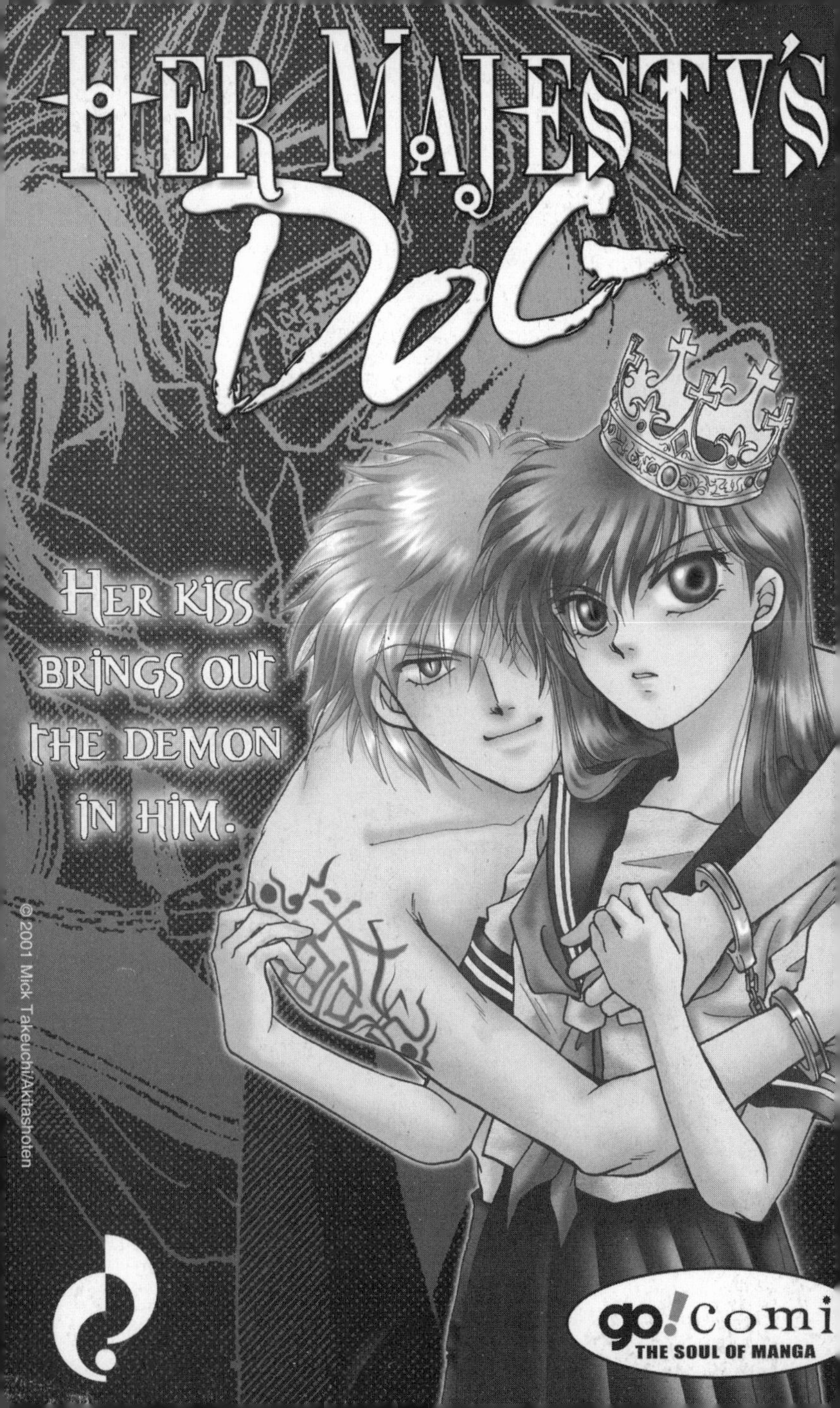

HER MAJESTY'S DOG
HER KISS BRINGS OUT THE DEMON IN HIM.
© 2001 Mick Takeuchi/Akitashoten
go!comi
THE SOUL OF MANGA

AUTHOR'S NOTE

I went to Italy to gather reference material!
This time around I chanced to be there just as
they were holding a Borgia Exhibit and they
even had their flag raised in the middle town.
It was a sight to behold.

Now as I'm writing I'm wearing a
Borgia T-shirt I bought there.

Visit You Higuri online at
www.youhiguri.com